For Jobs
and Freedom

For Jobs and Freedom

Selected Speeches and Writings
of A. Philip Randolph

EDITED BY

Andrew E. Kersten

AND

David Lucander

University of Massachusetts Press ◆ *Amherst & Boston*

Copyright © 2014 by University of Massachusetts Press
Printed in the United States of America

ISBN 978-1-62534-116-7 (paper); 115-0 (hardcover)

Designed by Jack Harrison
Set in Adobe Minion Pro
Printed and bound by Sheridan Books, Inc.

Library of Congress Cataloging-in-Publication Data
Randolph, A. Philip (Asa Philip), 1889–1979.
[Works. Selections]
For jobs and freedom : the selected speeches and writings of A. Philip Randolph /
edited by Andrew E. Kersten and David Lucander.
    pages cm
Includes bibliographical references and index.
ISBN 978-1-62534-116-7 (pbk. : alk. paper) — ISBN 978-1-62534-115-0 (hardcover : alk. paper)
1. United States—Race relations. 2. United States—Economic conditions.
3. African Americans—Civil rights. 4. Civil rights movements—United States.
5. Brotherhood of Sleeping Car Porters.
I. Kersten, Andrew Edmund, 1969– editor. II. Lucander, David, 1980– editor. III. Title.
E185.97.R27A25 2014
305.800973—dc23

                                        2014026025

British Library Cataloguing-in-Publication Data
A catalogue record for this book is available from the British Library.

Publication of this volume and other titles in the series In the Spirit of W. E. B. Du Bois, edited by
John H. Bracey Jr., is supported by the Office of the Dean, College of Humanities and Fine Arts,
University of Massachusetts Amherst.

PUBLICATION OF THESE PAGES

IS SUPPORTED BY A GRANT FROM

JEWISH FEDERATION OF GREATER HARTFORD

To my wife, Vickie, and my daughters, Bethany and Emily
—A. E. K.

To Kamal Ali and Joan E. Fuller, because you dedicated
so much to making opportunities for others
—D. L.

If there is anything more reprehensible than the practice of discrimination upon a people because of race, color, religion, national origin or ancestry, it is for the people discriminated against to accept it without protest or resistance. It is an evidence of an utter lack of self-respect, the most priceless possession an individual or a group can have, without which there can be no human dignity.

A. PHILIP RANDOLPH, 1959

Contents

A Note from the Editors on the Text and Sources

The primary sources assembled in this book were collected from various archives, presidential libraries, public records, newspapers, journals, and other publications. Our unwieldy "short list" of favorite documents was well over two hundred. When transcribed, this tallied nearly one million words. Difficult choices were made while cutting this project down to size. Serious Randolph scholars will notice that relatively few samples of his private correspondence are included. These files are voluminous enough to fill another book, and they offer an insider's view on how Randolph worked as an organizer. Instead, we chose to emphasize Randolph's public life, because this aspect of his career is what solidified his enduring place in history.

As editors, we sought to make this book useful for professional historians, classroom teachers, and general readers. As such, slight revisions were made to the text in order to modernize the works for contemporary audiences. Examples include removing the word "And" at the beginning of sentences, modifying verb tenses, and adding words such as "the" or "a" to smooth out syntax. Through it all, we were careful to retain Randolph's authentic voice. If not in the original document, the first names of historical figures were placed in [brackets], as were occasional transitional words or phrases that help with sentence structure. The use of an ellipsis (. . .) signifies that portions of the text were cut from the original document. Commas were added or removed to smooth out the syntax and make it more readable, but we retained the Oxford comma that Randolph used throughout his life. Capitalization and spelling were standardized throughout the text, but variations of the words "Race" and "Negro" appear in the original case that Randolph used them.

Acknowledgments

Institutional support for this project came from University of Wisconsin-Green Bay, the Center for Excellence in Teaching and Learning at Rockland Community College, and a National Endowment for the Humanities seminar hosted by the W. E. B. Du Bois Institute at Harvard University.

Bruce Wilcox, former director of the University of Massachusetts Press, was an exceptionally supportive and attentive editor. Carol Betsch and Mary Bellino moved the manuscript through production, and Barbara Folsom lent her editorial eye toward the improvement of the text.

Clayola Brown at the A. Philip Randolph Institute graciously gave her blessing early on, and Bill Fletcher Jr. was instrumental in the formative stages of this project. This would be a very different book without their backing.

Many archivists and librarians helped along the way, but a few standouts must be recognized. Tammy K. Williams at the Harry S. Truman Presidential Library and Museum graciously tracked down documents from afar, and Virginia Letwick at the Franklin D. Roosevelt Presidential Library and Museum lent her expertise. Sarah Levy at Rockland Community College tracked down hard to find sources with her usual efficiency. We also appreciate Jeff Brunner and Mitchell Scott at the University of Wisconsin–Green Bay's Cofrin Library for their assistance.

Andrew Kersten would also like to thank his History Seminar from the Spring of 2011. The following helped transcribe dozens of documents: Jessie Baehman, Amanda Becks, Casey Berg, Jessie Claymore, Aaron Damrau, Mathew De Meuse, Taylor Duxbury, Michael Gabriel, Angela King, Jennifer Kupsky, Danielle Le-Fevre, Alex Leonhard, Samantha Machalik, Stephanie Miller, Johnathan Nelson, Sara Rogatzki, Dave Starkey, Thomas Sutphin, David Tucker, Brooke Uhl, Megan Whelan, and Thai Xiong.

A number of scholars read sections of this book, gave their opinions, shared resources, and helped shape this project. Although far from comprehensive, the following deserve recognition for their contributions: Shawn Leigh Alexander, John Bracey, Bruce Delfini, Collette Fournier, Erik S. Gellman, Rhonney Grant, Andrew Jacobs, Clarence Lang, Shamika Mitchell, Christina Roukis-Stern, James

Smethurst, Jeanne Theoharis, Christopher Tinson, Kimberley Weston, and Thai Xiong.

David Lucander would like to thank Ursula Lucander for being a supportive spouse, insightful editor, and masterful typist.

Andrew Kersten would like to thank the three women with whom he lives—Vickie, Bethany, and Emily—for their support of yet another book project.

For Jobs
and Freedom

Introduction

This book is the first of its kind dedicated to the ideas of A. Philip Randolph, a charismatic civil rights and labor movement leader whose words inspired many to push forward an agenda set on advancing the interests of working-class African Americans. Randolph's lengthy involvement as an activist and intellectual spanned six decades that encompassed the years from the First World War through the end of the 1960s. During that time, he contributed to the transformation of American democracy by championing the causes of equal opportunity and democracy for all Americans. Randolph's success as a leader rested in part on his ability to organize and inspire those around him to do exceptional work. The speeches and writings chosen for this book exemplify the many ways in which Randolph understood key events of the twentieth century and used his influence to convince others of joining the various causes he supported. These documents provide a portrait of a trenchant intellectual who committed his life to fighting inequality and unfairness. Randolph was a politically engaged thinker who had prescient insights about the effect of racism on American society, and he acted to solve the social, political, and economic crises that bigotry and discrimination caused.

Randolph lived ninety years, and he was in the public eye for much of that time. As one of Randolph's recent biographers has noted, "it is difficult to comprehend the full measure of America's social and political development in the years between World War I and King's assassination in 1968 without fully grasping Randolph's social, political, and economic ideas."[1] This son of Florida who adopted Harlem as his home wrestled with competing ideologies about the struggles of African Americans as they moved from a predominantly rural population into a largely urban working class. The sheer longevity of his political engagement lends itself to a biographical case study for exploring the concept of a "long civil rights movement."[2] He fused civil rights, civil liberties, and radicalism in the 1910s; weighed in on various black nationalist programs beginning with his opposition to Marcus Garvey's "Back to Africa" plans; organized African American workers from the 1910s through the 1960s; and impacted national politics by directly challenging every American president from Franklin Roosevelt to Lyndon Johnson. Perhaps most important, as head of the Brotherhood of Sleeping Car Porters (BSCP) he represented the interests of the nation's largest contingent of unionized African American workers. Through his efforts on behalf of progressive causes, Randolph pioneered methods of civic engagement and sowed the seeds of the modern civil rights movement. He did this by experimenting with nonviolent civil disobedience such as sit-ins and marches and envisioning new directions in protest politics that brought oppressed minority groups into the national spotlight.

Randolph was a household name before America's foremost civil rights icon, Martin Luther King Jr., was born in 1929. As Randolph's longtime associate Bayard Rustin noted, he represented a new breed of African American leader, "a product both of the Negro experience and the radical political tradition."[3] Randolph challenged Booker T. Washington's gradualism, he derided Marcus Garvey's nationalism, and he opposed W. E. B. Du Bois's formula for uplift through the "Talented Tenth" working to elevate the masses. Randolph spent his cache of political and cultural capital to harness the power of social movements during the 1960s. The 1963 March on Washington for Jobs and Freedom was arguably the capstone of his career as an activist, but Randolph did not rest there. "Mr. Black Labor" remained immersed in campaigns for worker's rights and African American freedom struggles well into his seventies, making him "the dean of black activism" at a time when struggles for racial equality were at their most effervescent.[4]

For most of his journey, Randolph can be characterized as a critical patriot. He remained loyal to the United States throughout his life, but he did not curtail his scathing critique of America for failing to live up to its national ideals as an egalitarian and culturally pluralistic society. At a high school graduation speech in West Virginia, Randolph called on all Americans to realize that the nation "does not belong to any particular race." Rather, it belonged to everyone who believed in the democratic creed and "who fought to take it from British parents, worked to build it, bled and died to save it from enemies within and without."[5] In his view, the American experiment in multiracial democracy was worth believing in and sacrificing for, and he devoted his life to working for causes such as unfettered voting rights, fair wages for all workers, and the protection of minority groups from exploitation or intolerance.

A. Philip Randolph was a model of leadership for both the civil rights and the labor movements. His strategy and methods were sound; his positions were concrete; and his politics, though guided by ideals, were an amalgam of radicalism and pragmatism. As William H. Harris, a noted scholar of Randolph's work within the labor movement, put it: "Although he talked big, he moved with caution."[6] To Randolph, "the unfinished task of emancipation" could only be fulfilled by creating a society in which all Americans participated in the nation's political, economic, and cultural life as equals.[7] Randolph had an extraordinary sense of timing for his agitation. In the words of the journalist Roi Ottley, Randolph understood that "only in periods of great social upheaval can Negroes make fundamental gains."[8] His knack for picking the right fight at the right moment when it could gain traction is evidenced in the BSCP's campaign for union recognition, the various marches on Washington that he helped organize, and the push for military desegregation. In selecting these documents, we kept an eye on sources that illuminate the principles that guided Randolph while accomplishing these ends.

Randolph's story is rooted in the Jim Crow South. Born in 1889 in Crescent City, Florida, to James W. and Elizabeth Randolph, Asa and his older brother, James William Jr., shared a childhood marked by love and insecurity that one writer aptly described as "short on material resources but rich in intellectual and moral depth."[9] In preparing a biographical portrait of Randolph for *13 Against the Odds* (1944), Edwin Embree noted that Randolph sidestepped questions about his upbringing because he preferred to focus on "serious things" like organizing for social change.[10] With the exception of reminiscences in oral histories recorded in his later years, there is little documentation detailing Randolph's youth because many of the papers pertaining to this period were reportedly lost in a fire at the New York BSCP offices in 1930. The lack of hard evidence about Randolph's early life notwithstanding, his memory of a boyhood filled with "prayer, poverty, and pride" concisely captures the spirit of his youthful experiences.[11]

In the Randolph household, principle and dignity were just as important as money and comfort. James W. Randolph cobbled a livelihood together working as a clothier, shopkeeper, firewood seller, and minister in the African Methodist Episcopal Church. James and Elizabeth taught their sons the values of pride, dignity, and respectability. James held court at "fireplace kindergarten," and the informal curriculum imbued Asa with an intellectual curiosity that complemented his fighting spirit. From an early age the Randolph boys were told stories of Toussaint L'Overture, Nat Turner, Frederick Douglass, and others who embodied the heroic tradition of black liberation. Little did James and Elizabeth Randolph know it, but their second son was being prepared for a lifetime as a "race man." Even his name seemed fitting: Asa was an Old Testament king known for his altruism and selflessness. Like his father, a circuit preacher serving impoverished rural communities, Asa devoted his life to doing important and fulfilling work that did not pay well.[12] Randolph's mother was a Virginian and a descendent of enslaved parents. She instilled a sense of self-esteem in her sons, and she admonished them to "fight anybody who fought us."[13] Asa learned these lessons, and throughout his career he would prove incorruptible.

Randolph's formative years were spent in Jacksonville, Florida, a city described by its former resident James Weldon Johnson as "a one hundred percent cracker town."[14] The high-profile backlash to civil rights activism by ardent segregationists such as James O. Eastland and Eugene "Bull" Connor cemented the reputation of Mississippi and Alabama as particularly recalcitrant, but lying behind Florida's sunny reputation is the fact that it had the highest per capita lynching rate of any state between 1882 and 1930, a span of time that included Randolph's childhood.[15] As it was throughout much of the South, legally codified white supremacy structured race relations in the Sunshine State and violence enforced the many unwritten rules of racial etiquette.[16] Writing about coming of age in Oklahoma, the historian John Hope Franklin described this kind of "racial climate" as "stifling to my senses and damaging to my emotional health and well-being."[17] Rosa Parks, a contemporary of Randolph, remarked that daily survival in these conditions meant deftly "treading the tightrope of Jim Crow. . . . I felt that I was lynched many times in mind and spirit. I grew up in a world of white power used most cruelly and cunningly to suppress poor helpless black people."[18]

Despite the harshness of segregation and bigotry in the Jim Crow South, Randolph grew up in an all-black world that did its best to insulate him from the brutalities that scarred countless African American childhoods and adolescences. "We never felt that we were inferior to any white boy," he proudly recalled. Still, the first encounter with the color bar was a veritable coming-of-age ritual for African American children no matter how carefully parents tried to shield them.[19] For Randolph, this included being pushed to the back of the line by other newsboys when picking up the *Times-Union* and watching his father be meanly berated by whites for minor breaches of racial protocol.[20]

As a segregated city, Jacksonville presented all of the indignities and limitations that one would expect, but it also offered Asa some unique opportunities.[21] Histories of segregated public education often overlook the fact that some African American schools offered very well trained teachers who were dedicated to preparing students both academically and emotionally.[22] As the first high school in Florida open to African Americans, the Cookman Institute (now Bethune-Cookman College) offered instruction in trades such as shoemaking, husbandry, and home economics, but also provided courses in French, Latin, Greek, philosophy, music, and the natural sciences. The

Randolph home was close enough that he could attend classes, and young Asa thrived in this environment. He delved into literature, excelled in public speaking, honed his performance skills with drama, played on the baseball team, was a soloist in the choir, and, not surprisingly for a boy who was raised to love learning, graduated as class valedictorian in 1907.

The education he received at Cookman had an impact on shaping Randolph's personality, and in retrospect, the experience he had there suited his career as a writer, orator, and organizer.[23] Asa had the intellectual makings of an up-and-coming member of the "Talented Tenth," but the Randolph family was too poor for him even to think about pursuing further studies. He stayed in Florida another four years after graduating, apparently following in his father's footsteps by working odd jobs involving low-paid manual labor. Hard work did not dull Randolph's intellectual spirit, however, and he continued to act, sing, and read. His favorite book was *The Souls of Black Folk* (1903) by W. E. B. Du Bois, an influential text that has been widely praised by scholars and had a profound impact on generations of African American readers. Du Bois's accomplishments as a scholar and activist are legendary, but he also awakened the minds of individuals like Randolph. In fact, Randolph called *Souls of Black Folk* the "most influential book" he ever encountered and credited Du Bois's words with giving him a sense of direction at a critical point in his life.[24]

For a young man like Randolph, full of ideas and yearning for possibilities, it was only a matter of time before he acted on what must have been a gnawing sense of dissatisfaction. In the early twentieth century, hundreds of thousands of African Americans joined the Great Migration and fled the land of their ancestors. In search of greater opportunities and more personal freedom, they streamed into America's expanding cities, especially those of the North and Midwest. By doing so, they transformed from a predominantly rural peasant working class to a gritty urban industrial proletariat.[25] This massive drain of talent exacerbated the South's reputation for poverty, ignorance, and backwardness. Indeed, the ranks of noteworthy African Americans who, like Randolph, left the state of Florida were sufficient to start a respectable liberal arts college: the newspaper editor T. Thomas Fortune, the writer James Weldon Johnson and his brother, the musician and actor J. Rosamond Johnson, the artist Augusta Savage, and the anthropologist and writer Zora Neale Hurston. This very brief list hints at the vast human capital that moved out of the South as part of what the pioneering African American historian Carter G. Woodson dubbed the "northern migration of the talented tenth."[26]

Not content with living in a place where skin color so rigidly circumscribed his opportunities, Randolph and his childhood friend Beaman Hearn joined the more than sixty thousand African Americans who called Harlem home in 1911.[27] Being in Harlem as it was developing into the "Capital of the Black World" put Randolph in a vibrant city awash in social and political movements, and living there had a lasting impact on the evolution of his radical politics.[28] To symbolize his more mature and sophisticated identity, Asa chose the stately sounding name that he carried for the rest of his life, A. Philip.[29] Although his goal of establishing a career as an actor quickly fell through, the skills that he refined by practicing and performing were soon utilized in public speaking. Randolph's beautiful baritone voice was an asset when he stumped on Lenox Avenue making a case for socialism and advancing a peaceful revolution in American class and racial relations. He was naturally gifted as an orator, but courses in humanities and social sciences at City College of New York, a publicly funded school that at the time did not charge tuition, helped Randolph perfect his rhetoric and polish his diction.[30] As it was for Frederick Douglass and Malcolm X, literacy and reading were fundamental to Randolph's developing political consciousness.[31] As an analytical thinker who pondered big questions, Randolph sought explanations for the glaring inequalities that were so noticeable in America's rapidly expanding cities. A hungry intellect, Randolph said that he read Marx as avidly "as children read *Alice in Wonderland*." These writings impressed on Randolph a sense of the inherent unfairness of unregulated free markets and equipped him with an intellectual framework for understanding the profound concentration of wealth that bothered him so deeply.[32]

Randolph's early years in Harlem also introduced him to Lucille Campbell Green, the woman he wed and remained committed to for the rest of her life. The two met in 1913 and married later that year. They crossed paths because both worked in the same building, Asa for an employment agency and Lucille as a beautician.[33] The pair shared similar socialist leanings and an inclination toward public service, but, most important, they genuinely appreciated each other's company. They were the closest of friends, calling each other "Buddy" in correspondence for almost fifty years, until Lucille died shortly before the 1963 March on Washington. Lucille played a major role in her husband's rise as an activist. A Howard University graduate and small business owner with a salon that followed Madame C. J. Walker's beauty regimen by selling hair and skin products marketed toward African Americans, Lucille kept the household afloat when A. Philip's work for fledgling progressive causes failed to produce income during their early years together. "Without her money," Randolph told one writer, "we couldn't have started."[34] Lucille's financial support for *The Messenger* and Randolph's other ventures made her a quiet but substantial underwriter of radicalism during that period.[35]

Lucille, however, was only one of many women Randolph counted on to accomplish a shared political agenda. A short list of the others who worked with him at various times is a pantheon of twentieth-century African American woman activists: Anna Arnold Hedgeman, executive secretary of the National Council for a Permanent Fair Employment Practices Commission; Ella Baker, visionary of the Student Nonviolent Coordinating Committee; Pauli Murray, a founder of the National Organization of Women and a Yale faculty member; Layle Lane, vice president of the American Federation of Teachers; and Maida Springer Kemp, an organizer for the International Ladies' Garment Workers Union. Women were vital supporters of Randolph's many causes, and their work in organizations such as the Brotherhood of Sleeping Car Porters Ladies' Auxiliary and the March on Washington Movement was indispensible. For much of Randolph's career he relied on and employed women as fundraisers, grassroots organizers, and office workers. Although women planned and participated in marches, sit-ins, and other civil rights activities, they were rarely sought out as spokespeople by the national or local African American press. In the eyes of journalists and other outside observers, men were the movement's public leaders.[36] Randolph himself also made a practice of pushing aside or ignoring female leaders when the spotlight shined. The most extreme example occurred around the biggest event he had a hand in, the 1963 March on Washington for Jobs and Freedom. A longtime and well-respected associate, Anna Arnold Hedgeman, as well as many others, pressed Randolph and march organizers for greater representation of women in roles other than as entertainers.[37] However, as Dorothy Height, president of the National Council of Negro Women, lamented, "nothing that women said or did broke the impasse blocking their participation." Randolph, she astutely observed, understood that "women were part of the human family," but in his mind "there was no question as to who headed the household!"[38]

Like many charismatic leaders, Randolph used fiery words to advance his causes. His editorial leadership of *The Messenger,* a leading periodical during the Harlem Renaissance, cemented his reputation as a radical on the rise, but his publishing roots were planted in 1917 when the magazine debuted as the *Hotel Messenger.* With office space and equipment provided by the Headwaiters and Sidewaiters Society of Greater New York, he and cofounder Chandler Owen gained experience in publishing and familiarized themselves with the routines associated with running a periodical. The union's space at 486 Lenox Avenue was often bustling with activity. Adding to the excitement was that it was not uncommon for prominent figures of Harlem's Left such as the radical Texan Lovett Fort-Whiteman, the Dutch West Indian Cyril Briggs, the Jamaican nationalist and socialist W. A. Domingo, and the "black Socrates," Hubert Harrison, to come by and chat.[39] The first issues of the *Hotel Messenger* emphasized the exploitation of low-skilled laborers, something Randolph

A. Philip Randolph and Dorothy Height celebrate their long careers in the civil rights movement. (Library of Congress, Prints & Photographs Division, A. Philip Randolph Papers, LC-USZ62-134698)

experienced firsthand during his brief stint as an elevator operator earlier that year. Whether through a lack of tact or an unwavering commitment to exposing injustice, Randolph and Owen quickly ran afoul of their underwriters when they published an exposé of corruption within the union that detailed how headwaiters sold uniforms to their underlings at inflated prices and pocketed the difference. Predictably, the union pulled its support for the periodical.

Randolph's quest to build a forum on which socialist causes could be espoused was on the brink of collapse. Without free office space, furniture, and typing equipment at its editors' disposal, the fledgling magazine nearly disappeared. Neither Randolph nor Owen had developed any serious business acumen—in Randolph's words, "all we had were ideals."[40] Undeterred, and financially supported by Lucille, Randolph and Owen opened a new office on 513 Lenox Avenue and changed the magazine's title to *The Messenger*. The change signaled a new direction, and *The Messenger* came onto the scene as a voice of uncompromising radicalism.[41] A bold mission statement accompanied the first issue:

> Our aim is to appeal to reason, to lift our pens above the cringing demagogy of the times, and above the cheap peanut politics of the old reactionary Negro leaders. Patriotism has no appeal to us; justice has. Party has no weight with us;

principle has. Loyalty is meaningless; it depends on what one is loyal to. Prayer is not one of our remedies; it depends on what one is praying for. We consider prayer as nothing more than a fervent wish; consequently the merit and worth of a prayer depend upon what the fervent wish is.[42]

Randolph and Owen built on the tradition of militant journalism pioneered in the twentieth century by William Monroe Trotter's *Boston Guardian* and Robert Abbott's *Chicago Defender*.[43] *The Messenger* was a leading voice of the "New Negro" during the Harlem Renaissance. Its combination of sharp political commentary and support for literary arts made it a contemporary to organizationally supported periodicals like the NAACP's *The Crisis* and the National Urban League's *Opportunity* as well as a peer to lesser-known publications such as Cyril Briggs's *Crusader,* Hubert Harrison's *Negro Voice,* and W. A. Domingo's *Emancipator.* Together, these magazines and newspapers advanced a tradition in African American publishing that was forged during the nineteenth-century abolitionist movement and carried into the civil rights movement. After *The Messenger* folded, notable magazines such as *Fire!!* and *Freedomways* carried the torch of using words as weapons in the fight for racial equality.

The Messenger's pages attacked President Woodrow Wilson's hypocrisy of bringing the United States into war "to make the world safe for democracy" while disenfranchisement and racial violence in the American South represented such an obvious stain on the country's professed ideals.[44] Instead of enlisting in the military, *The Messenger* argued, African Americans could best serve democracy by fighting to "make Georgia safe for the Negro."[45] Decades before he became a leading proponent of nonviolent direct action in the 1940s, Randolph wrote in *The Messenger* that fighting back was the most effective way to stop a lynching. Drawing on a boyhood lesson learned when his father and other African American men prevented a mob action in Florida, Randolph advised, "If a choice has to be made," it was better to save one's own life and "destroy that of a lynch mob."[46] Two years later, Randolph boldly told readers that they should "shoot to kill anyone who encroaches upon their lives."[47]

No one was safe from Randolph's acerbic pen while he ran *The Messenger.* Indeed, at least one writer commented that the magazine was "against everything and everybody, particularly Colored men of prominence."[48] Randolph and Owen went after W. E. B. Du Bois for encouraging African Americans to halt their wartime protests and support President Wilson when the United States got involved in the Great War. They criticized Du Bois's "close ranks" position as one that "will rank in shame and reeking disgrace with the Atlanta Compromise speech of Booker Washington."[49] Randolph and Owen also waged an increasingly shrill attack against the popular nationalist leader

Marcus Garvey. The hostile tone of their editorials escalated in response to Garvey's meeting with the Ku Klux Klan to discuss a far-flung plan of repatriating African Americans outside of the United States.[50] The "Garvey Must Go" campaign was tinged with nativism, and *Messenger* editorials derided the bombastic leader as a "Jamaican jackass."[51] Obscured by this animosity was the unfortunate fact that neither Randolph nor Garvey offered an immediately workable solution to the problems of racism in America. While Garvey and the Universal Negro Improvement Association lacked the basic capital necessary to establish a black nation, few whites proved receptive to Randolph's message of interracial working-class solidarity.[52]

The staunch anti-war position taken by Randolph and Owen drew the attention of the Justice Department, and Attorney General A. Mitchell Palmer considered *The Messenger* "by long odds the most dangerous of all the Negro publications" in America.[53] In a nighttime raid on the magazine's office, files were ransacked, back issues were confiscated, and office furniture was broken.[54] Like Eugene Debs, a perennial Socialist Party presidential candidate, Randolph and Owen were charged with violating the Sedition Act. Unlike Debs, they escaped punishment because the judge in Cleveland believed that the two youthful-looking men were not "old enough, or, being black, smart enough to write that red-hot stuff." Convinced that white socialists were ghostwriters of the inflammatory editorials, the judge canceled the trial and ordered the pair to leave town immediately and return to their parents. Undaunted, they returned to Chicago and resumed propounding a strong anti-war position.[55]

Much of Randolph's reputation as a leading radical was established during these heady wartime years, but his political and social outlook was dynamic, and change was evident by the early 1920s. During this period, Randolph moved from the Far Left toward a more centrist democratic socialist ideology that he espoused for the rest of his life. At this time the Harlem Renaissance was gaining cultural capital, and *The Messenger* responded by increasing its coverage of the arts and devoting more space to bourgeoning writers. The magazine's masthead reflects its more tempered tone: instead of proclaiming "A Journal of Scientific Radicalism," it now read "The World's Greatest Negro Monthly." An analysis of 101 issues published across a span of eleven years showed that *The Messenger* printed over 250 poems written by ninety different writers.[56] Many of these authors became obscure with time, but the magazine's pages also included works by luminaries such as Langston Hughes, Zora Neale Hurston, George Schuyler, Jessie Fauset, E. Franklin Frazier, Arna Bontemps, Countee Cullen, J. A. Rogers, and Claude McKay. Despite its impressive literary merits, however, *The Messenger* remained financially unstable. James Weldon Johnson helped secure a one-time grant of more than $10,000 from the Garland Fund, but the magazine, which always sold for fifteen cents, was forever on the brink of bankruptcy.[57] Writers were rarely paid; theater reviewers were lucky to get complimentary tickets or car fare; and printer's bills piled up. In a last-ditch effort, the magazine's offices were moved several times to less expensive locations before its final issue appeared in 1928.[58]

The decline and eventual end of *The Messenger* forced Randolph to redirect his political energies into new areas, and in 1925 he helped form the all-black labor union, the Brotherhood of Sleeping Car Porters. His writing interests were rechanneled as well, into his next magazine, *Black Worker*. Published from 1929 to 1968 as the voice of the BSCP, *Black Worker* heralded itself as "The Mouthpiece of the Negro Workers of America." In comparison to *The Messenger,* it was printed on less expensive paper, appeared somewhat irregularly, and had far fewer journalistic frills such as photographs and experienced reporters. Despite its lack of niceties, however, this new periodical further solidified Randolph's position as a leading spokesman for the black working class by unapologetically attacking racism with as much page space as it devoted to covering the fledgling union's internal affairs. Randolph's quixotic quest to establish, maintain, and receive recognition for the BSCP was possibly his riskiest venture, and he probably would have fallen into obscurity if it had failed.

Having no experience of the job, Randolph was an unlikely person to head a union of railroad porters, but his unique position as an independent radical who controlled his own media outlet made him an effective voice for the railroad porters who worked for the gargantuan Pullman Company. As the largest private employer of African Americans in the United States, Pullman gave thousands of families a precious toehold in the middle class and launched countless children of porters on the path of upward mobility.[59] Being a porter was one of the better jobs available to working-class African American men, and it was also something of a coming-of-age ritual for upwardly mobile young adults. Indeed, the New York City radical Frank Crosswaith, the poet Claude McKay, Morehouse College president Benjamin E. Mays, and Supreme Court Justice Thurgood Marshall all did the job at one point in their lives.[60] E. D. Nixon, the BSCP member who was integral to the 1955–1956 Montgomery Bus Boycott that followed the arrest of Rosa Parks, called being a porter "the best thing in the world that ever happened to me."[61] The position was steady, the pay was reliable, and more important, working the rails took Nixon beyond his solidly segregated state of Alabama. Exposure to other regions showed him that racial segregation was not ubiquitous, and the implication was radical: life in Alabama didn't have to be that way.[62]

Porters routinely worked hundreds of hours per month making beds, cleaning bathrooms and spittoons, shining shoes, carrying luggage, and attending to every passenger's whim and wish.[63] According to one porter, "the work was hard, the hours long, and the pay poor," while another added, "and where the boss man was mean."[64] This was, as one porter told Randolph, "a tough road to travel."[65] Doing the job necessitated spending many days away from home. Wages were low—half what a white conductor was paid—and there was no compensation for time spent "deadheading" on empty trains traveling to and from assignments. Most of a porter's pay came in the form of tips.[66] Sometimes a particularly generous passenger might make the long hours worthwhile, but Randolph and other union leaders objected to the servile implications associated with tipping. As they saw it, working for little pay and relying on the good graces of primarily white passengers was especially offensive given that many porters were only one generation removed from slavery.[67]

Adding insult, white passengers commonly addressed every porter generically as "George" (the name of their employer, George Pullman). The practice was so common that the Chicago lumber dealer George W. Delany half-jokingly formed The Society for the Prevention of Calling Sleeping Car Porters George, with the mission of protecting whites from the racially charged name association. Formed in 1916, the group claimed support from 33,000 individuals including political leaders and celebrities such as King George V of England, Georgia senator Walter F. George, and New York Yankee slugger George Herman "Babe" Ruth. The condescending practice was challenged in more serious ways by the working men themselves. Porters repeatedly filed complaints with the company, calling for Pullman to discourage the insult, and individual porters sometimes had heated arguments with passengers. Seeing the potential for a public relations disaster, Pullman finally issued name tags to porters.[68]

Porters such as Ashley Totten had tried organizing an independent union before but failed because the company easily disrupted their efforts and intimidated supporters.[69] What was needed, the St. Croix native thought, was a man of unimpeachable character, strong principles, and financial independence that placed him beyond the reach of Pullman's economic sanctions.[70] The fledgling union lacked a spokesman, and Totten was among the first to realize that A. Philip Randolph was that man. The rest, it could be said, is history. A. Philip Randolph and the BSCP became synonymous, and for good reason. He was elected union president in 1925, and he remained in that position until his resignation in 1968. With the union as his base of power, Randolph spent the next four decades agitating to break racial barriers in the labor movement and to advance civil rights reforms.[71]

Building the BSCP from the ground up did not happen simply or quickly. Two $10,000 grants from the Garland Fund energized an early organizing campaign, and within one year more than half of all porters were enrolled.[72] This early success was fleeting, however, and the BSCP's ranks plummeted after a 1928 strike threat brought little gain.[73] The embattled union had only 771 members in 1932 and was on the verge of dissolution, but its fortunes reversed when Franklin D. Roosevelt moved into the White House. As one Randolph biographer put it, "the New Deal came just in time" to save the BSCP.[74] The Roosevelt administration provided a new legal framework to support workers and the union movement. Amendments to the Railway Labor Act further empowered the porters, and union membership jumped to more than 7,000. Pullman started to negotiate with the BSCP in 1935, and two years later an agreement was reached that included more than $2 million in base pay increases, additional overtime pay, and a shorter workweek.[75] To Randolph, this hard-won success that was more than a decade in the making confirmed that the labor movement was a viable way to generate reforms.[76]

Randolph was not content with improving the lot only of Pullman porters; he wanted a better life for all black workers. The "Roaring Twenties" were rough times for the upstart union, but the economic collapse of 1929 and ensuing depression hurtled working-class African Americans into destitution. Government studies showed in 1930 that an astonishing 38 percent of African Americans could not survive without federal aid—more than double the estimated 17 percent of the white population that was in a similar predicament. Black industrial workers were especially vulnerable because in many industries they were the "last hired, first fired." Moreover, African American workers who held their positions were not guaranteed a fair or equitable wage in comparison to other racial groups in their respective industries.[77] The black middle class of accountants, dentists, lawyers, and other professionals soon experienced the ripple effect of these layoffs, as their primary clients were often too poor to pay for services.[78] The problems caused by discriminatory employment patterns were reinforced by New Deal programs that distributed relief unequally along racial lines.[79]

The National Negro Congress (NNC) was organized to unite activists from across the left-liberal spectrum into a coordinated fight against political exclusion, racial segregation, economic disparity, and what Randolph called the "deepening crisis of monopoly capitalism."[80] The NNC's first national meeting in 1936 drew 817 delegates from 585 different organizations. The high turnout suggested the enormous potential of the congress, and Randolph's election as its president confirmed his stature as a rising star in the world of African American political leadership.[81] Randolph's inaugural address outlined the NNC's goal of uniting African American organizations and CIO-affiliated trade unions for an assault against all of the many manifestations of racism.

Labeling the NNC "a Negro movement," Randolph described its mission of galvanizing "Negroes of all political faiths as well as Negroes of various religious creeds and denominations" into a broad organizational base.[82] Given that the BSCP consumed most of Randolph's time, his position as head of the NNC was largely symbolic. Nevertheless, in the years under Randolph the NNC held three national conventions, joined the ongoing anti-lynching crusade, and coordinated local activities such as rent strikes and "Don't Buy Where You Can't Work" campaigns.[83]

Various ideological factions struggled for influence within the NNC, and a breaking point came in 1939 when the Nazi-Soviet Pact triggered an about-face by doctrinaire Communists on the issue of support for American involvement in World War II.[84] Randolph loudly left the NNC the following year. His parting message at the 1940 national convention was, in Ralph Bunche's words, "a bombshell."[85] Randolph denounced Communism and lambasted the once-promising NNC for being taken over by whites and radicals who were out of touch with the needs and desires of ordinary African Americans.[86] There was an element of truth to Randolph's charges, as 370 of the 1,264 delegates assembled were white.[87] Clearly, much had changed in the four years since Randolph temperately defended Communists as "a legitimate political party" and charged that red-baiters were intentionally obstructing "those who aggressively fight for human and race rights."[88] The increasing radicalism of the thirties made it difficult for Randolph to contain centrifugal forces within the NNC, and he believed that heightened visibility of Communists would make centrists and moderates wary of associating with the congress. Without mainstream support, the NNC could never serve as the voice of mass protest that Randolph hoped it would be.

Randolph's time with the NNC ended bitterly, but the experience awakened him to the potential of fighting segregation and discrimination through a national organization composed of pre-existing and autonomous groups. His next venture in coalition-building, the World War II–era March on Washington Movement (MOWM), followed that model. The bold idea for a march on Washington germinated while Randolph was traveling on an organizing and speaking tour for the BSCP.[89] Everywhere Randolph went, the audacious plan gained support, and in short time, according to one reporter, "it had caught fire . . . everybody was talking March on Washington."[90] Emboldened by enthusiasm at BSCP meetings, Randolph issued a press release calling for the mass demonstration to occur July 1, 1941.[91] He proceeded in a spirit of unity, collaborating with other leaders including Walter White of the National Association for the Advancement of Colored People (NAACP), the National Urban League's Lester Granger, Rayford Logan from Howard University, and Layle Lane of the American Federation of Teachers.[92] As the movement built momentum and gained credibility, estimates of expected marchers ballooned from 10,000 to 100,000.[93]

There was some doubt as to whether anyone could "get 10,000 Negroes assembled in one spot," the *Chicago Defender* reported, commenting that it would be "the miracle of the century" if Randolph could pull off the event.[94] Randolph himself waffled, and maintained that the number of marchers did not really matter—even 2,000 demonstrators, he argued, would "startle the country and win the respect of the American people."[95] He was right: the threat to march forced Roosevelt's hand, and Randolph was head of a delegation that met with the president at the White House. In exchange for canceling the march, Roosevelt issued Executive Order 8802 establishing the Fair Employment Practice Committee (FEPC) to ensure that "there shall be no discrimination in the employment of workers in defense industries or Government because of race, creed, color, or national origin."[96]

Despite the victory that E.O. 8802 represented, however, it failed to answer one of MOWM's principal demands, the desegregation of the armed forces. Randolph's experience in BSCP labor negotiations influenced his decision to call off the march in exchange for what seemed like limited concessions. It was preferable to secure one concrete gain, Randolph reasoned, than to follow through with a demonstration that might reap nothing.[97] The African American press overwhelmingly praised his handling of the march and lionized Randolph. The *Amsterdam News,* for example, hailed Randolph as "the number one Negro leader in America" and ranked him with such historical figures as Frederick Douglass.[98]

"Once the FEPC order was issued," the former MOWM member Bayard Rustin remarked, "the real activity began."[99] In the message after canceling the march, Randolph urged MOWM's local branches to "remain intact in order to watch and check how industries are observing the executive order."[100] A groundswell of grassroots support that brought tens of thousands to MOWM rallies in New York City, Chicago, and St. Louis signaled to Randolph that there was reason to keep the organization together.[101] MOWM encouraged grassroots activists to do what was necessary in each "local situation" to ensure compliance with the anti-discrimination policy, and prompted them to stage "simultaneous marches on local city halls, on state capitols, [and] on defense plants" whenever necessary.[102] More than two dozen chapters of MOWM were formed, and BSCP members figured prominently in the new organization's local campaigns. With a broader appeal than a labor union, MOWM also attracted many young activists who were discovering their voices. For individuals like Pauli Murray, James Forman, Bayard Rustin, and others who would go on to make an impact on the civil rights movement, participating in MOWM was a stepping-stone in a lifetime of activism.

MOWM was positioned at a pivotal point in twentieth-century struggles for civil rights, and the philosophical and theoretical controversies that Randolph navigated were issues that the next generation of civil rights activists also grappled with in the 1950s and 1960s.[103] Through MOWM, Randolph was a key intermediary in the transmission of nonviolent Gandhian civil disobedience tactics to African American civil rights protests.[104] Gandhi's method, Randolph explained, "is applied Christianity. It is applied democracy. It is Christianity and democracy brought out of gilded churches and solemn legislative halls and made to work as a dynamic force in our day to day life."[105] Such socially engaged religion became a hallmark of direct-action campaigns and major demonstrations of the civil rights movement. Likewise, MOWM's all-black membership policy was one of the organization's most controversial positions. Randolph was clear that the exclusion of whites should not be interpreted as a disavowal of his broader goal of integrating America's political and economic institutions, explaining that the racially exclusive membership policy was necessary to break "slave psychology" and to mitigate against communist intrusion. In his experience, being labeled "red" put an organization outside the bounds of potentially effective protest.[106] Randolph believed that African Americans needed to "take the initiative and make the fight and sacrifice and free themselves."[107] "White liberals and labor may sympathize with the Negro's fight against Jim Crow," he stated, but "they are not going to lead that fight. They never have and they never will."[108] As Randolph saw it, solidarity was an essential organizing principle, and throughout his career he called on African Americans to work together for a common cause.

The President's Committee on Fair Employment Practice was the first federal agency since Reconstruction to be concerned with civil rights—a reason why an early historian described it as one of the "most significant creations of the Roosevelt Administration."[109] Although the FEPC had no legal enforcement power and the agency never moved to have a defense contract revoked, its existence represented a groundbreaking shift in governmental responsiveness to minority interests.[110] The number of jobs that African Americans obtained directly or indirectly because of the FEPC is impossible to determine, but the proportion of racial minorities working in defense plants increased from 3 percent in 1941 to 7.3 percent in 1944.[111] Although their employment cannot be directly traced to the new anti-discrimination policy, some of the noteworthy individuals who started working in defense factories at this time included the Jackie Robinson and Irene Morgan (whose arrest for refusing to sit at the back of an interstate bus catalyzed the Supreme Court case of *Morgan v. Virginia*, 1946).[112] For them, and for tens of thousands of other black workers, the crisis of war meant a rare opportunity to earn a better living.

These were important gains, and Randolph realized that it was critical to support the beleaguered federal agency as it sustained attack from conservative forces. In aid of the effort to push for legislation to institutionalize the FEPC as a federal agency, Randolph appointed a former MOWM staffer, Anna Arnold Hedgeman, to handle the daily operations of the National Council for a Permanent FEPC.[113] Although the effort failed in the short term, the FEPC did herald a new era in fair labor practices because it was the model for state, local, and federal fair employment agencies that sprang up in the postwar years. By 1964, thirty-six states and more than two hundred cities had their own variant of the FEPC.[114] The BSCP was the foundation of Randolph's influence for this and other campaigns. "Without the porters," he acknowledged, "I couldn't have carried on the fight for fair employment, or the fight against racial discrimination in the armed forces."[115] With their support, he faced two presidents in the 1940s, Roosevelt and Truman, and boldly threatened to organize nonviolent direct-action campaigns against segregation and discrimination. In both instances, he canceled the protest after securing executive orders that appeased some of his demands. "In this period of power politics," Randolph wrote, "nothing but pressure, more pressure, and still more pressure" directed at the White House could win concessions for minority groups. The techniques of mass pressure politics matured through these campaigns, and this tactic eventually became a primary way for underrepresented groups in America to advance their interests.[116]

Randolph's quest to end inequality by eliminating segregation brought him to a confrontation with what was then the nation's largest single employer of African Americans, the armed forces. Integrating the military was something that Randolph advocated since the initial call to march on Washington in 1941, and he restated this position in his contribution to Rayford Logan's *What the Negro Wants* (1944). It was a difficult battle, and powerful interests opposed interference with the deeply entrenched tradition of military segregation. Undersecretary of War Robert Patterson, for example, rejected any reforms because the army was not a "sociological laboratory."[117] After World War I, Army War College staff had concluded that African Americans were physically unfit for duty and psychologically incapable of performing under the stress of combat. During the Second World War, black soldiers were primarily utilized as quartermasters and in menial support roles.[118] More than one million African American men and women experienced the hypocrisy of fighting for freedom in a segregated army during World War II, and Randolph capitalized on their resentment to revitalize the effort to end segregation within ranks.[119] The separate and unequal place of African Americans in the armed forces was reaffirmed in the aftermath of World War II by the 1946 Gillem Board Report, an officially sanctioned study of military manpower that did

A. Philip Randolph and Grant Reynolds testify before the Senate Armed Services Committee, 1948. (Library of Congress, Prints & Photographs Division, NYWT&S Collection, LC-USZ62-128074)

not call for any substantial modification of the army's well-established racial practices.[120]

To confront this seemingly ineradicable problem, Randolph joined the former Harlem congressman Grant Reynolds in 1947 to form the Committee against Jim Crow in Military Service and Training, a group that quickly rebranded itself as the League for Non-Violent Civil Disobedience Against Military Segregation. Randolph, now over sixty years old, advised young African American men to protest the military's racial barriers by refusing induction under the peacetime conscription proposed by Truman. His bold opposition was expressed unequivocally during his testimony before a U.S. Senate hearing when he stated: "I personally will advise Negroes to refuse to fight as slaves for a democracy they cannot possess and cannot enjoy." Eloquently justifying the necessity of nonviolent resistance in a democracy, he went on record as being ready for imprisonment if charged with treason: "I personally pledge myself to openly counsel, and abet youth, both white and Negro, to quarantine any Jim Crow conscription system."[121] For this defiant stand, Roy Wilkins later called Randolph the "spiritual and historical father" to draft resisters during the Vietnam War.[122]

Modern historians have favorably assessed Truman's record on civil rights, but it was individuals like Randolph who pushed him to act progressively on racial issues.[123] In an attempt to stop the post–World War II rash of violence targeting African American veterans and lay the groundwork for new civil rights legislation, Truman created the President's Commission on Civil Rights, whose report, *To Secure These Rights,* became a blueprint for the civil rights movement.[124] In 1948, Truman signed Executive Order 9981, which declared that "there shall be equality of treatment and opportunity for all persons in the armed services without regard to race, religion, or national origin." The lack of a timetable for implementation ("shall be put into effect as rapidly as possible") contributed to the unevenness with which racial barriers came down in the different branches of the armed forces.[125] Much like Roosevelt's E.O. 8802, Truman's order was substantially weaker than both its champions and its opponents asserted it was. Although E.O. 9981 did not explicitly mandate integration, its historical impact was significant because the military was among the first major institutions in America to desegregate, and it remains one of the only branches of the federal government that has consistently utilized racial minorities at a level close to their proportion of the population.[126]

Randolph's achievements during the 1940s solidified his reputation as an elder statesman in the struggle and gave him considerable political capital that allowed him to influence the next generation of civil rights activists. The Montgomery Bus Boycott is renowned for launching the career of Martin Luther King Jr. and for the community cohesion that sustained the protest for over a year, but Randolph made an impact from afar through his association with longtime local BSCP leader E. D. Nixon. In the years before the boycott, Nixon and Rosa Parks worked closely together as officers in the local NAACP. His status in the community as a preeminent voice of protest and the trust built through their long-standing work relationship are why Parks sought Nixon's advice on how to handle her arrest.[127] Nixon's affiliation with the BSCP connected him to Randolph, who authorized the union to send $10,000 in support of the boycott. In effect, the BSCP (and by extension Randolph) underwrote the beginnings of what became one of the most effective protests in modern history.[128]

In addition to financial support, Randolph aided the bus boycott in indirect ways. Bayard Rustin, Randolph's longtime friend and former collaborator in MOWM, was dispatched to Montgomery by the War Resister's League so that he could tutor the twenty-six-year-old King in peaceful, direct-action protest methods. Rustin was an outsider to the community, an acknowledged ex-Communist, a draft resister who had served time for avoiding conscription during World War II, and a convicted homosexual who had been imprisoned in 1953. Rustin was not the kind of character that the thoroughly respectable reverend would normally work with, but he came to Montgomery with Randolph's blessing and therefore was warmly received by Nixon, who then introduced him to King. The meeting was fortuitous. As a veteran activist, Rustin advised King on alternative transportation arrangements that helped sustain the boycott, and he also offered clarification on applying Gandhian principles. The two men stayed in contact after the boycott ended, and Rustin helped establish the Southern Christian Leadership Conference, King's base of power for the remainder of his life.[129]

Also during the late fifties, Randolph helped to organize three assemblies in Washington, DC, designed to pressure President Dwight D. Eisenhower to take a stand against the rising tide of racial violence and to encourage faster desegregation of American schools. The first, the 1957 Prayer Pilgrimage, attracted 25,000 demonstrators at the Lincoln Memorial. Held on May 17 to mark the third anniversary of the Supreme Court's *Brown v. Board of Education* decision, the three-hour outdoor religious service featured songs, scripture readings, and prayers.[130] In his remarks that afternoon, Randolph described the Prayer Pilgrimage as the product of unity between African Americans and "their allies, labor, liberal, and the Church," an emphasis on collaboration that was characteristic of his work in both civil rights and the labor movement.[131] Randolph, once again together with Bayard Rustin, was a lead planner in the 1958 and 1959 Youth Marches for Integrated Schools. At the 1958 action, Harry Belafonte, Jackie Robinson, and Coretta Scott King (representing her husband, who was recuperating after being stabbed at a book signing) joined a crowd of 10,000 to show their solidarity with students in Little Rock and elsewhere during the tumultuous early years of mandated public school desegregation. Martin Luther King Jr. and Roy Wilkins were two of the most prominent speakers at the 1959 event, which drew twice as many attendees as the previous year's assembly. The marches on Washington during the fifties gave Randolph and Rustin experience in handling the logistics of moving thousands of people into and out of the capital for a daylong protest, expertise that proved vital during the nearly flawless coordination of the 1963 March on Washington. Of themselves, however, the Youth Marches were scarcely covered by the national media and they have been largely forgotten in popular memory.[132]

In contrast to the demonstrations of the fifties, the 1963 March on Washington for Jobs and Freedom is an iconic moment of the American experience and the event was, as one Randolph biographer put it, "a culminating achievement that succinctly employed all the various aspects of his social, political, and economic thinking."[133] Randolph's socialism and his marriage of labor and civil rights were clear in the name of the action—jobs came before freedom, but opportunity and equality were inseparable. With the help of his longtime associate Bayard Rustin, the seventy-three-year-old Randolph had his day in the sun. On August 28, 1963, more than 200,000 demonstrators assembled at the foot of the Lincoln Memorial to hear speeches, songs, and prayers from activists, musicians, and religious leaders. Although the event was scaled back from Randolph's original vision of a "two-day action program" including acts of civil disobedience on Capitol Hill, the demonstration became the symbol of effective peaceful protest in the United States.[134] For good reason, King's "I Have a Dream" speech is synonymous with the day's proceedings, but celebrating this masterpiece of American oratory leads many people to overlook the fact that nine other leaders addressed the crowd that afternoon; one of them was A. Philip Randolph. Looking out at an interracial crowd that included supporters from the labor movement, various religious communities, and reformers from across the nation must have made him proud. Indeed, this event was more than twenty years in the making.

"Fellow Americans," Randolph began, "we are gathered here in the largest demonstration in the history of this nation. Let the nation and the world know the meaning of our numbers. We are not a pressure group . . . we are not a mob." With his experience in public speaking stretching back to his soapbox days in Harlem, Randolph slowed his cadence to let his words resonate: "We are the advance guard of a massive moral revolution."[135] The steadiness with which he spoke kept from view that he had just resolved a crisis brewing behind the scenes. John Lewis, of the Student Non-Violent Coordinating Committee, in his prepared remarks criticized John F. Kennedy's support for civil rights as "too little and too late." Catholic leaders threatened to pull their support for the event if the speech was given as written. Lewis refused to compromise and revise the speech. Only Randolph, a respected movement veteran, who at this point in his career was seen to be above organizational and territorial jealousies, was positioned to reason with the resolute SNCC leader.[136] Disobeying a venerated elder like Randolph, Lewis later reflected, was "like saying no to Mother Teresa," and a short conversation with Randolph was all it took to convince Lewis to change his words.[137]

The civil rights movement made its most significant legislative gains in the years immediately following the March on Washington. Indeed, the 1964 Civil Rights Act, the 1965 Voting Rights Act, and the 1968 Fair Housing Act all had roots in this demonstration. Martin Luther King and the thousands of activists he represented are rightly acknowledged for these advances, as are the principled politicians who drafted and signed the laws, but these developments owed much to the vision and legacy of A. Philip Randolph.

By the mid-1960s, Randolph was falling out of step as a leader, and his power base was shrinking because decreased rail travel reduced the BSCP to a shadow of its former self. Moreover, his political perspectives had become opposed to the more radical positions taken by civil rights groups such as SNCC and the increasingly militant Congress of Racial Equality. The conflict of positions first erupted around the 1964 Democratic National Convention. Randolph, at President Lyndon B. Johnson's behest, advised the Mississippi Freedom Democratic Party to take the two at-large delegate seats offered by the Democratic National Committee, but SNCC activists roundly rejected the deal. Randolph wanted to help President Johnson maintain control of the Democratic Party, and he also hoped to gain Johnson's support for further civil rights legislation. SNCC organizers had spent the past year registering voters in Mississippi to overthrow the state's notoriously racist Democratic Party, and two at-large seats were not going to accomplish the goals that homegrown activists such as Fannie Lou Hamer had risked so much for.[138] Randolph saw the compromise as an inroad for African Americans in the Democratic Party, but younger radicals viewed this as a betrayal.[139]

Ultimately, national politics and politicians failed Randolph. Under the auspices of the newly established A. Philip Randolph Institute (APRI), Randolph and Rustin spearheaded a 1966 campaign in support of the Freedom Budget. In a proposal unveiled at a White House press conference, Randolph called for spending more than $100 billion over the next ten years to upgrade and stabilize Social Security, guarantee health care for all Americans, and eradicate slums through a massive housing construction program. This was, in effect, a democratic-socialist agenda that ambitiously sought to break the multigenerational cycle of poverty which had taken root in America's inner cities. The Freedom Budget made it to the floor of Congress but went nowhere. Costly expenditures including the space program and the accelerating war in Vietnam undercut whatever political will there was for an expanded War on Poverty or a more expansive Great Society. As a result, vast disparities in economic opportunity and quality of life remained largely unchanged by the civil rights movement.[140]

After the failure of the Freedom Budget, Randolph stepped back from public life. Although he withdrew from the daily grind of organizing, Randolph remained active through the APRI as a public intellectual and theorist of change. Under Rustin's leadership, the APRI was much more than a think-tank. With financial support from the AFL-CIO, for example, the APRI aided Memphis sanitation workers in their 1968 strike (during which Martin Luther King was assassinated).[141] The group also assisted César Chávez and the United Farm Workers in the effort to organize California's vineyard workers.[142]

Despite this continued affiliation with causes for economic justice, Randolph became disconnected from the prevailing course of struggles against racism. For so many years, Randolph was in touch with the mood of the African American working class, but his response to the idea of Black Power revealed how removed he had grown from what was once his base. In an era when one's reaction to the phrase "Black Power" was something of a litmus test, Randolph took a staunch position against the Black Power movement and its associated nationalist spin-offs. Underestimating the resonance of Stokely Carmichael's message laid out in *Black Power* (1967) and various speeches given since he popularized the phrase on a hot Mississippi night during the March Against Fear, Randolph disingenuously dismissed it as "only an emotional slogan," saying, "it has no programmatic plan."[143]

The controversy surrounding the 1968 New York City teachers' strike illuminates the competing tensions that characterized Randolph's dual commitments to black liberation and the labor movement. Inspired by the Black Power ethos of community control, school board leaders in Ocean Hill–Brownsville, a predominantly African American section of Brooklyn, led a push to have more input in the administration of public schools. A wave of strikes and protests was sparked by the dismissal of several teachers, many of whom were Jewish, on short notice.[144] This was a local political crisis that pitted the black working class against a predominantly white trade union, and the most contentious arguments were fundamentally economic issues because they involved questions of personnel and staffing. Randolph came out on the side of the union, arguing that employees should be entitled to a hearing before termination. A full-page advertisement in the *New York Times* paid for by the APRI affirmed "the right of every worker to be judged on his merits—not his color or creed." In an era when phrases such as "community control" were being used by activists on both ends of the ideological spectrum in debates about race and the distribution of educational resources, the APRI reasoned, "Injustice must not be camouflaged by appeals to racial solidarity. . . . If due process is not won out in Ocean Hill–Brownsville, what could prevent white community groups in Queens from firing black teachers—or white teachers with liberal views?"[145]

Aligning with the teachers during the Ocean Hill–Brownsville controversy further alienated Randolph from many African Americans, and from this point on it was obvious that there was a rupture between him and a new generation of leaders. Much as Du Bois had been with Randolph's attacks against him earlier in the century, Randolph was finally being eclipsed as a voice at the vanguard of the struggle, and to him this was a natural development. "The black militants of today are standing upon the shoulders of the New Negro radicals of my day, the twenties, thirties, and forties," he proclaimed. "We stood upon the shoulders of the civil rights fighters of the Reconstruction era, and they stood upon the shoulders of the black abolitionists."[146] Randolph differed with the current generation, but he did not disavow them. "I don't agree with their methods," Randolph said in a 1969 CBS interview, but he admired the "romance in their heart for freedom . . . they remind me of my own self in the 20s."[147] This tacit support was lost on some commentators. That same year, a writer in *Ebony* remarked that Randolph held the dubious distinction of being "Uncle Tom No. 2" behind the movement's narcissistic archconservative, Roy Wilkins.

Perceptions of Randolph were changing, but his focus remained consistent throughout his career—access to jobs and workplace rights were his primary concerns. "The forces of advancing technology are not limited by national boundaries and they are sweeping the world," Randolph warned, and young African Americans "must make certain they are not left behind in the scientific and technological revolution." Economic disaster awaited "if the young Negro cannot become a part of this advancing technology," he predicted, and "his whole revolution will have been in vain." The elderly Randolph's message of economic integration through a state-centered class-based solution was out of step with popular discourse advancing cultural nationalism and self-determination.[148]

In the early 1970s, Randolph left his longtime residence at the once-fashionable but increasingly run-down Dunbar Apartments in Harlem. His move to a housing cooperative owned by the International Ladies' Garment Workers Union was precipitated by his being mugged by three young men in his doorway, a sad event that showed how unrecognizable the formerly venerated leader had become to the generation who would have been his grandchildren.[149] Randolph lived a sort of voluntary poverty. He may have had the demeanor of an old-fashioned Harvard-educated aristocrat, but this son of a hardscrabble preacher never pursued a line of work that offered much in monetary reward. Of course, this is just how he wanted it. "It is the lot of some people to be poor and it is my lot," the elderly Randolph wrote his old friend Chandler Owen. "I do not have any remorse about that."[150] The only luxury items that Randolph kept in his elder years were an old watch given to him by the BSCP for his decades of meritorious service and two black-and-white televisions that he used to watch baseball.[151] "Although I have never had a desire for wealth," Randolph wrote in 1963, "I have had a passion to create a significant movement which would also benefit others."[152]

If we measure Randolph's life on his own stated terms, his was a life well lived and it was one that made an impact on generations for years to come. E. D. Nixon, like so many longtime BSCP members, credited him for having "done more to bring me in the fight for civil rights than anybody."[153] After his death, Randolph's leading protégée, Bayard Rustin, reflected, "No individual did more to help the poor, the dispossessed and the working class in the

United States and around the world than A. Philip Randolph."[154] The conservative George Schuyler fondly remembered Randolph's ability to find humor in the toughest of times and praised him as "one of the finest, most engaging men I had ever met."[155] The white journalist Oswald Garrison Villard said of Randolph, "He is steeped in principle, and he has the complete certainty of a true reformer."[156] These remarks hint at the essence of A. Philip Randolph: inspiring, altruistic, personable, and confident. "I've said this many times," remarked the SNCC stalwart and Georgia congressman John Lewis: "If he had been born in another time, in another place, or of another race, A. Philip Randolph would have been a prime minister, or a president, or a king."[157]

Beyond the hagiography of his admirers, Randolph's life can also be assessed within the context of historical concerns such as the primacy of race in the American labor movement.[158] As the "conscience of organized labor," Randolph was a solitary figure at its meetings, and he was virtually unknown outside of progressive circles.[159] Randolph's remarks during the 1943 AFL convention in Boston were typical of his message: "The race problem is the number one problem of America today. It is the number one problem of American labor. It is the number one problem of the American Federation of Labor."[160] Year after year, delegates dismissed and ignored Randolph when he took the podium, and those who did not walk out for a cigarette often heckled or interrupted him. Despite this disrespect, Randolph felt obligated to keep the BSCP in the AFL because he thought it was important to have at least one African American voice represented within the ranks of the nation's most powerful labor federation.[161]

Randolph handled disrespectful racial incidents in the AFL stoically, but he never backed down from a good debate. His most memorable sparring matches were with George Meany, longtime president of the AFL and AFL-CIO, who reacted to one of Randolph's proposals by lashing out, "Who the hell appointed you as guardian of all the Negro members in America?"[162] As if in response, Randolph helped found the Negro American Labor Council (NALC) to assist in resolving the problems of racism and discrimination within the labor movement. In the early 1960s, African Americans held less than 1 percent of trade union apprenticeship positions, and exclusionary labor practices contributed to African American unemployment rates of nearly 20 percent, more than double of the rate for white workers.[163] In an era known for dramatic street protests, the NALC has been forgotten because it chiefly operated behind the scenes through lobbying efforts. To be sure, the NALC did not completely avoid mass action. In 1964, for example, it led a successful demonstration in Albany, New York, to raise the state's minimum wage. Randolph's advancement of such causes illustrates his links with the tradition of social democracy propounded by Ferdinand Lassalle, the nineteenth-century

German socialist theorist who advocated using existing political and government institutions to create socialist reforms.[164]

Black Nationalism presents another context in which to locate Randolph's
life and work. Throughout his career, Randolph was an integrationist. He
rejected the nationalist tenants of Garveyism in the early twentieth century,
and most of his efforts were aimed at integrating African Americans into
the political system and labor market. He criticized the idea of "a separate
black economy" as unrealistic and undesirable, working instead toward carv-
ing greater space for African Americans in "the mainstream of the economy
where the best jobs are to be found."[165] Writing in 1967, Randolph applauded
gains of "basic democratic rights," but he called attention to "the new frontier
of the civil rights crusade: working for higher wages, better schools, better
houses, more jobs."[166] Although the term "integration" became anathema to
many, none other than Malcolm X described Randolph as "less confused than
the rest," backhanded but high praise from the man who famously characterized integration as akin to moving into a burning house.[167] Statements such as
"Freedom is never granted; it is won. Justice is never given; it is exacted" could
easily be attributed to Malcolm X, but this quote, of course, is vintage A. Philip
Randolph. The two saw the problem of racism in America quite differently,
but they shared a work ethic and devotion to their causes that was impressive,
and they were in agreement that the economic impact of discrimination was
especially troubling.[168]

In 2002, the Afrocentric scholar Molefi K. Asante listed A. Philip Randolph
as one of the "100 Greatest African Americans."[169] Several schools are named
in Randolph's honor (including in New York City, Philadelphia, Atlanta, and
Jacksonville), two museums are dedicated to memorializing his work (the A.
Philip Randolph Porter Museum in Chicago and a permanent installation at
Edward Waters College in Jacksonville), statues of him have been placed in
Union Station in Washington, DC, and in Boston's Back Bay Station, and a
U.S. postage stamp commemorating him was issued in 1989. Housed in Washington, the A. Philip Randolph Institute carries on his legacy of organizing for
equal economic opportunity and civil rights for all.[170] A critically praised and
beautifully illustrated biography for young readers portrays Randolph's life as
a series of heroic fights against injustice.[171] Despite these efforts to maintain
the causes he advanced and to preserve his place in public consciousness,
few associate A. Philip Randolph with the towering achievements of the civil
rights movement.

There are several reasons for Randolph's obscurity in popular memory. The
label "socialist" is a political liability in the contemporary United States, and
the position of "integrationist" was a taboo among many of the activists who
inherited the causes he championed. Moreover, his home within the labor

movement seems irrelevant to a generation of people coming of age in an era when union-busting and "right to work" laws have devastated the labor movement. Union membership in the United States has steadily declined since the 1950s, and structural changes in the global economy suggest that it is unlikely that labor's World War II–era heyday will reoccur.[172] Responses to a 1969 *Ebony* article on Randolph as "Labor's Grand Old Man" indicate the ways he has been remembered and hint at the reasons why so many people have forgotten him. "All I can say is no wonder we never got anywhere," wrote one reader. "It is amazing to see a man of his age with such erect bearing, after such a long time on his knees." While some criticized Randolph's socialism, others were positive in their regard. "Without men like Mr. Randolph, there would be no black militants today. Those who consider him an Uncle Tom do not know they history"; and another commented: "I'm so proud of him and all that he's done not only for blacks but for America as well. He was out working for the cause of justice in a time more wicked than ours."[173]

As editors of this volume, we hope that the primary sources in this collection encourage further scholarship on Randolph and inspire a new generation to confront the issues of their time with the boldness that he exemplified. We have selected more than seventy documents from the hundreds attributable to Randolph. These materials were gathered from archival and manuscript collections, clipped from newspapers, and tracked down in presidential libraries. A majority of these selections are not available in a digital format and have not been reproduced elsewhere. Unlike most major African American leaders, Randolph never published an autobiography or book supporting the causes he represented. In the absence of such a work, we have aimed to approximate in this volume what Randolph might have compiled. We believe that the documents assembled here represent the best of Randolph's writings, and we hope that we have presented his work in a manner that proves useful for educators, students, and aficionados of African American history.

The volume is organized thematically in eight chapters, the first of which features documentary sources spanning Randolph's long association (1925–1966) with the Brotherhood of Sleeping Car Porters. Composed largely of congressional testimony, AFL transcripts, and Randolph's writings in African American newspapers, this chapter offers a broad view of Randolph's role within the BSCP.

As the leader of a labor union that exclusively represented black workers, Randolph was symbolically important. In this capacity, Randolph used annual AFL conventions to raise awareness about opportunities and limitations African Americans faced in a variety of industries. His reports on the state of the black working class given to AFL audiences, as well as his remarks on a variety of issues ranging from African American small business owner-ship to the necessity of a federal minimum wage comprise chapter 2.

Throughout the nearly half century that he was an iconic figure in the black freedom struggle, Randolph voiced his opinion on everything from lynching to the lessons of African American history. The documents in chapter 3 are collected from obvious sources such as *The Messenger* and *Black Worker* but also include a commencement speech, a keynote address from the NALC, and remarks made at an African Methodist Episcopal meeting in Bermuda.

Chapter 4 contains Randolph's political writings. These are particularly salient because he witnessed the dramatic party alignments during the 1930s, remained a committed socialist, and took a hard-line anti-Communist stance. He critiqued America's two-party democracy, but he also saw the potential of African Americans to form a key political block as swing voters in closely contested elections.

In some aspects, Randolph's leadership in the March on Washington Move-ment represents the apex of his political power. Chapter 5 includes the initial call to march, letters to Walter White and Franklin D. Roosevelt leading up to the event, official MOWM documents, and a lengthy essay published by Ray-ford Logan in his edited anthology, *What the Negro Wants*. The Fair Employ-ment Practices Committee is inseparable from MOWM, and this chapter concludes with Randolph's testimony about the importance of making this agency a permanent fixture in the federal government.

Chapter 6 encompasses Randolph's contributions to, and impressions of, the sweep of civil rights activities during the 1950s and 1960s. Beginning with his reaction to the murder of Emmett Till and ending with a letter to an old friend about the Ocean Hill–Brownsville crisis, this chapter covers much of the "golden age" of the civil rights movement. Transcripts of Ran-dolph's speeches at the 1963 March on Washington and other major events are highlights, as are excerpts from his *Amsterdam News* column, The Crisis of Victory.

Randolph lived through two world wars, the Korean War, and the tensions of the cold war. The documents in chapter 7 illuminate his understanding that military desegregation was a necessary step in the struggle for equality and highlight some of the ways in which Randolph pressured President Truman to sign Executive Order 9066. Remarks from the *Congressional Record* are included, as are letters to the White House and correspondence with Jackie Robinson and George Houser.

Randolph's vision for a just racial and economic order extended beyond America's geo-political boundaries. Randolph traveled the world, thought about how race reflected the global economic order, and saw decolonization as a unique possibility to reform the international status quo. The documents in the final chapter range from writings on Africa to Randolph's impressions of American tourists in Europe. Equal parts political commentary and observations on international developments, a common thread uniting these pieces is Randolph's belief that international affairs impacted race relations in the United States.

NOTES

1. Cornelius Bynum, *A. Philip Randolph and the Struggle for Civil Rights* (Urbana: University of Illinois Press, 2010), xix.

2. Jacquelyn Dowd Hall, "The Long Civil Rights Movement and the Political Uses of the Past," *Journal of American History* 91, no. 4 (March 2005): 1233–63; Robert Korstad and Nelson Lichtenstein, "Opportunities Found and Lost: Labor, Radicals, and the Early Civil Rights Movement," *Journal of American History* 75, no. 3 (December 1988): 1233–63; Richard Dalfiume, "The Forgotten Years of the Negro Revolution," *Journal of American History* 55, no. 1 (June 1968): 90–106; also see Sundiata Cha-Jua and Clarence Lang, "The Long Movement as Vampire: Temporal and Spatial Fallacies in Recent Black Freedom Studies," *Journal of African American History* 92, no. 2 (Spring 2007): 265, and Hassan Kwame Jeffries, *Bloody Lowndes: Civil Rights and Black Power in Alabama's Black Belt* (New York: New York University Press, 2009), 257n15.

3. Bayard Rustin, *Strategies for Freedom: The Changing Patterns of Black Protest* (New York: Columbia University Press, 1976), 14.

4. Quote from Eric Arnesen, "A. Philip Randolph: Labor and the New Black Politics," in *The Human Tradition in American Labor History*, ed. Eric Arnesen (Wilmington, Del.: Scholarly Resources, 2004), 174.

5. A. Philip Randolph, "The Spirit of Human Rights," box 2, A. Philip Randolph Collection, Manuscripts, Archives and Rare Books Division, Schomburg Center for Research in Black Culture, New York (hereafter cited as Randolph Collection).

6. William H. Harris, "A. Philip Randolph, Black Workers, and the Labor Movement," in *Labor Leaders in America*, ed. Melvyn Dubofsky and Warren Van Tine (Urbana: University of Illinois Press, 1987), 263.

7. "The Indictment," *The Messenger*, April 1926.

8. Roi Ottley, *New World A-Coming* (1943; repr., New York: Arno Press, 1968), 251.

9. Theodore Kornweibel, *No Crystal Stair: Black Life and the "Messenger," 1917–1928* (Westport, Conn.: Greenwood Press, 1975), 27.

10. Edwin Embree, *13 Against the Odds* (Port Washington, N.Y.: Kennikat Press, 1944), 216.

11. "A. Philip Randolph, Outline—Autobiography," box 42, A. Philip Randolph Papers, Library of Congress (hereafter cited as Randolph Papers); on BSCP fire, see Jervis Anderson, *A. Philip Randolph: A Biographical Portrait* (New York: Harcourt Brace Jovanovich, 1973), 354.

12. Quote from "Draft of 'The Black Militants of the Sixties Stand Upon the Shoulders of the Black Radicals of the Twenties,'" box 42, Randolph Papers. On religion and Randolph's childhood, see Bynum, *A. Philip Randolph and the Struggle for Civil Rights*, 1–23, Cynthia Taylor, *A. Philip Randolph: The Religious Journey of an African American Labor Leader* (New York: New York University Press, 2006), 7–36.

13. A. Philip Randolph, "Vita," box 41, Randolph Papers.

14. James Weldon Johnson, *Along This Way: The Autobiography of James Weldon Johnson* (New York: Viking Press, 1933), 45; on Jacksonville during Randolph's boyhood, see Abel A. Bartley, *Keeping the Faith: Race, Politics, and Social Development in Jacksonville, Florida, 1940–1970* (Westport, Conn.: Greenwood Press, 2000), 1–5, and Edwin Akins, "When a Minority Becomes a Majority: Blacks in Jacksonville Politics, 1887–1907," *Florida Historical Quarterly* 53, no. 2 (October 1974): 123–45.

15. Marvin Dunn, *The Beast in Florida: A History of Anti-Black Violence* (Gainesville: University Press of Florida, 2013), 2, 37; Michael Newton, *The Invisible Empire: The Ku Klux Klan in Florida* (Gainesville: University Press of Florida, 2001), 33.

16. Paul Ortiz, *Emancipation Betrayed: The Hidden History of Black Organizing and White Violence in Florida from Reconstruction to the Bloody Election of 1920* (Berkeley: University of California Press, 2005), 61–83.

17. John Hope Franklin, *Mirror to America: The Autobiography of John Hope Franklin* (New York: Farrar, Straus and Giroux, 2005), 3–4.

18. Parks quoted in Jeanne Theoharis, *The Rebellious Life of Mrs. Rosa Parks* (Boston: Beacon, 2013), 1, 7.

19. "Interview with Mr. A. Philip Randolph by Wendell Wray, New York City, June 20, 1972," 73, Columbia Center for Oral History, Butler Library, Columbia University; on childhood experiences of racism, see William H. Chafe and Raymond Gavins, eds., *Remembering Jim Crow: African Americans Tell about Life in the Segregated South* (New York: New Press, 2001), 152–206; also see Jennifer Ritterhouse, *Growing Up Jim Crow: How Black and White Children Learned Race* (Chapel Hill: University of North Carolina Press, 2006), and John Dollard and Allison Davis, *Children of Bondage: The Personality Development of Negro Youth in the Urban South* (Washington, D.C.: American Council on Education, 1940).

20. Anderson, *A. Philip Randolph*, 36.

21. Robert Cassanello, *To Render Invisible: Jim Crow and Public Life in New South Jacksonville* (Gainesville: University Press of Florida, 2013), 59–68.

22. Sarah Garland, *Divided We Fail: The Story of an African American Community that Ended the Era of School Desegregation* (Boston: Beacon, 2013), 30–59; Leon Litwack, *Trouble in Mind: Black Southerners in the Age of Jim Crow* (New York: Knopf, 1998), 61–68; Winfred E. Pitts, *A Victory of Sorts: Desegregation in a Southern Community* (Lanham, Md.: University Press of America, 2003), 109–42.

23. Andrew E. Kersten, *A. Philip Randolph: A Life in the Vanguard* (Lanham, Md.: Rowman & Littlefield, 2007), 4.

24. Randolph quoted in Anderson, *A. Philip Randolph*, 52.

25. James Weldon Johnson, *Black Manhattan* (1930; repr., New York: Da Capo Press, 1991), 145–69; Seth M. Scheiner, *Negro Mecca: A History of the Negro in New York City, 1865–1920* (New York: New York University Press, 1965), 6–12. A comprehensive survey of works exploring themes of migration, urbanization, and proletarianization is beyond the scope of this essay. For a general overview of the literature, see Kenneth Kusmer, "The Black Urban Experience in American History," in *The State of Afro-American History: Past, Present, and Future,* ed. Darlene Clark Hine (Baton Rouge: Louisiana State University Press, 1986), 91–122. Some important works on the subject are Beth Tompkins Bates, *The Making of Black Detroit in the Age of Henry Ford* (Chapel Hill: University of North Carolina Press, 2012); Jack Conroy, *They Seek a City* (New York: Doubleday, 1945); Joe William Trotter, *Black Milwaukee: The Making of an Industrial Proletariat, 1915–1945* (Chicago: University of Chicago Press, 1985); Joe William Trotter, ed., *The Great Migration in His-*

torical Perspective: New Dimensions of Race, Class, and Gender (Bloomington: University of Indiana Press, 1991); and Isabel Wilkerson, *The Warmth of Other Suns: The Epic Story of America's Great Migration* (New York: Random House, 2010).

26. Carter G. Woodson, *A Century of Negro Migration* (Washington, D.C.: Association for the Study of Negro Life and History, 1918), 147–66; also see Ortiz, *Emancipation Betrayed,* 128–41.

27. Nat Brandt, *Harlem at War: The Black Experience in World War II* (New York: Knopf, 1996), 27–34.

28. Quote from Nathan I. Huggins, *Harlem Renaissance* (New York: Oxford University Press, 1971), 13; on Harlem's multinational character, see Roi Ottley, *The Negro in New York: An Informal Social History* (New York: New York Public Library, 1967), 188–94.

29. Bynum, *A. Philip Randolph and the Struggle for Civil Rights,* 48.

30. Kersten, *A. Philip Randolph,* 12; on Randolph's speaking ability, see William H. Harris, "A. Philip Randolph as a Charismatic Leader, 1925–1941," *Journal of Negro History* 64, no. 4 (Autumn 1979): 303.

31. On empowerment and literacy as themes of the African American experience, see Heather Andrea Williams, *Self-Taught: African American Education in Slavery and Freedom* (Chapel Hill: University of North Carolina Press, 2005), 30–44; Jacqueline Jones Royster, *Traces of a Stream: Literacy and Social Change among African American Women* (Pittsburgh, Pa.: University of Pittsburgh Press, 2000), 42–76; and James Collins, "Literacy and Literacies," *Annual Review of Anthropology* 24 (1995): 75–93.

32. "Interview with Mr. A. Philip Randolph by Wendell Wray, New York City, June 20, 1972," Columbia Center for Oral History, 157.

33. Kersten, *A. Philip Randolph,* 13.

34. Randolph quoted in Anderson, *A. Philip Randolph,* 82.

35. Tiffany Gill, *Beauty Shop Politics: African American Women's Activism in the Beauty Industry* (Urbana: University of Illinois Press, 2010), 51–52; Paula F. Pfeffer, *A. Phillip Randolph: Pioneer of the Civil Rights Movement* (Baton Rouge: Louisiana State University Press, 1996), 8–9.

36. On gender and civil rights activism, see Kathryn L. Nasstrom, "Down to Now: Memory, Narrative, and Women's Leadership in the Civil Rights Movement in Atlanta, Georgia," *Gender and History* 11, no. 1 (April 1999): 114; Charles Payne, "Men Led, but Women Organized: Movement Participation in the Mississippi Delta," in *Women and the Civil Rights Movement: Trailblazers and Torchbearers,* ed. Vicki L. Crawford, Jacqueline Anne Rouse, and Barbara Woods (Bloomington: Indiana University Press, 1993), 1–12; Danielle L. McGuire, *At the Dark End of the Street: Black Women, Rape, and Resistance—A New History of the Civil Rights Movement from Rosa Parks to the Rise of Black Power* (New York: Knopf, 2010), 84–89; and Peter J. Ling and Sharon Monteith, eds., *Gender and the Civil Rights Movement* (New Brunswick, N.J.: Rutgers University Press, 2004), 6.

37. Anna Arnold Hedgeman, *The Trumpet Sounds: A Memoir of Negro Leadership* (New York: Holt, Rinehart and Winston, 1964), 176–81; Lynne Olson, *Freedom's Daughters: The Unsung Heroines of the Civil Rights Movement from 1830–1970* (New York: Scribner, 2002), 283–90; Charles Euchner, *Nobody Turn Me Around: A People's History of the 1963 March on Washington* (Boston: Beacon, 2010), 156–57; William P. Jones, *The March on Washington: Jobs, Freedom, and the Forgotten History of Civil Rights* (New York: Norton, 2013), 165–66, 175–76.

38. Dorothy I. Height, *Open Wide the Freedom Gates: A Memoir* (New York: Public Affairs, 2003), 145–46, and "We Wanted the Voice of a Women to Be Heard," in *Sisters in*

the Struggle: African American Women in the Civil Rights-Black Power Movement, ed. Bettye Collier-Thomas and V. P. Franklin (New York: New York University Press, 2001), 86–87.

39. On the multinational aspects of Harlem radicalism during this period, see Winston James, *Holding Aloft the Banner of Ethiopia: Caribbean Radicalism in Early Twentieth-Century America* (New York: Verso, 1998); Minkah Makalani, *In the Cause of Freedom: Radical Black Internationalism from Harlem to London, 1917–1939* (Chapel Hill: University of North Carolina Press, 2011); Jeffrey B. Perry, *Hubert Harrison: The Voice of Harlem Radicalism, 1883–1918* (New York: Columbia University Press, 2009); Joyce Moore Turner, *Caribbean Crusaders and the Harlem Renaissance* (Urbana: University of Illinois Press, 2005); and Irma Watkins-Owens, *Blood Relations: Caribbean Immigrants and the Harlem Community, 1900–1930* (Bloomington: University of Indiana Press, 1996).

40. "Interview: A. Philip Randolph & Richard Parrish," May 1, 1975, box 1, Randolph Collection.

41. Sondra K. Wilson, ed., *The Messenger Reader: Stories, Poetry, and Essays from* The Messenger *Magazine* (New York: Modern Library, 2000); also see Jacob C. Jenkins, "*The Messenger* and the Case for Black Scientific Radicalism" (MA thesis, Southern Illinois University Edwardsville, 2010).

42. "The Messenger Is the Only Magazine of Scientific Radicalism in the World Published by Negroes," *The Messenger* 1 (November 1917).

43. Kornweibel, *No Crystal Stair,* 45.

44. Woodrow Wilson's speech in *A Day of Dedication: The Essential Writings and Speeches of Woodrow Wilson,* ed. Alfred Fried (New York: Macmillan, 1965), 308.

45. "Making the World Safe for Democracy," *The Messenger* 1 (November 1917).

46. "How to Stop a Lynching," *The Messenger* 3 (August 1919).

47. "The Ku Klux Klan—How to Fight It," *The Messenger* 5 (November 1921).

48. "The Week," *Chicago Defender,* July 15, 1922.

49. "New Leadership for the New Negro," *The Messenger* 3 (May–June 1919); also see "The Crisis of the Crisis," *The Messenger* 3 (July 1919); "The Negro Radicals," *The Messenger* 3 (October 1919); for Du Bois's call to close ranks, see *The Crisis* 16 (July 1918). Much has been written about Du Bois in World War I; for a sampling, see Nina Mjagkij, *Loyalty in Time of Trial: The African American Experience in World War I* (Lanham, Md.: Rowman & Littlefield, 2011), 121–40; Mark Ellis, "Closing Ranks and Seeking Honors: W. E. B. Du Bois and World War I," *Journal of American History* 79, no. 1 (June 1992): 96–124; Mark Ellis, "W. E. B. Du Bois and the Formation of Black Opinion in World War I: A Commentary on The Damnable Dilemma," *Journal of American History* 81, no. 4 (March 1995): 1584–90; and William Jordan, "The Damnable Dilemma: African-American Accommodation and Protest during World War I," *Journal of American History* 81, no. 4 (March 1995): 1562–83.

50. Anderson, *A. Philip Randolph,* 120–37; David E. Cronon, *Black Moses: The Story of Marcus Garvey and the Universal Negro Improvement Association* (Madison: University of Wisconsin Press, 1969), 188–92; Judith Stein, *The World of Marcus Garvey: Race and Class in Modern Society* (Baton Rouge: Louisiana State University Press, 1986), 153–170; Wilson Jeremiah Moses, *The Golden Age of Black Nationalism, 1850–1925* (New York: Oxford University Press, 1978), 265–66.

51. For examples, see *The Messenger* 6 (July and October 1922). Makalani, *In the Cause of Freedom,* 106–9, attributes the vitriolic nativist attacks on Garvey to Randolph's coeditor, Chandler Owen.

52. "Reasons Why Black and White Workers Should Combine in Labor Unions," *The Messenger* 3 (July 1919); Bynum, *A. Philip Randolph and the Struggle for Civil Rights,* 101–14.

53. Palmer quoted in Kersten, *A. Philip Randolph,* 17.

54. Theodore Kornweibel, *Seeing Red: Federal Campaigns against Black Militancy, 1919–1925* (Bloomington: Indiana University Press, 1999), 76–99.

55. Kornweibel, *No Crystal Stair,* 3–4; on the arrest, also see Special Agent Sawken, August 10, 1918, box 29, FBI Files, Library of Congress (also available in OG 265716, RG 65, National Archives).

56. Kornweibel, *No Crystal Stair,* 121.

57. On the Garland Fund, see Gloria Garrett Samson, *The American Fund for Public Service: Charles Garland and Radical Philanthropy, 1922–1941* (Greenwich, Conn.: Greenwood Press, 1996).

58. Rhone Fraser, "Publishing Freedom: African American Editors and the Long Civil Rights Struggle" (PhD diss., Temple University, 2012), 140–54.

59. Jack Santino, *Miles of Smiles, Years of Struggles: Stories of Black Pullman Porters* (Urbana: University of Illinois Press, 1981), 52; Larry Tye, *Rising from the Rails: Pullman Porters and the Makings of the Black Middle Class* (New York: Henry Holt, 2005).

60. Kersten, *A. Philip Randolph,* 27–28; Juan Williams, *Thurgood Marshall: American Revolutionary* (New York: Random House, 1998), 38.

61. Nixon quoted in Theoharis, *The Rebellious Life of Mrs. Rosa Parks,* 19.

62. E. D. Nixon, "When Montgomery Was Not Like St. Louis," in *Refuse to Stand Silently By: An Oral History of Grass Roots Social Activism in America, 1921–1964,* ed. Eliot Wigginton (New York: Doubleday, 1992), 22–28, 219–28.

63. William H. Harris, *The Harder We Run: Black Workers since the Civil War* (New York: Oxford University Press, 1982), 78; Bernard Mergen, "The Pullman Porter: From 'George' to Brotherhood," *South Atlantic Quarterly* 73 (1974): 224–25, 228.

64. Quotations from Anderson, *A. Philip Randolph,* 158, and Stanley Buder, *Pullman: An Experiment in Industrial Order and Community Planning* (New York: Oxford University Press, 1967), 15–17.

65. Bynum, *A. Philip Randolph and the Struggle for Civil Rights,* 123; for an excellent autobiography that includes dozens of reminiscences about working during this era, see Robert E. Turner, *Memories of a Retired Pullman Porter* (New York: Exposition Press, 1954); also of interest is Lyn Hughes, ed., *An Anthology of Respect: The Pullman Porters National Historic Registry of African American Railroad Employees* (Chicago: Hughes Peterson, 2007).

66. William H. Harris, *Keeping the Faith: A. Philip Randolph, Milton P. Webster, and the Brotherhood of Sleeping Car Porters, 1925–37* (Urbana: University of Illinois Press, 1977), 101–4; Eric Arnesen, *Brotherhoods of Color: Black Railroad Workers and the Struggle for Equality* (Cambridge: Harvard University Press, 2001), 16–23.

67. On the image of Pullman porters, see Janet L. Reiff and Susan E. Hirsch, "Pullman and Its Public: Image and Aim in Making and Interpreting History," *Public Historian* 11, no. 4 (Autumn 1989): 102, and Joseph Husband, *The Story of the Pullman Car* (Chicago: A. C. McClurg, 1917), 155–56.

68. Murray Kempton, *Part of Our Time: Some Ruins and Monuments of the Thirties* (New York: Simon and Schuster, 1955), 259; the TV movie *10,000 Black Men Named George* (2002, dir. Robert Townsend) tells the story of Randolph and the BSPC.

69. Arnesen, *Brotherhoods of Color,* 58–61; Harris, *Keeping the Faith,* 17–18; and "A. Philip Randolph," *American Labor* (August 1968): 44–49, box 43, Randolph Papers.

70. Kersten, *A. Philip Randolph,* 25–26.

71. Beth Tompkins Bates, *Pullman Porters and the Rise of Protest Politics in Black America, 1925–1945* (Chapel Hill: University of North Carolina Press, 2001), 10–16, 126–47;

Sterling D. Spero and Abram L. Harris, *The Black Worker: The Negro and the Labor Movement* (1959; repr., New York: Atheneum, 1968), 430–60.

72. Anderson, *A. Philip Randolph*, 207.

73. Harris, "A. Philip Randolph, Black Workers, and the Labor Movement," in Dubofsky and Van Tine, *Labor Leaders in America*, 264–66; Bruce Minton and John Stuart, *Men Who Lead Labor* (1937; repr., Freeport, N.Y.: Books for Libraries Press [1969]), 155–58.

74. Pfeffer, *A. Philip Randolph*, 24–25.

75. Kersten, *A. Philip Randolph*, 44–45; Anderson, *A. Philip Randolph*, 217–25.

76. Harris, *Keeping the Faith*, 183–216; Bynum, *A. Philip Randolph and the Struggle for Civil Rights*, 127; "U.S. Supreme Court Decision Seen as Aid to Brotherhood," *Amsterdam News*, July 9, 1930; also see Brailsford Brazeal, *The Brotherhood of Sleeping Car Porters: Its Origin and Development* (New York: Harper, 1946).

77. John P. Davis, "A Survey of Problems under the New Deal," *Journal of Negro Education* 5 (Winter 1936): 8–11; John P. Davis, "A Black Inventory of the New Deal," *The Crisis* 42 (May 1935): 141–42, 154. Raymond Wolters, *Negroes and the Great Depression: The Problem of Economic Recovery* (Westport, Conn.: Greenwood, 1970), remains a useful general study of African Americans during the depression and New Deal.

78. Cheryl Lynn Greenberg, *To Ask for an Equal Chance: African Americans in the Great Depression* (Lanham, Md.: Rowman & Littlefield, 2009), 21–41; Michael Goldfield, *The Color of Politics: Race and the Mainsprings of American Politics* (New York: New Press, 1997), 202–5.

79. John B. Kirby, *Black Americans in the Roosevelt Era: Liberalism and Race* (Knoxville: University of Tennessee Press, 1980), 218–35; Patricia Sullivan, *Days of Hope: Race and Democracy in the New Deal Era* (Chapel Hill: University of North Carolina Press, 1996), 1–9; Roger Biles, *The South and the New Deal* (Lexington: University Press of Kentucky, 1994), 58–82; Harvard Sitkoff, *A New Deal for Blacks: The Emergence of Civil Rights as a National Issue* (New York: Oxford University Press, 1978), 34–57; Richard Sterner, *The Negro's Share: A Study of Income, Consumption, Housing, and Public Assistance* (New York: Harper, 1943), 219–38.

80. Randolph quote from John P. Davis, *Let Us Build a National Negro Congress* (Washington, D.C.: National Sponsoring Committee, National Negro Congress, 1935), 3; for an overview of the National Negro Congress, see John Baxter Streater, *The National Negro Congress, 1936–1947* (Cincinnati, OH: University of Cincinnati Press, 1981), and Lawrence S. Wittner, "The National Negro Congress: A Reassessment," *American Quarterly* 12 (Winter 1970): 883–901.

81. Erik S. Gellman, *Death Blow to Jim Crow: The National Negro Congress and the Rise of Militant Civil Rights* (Chapel Hill: University of North Carolina Press, 2012), 1–5.

82. Randolph quoted in Anderson, *A. Philip Randolph*, 234.

83. Erik S. Gellman, "Carthage Must Be Destroyed: Race, City Politics, and the Campaign to Integrate Chicago Transportation Work, 1929–1943," *Labor: Studies in Working-Class History of the Americas* 2, no. 2 (2005): 81–114.

84. On the Nazi-Soviet Pact and its impact on African American activists, see Mark Naison, *Communists in Harlem during the Great Depression* (Urbana: University of Illinois Press, 1983), 232–33; Doug Rossinow, *Visions of Progress: The Left-Liberal Tradition in America* (Philadelphia: University of Pennsylvania Press, 2008), 157–62; Frank A. Warren III, *Liberals and Communism: The 'Red Decade' Revisited* (Westport, Conn.: Greenwood Press, 1966), 163–215; and Maurice Isserman, *Which Side Were You On? The American Communist Party during the Second World War* (Middletown, Conn.: Wesleyan University Press, 1988).

85. Gellman, *Death Blow to Jim Crow,* 149–64; Bunche quoted in Ralph Ellison, "A Congress Jim Crow Didn't Attend," *New Masses,* May 14, 1940.

86. A. Philip Randolph, "Why I Would Not Stand for Re-election in the National Negro Congress," *Black Worker* 12 (May 1940).

87. Gellman, *Death Blow to Jim Crow,* 156.

88. "Randolph Says Race Congress Not Communist," *Chicago Defender,* February 29, 1936; "Randolph Defends the Negro Congress," *Daily Worker,* March 5, 1936; also see Eric Arnesen, "No 'Graver Danger': Black Anticommunism, the Communist Party, and the Race Question," *Labor: Studies in Working-Class History of the Americas* 3, no. 4 (2006): 13–41.

89. Anderson, *A. Philip Randolph,* 248; Brazeal, *The Brotherhood of Sleeping Car Porters,* 234–35; Kempton, *Part of Our Time,* 250; Turner, *Memories of a Retired Pullman Porter,* 138; Lerone Bennett, "The Day They Didn't March," *Ebony* 32, no. 4 (February 1977): 132; Ted Potson, "From Shakespeare to FEPC," *New York Post,* February 13, 1946, box 1, Randolph Collection.

90. "1941: The Pullman Porters March on Washington," *The New Leader,* July 11, 1955, FSN Sc 002, 968-4 (microfiche), Clipping Files, Schomburg Center for Research in Black Culture, New York.

91. "Let's March on Capital 10,000 Strong," *Pittsburgh Courier,* January 25, 1941.

92. A. Philip Randolph, "March on Washington Movement Presents Program for the Negro," in *What the Negro Wants,* ed. Rayford Logan (Chapel Hill: University of North Carolina Press, 1944), 144–45; Herbert Garfinkel, *When Negroes March: The March on Washington Movement in the Organizational Politics for FEPC* (1959; repr., New York: Atheneum, 1969), 38–42; David Lucander, *Winning the War for Democracy: The March on Washington Movement, 1941–1946* (Urbana: University of Illinois Press, 2014), 29–40.

93. The low estimate of 10,000 marchers was from Randolph's initial call in early 1941; projected estimates of anticipated attendees steadily increased throughout the summer. For a chronology of the projections, see Benjamin Quarles, "A. Philip Randolph: Labor Leader at Large," in *Black Leaders of the Twentieth Century,* ed. John Hope Franklin and August Meier (Urbana: University of Illinois Press, 1982), 155.

94. "A. Philip Randolph," *Chicago Defender,* February 8, 1941.

95. "The Randolph Plan," *Chicago Defender,* March 15, 1941.

96. "Executive Order 8802," *Federal Register* 6, no. 125 (June 27, 1941): 4544; June 18, 1941, Franklin D. Roosevelt Day by Day Project, Pare Lorentz Center, FDR Presidential Library, available at www.fdrlibrary.marist.edu. No notes were taken or recordings made of the White House meeting, but historians have assembled accounts of the discussion from various sources: see Anderson, *A. Philip Randolph,* 256–58; Bates, *Pullman Porters,* 158–59; Lerone Bennett, *Confrontation: Black and White* (Chicago: Johnson, 1965), 176–77; Garfinkel, *When Negroes March,* 53–57; Doris Kearns Goodwin, *No Ordinary Time: Franklin & Eleanor Roosevelt—The Home Front in World War II* (New York: Simon & Schuster, 1994), 249–53; Kenneth R. Janken, *Walter White: Mr. NAACP* (Chapel Hill: University of North Carolina Press, 2006), 257; and David Welky, *Marching Across the Color Line: A. Philip Randolph and Civil Rights in the World War II Era* (New York: Oxford University Press, 2013), 72–74.

97. A. Philip Randolph, "How and Why the March Was Postponed," *Black Worker* 13 (August 1941).

98. "A. Philip Randolph, Leader," *Amsterdam News,* July 12, 1941.

99. "Interview with Bayard Rustin," March 28, 1974, box 58, August Meier Papers, Schomburg Center for Research in Black Culture, New York.

100. "Randolph's Speech Explains Why He Called Off the March," *Amsterdam News,* July 19, 1941.

101. Lucander, *Winning the War for Democracy,* 48–54.

102. "Report of Committee on Resolutions to National Policy Conference," Proceedings of Conference Held in Detroit, September 26–27, 1942, 35, FSN Sc 002, 968-3 (microfiche), Clipping Files, Schomburg Center for Research in Black Culture, New York.

103. August Meier and Elliot Rudwick, *Along the Color Line: Explorations of the Black Experience* (Urbana: University of Illinois Press, 1976), 344–53; John H. Bracey Jr. and August Meier, "Allies or Adversaries?: The NAACP, A. Philip Randolph, and the 1941 March on Washington," *Georgia Historical Quarterly* 75, no. 1 (Spring 1991): 1–17; Rustin, *Strategies for Freedom,* 18; Wallace Lee, "Is Civil Disobedience Practical to Win Full Rights for Negroes?," *Negro Digest* 1 (March 1943): 25.

104. Joseph Kip Kosek, *Acts of Conscience: Christian Nonviolence and Modern American Democracy* (New York: Columbia University Press, 2009), 183–85; Marian Mollin, *Radical Pacifism in Modern America: Egalitarianism and Protest* (Philadelphia: University of Pennsylvania Press, 2006), 9; also see Erik Erikson, *Gandhi's Truth: On the Origins of Militant Nonviolence* (New York: Norton, 1969), 413–34.

105. Randolph quoted in George M. Houser, *Erasing the Color Line* (New York: Fellowship Publications, 1945), 7.

106. "Slave psychology" from "MOWM Not Anti-White," press release, August 19, 1943, box 26, Randolph Papers; for an excellent discussion of Randolph's motives for keeping the organization all-black, see Pfeffer, *A. Philip Randolph,* 55–57.

107. "Weeping for the Poor White Folks," speech, 1943, box 34, Randolph Papers.

108. Randolph, "March on Washington Movement Presents Program for the Negro," 155.

109. Louis Ruchames, *Race, Jobs, and Politics: The Story of FEPC* (New York: Columbia University Press, 1953), 22.

110. A sampling of the many FEPC histories includes Andrew E. Kersten, *Race, Jobs, and the War: The FEPC in the Midwest, 1941–1946* (Urbana: University of Illinois Press, 2000); Louis Kesselman, *The Social Politics of FEPC* (Chapel Hill: University of North Carolina Press, 1948); Paul D. Moreno, *From Direct Action to Affirmative Action: Fair Employment Law and Policy in America, 1933–1972* (Baton Rouge: Louisiana University Press, 1997); Paul F. Norgrent and Samuel Hill, *Toward Fair Employment* (New York: Columbia University Press, 1964); Merl E. Reed, *Seedtime for the Modern Civil Rights Movement: The President's Committee on Fair Employment Practice, 1941–1946* (Baton Rouge: Louisiana State University Press, 1991); and Ruchames, *Race, Jobs, and Politics.*

111. Robert C. Weaver, "Racial Employment Trends in National Defense," *Phylon* 2 (4th Quarter, 1941): 337–58; William J. Collins, "Race, Roosevelt, and Wartime Production: Fair Employment in World War II Labor Markets," *American Economic Review,* 91, no. 1 (March 2001): 272–86.

112. On Robinson's work at Lockheed, see Arnold Rampersad, *Jackie Robinson: A Biography* (Knopf: New York, 1997), 87; on Irene Morgan, see Raymond Arsenault, *Freedom Riders: 1961 and the Struggle for Racial Justice* (New York: Oxford University Press, 2006), 11–21, and Derek Charles Catsam, *Freedom's Main Line: The Journey of Reconciliation and the Freedom Rides* (Lexington: University Press of Kentucky, 2009), 14–18.

113. Hedgeman, *The Trumpet Sounds,* 87–96.

114. Anthony S. Chen, *The Fifth Freedom: Jobs, Politics, and Civil Rights in the United States, 1941–1972* (Princeton: Princeton University Press, 2009), 117–20.

115. Randolph quoted in Anderson, *A. Philip Randolph,* 227.

116. "Call to Negro America to March on Washington for Jobs and Equal Participation in National Defense," *Black Worker* 13, May 1941; on pressure politics, see Bates, *Pullman Porters,* 148–74.

117. Patterson quoted in Albert Russell Buchanan, *Black Americans in World War II* (Santa Barbara, Calif.: Clio Books, 1977), 67.

118. There are many studies of African Americans in the U.S. armed forces during World War II; among the most useful are Ulysses Lee, *The Employment of Negro Troops: Special Studies, The United States Army in World War II* (Washington, D.C.: Office of the Chief of Military History, 1966); Mattie E. Treadwell, *United States Army in World War II—Special Studies: The Women's Army Corps* (Washington, D.C.: Office of the Chief of Military History, 1954); Phillip McGuire, *Taps for a Jim Crow Army: Letters from Black Soldiers in World War II* (Lexington: University Press of Kentucky, 1983); and Charles C. Moskos, Jr., "Racial Integration in the Armed Forces," *American Journal of Sociology* 72, no. 2 (September 1966): 132–48.

119. "The Negro and the Army: A Critical Problem in Race Relations," *Washington Post,* March 19, 1944; Richard M. Dalfiume, *Desegregating the U.S. Armed Forces: Fighting on Two Fronts, 1939–1953* (Columbia: University of Missouri Press, 1969), 105–31; Pfeffer, *A. Philip Randolph,* 133–68.

120. Kimberley L. Phillips, *War! What Is It Good For?: Black Freedom Struggles and the U.S. Military from World War II to Iraq* (Chapel Hill: University of North Carolina Press, 2012): 82–86; Richard J. Stillman II, *Integration of the Negro in the U.S. Armed Forces* (New York: Praeger, 1968), 34–36.

121. *Congressional Record,* 80th Cong., 2nd sess., Senate, April 12, 1948, 4416–18; *New York Times,* April 1, 1948.

122. Roy Wilkins, *Standing Fast: The Autobiography of Roy Wilkins* (1982; repr., New York: Da Capo, 1994), 202.

123. Michael Gardner, *Harry Truman and Civil Rights: Moral Courage and Political Risks* (Carbondale: Southern Illinois University Press, 2002); Richard M. Yon and Tom Lansford, "Political Pragmatism and Civil Rights Policy: Truman and Integration of the Military," in *The Civil Rights Legacy of Harry S. Truman,* ed. Raymond H. Geselbracht (Kirksville, MO: Truman State University Press, 2007), 103–16; for a time-tested account of Truman and American race relations, see William C. Berman, *The Politics of Civil Rights in the Truman Administration* (Columbus: Ohio State University Press, 1970).

124. Steven F. Lawson, ed., *To Secure These Rights: The Report of President Harry S. Truman's Committee on Civil Rights* (Boston: Bedford, 2004), 1–41.

125. Harry S. Truman, "Executive Order 9981," in *A Documentary History of the Truman Presidency: The Truman Administration's Civil Rights Program,* ed. Dennis Merrill (New York: University Publications of America, 1996), 741.

126. Charles C. Moskos and John Sibley Butler, *All That We Can Be: Black Leadership and Racial Integration the Army Way* (New York: Basic Books, 1996), 1–14; Phillips, *War!,* 275.

127. Theoharis, *The Rebellious Life of Mrs. Rosa Parks,* 72–77.

128. Gail Milissa Grant, *At the Elbows of My Elders: One Family's Journey toward Civil Rights* (St. Louis: Missouri History Museum, 2008), 129–30.

129. Jervis Anderson, *Bayard Rustin: Troubles I've Seen* (New York: Harper, 1997), 183–90, 197–212; John D'Emilio, *Lost Prophet: The Life and Times of Bayard Rustin* (New York: Free Press, 2003), 226–41; Gerald Podair, *Bayard Rustin: American Dreamer* (Lanham, Md.: Rowman & Littlefield, 2009), 38–43; also see David L. Chappell, *A Stone of Hope:*

Prophetic Religion and the Death of Jim Crow (Chapel Hill: University of North Carolina Press, 2004), 54–62.

130. *Ebony* 12, no. 10 (August 1957): 18–19; *New York Times,* May 18, 1957; and Scott A. Sandage, "A Marble House Divided: The Lincoln Memorial, the Civil Rights Movement, and the Politics of Memory, 1939–1963," *Journal of American History* 80, no. 1 (June 1993): 154–55.

131. "Statement by A. Philip Randolph to the Prayer Pilgrimage for Freedom at the Lincoln Memorial," May 17, 1957, box 35, Randolph Papers.

132. Kersten, *A. Philip Randolph,* 94–96.

133. Bynum, *A. Philip Randolph and the Struggle for Civil Rights,* x.

134. Lerone Bennett Jr., "The March," in *The Day They Marched,* ed. Doris E. Saunders (Chicago: Johnson Publishing, 1963), 3–14; Mary L. Dudziak, *Cold War Civil Rights: Race and the Image of American Democracy* (Princeton, N.J.: Princeton University Press, 2000), 187–218; Jones, *The March on Washington,* 201–2.

135. "Address of A. Philip Randolph at the March on Washington for Jobs and Freedom," box 36, Randolph Papers.

136. Euchner, *Nobody Turn Me Around,* 150–53; for Lewis's speech, see "The March on Washington, Original Draft of SNCC Chairman John Lewis' Speech to the March," available at www.crmvet.org.

137. John Lewis with Michael D'Orso, *Walking with the Wind: A Memoir of the Movement* (New York: Simon & Schuster, 1998), 222–24.

138. Bruce Watson, *Freedom Summer: The Savage Season of 1964 That Made Mississippi Burn and Made America a Democracy* (New York: Penguin, 2010), 237–61; on Hamer, see Chana Kai Lee, *For Freedom's Sake: The Life of Fannie Lou Hamer* (Urbana: University of Illinois Press, 2000), and Chris Myers Asch, *The Senator and the Sharecropper: The Freedom Struggles of James O. Eastland and Fannie Lou Hamer* (New York: New Press, 2008).

139. Stokely Carmichael with Ekwueme Michael Thelwell, *Ready for Revolution: The Life and Struggles of Stokely Carmichael* (New York: Scribner, 2003), 382–413.

140. Dona C. Hamilton and Charles V. Hamilton, *The Dual Agenda: Race and Social Welfare Policies of Civil Rights Organizations* (New York: Columbia University Press, 1997), 147–52; William Julius Wilson, *More Than Just Race: Being Black and Poor in the Inner City* (New York: Norton, 2009), 25–61; Pfeffer, *A. Philip Randolph,* 288–91.

141. David J. Garrow, *Bearing the Cross: Martin Luther King, Jr., and the Southern Christian Leadership Conference* (New York: Perennial, 1986), 575–624.

142. Pfeffer, *A. Philip Randolph,* 283; on Chavez and labor organizing, see Susan Ferriss and Ricardo Sandoval, *The Fight in the Fields: Cesar Chavez and the Farmworkers Movement* (New York: Harcourt Brace, 1997).

143. "Black Power—A Promise or a Menace," *Black Worker,* December 1966. For discussions on the meaning and substance of Black Power, see Stokely Carmichael (Kwame Toure) and Charles V. Hamilton, *Black Power: The Politics of Liberation* (1967; repr., New York: Vintage, 1992), 34–57, and Peniel Joseph, *Waiting 'Til The Midnight Hour: A Narrative History of Black Power in America* (New York: Henry Holt, 2006), 132–73.

144. Jerald Podair, *The Strike That Changed New York: Blacks, Whites, and the Ocean Hill–Brownsville Crisis* (New Haven, Conn.: Yale University Press, 2002); Jane Anna Gordon, *Why They Couldn't Wait: A Critique of Black-Jewish Conflict over Community Control in Ocean Hill–Brownsville* (New York: Routledge, 2001); Derek Edgell, *The Movement for Community Control of New York City's Schools, 1966–1970: Class Wars* (Lewiston, N.Y.: Edwin Mellen Press, 1998); Marilyn Gittell and Maurice Berube, eds., *Confrontation at Ocean Hill–Brownsville* (New York: Praeger, 1969).

145. "An Appeal to the Community from Black Trade Unionists," *New York Times,* September 19, 1968; on white segregationists and community control, see Ronald P. Formisano, *Boston against Busing: Race, Class, and Ethnicity in the 1960s and 1970s* (Chapel Hill: University of North Carolina Press, 1991), 172–202.

146. Randolph quoted in Phyl Garland, "A. Philip Randolph: Labor's Grand Old Man," *Ebony* 24, no. 7 (May 1969): 31; for a variant of this sentiment, see "The Black Militants of the Sixties Stand Upon the Shoulders of the Negro Radicals of the Twenties," box 37, Randolph Papers.

147. Randolph quoted in Anderson, *A. Philip Randolph,* 346.

148. Randolph quoted in Garland, "A. Philip Randolph," 31, 38; also see John Henrick Clarke, "A. Philip Randolph: Portrait of an Afro-American Radical," *Negro Digest* 16, no. 5 (March 1967): 16–23, and Rhonda Jones, "A. Philip Randolph, Early Pioneer: The Brotherhood of Sleeping Car Porters, National Negro Congress, and the March on Washington Movement," in *The Economic Civil Rights Movement: African Americans and the Struggle for Economic Power,* ed. Michael Ezra (New York: Routledge, 2013), 9–21.

149. Kersten, *A. Philip Randolph,* 110; on the history of Dunbar Apartments, see Gilbert Osofsky, *Harlem: The Making of a Ghetto, 1890–1930* (New York: Harper, 1971), 155–58.

150. Randolph quoted in Anderson, *A. Philip Randolph,* 339.

151. "A. Philip Randolph Is Dead," *New York Times,* May 17, 1979.

152. A. Philip Randolph, "If I Were Young Today," *Ebony* 18, no. 9 (July 1963): 82.

153. Nixon quoted in Studs Terkel, ed., *Hard Times: An Oral History of the Great Depression* (New York: Pantheon, 1970), 119.

154. "A. Philip Randolph Is Dead," *New York Times,* May 17, 1979.

155. George S. Schuyler, *Black and Conservative: The Autobiography of George S. Schuyler* (New Rochelle, N.Y.: Arlington House, 1966), 135–37; on Randolph and Schuyler, see Jeffrey B. Ferguson, *The Sage of Sugar Hill: George S. Schuyler and the Harlem Renaissance* (New Haven, Conn.: Yale University Press, 2005), 17, 63, 259n31.

156. Villard quoted in Anderson, *A. Philip Randolph,* vii.

157. Lewis, *Walking with the Wind,* 205.

158. Benjamin Quarles, *Black Mosaic: Essays in Afro-American History and Historiography* (Amherst: University of Massachusetts Press, 1988), 151–77.

159. C. Wright Mills, *The New Men of Power: America's Labor Leaders* (New York: Harcourt, Brace, 1948), 43–45, cites public opinion surveys in the 1940s suggesting that most Americans were unaware of Randolph.

160. American Federation of Labor, *Report of the Proceedings of the Sixty-Second Convention* (Washington, D.C.: AFL, 1943).

161. Kersten, *A. Philip Randolph,* 87; for summaries of race relations in AFL and CIO affiliates prior to 1955, see Philip S. Foner, *Organized Labor and the Black Worker, 1619–1973* (New York: International Publishers, 1974), 158–76, 215–37, and Herbert Hill, "The Problem of Race in American Labor History," *Reviews in American History* 24, no. 2 (June 1996): 189–208.

162. "Meany, in a Fiery Debate, Denounces Negro Unionist," *New York Times,* September 24, 1959. The remarks were amended in the record of official proceedings to "Who appointed you as the guardian of the Negro members in America?"; see Anderson, *A. Philip Randolph,* 302.

163. Pfeffer, *A. Philip Randolph,* 206–39; Hamilton and Hamilton, *The Dual Agenda,* 114–21.

164. On Lassale and Lassaleans, see Kersten, *A. Philip Randolph,*10–11; on the campaign

to increase New York's minimum wage, see Hedgeman, *The Trumpet Sounds,* 168; for state wage statistics, see www.labor.ny.gov/stats/minimum_wage.asp.

165. Randolph, "The Economics of Black America," box 2, Randolph Collection.

166. Randolph, *The Civil Rights Movement Re-examined,* pamphlet (New York: A. Philip Randolph Educational Fund, 1967), 6.

167. Malcolm X quoted in Anderson, *A. Philip Randolph,* 13; Manning Marable, *Malcolm X: A Life of Reinvention* (New York: Viking, 2011), 191, indicates that Malcolm still chided Randolph as "Uncle A. Philip."

168. *A. Philip Randolph at 80: Tributes and Recollections, May 6, 1969* (New York: A. Philip Randolph Institute, 1969), 27–29.

169. Molefi Kete Asante, *100 Greatest African Americans: A Biographical Encyclopedia* (Amherst, N.Y.: Prometheus Books, 2002), 255–59.

170. A. Philip Randolph Institute website, www.apri.org.

171. Calvin Craig Miller, *A. Philip Randolph and the African American Labor Movement* (Greensboro, N.C.: Morgan Reynolds Publishing, 2005); also see Daniel S. Davis, *Mr. Black Labor* (New York: Dutton, 1972).

172. Some of the voluminous literature on the decline of America's labor movement includes Rick Fantasia and Kim Voss, *Hard Work: Rebuilding the American Labor Movement* (Ithaca, N.Y.: ILR Press, 2004); Ruth Milkman and Kim Voss, eds., *Rebuilding Labor: Organizing and Organizers in the New Union Movement* (Ithaca, N.Y.: ILR Press, 2004); Nelson Lichtenstein, *State of the Union: A Century of American Labor* (Princeton, N.J.: Princeton University Press, 2002); Vernon M. Briggs, *Immigration and American Unionism* (Ithaca, N.Y.: ILR Press, 2001); Stanley Aronowitz, *From the Ashes of Old: American Labor and America's Future* (New York: Basic Books, 1998); Peter J. Rachleff, *Hard-Pressed in the Heartland: The Hormel Strike and the Future of the Labor Movement* (Boston: South End Press, 1992); and Michael Goldfield, *The Decline of Organized Labor in the United States* (Chicago: University of Chicago Press, 1987).

173. Letters to the Editor, *Ebony* 24, no. 9 (July 1969): 18–20.

1

The Brotherhood of Sleeping Car Porters

In 1911, Asa Philip Randolph moved to New York City and quickly got caught up in radical politics. Engaging in the big debates of the day, in 1917 he and his collaborator, Chandler Owen, decided to publish a magazine, named *The Messenger*, devoted to advancing radicalism and African American civil rights. This socialist periodical commented on a range of topics including religion, the world war, and unionism. By the mid-1920s, however, *The Messenger* was failing, and Randolph was looking for new ways to advance his political and social causes. An opportunity soon appeared. In 1925, an employee of the Pullman Company, Ashley Totten, approached Randolph with a job offer: organizing the Pullman porters into a union. If Randolph did his work well, he would be forging the first modern all-black labor organization. It took a decade and a half, but his efforts to form the Brotherhood of Sleeping Car Porters (BSCP) were finally successful. The union survived into the late 1960s until its base eroded when passenger rail travel all but disappeared in the United States.

The documents in this chapter chronicle the rise and fall of the BSCP amid the struggles that Randolph and his lieutenants had to maintain the union against such forces as the fierce resistance of the Pullman Company, the skepticism of black communities, the lethargy of the labor movement, and the transformations of the American economy. As if fighting for recognition from one of America's most powerful companies was not enough, the union had to face racism within the labor movement itself. The first document in this chapter, "The Case of the Pullman Porter" elucidates the porters' grievances and illustrate their difficulties in winning the hearts and minds of porters and African Americans generally. The next set of documents, particularly "Why a Trade Union?," show Randolph at the pinnacle of his union leadership.

Randolph's political power within the labor movement and in various progressive causes rested on the shoulders of his BSCP members. Consequently, his stature waned alongside their steady decline in numbers after World War II. In the last document of this chapter, "Report by International President A. Philip Randolph to the Sixth Triennial Convention and Forty-Third Anniversary of the Brotherhood of Sleeping Car Porters," Randolph summarizes the achievements of the Brotherhood and argues that unionism, not the various forms of black radicalism of the 1960s, is the surest path toward lasting social, economic, and political power.

FOR FURTHER READING

Arensen, Eric. *Brotherhoods of Color: Black Railroad Workers and the Struggle for Equality.* Cambridge, Mass.: Harvard University Press, 2001.

Bates, Beth Tompkins. *Pullman Porters and the Rise of Protest Politics in Black America, 1925-1945.* Chapel Hill: University of North Carolina Press, 2000.

Chateauvert, Melinda. *Marching Together: Women of the Brotherhood of Sleeping Car Porters.* Urbana: University of Illinois Press, 1997.

Harris, William Hamilton. *Keeping the Faith: A. Philip Randolph, Milton P. Webster, and the Brotherhood of Sleeping Car Porters, 1925-37.* Urbana: University of Illinois Press, 1977.

Kornweibel, Theodore. *Railroads in the African American Experience: A Photographic Journey.* Baltimore: Johns Hopkins University Press, 2010.

Mathieu, Sarah-Jane. *North of the Color Line: Migration and Black Resistance in Canada, 1870-1955.* Chapel Hill: University of North Carolina Press, 2010.

McWatt, Arthur C. "'A Greater Victory': The Brotherhood Of Sleeping Car Porters in St. Paul." *Minnesota History* 55, no. 5 (April 1997): 202-16.

Pfeffer, Paul F. "The Women behind the Union: Halena Wilson, Rosina Tucker, and the Ladies' Auxiliary to the Brotherhood of Sleeping Car Porters." *Labor History* 36, no. 4 (Fall 1995): 557-78.

Santino, Jack. *Miles of Smiles, Years of Struggle: Stories of Black Pullman Porters.* Urbana: University of Illinois Press, 1991.

Tye, Larry. *Rising from the Rails: Pullman Porters and the Making of the Black Middle Class.* New York: Henry Holt and Co., 2004.

Wilson, Joseph F. *Tearing Down the Color Bar: A Documentary History and Analysis of the Brotherhood of Sleeping Car Porters.* New York: Columbia University Press, 1989.

The Case of the Pullman Porters (1925)

A. Philip Randolph successfully developed a supportive relationship with the American Federation of Labor. In this article, which appeared in the AFL's house organ, *American Federationist,* Randolph makes the case that the AFL should support African American railroad porters because they were challenging exploitative working conditions such as unpaid hours on the job, low wages, and the degrading practice of tipping—something that Randolph saw as enforcing servility. Toward the conclusion, he also argues that the BSCP is especially important to the future of the labor movement and that unionization will make African Americans become "better men and more useful citizens."

Brotherhood Conditions — Well-nigh proverbially one thinks of the Pullman porter as happy and contented, smiling and jaunty; his *esprit de corps* is at once catching. One little imagines that his big heart is twitching with a deadly uneasiness and fear which arises chiefly from economic uncertainty and insecurity. Few passengers, whose every whim is carefully catered to and oft-times anticipated by the untiring men of the whisk broom and the white coat, realize that these men get a wage to begin with of only $72.50 a month and whose maximum is $104. And unlike other railroad workers, they operate on a mileage basis of 11,000 a month or a little over 330 hours. Overtime is seldom possible under such conditions. On a number of runs throughout the country, preparatory time from one to five hours and more are exacted from porters without pay. Preparatory time means making ready a car and receiving passengers until the train leaves. Wages-time only begins upon the departure of train.

It is seldom realized that though a porter is supposed to have three hours' sleep-time, he has no assurance of ever sleeping one hour at a time without interruption by a call to duty, in the form of a geographical guide, a valet or wet-nurse, etcetera. He is the guardian of the lives, the honor and the property of the car, and, according to the records of the Pullman Company, a very good one. While he is supposed to get three hours' sleep, it is merely a supposition contrary to fact; for to fail to answer a bell may mean a suspension of fifteen days on the street, and, of course, without pay.

Tips — But what about the tips, fat (?) tips, the porter receives? Twenty-five or thirty years ago, perhaps, a porter received some sizable tips. But, according to the old men, "them days have gone forever." Good size tips were indispensable then since wages were low, that is, much lower than the present low wage. Today, the average porter's tips run around twenty to twenty-five dollars a month; exceptional runs, more, some, less. Withal the total income, including wages and tips, is far below a wage sufficient to maintain a family according to a decent American standard of living. But besides tips being uncertain, inadequate and irregular, they are morally and spiritually indefensible, un-American and undemocratic. Moreover, the system of rewarding labor with charity demoralizes and compromises the manhood of the wage earners.

In fact, the public is not tipping the porter. It is tipping the Pullman Company, which made a net income, according to its fiscal report, July 1, 1925, of seventeen million dollars. The company has relied upon the public to pay part of the wages of the porter in tips. The Pullman Company's reports, according [to] the Wall Street Journal, show that in eleven months ending June, 1926, it has revenue of $74,654,133 as against $68,735,392 for the same period in 1925. The net income is $10,143,500, against $8,347,636 [for] the corresponding period last year. Evidently from the reports of the company, it is fully able to pay a living wage and still annually cut a luscious melon.

Efforts of the Porters to Organize — To the end of improving the foregoing conditions, Pullman porters have made three or four attempts at organization. Each succeeding effort created a deeper consciousness among the porters of the need for an organization of, by and for themselves. The last attempt was made during the war. It was aided considerably by the favorable attitude of the government toward organized labor. Still it failed, largely because the leaders attempted to remain in the service while organizing the men and [porters] were intimidated by the company.

From the beginning of attempts of the porters to organize, the company began planning a company union. The first organization was a benevolent edition of the company union, if that's possible. It is known as the Pullman Porters' Benefit Association. For $26, it gives a porter death and sick benefits. Should a porter leave the service, his dues are increased 50 percent, although his risk is considerably less since he no longer is on the road. The increase in dues is calculated to discourage a porter from supposedly risking his job by joining a union, the vices of which are amply magnified by Pullman agents.

The Pullman Porters' Benefit Association is the breeding grounds of porter-instructors and "welfare workers." A whispering campaign has pretty effectively established the idea among the porters that if they want to "get in right" with the company they had better join the Pullman Porters' Benefit Association, which is nominally a porters' organization, but actually a company's proposition, since all expenditures by the Pullman Porters' Benefit Association are subject to supervision by the treasurer of the Pullman Company. It's an old but true adage that "he who pays the fiddler calls the tune." And in order securely to fasten the yoke of this benevolent feudalism upon the necks of the porters, the company has adroitly thrown a sop to the Negroes' race pride by taking $10,000 of their own money in the Pullman Porters' Benefit Association and depositing same in a Negro bank in Chicago. The Brotherhood of Sleeping Car Porters, which was formed on August 25 in New York

City, is successfully exposing this organization as the benevolent wing of the company union, sugarcoated by the employee representation plan. . . .

Porters' Attitude—When the Brotherhood first began it was apparently ignored. Few ever dreamed that it would grow; certainly not the Pullman Company. Many of the older men were favorable but skeptical, as well as afraid. They took the position: "If it succeeds, we are with it; If it doesn't, we are agin' it."

After the movement had steadily made progress over a period of several months, the older men, in common parlance began to "loosen up," until today the union can boast of having 90 percent or more of the oldest and most responsible and stable porters in the service. One of the policies which won their confidence was the secrecy of membership under which the organization was protected and maintained. While a few porters have been discharged for union activities under the blanket cause of unsatisfactory service, since the company was naturally too clever to state the real reasons for the discharge, the Pullman Company could not swear in a court of law and produce the evidence to show that it knows that a single porter in the service is a member of the union, unless the porter has supplied such information himself. Such was not the case with former attempts at organization, since the organizers attempted to remain in the service while they were forming the union. The younger men show little or no fear, though a few show little concern.

Opposition—In the beginning of the movement, opposition was expected both from the Pullman Company and from some of the leaders of the Negroes, because of ignorance on the one hand, or corruption on the other. The most prominent leader of the opposition was Perry W. Howard, Special Assistant to the United States Attorney General. He debated the writer in Chicago during the early stages of the movement on the right, necessity and value of the Pullman porters organizing. The leading negro papers, such as the *Chicago Defender,* the *Chicago Whip* and the *St. Louis Argus,* pretended that they were opposing the movement because of the alleged intention of the writer to put the union into the American Federation of Labor, although they had been formerly fighting the American Federation of Labor on the grounds that it discriminated against negro workers joining trade unions. Of course, this was merely a smoke screen. The real reasons were more subtle and questionable. They simply sought to capitalize on the distrust which various unfavorable work and wage conditions for black workers had naturally built up in them against their white brothers.

Many of the Negro clergy, too, allied themselves with the Pullman interests.

Huge, elaborate, expensive conferences and banquets for Negro leaders have been planned and paid for by the Pullman agents; letters condemning the union have been signed, if not written, by welfare workers and Pullman porter-instructors; thousands of Negro papers attacking the brotherhood have been bought and given away to the porters in the offices of the Pullman Company. And as a threat to the men, should they join the union, Filipinos were dressed up and put on some of the club cars in utter and flagrant violation of the seniority right of Negro porters who had given their best years in the service. But every form of opposition has merely served to fire the men with stronger determination to carry on.

Spies — In addition to other forms of opposition, the company has organized and let loose on the movement a swarm of stool-pigeons, spies and confidence men, white and black. Their policy has been to pose as strong union men with a view to discovering who the strong brotherhood men are in order that they might frame them for discharge. Several men have been victimized as a result of the operation of the Pullman spy system. But the spirit of the men surges high, undaunted. . . .

Progress of the Brotherhood — The movement to organize the Pullman porters has gone promisingly forward for many reasons. It has met with widespread cooperation from the American Federation of Labor in various cities and the standard railroad unions. Practically all of the conventions of powerful national Negro organizations held during this year have adopted resolutions endorsing the brotherhood. This includes such movements as the National Association for the Advancement of Colored People, the National Federation of Colored Women's Clubs, the leaders of the National Urban League, the Nobles of the Mystic Shrine and Knight Templars, the Knights of Pythias, the Elks, the Lott Carey Baptist Convention, etcetera. Practically all the opponents mobilized by the Pullman Company have become quiescent, probably due to the fact that the company is not paying for very much opposition now, realizing that it is ineffective in holding back the rising tide of organization. The company, however, has not lessened its determination to maintain the company union against the porters union.

What it Means to Black and White Wage Earners — The movement to organize the Pullman porters is the most successful serious effort to organize a large industry of Negro wage earners yet made. Its significance to organized labor and the Negroes generally is much bigger than the benefits that will come to the Pullman porters and maids. The movement bids fair to awaken and stimulate the spirit of organization among Negro wage earners in every industry in the country. It will serve as a most effective agency in breaking down the superstition among white workers and the public that the Negro workers are un-organizable. It will do much to eliminate the stigma of the scab from the name of the Negro wage earner. It will help to break down the barriers of race discrimination to Negro wage earners. It will tend to introduce sanity and reason and justice and vision into the relations between the races in America. This social achievement will be all the more manifest should the handling of this new instrument of power be characterized by sobriety and common sense, understanding and an unselfish devotion to decent fair-dealing and creative efficiency.

Aims of the Brotherhood — The Brotherhood is a service organization as well as an organization to protect and advance the interests of its members. Its policy is to develop and employ the initiative, intelligence, and a sense of responsibility with a view to maintaining helpful and constructive cooperation with the Pullman Company. It realizes that when a group of wage earners accumulate power through unity, they must expect also to assume responsibilities, duties and obligations to the Pullman Company and the great public, as well as enjoy privileges and rights; that its aim is not merely to fight to raise wages, but also to study, understand and appreciate the industry of which they are a part, in order that they might make it bigger and better.

The Brotherhood of the Sleeping Car Porters will also fulfill the high mission of creating out of the Pullman porters better men and more useful citizens; to develop a higher measure of independence and manhood; to appreciate the dignity and social work of service; to recognize the common aim and brotherhood of wage earners regardless of race, creed, color, sex or nationality.

To this end, it is the writer's wish that the Brotherhood of the Sleeping Car Porters will take its logical and natural place in the not distant future in the American Federation of Labor and play a constructive role in the broad stream of American labor that they may not only help themselves, but all Negro workers in particular and the labor movement in general. For it may be that the Negro workers have a distinct spiritual contribution to make to the American labor movement. More than any other group of wage earners they have drunk deep of the bitter dregs of economic exploitation; more than any other group of wage earners, they have borne the poignant pain of social misery. Only they, of all American wage earners, have sat in the silent shadows singing songs of sorrow. Thus it may be that out of the tragic depths of their sufferings they may bring forth a new, vital, stirring message for industrial peace with justice which will enrich, ennoble and inspire the life of labor, thereby advancing the cause of humanity.

SOURCE: *American Federationist*, November 1926, 1334–39 (Copyright © AFL-CIO).

Randolph Replies to *Chicago "Surrender"* Misnamed *Defender* (1927)

Chicago Defender editor Robert Sengstacke Abbott and Randolph fought a very public battle for the hearts and minds of the black community in Chicago. Because of the *Defender*'s reach, their debate over the expediency of unionism spread to many other places where the newspaper had influence. Although the Pullman Company supported the newspaper financially, Randolph eventually won the allegiance of Abbott and his readers, but before that, he had to vociferously defend his union against criticism. As often occurred in journalism of that era, the attacks sometimes became personal.

In your issue of August 20th in an editorial entitled "The Pullman Porters' Case" your flagrant misrepresentations, inexcusable and obvious distortions and bold, downright lies, are an insult to the Negro race, a travesty upon decent journalism and an outrage on commonsense.

In the first paragraph, you say "The fight between the Pullman Company and its employees, if a fight actually existed, has come to an end." *Lie Number One*. The Brotherhood and not you, Brother Abbott, will determine that. You printed that same lie only a week before the United States Mediation Board began the hearings on the porters' case.

You continue, perfectly unaware of what it is all about: "Since the Boards of Mediation could only act where both parties concerned submit their grievances to it, there was nothing for it to do but drop the matter after it found that no dispute existed between the Pullman Company and its employees." That's not true. In the first place, the Board can act even if only one party to a dispute submits its case. When one party submits its case, it is known as an ex-parte presentation, if this means anything to Brother Abbott, our "pathetic journalistic intellectual Lilliputian." Besides, the *Mediation Board found that there was a dispute* and urged and recommended that the Pullman Company and the Brotherhood arbitrate said dispute. This is stated in clear English in the letters of Mr. Morrow to the Pullman Company and the Brotherhood. Abbott attempts deliberately to juggle the correspondence for deception.

You say that "the porters have spent money in wrangling, that the Company Union has race members sitting in judgment on disputes." How naïve and childish! What if the porters have spent money? It's theirs and it would have been wisely spent even if they knew that they would lose before they began. All money spent for freedom and justice is wisely spent.

As to Negroes on the Company Union, what kind of Negroes are they? Their mouths are sealed and hands are tied by the Company just as yours are.

The Pullman Company itself appears not to have been injured, you say. Then what are you crying about? Are you such a moron as to think that the Pullman Company needs the big brain (?) of the World's Greatest *Weakly?*

You say "porters who have been active against their employers . . . should forget the past and spend the ensuing years building up the service." Your slave psychology is so strong that you think that because a porter fights for more wages and better working conditions as the Pullman conductors do they are acting against their employers. What about the conductors, engineers, firemen, trainmen? Are they active against their employers? If they are, they will never be less active, and if the porters have any brains and stamina, they will not be less active for their rights.

"Who knows what recognitions, promotions, and salary increases the porters and maids have been deprived of by virtue of the past two years' agitation?" you continue. This is pure nonsense. The Pullman Company has had over fifty years in which to give the porters a living wage and promotions, and what have they given? Seventy a month, the right to beg the public, and promotion to a stool-pigeon's job and work nearly 400 hours a month, while the Pullman conductors get $150 and work only 240. Of course, the conductors are organized, Brother Abbott. The Company makes porters do conductors' work now, and won't even give them the satisfaction of having the title. They are called *porters-in-charge* and paid $10.00 additional. And this slavery is what Abbott wants the porters, who peddled his paper all over the country years ago and got him a circulation, ought to be happy and glad about. Not on your life, Brother Abbott. You are really a bigger joke than you look like.

You say, "let the Pullman Company be fair and let all of its employees advance according to their ability." Your gullibility would be refreshing were it not so tragic. Such is the reason for the Negroes' weakness today. Some of their leaders will believe anything a white man tells them. Who in the name of commonsense believes the Pullman Company will advance a porter according to his ability? Not even the stool-pigeons believe this "moonshine." It's to laugh. The Company chuckles up its sleeve at such ravings of a big, fat, stupid, lucky Negro "iditor." Poor old Abbott, pitiful Pullman puppet! Probably his heart is right, but his head is wrong.

Continues the *"Surrender,"* "We have always been for justice in American industries." Is that so? No one would even know it unless you said it. "It does not, however, feel that the points desired can be gained through antagonistic methods." Whatever that is. How much did Abbott get for his dumb crack? Think of a black man helping a group of rich white men to rob the very black men who made him what he is today!

"The Pullman Company is not merely a local concern, but one in which the entire nation is interested. The nation which supports it depends upon it for the best service that it can afford," says the *"Surrender."* True, that's just why the Company has no right, in law or morals, to pay its porters who supply the service it sells a starvation wage. The Company bought thousands of *"Surrenders"* to *give,* not *sell* the porters. The Company loves to have the porters read

Negro papers, that is, those papers that oppose organization. The Company never gave porters any papers before the birth of the Brotherhood of Sleeping Car Porters. That's funny, isn't it?

Now listen to this: "The *Defender* suggests that the Pullman Company even reinstate those who left the Company during the dispute and who now seek reinstatement. . . ." This is an indictment of the Company. The *"Surrender"* admits that the Company fired porters for exercising their moral right to join a union of which the Company says it permits in its own plan. But, of course, what it says in its plan means nothing. It's for the public's consumption and the porters' deception. If porters discharged ought to be reinstated, it shows plainly that there was no just cause for their ever having been discharged. If there was a just cause why porters were discharged, then they ought not to be reinstated. So the *"Surrender's"* plea is superfluous, unnecessary, ridiculous and futile.

The Pullman Company recognizes nothing but power, and that the porters have when they are organized. The Company cannot injure them and they do not want to injure the Company. They want only justice, which they must and will have. This means a fight to [the] finish, regardless of cost or consequences. We are winners not quitters, Brother Abbott.

SOURCE: *The Messenger* 9 (October 1927): 304, 313–14.

A. F. of L. Redoubles Its Support for Porters' Victory (1930)

Randolph's controversial strategy of seeking an alliance with the American Federation of Labor, a labor union with a disappointing record on racial affairs, eventually proved to be a productive one. Once allied, the AFL helped by lending its organizers, paying for expenses, and giving its stature to the BSCP. The alliance paid dividends, as the new union grew quickly in cities across the North and South.

The entrance of the Brotherhood of Sleeping Car Porters into the American Federation of Labor was of far-reaching significance, not only to the porters but to Negro workers everywhere. It was the signal for white organized labor to throw its forces behind the struggle of the porters. Cooperation has been not only promised but generously given by the national officers of the American Federation of Labor proper and the central labor councils in the various cities in general. This support is of incalculable value to the movement, the A. F. of L. organizers all over the country are available to the brotherhood local organizations.

President Green of the A. F. of L., to the end of mobilizing the great forces of this organization behind the porter's union, recently sent a letter to the presidents of the central labor councils advising them to give whole-hearted support to the sleeping car porters' locals. Results are already manifest from this move that promise great additional strength to the Brotherhood. Cincinnati will soon be captured by the central labor council for the Brotherhood. A. F. of L. officials have gone out on the field to round up the porters and bring them into the local. This individual contact of A. F. of L. leaders with the porters is irrefutable evidence of the value of affiliation on the part of the Brotherhood with the federation, as organization work is rendered possible in places where the Brotherhood has no organizers. Louisville has already surrendered to the aggressive attacks of the local A. F. of L. officials of the Central Labor Council. Word has come to the national office advising that out of 135 porters in the district all but six have indicated their willingness to join the forces of the union. This is a notable piece of work on the part of the Louisville A. F. of L. organizers. They went out and met the men individually and successfully convinced them that the Brotherhood was their only hope and that the A. F. of L. expected each porter to do his bit by allying himself with the organization and paying his dues.

The cooperation of the A. F. of L. is the key in the solution of the organization problem of the Brotherhood in the South. In Jacksonville, Savannah, Atlanta, New Orleans, Nashville, Memphis, Little Rock, and other southern centers, A. F. of L. organizers are making determined efforts to enlist every Pullman porter in the Brotherhood and have indicated and spread the news among them that they have only to bring their joining fee and dues to the office of the Central Labor Council and be enlisted as a member of the movement. Reports are flowing into the Brotherhood headquarters to the effect that the porters are taking advantage of this cooperation of the A. F. of L. leaders and are going voluntarily to the local offices and signing the questionnaires and enlisting as members. From the trend in the organization's drive in the southern centers, a large majority of the porters will be mobilized in the Brotherhood very shortly, which will increase the already large majority of porters and maids already members in the union. . . .

The fight of the Brotherhood has met with widespread appreciation and commendation among organized labor. From all quarters come indications of the general credit and tribute given the porters for initiating and carrying through such a heroic and significant fight against so powerful an industrial combination as the Pullman Company. Great faith and confidence are shown by the leaders of labor in the ultimate victory of the porters. They are especially amazed and pleased at the spirit to stick, to undergo the necessary hardship and make the requisite sacrifice to build an organization which can protect and defend their interests and rights.

Many heads of labor organizations have expressed their skepticism that the porters would carry the fight through to a finish, but as a result of the militant and unremitting struggle these same heads have not only changed their opinions but expressed the belief that the porters were making a significant contribution to the American labor movement as a whole by their formidable attack on Pullman's company union. It is generally recognized that the overthrow of the employee representation plan of the Pullman Company, which was formed in 1920 (about the time the porters were trying to form a union of their own) will be one of the most outstanding and constructive achievements of American labor. It will virtually turn the tide against the company union movement which has sprung up since the World War.

The porters are to be congratulated that they have waged so vital and far-reaching a fight against the worst species of industrial despotism in America today. Their certainty of victory is practically recognized and conceded by all serious labor men. Because of their steadfast and unceasing resistance to Pullman company unionism, President William Green has sent the following message: "On behalf of other organized workers I extend most cordial Labor Day greetings to our fellow trade unionists in the sleeping car porters unions. You have thrown in your lot with the organized workers of America, realizing that economic problems are fundamental in your progress and the union is the instrumentality through which you can raise standards of work and pay.

"Sleeping car porters want to get on in the world. You want higher wages, definite agreements specifying the services to be rendered, representation to protect and advance your interests. By acting together, pooling your strength and influence and organizing to carry out definite plans you can make constructive progress. The most important thing is that you get together and stick together. That is the purpose of the union.

"Not only do the Pullman porters need a union, but you need the support and co-operation of all other unions. No group of workers can make sustained progress by keeping aloof from the general movement, by taking advantage of the misfortune of other workers.

"Progress and betterment come by getting more for all. If we all work together we shall all be the better for it.

"The Pullman porters have gained a constructive leadership by identifying themselves with the general labor movement. We respect your understanding of practical problems and your intelligent self-interest. We hope Negro workers in industry will follow the path on which you are pioneers."

This preaches a sermon of its own.

SOURCE: *Chicago Defender*, August 30, 1930.

Why a Trade Union? (1931)

In the second installment of a three-part series, Randolph argues that porters want to be treated just like any other union members working within the Pullman Company. By accepting the porters' union, Randolph writes, the company can guarantee itself a more efficient, profitable, and safe operation. This is because the BSCP presents an opportunity for African Americans to become sophisticated and urbane workers, the kind of employees who will best serve the company's interests.

The material progress of the Pullman service industry has been marvelous . . . [the] entire American public has been the beneficiary of the constructive resourcefulness and ingenuity of its management in mechanical elaboration and perfection of physical environment. From the wooden kerosene-lamp miniature sleeper has developed a magnificent yet richly decorated and furnished standard sixteen-section sleeper, and your very recent addition the fourteen-room car [. . .] probably represents the last word in luxury and comfort on the rails.

You spared no means in fashioning an environment of such a work of art for the traveling public as would elicit from it a response of aesthetic appreciation and enjoyment. To this end the late President [Edward] Carry in the annual report of July 31, 1926, stated that during the six years and five months since the property was released from federal control (March 1, 1920), $481,473,100 has been invested in new equipment, and that of this amount $17,274,313 was invested in 546 new cars in the fiscal years just closed. For the replacement of equipment you have long followed an exceedingly liberal depreciation policy. According to your balance sheet as of the aforementioned date, $86,423,333 of earnings have been charged in your company equipment depreciation account. Your cars and equipment trench hard upon two hundred millions, or more accurately, $196,311,691.

According to the Interstate Commerce Commission, the total cash investment of the Pullman Company up to 1924 was $32,602,238 and $200,238. Your capitalization as of 1925 however is $135,000,000 brought to that figure by the reinvestment of surplus earnings and issue of stocks as dividends and in exchange for property. Since 1897 the Pullman Company has distributed $345,675,000 cash dividends and $60,000,000 in stock dividends. Such is the stupendous and remarkable progress your company has made in material and mechanical refinement, in financing and organization.

In management technique, too, your company has moved apace. An extraordinary form of recent business expansion is the combination program in which the Pullman system will include these units, all subsidiary to Pullman Incorporated of Delaware: The Pullman Company, Chicago; Pullman

Car and Manufacturing of Alabama, Birmingham; Standard Osgood plants at Butler, Pennsylvania, Baltimore, Maryland, Richmond, Virginia, Sagamore, Massachusetts, Hammond, Indiana, St. Paul, Minnesota, Worcester, Massachusetts, Ellwood City, Pennsylvania, La Rochelle, France, Rio de Janeiro, Brazil; the Dickson Car Wheel Company, Houston, Texas; New Orleans Car Wheel Co., Inc., New Orleans; Pullman Railroad Company, Pullman, Illinois; Pullman Land Association, Chicago, Illinois; Harbor City Land Company, Michigan City, Indiana.

I need not tell you that in the nature of things it would be impossible for the porters and maids to be a part of this phenomenal progress, playing a considerable and basic share in giving it existence, without being profoundly influenced intellectually and spiritually. In very truth, the porter of 50 years ago, with the wicker-lamp, wooden-car mind, could no more properly handle the deluxe standard sleeping, parlor, buffet, room, observation steel cars of today than could the wooden, wicker-lamp cars of yesterday meet the rigid and exacting industrial and social requirements of modern travel. The former only required a porter with a primitive, rural mind; the latter, a porter with an alert urbanized mind. I think you will agree that the vast progress of the company would not have been possible with the porter with the slow-moving rural mind. A person needs much more urbanization to be able efficiently to handle the highly elaborated mechanism of the Pullman car. And along with the transformation of the rural mind of the porter into an urban mind goes a progressive change in worth, service technique, competency and productivity. But accompanying this urbanization and improvement in the productive ability of the porter go the needs, desires, interests, hopes and demands of an urban citizen.

The history of all social psychology shows that the latter inevitably follows the former. The wage increases you have granted, though small, are based upon the assumption that a porter of today, with an urban mind, is worth more to the company than a porter of yesterday with a rural mind. And it may be interesting for you to know that this demand of your porters and maids for higher standards of living, better wages, hourage and working conditions is merely a manifestation of a general movement forward of the Negro race. In the last 50 years the Race has accumulated $2,000,000,000 in property and its illiteracy has decreased over 85 percent. In 1930 there are practically 5,000 Negro doctors, 2,500 Negro dentists and 3,000 Negro lawyers. In 1920 there were 3,411 trained nurses. There are 100 Negro banks, 75 Negro insurance companies and 342 periodicals. In literature, art and science the Negro has made substantial and enduring contributions of unquestioned world merit in reaches and quality to society.

The above mentioned achievements indicate a progressive upward trend which should elicit the admiration of the most grudgingly critical. Their consequent implications are that the needs and desires of the Negro, like [those of] other race groups, cannot and will not and should not remain stationary or unsatisfied. Among the porters and maids are definite and insistent stirrings for higher living levels. Superficially considered, this unrest may be ascribed to agitators, the Brotherhood of Sleeping Car Porters. But this is far from the truth. The existing unrest among the porters was no more created by the Brotherhood than is a storm created by the weather bureau. The former pointed out the existence of unrest; the latter indicates the approach of a storm. Both the unrest and the storm arise out of conditions prior to and independent of the Brotherhood and the weather bureau. The Brotherhood, however, seeks to remedy the unrest by prescribing a program for reasonably revising wages, working conditions and hourage so as to achieve a greater measure of contentment among the porters and maids which will naturally reflect itself in a finer morale and service development.

Industrial unrest of the porters and maids cannot be removed through summary repression. If stopped at one point temporarily, it will find expression through other channels that may not be rational and constructive. Porters and maids could no more remain on the same hours with the conductors and on the same trains with other train crews who seek, through collective bargaining, to improve their conditions, and not seek to employ the very same method of collective bargaining to improve their conditions than could a man fail to seek food when hungry or water fail to seek its level. Even granting that the Brotherhood should fail, it would not amount to a destruction of the will of the porters to organize. The will to self-organization without interference, coercion or intimidation may be stifled, crushed for a while; and delayed, but it cannot be permanently destroyed—nor can it be killed by a mere increase in wages and better working conditions apparently secured through a company union. The company can get no relief from besetting unrest by temporary victories over attempts of porters and maids to organize, assuming that it can win such victories, for these victories are in reality but harbingers of ultimate permanent victory of the porters in bona fide self-organization. . . .

Conditions have convinced the porters and maids that they cannot rely upon anything to safeguard their interests but their own organization, which is untrammeled in the least, in the selection and designation of representatives for the formulation, presentation of their case and the handling of recurrent grievances. No benevolent, paternalistic, grievance adjusting system such as the company union will suffice. The rise and existence of the Brotherhood is incontrovertible evidence of the truth and soundness of this proposition.

May I say that I am quite reassured by your jointly setting up an adjustment board with the Order of Sleeping Car Conductors, under the provisions of the new Railway Labor act, which recognizes and sanctions the principle of collective bargaining on wages and working conditions, that you will not be disinclined consistently to pursue the same labor policy with the Brotherhood of Sleeping Car Porters which represents a majority of your employees in this class of service.

I cannot believe that you would entertain for one moment the idea or indulge the practice of making any morally unjustifiable and untenable distinction between your conductors and porters in the recognition and application of the principle of self-organization and the self-designation and selection of representatives for collective bargaining and the adjustment of disputes. I am certain that you must realize that there are no sound facts, scientific or industrial, for such a distinction and that such could not be construed as in harmony with the express language and implied spirit and intent of the federal statute.

I am sure you would not join hands in the adoption of a course of action which you thought was harmful to the company and conductors. Thus, I think you will agree that the porters and the public are justified in assuming by your recognition of the conductors' union that you do not consider the principle of self-organization, self-designation of representatives for collective bargaining as inimical to the welfare and interests of the company, the conductors or the porters and maids.

Therefore, I assume that the question of organization will not be an issue if it can be demonstrated that the porters and maids want it, which, of course, is a logical position. If the porters did not want organization, the Brotherhood could not well claim that they did, since such a claim is subject to verification by a disinterested government body, the United States Mediation Board. No legitimate objection can be raised against the organization of porters on the ground that it will destroy discipline, for in the first place a bona fide functioning organization of porters and maids has never existed, hence, no grounds of fact exist upon which to base such an assumption. Moreover, it is perfectly unfair to predicate attributes and behavior of a group of men and women under conditions they have never experienced. Instead of organization subverting discipline, it will greatly improve it, since the very organization of porters presupposed, implies and indicates their susceptibility to discipline, for discipline is nothing more than the implicit acceptance of and obedience to definite rules of conduct, which is the recognized condition of organization. But if organization is believed by you to be injurious to the discipline of the porters, why do you maintain the employee representative plan for them? It is my understanding that you allege the company union plan to be an organization; hence, rendering another form of organization superfluous and unnecessary.

Can the Brotherhood be of any actual value to the company? It decidedly can. It can effectively weed out the shiftless, irresponsible element from the service, which constitutes a definite liability, and attract and secure more men of pronounced character, industry and worth for the work. It can stabilize the turnover, thereby achieving a higher degree of efficiency through the attractive impressment of porters and maids into the service over longer periods. The development of efficiency in the handling of safety-first devices and methods can be greatly facilitated under the Brotherhood's stimulation and control. As to service, a more resourceful and constructive system of service education can be developed in the hands of the porters' own union. A more rational and higher conception of its social dignity and importance can be inculcated in the minds of the porters through the Brotherhood, which will express itself in definite productive value.

SOURCE: *Chicago Defender*, January 3, 1931.

Requesting International Charter for Sleeping Car Porters (1934)

Randolph was a frequent speaker at annual conventions of the American Federation of Labor (later the AFL-CIO). Typically, he lectured the assembly on civil rights and made motions to advance the cause of African American workers. In Resolution No. 144 at the 1934 AFL convention, Randolph successfully asked for international and independent status for the Brotherhood of Sleeping Car Porters.

WHEREAS, The Sleeping Car Porters have functioned since they were organized in 1925, through the Brotherhood of Sleeping Car Porters, international in scope, though affiliated with the American Federation of Labor under federal charters since 1929; and

WHEREAS, The Pullman Company is an international corporation which operates its sleeping cars in Mexico and Canada; and

WHEREAS, There are now thirteen federal locals of Sleeping Car Porters affiliated with the American Federation of Labor, with ten or more sleeping car locals in preparation for affiliation as federal locals, which fully satisfies the conditions and requirements for an international charter; and

WHEREAS, The Railway Labor Act, as amended by the Seventy-third Congress, specifically states under the general caption: National Board of Adjustment—Grievances—Interpretations of Agreements, Section 3, paragraph (a), "That the said Adjustment Board shall consist of thirty-six mem-

A. Philip Randolph meets with unionized railroad workers in Rangoon, Burma, ca. late 1940s or 1950s. Library of Congress, Prints & Photographs Division, A. Philip Randolph Papers, LC-USZ62-104694.

bers, eighteen of whom shall be selected by the carriers and eighteen by such labor organizations of employees, national in scope, as have been or may be organized in accordance with the provisions of Section 2 of this Act," and renders it imperative that railway workers, in order to function effectively in bargaining collectively in the negotiations of agreements concerning rates of pay and rules governing working conditions, be embraced in an organization national in structure and scope; and

WHEREAS, The tax of federal locals is too heavy a burden upon the Sleeping Car Porters to permit them adequately to handle the grievances and represent Sleeping Car Porters that are located in Pullman districts, extending from Miami, Florida, to the Twin Cities of Minnesota and from New York City to California; and

WHEREAS, The only sound structure of organization of Sleeping Car Porters is one which is co-extensive with the industry in which they are employed and the corporation with which it must fight for the right of self-organization and the selection and the designation of representatives of their own choosing; and

WHEREAS, Since the passage of the Railway Labor Act, as amended by the Seventy-third Congress, five or six thousand sleeping car porters and maids have joined the Brotherhood of Sleeping Car Porters, representing the large majority of porters and maids in the sleeping car industry; and

WHEREAS, The Sleeping Car Porters will soon institute action, through the Brotherhood of Sleeping Car Porters, to secure a conference with the Pullman Company, to make and maintain an agreement on wages, hours and rules governing working conditions; therefore be it

RESOLVED, That in view of the aforementioned facts and reasons, that the Fifty-fourth Annual Convention of the American Federation of Labor, in San Francisco assembled, herewith grant an international charter to the Sleeping Car Porters, the same to include within its scope of jurisdiction the red-caps, ushers and train porters.

As the subject matter of this resolution requires administrative action, your committee recommends that the resolution be referred to the Executive Council for their earnest consideration.

A motion was made and seconded to adopt the report of the committee.

SOURCE: American Federation of Labor, *Report of the Proceedings of the Fifty-Third Convention* (Washington, D.C.: AFL, 1934), 704–8.

Remarks before U.S. Senate Committee on Interstate Commerce (1934)

The 1934 Railway Labor Act transformed the Brotherhood of Sleeping Car Porters' chances for success in the struggle for union recognition and collective bargaining rights. Here Randolph speaks in favor of the bill and for his suggested revision, which directly included the BSCP in the grievance language to ensure that African American workers received equal protection. The fact that Randolph appeared before a Senate committee attests to his growing stature as a leading voice within the labor movement.

Mr. RANDOLPH. Mr. Chairman and gentlemen, my name is A. Philip Randolph. I am president of the Brotherhood of Sleeping Car Porters. My residence is New York City, 207 West One Hundred and Fortieth Street.

The Brotherhood of Sleeping Car Porters, which I represent, embraces a membership of some six or more thousand sleeping car porters and maids, and on behalf of this group I wish to register our approval and support of bill S. 3266, with the following amendment: In paragraph 1, of the third division, page 14, under general caption, National Board of Adjustment—Grievances—

Interpretation of Agreements, add the words: "sleeping car porters and maids and dining car employees," after the words, "sleeping car conductors."

My reason for making this request is that the sleeping car porters number some nine or more thousand workers in the railway industry and there are many thousands of dining car employees in the railway industry who logically belong under the jurisdiction of this act in general and the third division in particular. Unless this is done, it is apparent that endless complications will arise in attempts to adjust disputes that will arise between these classes of employees and the railway companies for which they work.

Since the various classes of carriers have been particularized and specifically designated along with definite classes of workers, to insure clarity and preciseness of intent and purpose with respect to the groups that fall under the scope of this act, it is proper, logical, and sound to name sleeping car porters and maids and dining car employees. These are basic and major groups of workers in the railway industry and should have access to the machinery of this act so as to be able to exercise their right of self-organization, free from intimidation and coercion.

The CHAIRMAN. Do you know how many of them there are? You say there are 9,000 porters; do you know how many there are of dining car employees and maids?

Mr. RANDOLPH. I don't know the number of dining car employees, but I think there are far more dining car employees than there are Pullman porters.

For almost a decade the porters and maids in the Pullman service have struggled to organize a union of their own but have found as their biggest obstacles the company union and the lack of power and definiteness of the Railway Labor Act with respect to getting decisive action on the principle of representation. When the Emergency Railroad Transportation Act of 1933 was enacted with its far-reaching provisions to safeguard the right of self-organization for railroad workers, the porters and maids thought that they would then be able to establish their right to select and designate representatives of their own choosing, but when their case was raised to the coordinator, they were informed that the Pullman Company did not come under [the] N.R.A. [National Recovery Administration] because it is a carrier, and that it does not come under [the] E.R.T.A. because it is not a carrier by railroad, and that the only remedy was to amend the act so as to include sleeping car companies. Now that the term "sleeping car companies" is included, it is the desire of the Brotherhood of Sleeping Car Porters that the term "sleeping car porters" be also included with the other groups of workers and also the term dining car employees.

I want to say a word, too, Mr. Chairman, in confirmation and justification for the amendments presented by Mr. Harrison in relation to the company union, and in order that you might get a concrete picture of what I want to say, or the basis that I want to present, if you will permit me I would like to describe briefly the structure of the company union the Pullman porters are up against. It will not take very long.

The CHAIRMAN. I hope you will not take very much time.

Mr. RANDOLPH. It will not take long. The matter of the company union is really the crux of this whole question, and you might get a concrete picture of it from this particular group. They have a company union which is divided into three groups.

They have what is known as a local grievance committee, which is the organization of original jurisdiction. All grievances are presented to this committee first. On that committee the superintendent of the various districts sits together with his assistants.

Mr. CHAIRMAN. The superintendent of what?

Mr. RANDOLPH. Of the Pullman Company. That is to say, he has the power to hire and fire. He sits on the committee; although he has just fired a porter, he sits on the committee and determines whether he was justified in having fired that porter or not. He is judge, jury and prosecutor.

The CHAIRMAN. He is like the judge in a contempt proceeding.

Senator HATCH. Does he ever decide against himself?

Mr. RANDOLPH. He never decides against himself. We have a case in Cleveland, Ohio, where even the committee decided—they had a sort of a decision in favor of putting a porter back to work, but the superintendent overruled it. So that the whole set-up of the company union, of the Pullman Company, is designed to contravene and submerge and destroy the ability and the right of the Pullman porters for self-organization.

Now, this first committee has the right of appeal to, they call it the Zone General Committee, supposed to be the circuit court of appeals, and on this Zone General Committee you also have the superintendents of the Pullman Company who have the power to hire and fire. Invariably anything that goes to the court of appeals or the Zone General Committee usually finds that same confirmation of the original committee, the grievance committee.

Then they have what is known as the "supreme court" or the industrial relation board. On that they have the general supervisor of industrial relations. This gentleman is paid by the Pullman Company a handsome salary, and he handles and controls the entire machinery of the employees' representation or the company union. On that board they once had a Pullman porter. I think he has disappeared now. [*Laughter*] Consequently, the whole machinery for adjudicating the disputes and grievances of the Pullman porters is entirely in the hands of the Pullman Company.

The CHAIRMAN. You said there were 6,000 of the 9,000 in your organization?

Mr. RANDOLPH. Yes.

The CHAIRMAN. And that is not a company union?

Mr. RANDOLPH. It is not a company union.

The CHAIRMAN. But your grievances must be decided by this board of which you speak?

Mr. RANDOLPH. Yes. We took our case to the United States Mediation Board, but the Board was unable to reach any decision, as they could not compel the company to meet us. Then we also went to the Federal District Court to get an injunction, to prevent the Pullman Company from maintaining a company union, and that decision went against us, and we are now taking an appeal.

The CHAIRMAN. To the Supreme Court?

Mr. RANDOLPH. To the circuit court of appeals, and finally, to the Supreme Court.

The CHAIRMAN. I thought possibly you might think that this being a labor bill, we ought to require that Pullman porters be American citizens in this law, too.

Mr. RANDOLPH. Well, the Pullman porters, who are American citizens, I might say built up the Pullman Company.

The CHAIRMAN. I notice that the Filipinos and Japanese are being used to replace the colored man on those jobs.

Mr. RANDOLPH. Yes, and I might say in connection to that, Senator, that the Filipino and the Japanese were employed by the Pullman Company purposely and fundamentally to break the Brotherhood of Sleeping Car Porters and prevent men from organizing. That was the primary purpose. Of course, I think their wages are lower, and consequently they are able by using them, to hold sort of a weapon over the heads of the Pullman porters who desire to join the union.

Mr. CHAIRMAN. I think the American public is pretty well pleased with the colored man as a Pullman porter. I don't think they want to get anyone else to handle the Pullman cars and the dining car system. But go ahead.

Mr. RANDOLPH. I want to say a word too about the matter of the company paying representatives of the company union. If you eliminate that phase of the bill, permitting the companies to pay the representatives of the company unions, then you really destroy the power of the bill, because if the companies are able to pay the representatives of the company union, then they will be able to intimidate the employees and practically prevent them from joining legitimate and bona-fide unions. So that I think is basic, because the power over a man's subsistence is the power over his will, and usually the man who pays the fiddler calls the tunes, so that the Pullman Company by paying these representatives of the company union, they make them do just what they want done.

Now, in the elections no doubt the representatives of the Pullman Company will tell you, when they are held, that 98 percent of the porters vote for the company union. We are willing to concede that probably they may take 101 percent if they want to, but these men, when they vote, vote under duress and intimidation, fear of losing their jobs. Many of them, especially the independent spirits, have been fired. For instance, negligible and insignificant derelictions of duty are piled up against these men. Then they are presented with a record card and shown, "here, your services have not been so good," despite the fact that some of these men have been in the service for 30 years.

The CHAIRMAN. And probably never had a serious complaint against them at any time.

Mr. RANDOLPH. No, sir; no serious complaint at all, and despite that fact these men are fired, and that is all done to break up the organization. So that we, the Brotherhood of Sleeping Car Porters, in harmony with the program presented by Mr. Harrison, and especially those amendments and recommendations designed to give freedom of choice in the selection of representatives to negotiate agreements and wages, rules and working conditions; and we are especially concerned about this matter because it relates to our ability to carry forward this work of enabling the porters to determine the conditions under which they work and the wages that they receive.

Senator HATCH. Who pays your expenses?

Mr. RANDOLPH. The Brotherhood of Sleeping Car Porters. And I might say, too, that I don't get any salary. Our organization—we use all the money that is available and put it into actual work carrying forward the movement. We, for instance, have about 15 or more organizers, and all those organizers today are working without pay.

April 12, 1934

SOURCE: Senate Committee on Interstate Commerce, *A Bill to Amend the Railway Labor Act Approved May 20, 1926, and to Provide for the Prompt Disposition of Disputes between Carriers and Their Employees,* 73rd Cong., 2nd sess., April 10, 11, 12, 18, 19, 1934 (Washington, D.C.: GPO, 1934), 50–53.

Pullman Porters Union Will Not Fold (1966)

By the 1960s, the porters' fortunes were in decline as the passenger rail industry waned. In response, the BSCP sought to provide a buffer against economic dislocation. In this article, Randolph predicts that rail service will continue as the nation's population grows. Gridlock on roadways, he reasoned, would make large-scale public transportation a necessity. Forces far larger than Randolph could confront were at work, however, but he did his part to ensure that individual workers who were displaced from their industry still had protection through their union.

I want to make it unmistakably clear that the Brotherhood of Sleeping Car Porters is not about to fold up. . . . I am persuaded to make this observation because of the possible impression one might get from the article: "Pullman Porters Face Extinction by Railroad Moves," appearing in the *Amsterdam News,* August 13, 1966.

There is less wrong with the facts presented than the conclusions deducted therefrom.

While it is true, as stated in the article, that New York Central has applied to the Interstate Commerce Commission for the right to discontinue its long distance trains, this reduction in Pullman services, if granted, will only affect some 250 porters, more or less, although I do not regard this as an inconsiderable loss. Of course, I shall appear before the I.C.C. to oppose it. This is standard procedure of railroad unions when railway carriers request permission from the Interstate Commerce Commission to change operations that affect union membership.

Of course, sleeping car porters on the New York Central, as a result of a job stabilization agreement the Brotherhood has negotiated with the New York Central, have job protection and will be paid even though they do not work, conditioned by the annual revenues of the carrier. . . .

As I observe the national transportation problem, as related to the population explosion, I am inclined to believe that the railroads that have been in decline as an industry are on the rebound. The movement of our growing population will require that railroads, buses, [and] airlines not only be retained but that they be developed and expanded to serve our national needs. Private automobiles that now transport 85 percent of the population between cities continue to congest the highways with increasing hazards. Moreover, even today, Pullman service on western and Southern roads is relatively good.

Finally, the Brotherhood of Sleeping Car Porters which represents Pullman porters, train porters and attendants is destined, along with other railway unions, to be around for many years to come.

SOURCE: *Amsterdam News,* August 27, 1966.

Report at Brotherhood of Sleeping Car Porters Convention (1968)

In his last major public speech before the Brotherhood of Sleeping Car Porters, Randolph summarizes almost forty-five years of union history. The scope of his remarks includes an account of the BSCP's early glory years and an explanation for its recent decline. He also explores the crises of the 1960s and provides a generous analysis of the radical movements that shaped the left wing of American politics. "Saint Philip of the Pullman Porters" praises the spirit of black militancy, but he argues that unionization remains the most reliable path that African American workers can follow to provide a better future for their families.

International Officers and Delegates of the Sixth Triennial Convention and Forty-third Anniversary of the Brotherhood of Sleeping Car Porters: Greetings!

Forty-three years ago, in the Elks' Auditorium at 126 Street and Seventh Avenue, New York City, the first meeting of Pullman Porters was held, which led to the organization of the Brotherhood of Sleeping Car Porters. It was the responsibility of your humble servant to plan and preside over that meeting. It was probably one of the strangest and most unorthodox meetings ever held to set up a union or a church or a fraternal society, or for any reason. As the chairman, I called the meeting to order, gave the prayer, began the singing of "Hold the Fort," followed by my address which dealt with the reasons for calling this meeting at the suggestion of some unknown Pullman Porters to form a bona fide labor union of Pullman Porters for Pullman Porters. But before beginning my speech, I advised and cautioned the audience which packed the hall that no porter in the meeting should make a speech, or a motion, or ask a question, to avoid being reported by stool pigeons to the Pullman superintendents, which, most likely, would result in his being fired. Before announcing the end of the meeting, I pointed out to the men that this meeting was conducted without porters' participation to avoid their victimization which would play into the hands of Pullman to wreck the movement by throwing some of our stouthearted men in the streets in the beginning of our crusade. I added that there would not be any future meetings like this one since the porters cannot hope to build a bona fide labor union without their taking the risks of joining the union and fighting for the union. Such is the start of the building of every trade union.

As I looked over that group of silent but stalwart men, I felt, with deep emotion, that there were porters who would become economic martyrs for the cause, yes, the cause, because the Brotherhood of Sleeping Car Porters, phoenix-like, would rise bloodied from its strenuous struggles as a great moral challenge, as well as a powerful economic force, in its victorious march for economic justice as a union and as a cause.

This dramatic, unforgettable meeting was held [on] August 25, 1925, forty-three years ago, seven years after the end of the First World War. The angry winds of reaction were rising. Powerful economic royalists, represented by the United States Chamber of Commerce and the National Association of Manufacturers, had contrived the so-called American Plan which was a euphemism for the Company Union, Yellow Dog Contract, and Right-to-Work laws.

Since William Gibbs McAdoo, son-in-law of President Woodrow Wilson, and a member of his Cabinet and Director of Transportation, had, in the interest of avoiding work stoppages during the war, proclaimed and issued General Orders asserting the right of workers in war production and related industries such as railroads to self-organization, Pullman, one of America's corporate giants, in order to relieve the Pullman Porters of the trouble of organizing a union, promptly set up the famous Plan of Employee Representation, a bona fide company union of the worst stripe.

Phony nationwide elections of officers of the Plan were held periodically. If a porter failed to vote right in the elections he was called in to give the reason why, suggesting some possible contamination by "that Randolph movement." As a rule, some question was raised concerning debts of the porter of which Pullman stool pigeons had informed the Superintendent, hinting to the porter that he might find it necessary to seek a job from Randolph who has no job himself.

Following the elections, conferences of the Plan, composed of the prearranged elected representatives in the various Pullman districts and agencies in the country, were held, usually in the YMCA in Chicago. It was addressed by one or two important officials of the Pullman Company and some Negro bishop, important preacher or politician. At the close of the conference, a so-called Agreement, written under Pullman supervision, was read and presented to the delegates for signatures. No porter in the conference, of course, would be so ungentlemanly as to suggest any changes in the Agreement or hesitate to sign on the dotted line.

Strangely enough there was one such instance. The culprit was our distinguished and courageous First International Vice President, Bennie Smith. The occasion scared the porter-delegates to death, shocked, startled and stunned Pullman officials in the headquarters in Chicago and throughout the country. Pullman officials, proud and powerful, some of whom were scions and Brahmins of the world of industry and finance, were livid with rage, chiefly over the fact that their stool-pigeon system had failed. It just was not understandable how a screened elected company union delegate to the prestigious Plan of Employee Representation conference could fail to sign the Agreement.

Despite the prayers of the stool-pigeon fraternity with Brother Smith, pleading with him, in the name of the future of the porters and the Negro race, to sign the Agreement, he refused. When it was all over he came over to the Vincennes Hotel where Brother Webster and myself, who knew what was going to happen, awaited him. We went out and celebrated the occasion in the nightspots on the Southside. This was one of the great victories of the Brotherhood over Pullman, and it was our major propaganda piece from then on. Of course Brother Smith was promptly fired. I immediately had him go South, especially to Jacksonville, to direct the organization campaign with Brother Darby who was representing the Brotherhood. Brother Smith proceeded to the South armed with bundles of *The Messenger* magazine for which he sought subscriptions from the porters and the public.

Pullman officials, aroused and troubled over the presence of Bennie Smith in Jacksonville, alerted the police about his activities. The police arrested him and he was charged with selling a magazine which advocated social equality. This was enough. He was hauled before a judge as an agent of a northern union to foment strife and trouble among the colored population. The judge told Brother Smith he would give him a few hours to get out of town or he would send him to the Blue Jay Farm. When he returned north, I assigned him to supervise the Detroit and Canadian area. He is there now.

Recognizing the growing involvement with and commitment of the porters to the Brotherhood of Sleeping Car Porters, Pullman strategists resorted to the age-old weapon of the discharge to halt the march of the union. In St. Louis, Oakland, Chicago and New York City, old porters nearing pension age and active in the Brotherhood were struck down for the slightest dereliction of duty. Naturally, this bare-knuckles attack tended to throw the fear of God into the hearts of the porters and their families. But it didn't break their spirit. They continued to attend the meetings of the Brotherhood and joined in singing "Hold the fort for we are coming, union men be strong." At the end of every year some of the most gallant warriors of the Brotherhood union army had fallen, but the army continued to march on.

Realizing that the porters needed the sustaining moral consciousness of membership in a wider community of union forces, the Brotherhood secured some ten, more or less, federal union charters from the American Federation of Labor which gave the porters' leadership a voice in the house of organized labor. Thus, in every annual convention of the AFL the voice of the porters was heard, demanding in resolutions the abolition of discrimination based upon race, color, religion or national origin in all unions affiliated with the Federation. While the resolutions were consistently rejected with attacks upon the porters' leaders, they were consistently presented from year to year. We missed only one convention from 1929. It was the convention which was held in Vancouver, British Columbia. Reason: unable to raise the railroad fare for Brother Webster and myself. It was reported that when it was certain the

Brotherhood delegates had not registered, some of the delegates laughingly called upon President Green, in the interest of peace, to hold future conventions in Vancouver.

But while President Green at times manifested irritation under bitter attacks of Brotherhood delegates on the Federation, he issued a statement of cooperation of the AFL with the Brotherhood when it set a strike date against Pullman. He counseled with Brotherhood leaders on strategy in handling the strike threat, assuring us of financial help in the event of the strike while advising that it would be an act of trade union wisdom to call it off and resume the building of membership.

And when the Brotherhood Memphis local division was denied the use of the city auditorium for a public labor education rally, President Green, upon being informed about the incident, ordered the Memphis Central Labor Council to call upon Mayor [Edward] Crump, the powerful boss of the city, and demand that the use of the city auditorium be granted the Brotherhood. The Mayor refused. President Green then ordered the Central Labor Council officers to cooperate with Brotherhood officials in securing a suitable place and to give the labor rally their full support. This was done. A monster meeting was held in one of the largest Negro churches in Memphis. It was opened by the president of the labor council, followed by your humble servant who paid his respects to Boss Crump much to the discomfort of the Negro leadership of the city who had urged the Brotherhood leaders to call the meeting off and leave town, expressing fear lest the city become the victim of racial violence.

In the early 1930's, President Green presented an international charter to the leaders of the Brotherhood at a meeting in a public school in Chicago. The Brotherhood was the first labor union under Negro leadership to be granted an international charter in the history of organized labor in the country. This was not because the AFL had refused to grant such a charter but because there was no bona fide union international in scope under Negro leadership to receive one. But this international charter was only available to the Brotherhood after it attained the structural status of an international union. It took the Brotherhood ten long years to achieve this goal. It required that the Brotherhood win a nationwide election against the Pullman company union under the supervision of the National Mediation Board. This was done in 1935. Following the certification of the Brotherhood as the duly authorized representative of Pullman porters and attendants, conferences for the negotiation of an agreement covering wages and rules governing working conditions began, and continued over a period of two years. When the Agreement was completed and signed by representatives of Pullman and the Brotherhood, an indeterminate period of the interpretation and application of the rules of the Agreement began.

The acknowledged master of interpreting and applying the rules of the Agreement for the settlement of claims and grievances for the members was Brother Milton P. Webster. There was nothing he enjoyed more than winning a case involving a claim or grievance against Pullman or a railroad. The international vice presidents and international field representatives of the Brotherhood attained their proficiency in the handling of claims and grievances largely under his tutelage. Fortunately for the members of the Brotherhood, the international and local officers of the organization in the United States and Canada are men of unimpeachable integrity, organizational knowledge, ability and expertise. Be it said to the eternal credit of the Brotherhood that it has lifted the porters and attendants, train and rail porters from a condition of semi-serfs to the status of middle-class wage earners with a sense of greater economic and social security. . . . Because of the continued discontinuance and deterioration of railway and Pullman passenger service, one of the most important and encouraging developments for Pullman and railway porters and attendants in recent years is a report of the Interstate Commerce Commission to the Congress appearing in the *New York Times,* June 26, 1968, which repeatedly criticized the federal government for not promoting rail passenger service and also pointed out that the lack of government promotion encouraged the railroads to allow the quality and quantity of their passenger service to deteriorate. G. E. Leighty, chairman of the Railway Labor Executives Association, said: "The report of Interstate Commerce Commission Hearing Examiner John Messer on the plight of the rail passenger service in the United States is indeed a hopeful sign that the Commission may now assume responsible leadership in the field of rail passenger service."

In contrast to the negative attitude of most of the railroad corporations, Mr. Stuart Saunders, chairman of Penn Central Company, on June 6, 1968, declared: "I would like to propose, either as corollary or an alternative to a congressional review, that a National Railroad Passenger Council be created by appropriate governmental action to expedite solution of this (passenger service) problem. This council should be a group representative of the public, the railroads, and the governmental agencies concerned with transportation policy. It should move promptly, in as brief a time as possible, to study the problem and issue a report as a basis for formulating a railroad passenger service program within the larger context of the national transportation policy. Such a report is fundamental in determining the extent to which the federal government must support rail passenger service." This statement by Mr. Saunders, who is undoubtedly the most powerful personality in the railway industry today, is the most encouraging ray of hope for the revival of the railway passenger which has appeared in the last decade. I want to suggest that he left out one of the most important factors, namely, organized railroad labor.

It is difficult to understand, in the light of a population explosion reflected in a continuing congestion of the airways with airplanes, and the highways with automobiles and trucks, how any single mode of existing transportation can be eliminated, and especially railroads that are indispensable in peace and war.

Now, it is a well-known fact that the Brotherhood was built by the porters, Pullman and railroad porters and attendants in the United States and Canada. Since the Brotherhood was born in the belly of the black ghettos in the United States and Canada, its life and struggles were naturally influenced and affected by the leadership and institutions, hatreds, poverty and prejudices of the Negro communities. Thus, white labor unions that were universally charged, with some justification, with the sin of having excluded Negro workers from membership were violently roasted as the enemy of the race. White capitalists, on the other hand, who contributed, though meagerly, financially to Negro colleges were viewed as benefactors of the race. Pullman naturally exploited this windfall of race bias. . . .

Let the Black Militants speak! This is not to suggest that I am in agreement with all of their tactics, strategy and methodology. Not at all! However, I am persuaded to agree that the Black Militants have been responsible for deepening the American consciousness of the immediacy, magnitude and danger of the racial crisis in the cities. They have quickened American concern about opportunity for jobs for Negroes in all areas of American life. They have challenged and stirred the American mind and conscience about the exclusion of the cultural achievements of Black Americans from the historiography of our American society. They have vigorously stressed the need of the Negro's interest in self-help. They have accented the search for identity and the Africans' contribution of an ancient glorious historical cultural heritage and endowment to world civilization. Such are the assets of the Black Militants. . . .

Now, a word about the Brotherhood Black Militants. We had some, you know, and I am immensely proud of them. They flourished in the early dark days. Bennie Smith, first International Vice President, was one. He stood up against the Pullman power establishment and refused to sign a Yellow Dog Contract despite the fact [that] every Pullman porter delegate to the conference signed on the dotted line. There was Ashley L. Totten, our first International Secretary-Treasurer. When I sent out the call and set the date for the porters' strike against Pullman, I made a brief trip to a number of Brotherhood divisions to make talks and note the state of the spirit of the men. I found Totten in a little hole in a Negro business building collecting sawed-off shotguns, railroad iron taps, boxes of matches, knives and billies. It scared me. I asked him what was he going to do with the ammunition. He said he wasn't going to let any stool pigeon get into the Pullman yards. I told him he was going to get all of the Brotherhood officials put in jail before we got a chance to strike. I persuaded him to dispense with the hardware.

When the debate on the value of a union to the Pullman porters was planned to be held in Chicago between a prominent Negro politician and myself, Totten arrived in Chicago on his run the morning of the day of the debate. He asked the Pullman superintendent for permission to lay over until the next day. The superintendent, naturally, knew why he wanted to lay over. He was refused. He laid over anyway, and he was fired. The day after the debate Totten was the main speaker at a big Pullman porters' rally. He paced up and down the platform shaking his fists at the stool-pigeon department. Brother Webster whispered in my ear when Totten finished, "That's our man. Take him to the coast with you." I did, and Totten laid on the stool pigeons at every stop. When Totten and I got to the coast we found [C. L.] Dellums and [Richard] Dad Moore, two red-hot firebrands on the stool pigeons. The meeting halls were packed with porters and Dellums called the roll of the stool pigeons and Dad Moore would cuss'em out. Dellums was threatening to put the secretary of the Oakland Division in jail for stealing the dues. He got the Brotherhood money from the bonding company.

In the Twin Cities we were met by Frank Boyd, short and fat, who came rocking down the platform cussing out the stool pigeons. He had rounded up a bunch of Wobblies, Communists, Socialists, and Milk Drivers' Union radicals to meet me. During the strike threat, Brother Boyd had planned to poison all the stool pigeons. He chuckled and shook his fists, exclaiming that he was going to put the stool pigeons in such a fix they couldn't get on the cars. When Benny and myself got to Canada we found [Arthur] Blanchette who had the figures on the Canadian officials and labor law. He demanded that everybody be required to toe the mark, Canadian official and delinquent porter alike. We found another crusader in Canada, Brother [Bud] Jones, who never faltered. . . .

And now permit me to hail and salute my good friend and co-worker, George Meany, distinguished, able and resourceful president of the AFL-CIO, a great labor statesman, a great American, and a great human being. While the battle for the elimination of racial discrimination in the House of Labor is not yet over, definite and positive progress is being made. Be it said to the great credit of Brother Meany that the AFL-CIO fought side by side with the NAACP and other civil rights organizations in the memorable struggle for the enactment of federal legislation against racial discrimination in public accommodations, voting rights, jobs and housing.

George Meany is wholly committed to the policy that racial bias in labor unions is unsound, indefensible and morally wrong, and must go. The time will come, and soon, when not a single labor union bars a worker from membership or a seat in its policy-making bodies because he is black, and for this we must ever fight. And the time will come, and soon, when no job will be denied a worker because of the color of his skin, and for this we must ever fight.

And now let me hail and salute the porters on Pullman and railroads in the United States and Canada. Let me hail and salute the distinguished gallant, though fallen, warriors and dauntless leaders of the long, hard, desperate years of the Twenties, Thirties, Forties, Fifties, and onward. Moneyless, friendless, but not hopeless, the Brotherhood held meetings every day or night in some divisions during the twelve years—from its birth to the first day of negotiation with the management of Pullman. Verily, the handful of porters who weathered the storms of Pullman oppression were the shock troops of Black Labor. They were the first black workers who had openly dared to beard the mighty industrial lion of Pullman in its den.

Yes, Pullman was fierce and cruel. It had brutally battered the railroad workers under the matchless leadership of the great Gene Debs in the celebrated Pullman strike of 1894. During the bitter, gray and hapless days there was not a single Negro organization which the Brotherhood could call its friend, and only one or two black papers, and not a single nationally known leader. The Brotherhood porters and leaders were the black untouchables. But the small band of militant, weather-beaten black proletarian brothers of the ghetto never faltered. With heads erect and souls uncurbed, porters who had been fired on account of membership in the union were stirred by the spirit of the labor hymn, "Solidarity Forever":

> *In our hands is placed a power greater than their hoarded gold,*
> *Greater than the might of armies magnified a thousand fold.*
> *We can bring to birth a new world from the ashes of the old,*
> *For the Union makes us strong.*

> *They have taken untold millions that they never toiled to earn.*
> *But without our brain and muscle not a single wheel could turn.*
> *We can break their mighty power, gain our freedom when we learn*
> *That the Union makes us strong.*

The Brotherhood preached this philosophy to the black worker in particular and the Negro communities in general. The Brotherhood gave the porter, and incidentally the Negro workers as a whole, a sense of racial and class identity and pride. While the Brotherhood fought to break down racial barriers in labor unions, it also fought against Negro workers permitting themselves to be used as scabs against their white brothers on strike.

The Brotherhood is supremely proud of the fact that its ceaseless struggle against race bias in the labor movement brought about the establishment of the Civil Rights Department of the AFL-CIO; the placing of two Negro trade unionists on the Executive Council of the AFL-CIO; the placement of an increasing number of Negro workers on policy-making committees of national, international and local unions, and a continuous increase in the number of black representatives in national, international and local unions.

The concept of fair employment practice was the gift of the Brotherhood to the Negro, union labor, and the country. . . . It was Brother Milton P. Webster, strongman of the Brotherhood, who put the steam behind the federal FEPC set up by President Roosevelt's executive order. In California, Brother C. L. Dellums, International Vice-President, served as chairman of the Fair Employment Practice Commission; and in the legislature of Missouri, brother T. D. McNeal wrote and secured the enactment of fair employment practice legislation. In Canada, Brother A. R. Blanchette, International Representative, piloted the movement for the enactment of civil rights legislation.

Today, Negroes have become high-ranking officers in practically all of the departments of the armed service because the Brotherhood led the fight which caused President Harry S. Truman to issue an executive order banning discrimination based upon race or color, religion or national origin in 1949.

William H. Bowe, International Secretary-Treasurer, is the Treasurer of the New York City Central Labor Council, the largest in the country with over a million members. B. F. McLaurin, Eastern Zone Supervisor, is a member of the Board of Higher Education of New York City, and recently was responsible for the appointment of a Negro educator as President of Bronx Community College, the highest post a Negro occupies in the educational system of New York City.

And there is a long host of aggressive, militant, dedicated rank-and-file porters who gave this great Brotherhood life, not only with their dues, taxes, and contributions but by the grandeur of their spirit. They built a labor movement which brought a new dimension of self-reliance, hope, strength, courage, faith and integrity which no other organization can claim. Black youth can take the deepest pride in the fact that for almost a half century there never has been a breath of scandal involving the mishandling of a single dollar by a leader or member of this Brotherhood.

And as I take my leave I want to thank every Pullman, train and mail porter and attendant, and our devoted and loyal sisters of the Ladies Auxiliary, in the United States and Canada, for having given me the opportunity to play a humble role in building this mighty movement. And may God give you strength, faith and fortitude that you march on and never falter.

SOURCE: Report by International President A. Philip Randolph to the Sixth Triennial Convention and Forty-Third Anniversary of the Brotherhood of Sleeping Car Porters, September 2, 1968, box 37, folder: Speeches, 1968, A. Philip Randolph Papers, Library of Congress.

2

Labor Leader at Large

Constructing and maintaining the Brotherhood of Sleeping Car Porters (BSCP) was A. Philip Randolph's top priority throughout his career, and he worked diligently for four decades to increase the union's strength. Although known for his humility, he was extraordinarily proud of his title as president of the BSCP. Randolph knew that running the union was important, but his activities extended far beyond workplace issues. From his position as head of the porters, he launched various civil rights and union initiatives.

This chapter focuses on Randolph's career as a labor leader at large. From his position as the head of the largest African American labor union, he spoke on topics ranging from the struggle to diminish the presence of racial discrimination within the American labor movement to the need for the federal government to take steps toward improving the lives of exploited and marginalized people. Although not all of his causes produced immediate results, Randolph nonetheless remained a prominent public voice for many decades. As a working-class spokesperson, he challenged such institutions as the federal government and the American Federation of Labor (AFL, later the American Federation of Labor–Congress of Industrial Organizations, AFL-CIO) to put the concerns of racial and ethnic minorities at the center of policy debates.

Randolph's decision to have the BSCP affiliate with the AFL was a fateful one. The AFL had a well-earned reputation of being the reserve of white trade unionists who had few sympathies for men and women of color. Many of its individual unions actively discriminated against minority workers by keeping them out entirely or only allowing their participation in a subordinate role. Some African American and Hispanic workers found their way into unions, but these auxiliary arrangements did not give the benefits of unionism equitably to all despite charging the same monthly dues. Aware that the porters and their special interests could easily get lost in this bastion of white privilege, Randolph gambled that their inclusion could transform the AFL—and eventually the entire labor movement. For him, fighting for democracy and equality inside the AFL (and later the AFL-CIO) was a calculated risk, and it was one that bore significant fruit. After years of battling union leaders at conventions, Randolph finally decided to create a new organization, the Negro American Labor Council (NALC). AFL-CIO leadership saw this as an encroachment on their territory and censored it. Randolph's spirited defense of the NALC and of his efforts to transform the labor movement is one of the most striking documents in this chapter.

Randolph was a keen observer of the economy and was especially sensitive to the ways in which modern American capitalism created enormous wealth yet seemed to perpetuate poverty. Through his writing and speaking, he exposed the hardships that African American workers endured because of structural inequalities in crucial areas such as education and the job market. To rectify the situation, Randolph called for cooperative action by African Americans and appealed to the federal government for intervention. As is evident from his various testimonies before congressional committees, he advocated the enactment of a law banning discrimination in employment and supported the creation of a federal agency to enforce this policy. He also championed the expansion of apprenticeships and the removal of barriers to minority workers for entrance into important job-training programs. Finally, he stridently fought against so-called right-to-work laws and called for federal legislation to end these Orwellian-named union-busting tactics.

Although Randolph was not successful in all of these endeavors, a major accomplishment was the establishment of the Equal Employment Opportunities Commission (EEOC). From his position as black America's labor leader at large, Randolph helped set a progressive agenda that he continued to champion until well into his eighties. His 1978 Labor Day message, one of Randolph's last public statements, attests to the consistency with which he argued that concerted action be taken against reactionary forces seeking to turn back the hard-won advances of the civil rights and labor movements. To the end, despite his long list of accomplishments, he somewhat tragically recognized the ongoing need for struggle.

FOR FURTHER READING

Gall, Gilbert J. *The Politics of Right to Work: The Labor Federations as Special Interests, 1943–1979*. New York: Praeger, 1988.

Goldberg, David, and Trevor Griffey, eds. *Black Power at Work: Community Control, Affirmative Action, and the Construction Industry*. Ithaca, N.Y.: Cornell University Press, 2010.

Graham, Hugh Davis. *The Civil Rights Era: Origins and Development of National Policy.* New York: Oxford University Press, 1990.

Holloway, Jonathan Scott. *Confronting the Veil: Abram Harris Jr., E. Franklin Frazier, and Ralph Bunche, 1919–1941.* Chapel Hill: University of North Carolina Press, 2002.

Honey, Michael, ed. *Black Workers Remember: An Oral History of Segregation, Unionism, and the Freedom Struggle.* Berkeley: University of California Press, 1999.

Jones, William P. "The 'Void at the Center of the Story': The Negro American Labor Council and the Long Civil Rights Movement." In Andrew E. Kersten and Clarence Lang, eds., *Reframing Randolph: Debating A. Philip Randolph's Legacies to Labor and Black Freedom.* New York: New York University Press, 2015.

Mann, Robert. *The Walls of Jericho: Lyndon Johnson, Hubert Humphrey, Richard Russell, and the Struggle for Civil Rights.* New York: Mariner Books, 1997.

Moreno, Paul D. *Black Americans and Organized Labor: A New History.* Baton Rouge: Louisiana University Press, 2006.

Nelson, Bruce. *Divided We Stand: American Workers and the Struggle for Black Equality.* Princeton, N.J.: Princeton University Press, 2001.

Zieger, Robert H. *For Jobs and Freedom: Race and Labor in American since 1865.* Lexington: University of Kentucky Press, 2010.

The Unemployment Crisis (1921)

In the face of the postwar economic downturn, Randolph provides a socialist critique of the war and of the capitalists who reaped profits during the fighting. It is important that nowhere in this article does he specifically make reference to race. At this early point in his public life, Randolph argued that the suffering brought on by structural economic changes unites all workers.

The crisis of unemployment grips the country. It is variously dubbed as a period of "transition," of "reconstruction," of "readjustment," of "back to normalcy," etcetera. What ever it may be called, the fact is, it is a period of economic chaos, political maladjustment, indescribable social suffering and distress. In short, it is an industrial and financial panic. The ground-work of the existing social structure has been rudely and violently shaken by the titanic economic forces unleashed by the great World War.

During the war the magic word was "produce!" "produce!" Then, the war dogs were yelping for blood, more blood. . . . In economic blood, the entire industrial man and machine power of the nation was mobilized. The national industrial mechanism reached the nth power of production. In obedience to the abnormal demand created by the war, high price levels reigned, stimulating a mad scramble on the part of the financial and industrial capitalists to reap huge profits out of this abnormal situation. Hence, with the aid of the "work or fight" order, the invention of new and more efficient machinery and methods of production, American capitalists carried on. The government of the people (?) guaranteed certain profits to certain business interests. The flag was pawned to the financial oligarchs, and they waved it feverishly mouthing [such] 'balderdash' as: "we are fighting to make the world safe for democracy," "Americanism," "100 per cent patriotism," etcetera. The pulpit, press and school sang praises to the "God of Production." Capitalists, drunk with the red wine of profits, unloosed their [Albert S.] Burelsons, [A. Mitchell] Palmers, [Clayton R.] Lusks and [Archibald] Stevensons upon him who dared to challenge their holy right to feed the "dogs of war" with men and munitions.

But the orgy of wanton destruction ended, and ended suddenly. The Armistice was signed. The abnormal war demand for munitions and goods ceased to exist. There being no market, production stopped. The mills, factories, mines and farms closed down. Lay-offs accompanied with rehiring at reduced wages began. Suddenly, a false alarm of "more production," "more efficiency," was raised as a pretext for redoubling with a vengeance the campaign of laying off and slashing wages.

Meanwhile the workers pined and whined, protested and cursed. For had they not worked to "make the world safe for democracy," had they not sacrificed and suffered? Had they not refused to strike, making uninterrupted production possible, and incidentally a saturnalia of profiteering, giving rise to a crop of 22,000 brand new millionaires? Naturally, memories, on the part of the workers of their privations during the war and of the glittering promises of their pay-trioteering [sic] bosses, soured and embittered them. In their breasts blazed the dangerous fires of hate and revenge against their employers. Nor are these fires of hate and revenge kindled by the "machinations of passionate and malevolent agitators," but they flare up out of the material conditions of the struggle for a living.

Of course, the workers, well-meaning but misguided, naive and credulous, did not reckon with the nature of the system under which they lived. They did not realize that business is run for profits and not for the service of the people. They knew nothing about the economics of production and distribution. It never occurred to them that their wages represented but a part of what they were producing and that the remainder went into the coffers of the owners of the mines, mills, factories, farms, railroads, steamships, telephones, traction lines, in short, the means of production and exchange. Inasmuch then, as the workers produce more than they receive in the form of wages, they can never buy back the entire product of their toil. They are continuously producing a surplus of commodities—wealth. This wealth seeks investment at the highest rate of interest. Thus foreign loans are made. Concessions of coal, iron, timber and oil resources are sought by the investment bankers of all capitalist nations, thereby creating rivalry and competition which result in a mad race in building huge navies and armies; in diplomatic intrigues, plots and conspiracies; in defensive and offensive alliance, such as cordiales, ententes; and finally, in wars.

The workers are unaware of the fact that they produce a surplus, that this surplus produces rivalry between the different world powers, and that this rivalry produces wars; that wars are followed by periods of unemployment, due to the lessening of demand for goods, and the existence of large inventories. In very truth, the workers, under the modern capitalist system, produce themselves out of jobs. They produce so much food that they must starve to death; so many clothes that they must go in rags. This is the frightful paradox of capitalism!

Today, it is variously estimated that from five to six million men are unemployed. Of course, I believe there are more. And the worst is yet to come! The peak of the unemployment wave has not yet been reached. Daily, the newspapers report of new layoffs; of new wage cuts. Dun's and Bradstreet's report the closing of numerous banks. The "first aid" of soup kitchens graces the big industrial centers. The machinery of credit has well-nigh collapsed. In common parlance, money is "tight."

During periods of this kind two groups suffer most: the petite bourgeoisie, or the small capitalists, and the workers. The former, trying to profit from the existence of high price levels during the war, piled up huge inventories at war prices. Now that a nation-wide liquidation of wages and prices has set in, the small business man finds that he is caught between the devil and the deep sea. His existence depends upon continuous and rapid turn-overs of his capital. When once his capital becomes frozen, he slides into bankruptcy. For his credit is too small to permit him to adopt the postponement of liquidation, such as the big trusts are able to do. Hence, if the little businesses liquidate, they are bankrupt; and if they don't liquidate, they are bankrupt.

As to the workers, in periods of prosperity, wages lag behind prices in the upward trend. In periods of depression, wages precede prices in the downward trend. Such is the case today. Nothing has fallen materially, save eggs. Food, clothes, rent and transportation are still high. But wage deflation marches on. Job deflation precedes wage deflation. Workers are first fired; then they are rehired at slashed wages. The doctors, preachers, and lawyers of the working-class suffer too, for their incomes come from the income of the people who toil.

Only big business benefits from panics. The trusts become bigger trusts. They become veritable empires of capital. Witness the Steel Trust, Coal Trust, Food Trust, Oil Trust, Money Trust, etcetera. These gigantic combinations of capital, like a mighty octopus, have reached out their long tentacles and drawn under their control the little, independent businesses engaged in their particular industries. . . .

When will it all end, you ask? Will it end when the international rates of exchange—the pound sterling, the franc, the lire, the mark and the kronen—reach their pre-war status, which will enable Europe to begin buying again? The answer must he made in the form of a question: When will this happen? Nobody knows. Unemployment is not indigenous to the soil of America. It is indigenous to the soil of capitalism. Today it is world-wide. We have not only the unemployed but we have also the more alarming phenomenon, the unemployable. It is highly doubtful whether the mechanism of production and distribution will ever again absorb but a very small section of the existing unemployed. Only a war between the United States and Japan or Great Britain can absorb the idle. This, of course, is too great a price to pay for the abolition of unemployment. Waiving aside this contingency, which would be but temporary, only to be followed by a greater wave of unemployment, there is no complete relief from unemployment except through the abolition of its cause, the profit system. For the nonce, palliatives may be applied, such as government employment bureaus; a building boom of houses; the improvement of public highways, work and buildings; unemployment insurance, etcetera. Needless to say, however, that these doles of charity and make-shift devices to patch up an economic system in collapse are only superficial.

SOURCE: *The Messenger* 3 (August 1921): 230–32.

The Negro and the Labor Movement (1925)

Cognizant of the forces within the labor movement that were trying to open opportunities for African American workers, Randolph and his magazine became increasingly pro-union. At the same time, however, he was wary of the Communists, whom he criticizes in the following piece. This combination of advancing the union cause while rhetorically attacking far left radicalism is one reason why some thought Randolph an excellent choice to launch the Brotherhood of Sleeping Car Porters.

It is gratifying to note that there is now considerable interest manifest in the organization of the Negro workers. Doubtless the real reason is that the white unions are slowly but surely awakening to the serious necessity of unionizing the Negro worker in self-defense. They are beginning to realize that Negro labor is playing an increasingly larger and more significant role in American industry. Especially is this true in the East, West and North, where large numbers of Negro workers have migrated and are competing in the labor market with organized labor. It is this competition which has jolted the organized white workers out of their state of chronic indifference, apathy and unconcern.

Of course, even now nothing definite has been done in the interest of Negro labor by the organized labor movement. Some of its leaders such as Hugh Frayne, Thomas J. Curtis and Ernest Bohm, are members of the Trade Union Committee for Organizing Negro Workers, but it is not apparent that this committee has anything as yet save the moral good will of some of the local unions of New York City. In order for it to succeed in its organization work, however, it must be financed by the white organized workers. So far its financial backing has come from the American Fund for Public Service. It has made possible the employment of Frank R. Crosswaith as Secretary.

Of course, this work is not new or original. *The Messenger* has been the pioneer in the field advocating the organization of Negro labor. Now the *Crisis* is belatedly taking up the fight for the next three years, and the Negro press generally has become sympathetic and active in advising Negroes to organize into labor unions wherever their white brothers will accept them. We are glad to note that Negro editors are learning their economic lessons slowly but surely.

Let no Negro fail in his duty of advancing the cause of Negro labor without let or hindrance. The time is rotten ripe. Immigration from Europe has been materially cut, which means that the yearly supply of labor is much less than it formerly was. This gives the organized workers an advantage, greater bargaining power by virtue of this limited supply. It also gives the Negro worker a strategic position. It gives him power to exact a higher wage from capitalists, on the one hand, and to compel organized labor to let down the bars of discrimination against him, on the other. Thus it benefits him in two ways. And the Negro workers cannot rely upon anything but the force of necessity, the self-interests of the white unions, and the fear of Negro workers' competition, to give them a union card.

Another potent force in the organization of Negro labor is education and agitation. A certain course of action may be to a group's interest to take, but if it doesn't realize [this] it is not likely to act upon it. Thus the Negro press and the enlightened white labor press have a big task before them. But the task of Negro workers consists in more than merely deciding to organize. They must guard against being lured up blind alleys by irresponsible labor talkers who present them all sorts of wild, impossible dreams such as are advocated by the Communists. No labor movement in America among white or black workers can solve the industrial problems of the American workers, white or black, whose seat of control is outside of the country. This ought to be too obvious to require argument. The Communist movement in America is a menace to the American labor movement. It is a menace to the Negro workers. While healthy, intelligent, constructive criticism is valuable and necessary to the American labor movement, criticism which starts from the premise that the existing organized labor movement should be disrupted and destroyed must be resolutely opposed. . . . It ought to be patent now that the social history and psychology of the American workers will not yield to Communists' methods and tactics. Thus, instead of advancing, the Communists have set back and retarded the cause of labor in America. If such is true of the white worker it is as equally true of the Negro worker.

SOURCE: *The Messenger* 7 (July 1925): 261, 275.

Race Workers Turning to the American Federation of Labor (1929)

Many African Americans were skeptical about the usefulness of labor unions, especially those belonging to the American Federation of Labor, because it had not been much of an advocate for organizing black workers or for equal rights. Randolph helped to change that. His partnership with the AFL ushered in a transformation of the labor movement, and although it took decades, the AFL eventually became quite supportive of unionism among black workers and of civil rights.

When the Brotherhood was born in New York, in August 1925, the question was raised, "What will be the attitude of the American Federation of Labor toward this movement?" The psychological background of this question was a general unbelief in the disposition of the A.F. of L. to receive Race workers as members; this unbelief also had a background. It arose out of fact that several international unions of the American Federation of Labor had refused to accept Race workers as members and the sins of the internationals in question were readily assigned to the American Federation of Labor as a general movement.

This form of reasoning, of course, was unsound, in the light of the nature of the structure of the American Federation of Labor. The constitution of the American Federation of Labor accords autonomy to its internationals, which permits them to conduct their own affairs with measurable independence, just as the Constitution of the United States government accords measurable autonomy to the individual states, permitting them to regulate their own local affairs very largely. . . .

There is discrimination in practically all of the church denominations of America, the high schools, colleges and universities, the Y. W. and Y. M. C. A.'s, the federal, state and municipal governments, and practically every other institution that [it] has been my privilege to observe and study. But no rational person would contend that because there are instances of race prejudice in the high schools, colleges and universities that Negros should keep out of them and thereby deny themselves the opportunity of securing an education. The same may be said with the respect to the various branches of the government: because there are forms of race discrimination in them is no sound reason why the Negro should not exercise his constitutional rights to vote and be voted for the privilege of sitting as representatives in the municipal, state and federal branches of the government.

The philosophy underlying this position is the one of self-interest. Institutions are instruments to be employed by groups and individuals for the accomplishments of certain definite things. They are useful because they are the occasion, reason and basis of forms of power. This is due to the fact that they are the expression of organization. Individuals or groups are able to advance their interests and secure larger advantage when they act through organized groups than when [they] are independent and isolated. The American Federation of Labor is an institution for the purpose of increasing wages and improving the hours and working conditions of wage earners. One's position is logically unassailable; therefore, it maintains that since Negroes are largely wage earners their interests are definitely and virtually tied up with [those of] all other wage earners, fighting for a common objective through the instrumentality of the A. F. of L.

The Negro workers, to the number of several thousands, have held memberships in the American Federation of Labor for many decades. They were members of local unions or internationals that were, in turn, affiliated with the A. F. of L, in the building trades especially. Negro workers have a large representation, especially in the South, and since the war, increasingly so in the North, East, and West. They have been the beneficiaries of higher wage standards and better working conditions [that] have been the consequences of organized and systematic fight of the A. F. of L. The recognition of the obvious and concrete benefits in wage increases and shorter work days and favorable working conditions, secured as a result of allegiance with the trade union movement, has been one of the greatest factors in bringing about a change of attitude on the part of Race wage earners toward the A. F. of L.

Undoubtedly, the most effective and far-reaching influence upon the attitude of the Negro in relation to the A. F. of L. has been the fact that the Brotherhood of Sleeping Car Porters, the only national Negro labor union in America, received a charter from the Federation this year. No one who will take a fair and realistic viewpoint on the American Federation of Labor and the Negro workers, in the light of the facts as they are, and especially in relation to the Brotherhood, can rationally persist in a policy either of indifference or hostility toward the organized American labor movement. Not only has the charter granted the porters' union been a beneficent influence on the psychology of the Race as a whole, but it has profoundly affected the psychology of the white wage earners toward Race workers.

Even in the South where greater antagonism to Negro efforts is expected than in the North, the labor papers of the various central trades and labor council in the large cities have carried favorable news articles and written strong editorials in the interest of the Pullman porters' fight for the recognition for the Brotherhood of Sleeping Car Porters—a living wage, the eight-hour day or 240 hours work month, and improved working conditions, despite the fact that the Pullman porters are Negroes and the Pullman company is a white corporation.

When it is recognized that the Southern labor press reaches the white men in the South, who heretofore have been inflamed against their brothers in black in the rails and mines, on the railroads and the farms, by certain white agitators for their personal political and economic aggrandizement, this favorable attitude of southern white workers is promising and significant. Now, with the rise of the Pullman porters' organization and its entrance into the A. F. of L., which embraces millions of white workers in the North, South, East, and West, the white wage earners of the South and other parts of the country are beginning to see the light of common interests between all wage earners, regardless of race or color, and are joining hands with the Pullman porters to help them put over their fight.

Nothing has probably ever occurred before in the life of the American Negro which has occasioned such widespread, favorable news and editorial comment on a Negro movement, such as the Brotherhood has provoked form the southern labor press. . . .

SOURCE: *Chicago Defender*, June 29, 1929.

Open Letter Opposing Proposal to Ban Migration (1943)

In this piece, Randolph argues that the federal government should not limit the migration of African Americans to war production centers, a measure then under consideration by some federal officials as a way to handle the rise in racially motivated violence that rocked places such as Detroit during World War II.

Honorable Francis Biddle
U.S. Attorney General
Department of Justice
Washington, D.C.

Dear Sir:

I note in a recent news item which states that you are recommending to the White House that the government limit and possibly prohibit further migration of Negroes to overcrowded war production centers. You can readily see how this will be interpreted in relation to the Negro. It will be used to limit the employment opportunities of Negroes in their efforts to secure work in war plants. Moreover, as I see it, it is a violation of the Constitution, because it limits the freedom of movement of American citizens. Instead of preventing race riots, it will help constitute a fuse which may touch off the social, economic, racial, political magazine of dynamite which is the result of a long series of injustices and abuse and discrimination and segregation to which the Negro people have been subjected.

As one who is interested in racial peace and the victory of the United nations over the Nazi theories of racialism and tyranny, I want to urge you to rescind this order, if it has been made, in the interest of racial co-operating and harmony. This proposed policy is the grossest kind of segregation and discrimination. What about the poor whites who are flowing from the rural districts of the South into the war production centers? Nothing is suggested about limiting their migration, but they are the main carriers of the germ of racial hatred and are certain to create trouble unless the causes of race riots are fearlessly and constructively dealt with. These causes are segregation in the armed forces, defense plants and government departments as well as on various means of transportation, housing, recreation, law enforcement, etc.

I am sure that upon a careful examination of the national situation in regard to race relations, you will see the fallacy of this proposed policy. It is not the increase of the Negro population in war production centers that causes race riots, but it is the fact that Negroes have never gotten a fair break and just and reasonable opportunities in any phase of American life that is at the bottom these conflicts. One of the most fundamental and immediate remedies for these social explosions at the present time would be for the President to issue a national proclamation abolishing segregation in the armed forces. Nothing would be more effective than this.

SOURCE: *Amsterdam News*, August 21, 1943.

Telegram, Judge Kennesaw Mountain Landis (1943)

Four years before Jackie Robinson broke the color barrier in baseball, Randolph pleaded with Judge Kennesaw Mountain Landis, the first commissioner of Major League Baseball, to integrate the leagues. Randolph appealed to Landis as a businessman, arguing that games played by integrated teams would generate more revenue in ticket sales. A staunch segregationist, Landis remained unconvinced, and the integration of professional baseball did not occur until three years after his death in 1944.

As the head of the Brotherhood of Sleeping Car Porters embracing twelve thousand members from coast to coast and in the dominion of Canada I herewith wish to request and urge that Negro baseball players be employed upon a basis of equality with white ball players by the big leagues and also the minor leagues because these Negro players are American citizens and many of them are now on the battlefields throughout the world and seven seas giving their lives and blood to save democracy and defend the traditions of our country. It is a matter of common knowledge that Negro baseball players have won just as high acclaim for their skill in this national sport as white players have. We call for a just and fair consideration of the Colored baseball players solely upon their merit and ability alone. Just as Negro boxers like Joe Louis are great box office attractions so Negro baseball players are too, fine box office attractions. As shown by the fact of the East-West games in Chicago record-breaking crowds to the extent of fifty thousand attend.

SOURCE: Box 1, folder: A-W 1943, A. Philip Randolph Papers, Library of Congress.

The Negro and CIO-AFL Merger (1955)

Randolph welcomed the unification of the labor movement under the banner of the AFL-CIO. As he saw it, the merger was a positive development for civil rights and for other aspects of the postwar liberal agenda such as national health insurance and a higher minimum wage.

When recently the two unity committees of the American Federation of Labor and Congress of Industrial Organizations agreed on a name, the final obstacle blocking a merger was removed. In the not too distant future, we can expect for the first time in twenty years unity between the two dominant labor bodies. The wholesome impact of such a movement is tremendous. The effect on the politico-economic life of the nation in bringing together more than 16 million organized workers staggers the imagination. I believe sincerely that the merging of the AF of L and CIO will serve the public welfare of the nation and will accelerate the efforts of the American Negro to eliminate racial bias from the American scene.

More than a million and a half Negroes are members of the AFL and CIO unions. Simply stated, one in every ten Negroes is a trade unionist. Three out of every four Negro families counts some member a dues payer in an AFL or CIO local union. The Negro has a twofold task in respect to his union membership. First, he must assume his responsibility as a member and participate with other members to improve his economic standard of living. He must make certain that the union develops policies and programs designed to achieve a dynamic industrial democratic society. It would seem, therefore, that the Negro's first job is to make certain that he as a member is a participant in every phase of his local union's program. Second, he must wage continuously an unrelenting campaign to remove those practices of union racial bias whether by virtue of constitutional provisions or the more subtle mannerisms far too prevalent in some local bodies.

Essentially the American Negro is a wage earner. This makes him potentially a trade unionist. The free trade union movement provides a medium through which he can accomplish much to improve his economic life. One hears a great deal pro and con about the responsibility of a democratic society to the economic welfare of the individual. Federal and state legislation dealing with maximum hours and minimum wages, women and child labor laws, social security, railroad retirement provisions, federal health programs, federal aid to education and federal aid to public housing are just a few of the legislative acts which concern officially the AFL and the CIO.

In recent months Negroes in and out of AFL and CIO locals together with thousands of interested fellow white citizens have expressed great interest in the anti-discrimination clause in the proposed constitution for the new AFL-CIO organization. It is an evidence of wisdom on the part of Presidents George Meany and Walter Reuther, the heads of the AFL and CIO respectively, and their colleagues on both unity committees, to recognize the clamor from men of good will of both races to eliminate racial segregation from the new body as one of major importance.

The new constitution states in simple terms that one of the objects and principles of this federation is "to encourage all workers without regard to race, creed, color or national origin to share in the full benefits of union organization." The constitution calls for the creation of a department of civil rights, and already George Meany, who will be the president of the new organization, has stated that such a department will be a major wheel in the new AFL-CIO operational machinery. It would seem that this department, buttressed with the support of the president and executive council of the new body, could do much in the beginning by starting the new department off with the firm determination to tackle racial bias and to use the organization's resources, influences and most of all its humanitarian purposes in eliminating racial discrimination.

There is no doubt that great progress has been made both by the AFL and CIO in eliminating racial discrimination. This is due essentially to an increased awareness of free labor's role in a free society. . . . Yet, one must be ever mindful that there still exists in far too many places both in the AFL and CIO, at times subtle, at other times not too subtle, practices which give evidence that perhaps some are not "their brothers' keeper." The new merged body can go far in giving leadership and vitality to the fight against racial discrimination. Such organizations as the NAACP, and numerous religious and welfare groups which are dedicated to improving human welfare, could move faster in their programs with cooperative assistance from the new AFL-CIO body.

Unions have great resources for not only cooperating with such organizations but can and should give leadership drawn from their wide experience in the industrial, political and legislative fields. Through their ability to accumulate and to spend great sums of money from their financial resources, the free trade union movement could do much to alleviate human misery from great masses of people in programs conceived and executed through democratic planning. Therefore, it is easily seen that such a movement is truly a force to be reckoned with in the civil rights fight of the American Negro. One cannot emphasize too strongly that the dues-paying member is the backbone of the labor movement. Functioning essentially through his local, he can exert constrictive pressures, not only for increasing his wages, reducing his hours of work and improving his working conditions, but also for effecting policies and programs designed to make his community a more wholesome place for all to enjoy.

It is in this context that the more than one and a half million Negroes who pay union dues can contribute to hastening the elimination of racial and religious discrimination from our national society. If the Negro is to make progress as a result of the merger he will have to do many things. He must willingly assume all of the financial responsibilities and accept the basic philosophy that governs the free trade union movement. For this is basic to the worker's salvation in a democratic society. Not only must he pay joining fees, regular dues and assessments, but he must function earnestly and consistently in every phase of the union's program. He must be seen and heard at meetings, participate in debates concerning issues before the local and national union body and run for local and national offices. . . .

No member should leave it to someone else in the local to do all the required tasks. For such lethargy can only assure a movement lack of growth and vision. If only a few Negroes occupy positions affecting the basic AFL and CIO policies and programs this cannot be blamed entirely on our white union brothers. The AFL and CIO can feel justly proud of the progress made in improving the wages, reducing the hours and improving the working conditions of all workers white and black, union and non-union members. Both the AFL and the CIO recognize that federal and state legislation are means for achieving or retarding a democratic Society.

On the credit side of the ledger, the recent increase in the federal minimum wage law to $1.00 an hour from 75¢ represents a notable legislative achievement for the trade union movement. Although the unions rightly attempted to get the figure for workers in interstate commerce at $1.25, Congress was unwilling to heed the plea for the higher figure. This increase not only benefits members of the trade union movement, but all workers are affected wholesomely. In fact the national economy is the beneficiary of such an achievement. When one recognizes also the great improvement in the Social Security and Railroad Retirement acts, the laws affecting child and women workers, federal funds for public housing, it can be seen that we have moved forward.

Yet, be aware that the trade union movement is still threatened in numerous places. Increased efforts are being made by powerful forces to place upon the state statute books a law which would limit unions in their efforts to achieve a semblance of union security. These laws, misnamed "right to work" laws, would nullify, if not completely wipe out the free trade union movement. All unionists must participate in alerting the public to the dangers inherit in such laws and the general public should repudiate legislators who favor such legislation. The Taft-Hartley Act after eight years is still on the federal statute books.

If recognized labor is to expand and continue to make its contribution to the general welfare of the nation, we must defeat the efforts of this anti-labor statute. Labor still seeks to get effective legislation establishing a national health program. More than 65 years have passed since Congress last enacted any civil rights legislation. We still seek earnestly a federal FEPC with sanctions and penalties. At the same time, we work ardently for an effective housing program, free from jim-crow, anti-lynch and anti-poll tax laws. These issues continue to be political footballs drawn out by both political parties at election time to be kicked around, with FEPC, for the Negro vote.

Therefore, the American Negroes who are privileged to be members or who have the opportunity to be members of a democratic free trade union movement, AFL or CIO have the responsibility to participate actively, vigorously and faithfully in every phase of his union's program. He must ever seek to use the free trade union movement, especially through his local, to make certain that his union is operating effectively to increase his wages, reduce his hours of work and improve his working conditions. . . . He must see that his union is participating aggressively in removing all practices that affect adversely any member in exercising his right to a job. He should hold his government responsible for leading the way in eliminating racial bias. The Negro worker can increase his effectiveness by being a union member and advancing the course of free trade unionism: a bulwark against Communism and Fascism and the advanced guard for freedom, peace and plenty.

SOURCE: *Chicago Defender*, August 13, 1955.

Why the National Negro Labor Council (1959)

In this statement to the steering committee of the National Negro Labor Council, Randolph gives an account of racial problems within the AFL-CIO and provides an overview of the work that the NNLC could undertake to remediate these issues. Randolph is careful to frame the NNLC as an organization complementary to the AFL-CIO, and he praises union leadership for the progress that has been made. A key component of his argument for the establishment of the NNLC is that it could bridge the gap between African American workers and the labor movement. By doing so, Randolph argues, the new organization could challenge growing Black Nationalist sentiments that he dismissed as reactionary "psychological compensation."

What Can the National Negro Labor Council Achieve?

It can give Negro trade unionists a sense of unity, both among themselves and with their white brothers. It can also provide them with a sense of purpose, direction and mission and dedication to the philosophy of trade unionism and the program for equality of Negro trade unionists in the labor movement. It can struggle to bring about the desegregation of the racially segregated unions, with a view to the integration of all workers into trade unions without regard to race or color. It can promulgate its philosophy to the effect that racially segregated or Jim Crow unions do not have the right to exist within the framework of a free trade union movement—but since they do exist, they do not have the right of final decision as to whether or when they shall cease to exist, and [must] conform with the national policy on discrimination and segregation as set forth in the Constitution.

The National Negro Labor Council can help the AFL-CIO to cleanse the House of Labor of color-caste discrimination and segregation which will help it win the confidence and faith in its declarations of democracy and freedom among the laboring masses of Africa and Asia. . . .

Why Is It Necessary?

It is necessary to achieve greater contact and communication among Negro trade unionists for the achievement of their common goals that invite their fight for equality. It is necessary because the AFL-CIO, though a national policy against discrimination and segregation based upon race or color, will not voluntarily move toward the implementation of this policy unless it is caused to move, and it cannot be caused to move except through an organization which is committed to the elimination of discrimination and segregation. This is no reflection upon the leadership of the AFL-CIO or the various national or international unions affiliated therewith.

The fact is, racial discrimination and segregation have reached the stage of institutionalization in the labor movement. They are taken for granted. They are viewed with utter complacency, apathy, unconcern, if not indifference. This has been true from the very foundation of the labor movement in the United States up to the present time. There are historical, socio-economic, political and ethnic reasons for this attitude, but it is important to point out that this is not peculiar to the labor movement. Racial discrimination and segregation have reached the state of institutionalization in government, in the church, in business and industry, in the schools, colleges and universities, in sports and entertainment. As a matter of fact, the racial discrimination and segregation system of various institutions of the country are given rigidity and resistance because they are encrusted with the dogma of white supremacy. The labor movement, being an integral factor of the American community, naturally reflects the mores and attitudes that prevail in the community.

It may not be amiss to observe that the proposed National Negro Labor Council is not a new phenomenon in the labor movement. The early Jewish immigrants to this country set up the United Hebrew Trades, the mouthpiece of which was the *Jewish Daily Forward* in New York and the country. The purpose of this movement was to advance the cause of the Jewish workers. Today, the Jewish workers have developed the Jewish Labor Committee, which is a movement of considerable proportions and has worked effectively in the civil rights field not only for Jews but other minorities. It is recognized and accepted as a legitimate phase of the American labor movement by the AFL-CIO. Jewish workers also receive moral and public relations support from the American Jewish Congress, the American Jewish Committee and B'nai B'rith. On account of the fact that the early Irish immigrants were the victims of religious persecution, they found it necessary to establish Catholic trade unions. In addition to Catholic trade unions, the Hibernians, the Knights of Columbus, the Holy Name Society, and other Catholic organizations work with vigor and determination to eliminate discrimination against Irish Catholics in this country. Realizing the futility of depending upon outside forces to advocate their cause against the evil practices of discrimination and segregation, Puerto Rican workers are now in the process of establishing a Puerto Rican Labor Committee.

The National Negro Labor Council can play an effective and progressive role in opposing anti-labor legislation such as the "right to work" laws. It is a well-known fact that although "right to work" laws were defeated in California and Ohio during 1959, the movement for the extension of "right to work" laws in various states and, finally, a federal right to work law, still has vitality and is pursuing the same program. Be it said to the credit of the NAACP, in cooperation with the Committee on Political Education of the AFL-CIO, waged a vigorous and effective campaign against "right to work laws" in the aforementioned states. It is an understatement to add that were it not for the relentless educational campaign of the NAACP against the "right to work" laws, they might not have been defeated. The National Negro Labor Council can be effective in joining hands with trade unions in opposing anti-labor politicians and supporting pro-labor political leaders in government and out of government.

Will The Proposed Council Promote Black Nationalism?

What is Black Nationalism?

1. It is basically the Negro's reaction behavior pattern to White Nation alism. White Nationalism is the cause—Black Nationalism is the effect.

2. Black Nationalism is a ghetto people's defense and offense mechanism against persecution, insult, oppression and poverty.

3. Black Nationalism is psychological compensation for social, economic and political rejection by the dominant racial power system.

4. It is a manifestation of disillusionment with the concepts, professions and practices of Christianity and democracy.

5. It is an expression of fear and frustration, despair and desperation, on the part of the Negro, with the violence of race hate.

6. It's a bitter outcry against the empty and mocking conservative, liberal, religious, and labor white paternalism.

7. It's a direct, if awkward, expression of belief in the simple fact that the salvation of a people must come from within—that our friends may help us but they cannot save us.

8. The basic remedy for Black Nationalism, which can become a danger to social peace as White Nationalism is a danger to social peace, is the abolition of White Nationalism which expresses itself in lynchings, mob law, disfranchisement, segregation and discrimination in schools, church, government, housing, political parties, labor unions, sports, stage and screen.

9. While Black Nationalism, like White Nationalism, is unsound and leads to violent forms of extremism, it is not to be equated with rational racial unity which may be constructive, creative and healthy for self-defense and various forms of cultural, political, economic and social achievement.

10. One of the dangers of Black Nationalism is that it tends to breed hatred against white people merely because they are white, not because they have committed some wrong against Negroes. This is the behavior pattern of white nationalists.

11. Black Nationalism's violent hatred and propaganda against white people can lead to violence, which will worsen racial relations and injure both Negroes and whites.

12. Black Nationalism tends to direct its venomous attacks upon white people instead of [the] discriminatory practices of some white people.

13. It is based upon the false assumption of the capacity of Negroes for self-sufficiency in the age of science, industrialism and technology.

14. Black Nationalism tends to develop into a conspiracy against Negroes themselves, by opposing the Negroes' fight for freedom on the grounds that freedom from discrimination and segregation will lead to racial mixing and the loss of proper devotion to the black man's African heritage—which is both a folly and a fallacy.

15. Black Nationalism also tends to lead to division and weakness of the Negro masses from within because of internal color bias.

16. Black Nationalism is unsound because it disallows contact between the races. Without contact, there can be no communication, and without communication, there breeds suspicions, doubts, fears and frustrations that prevent understanding, confidence and cooperation.

To the question, "Will the National Negro Labor Council promote Black Nationalism?" the answer is naturally, "No." Instead of the Council promoting Black Nationalism, it will serve to remove the basis of Black Nationalism by working to the end of eliminating discrimination and segregation in the labor movement and the government. Finally, it is said in Holy Writ: "For the trumpet give an uncertain sound, who shall prepare himself for battle."

SOURCE: Box 35, folder: Speeches, September 7, 1959–December 4, 1959, A. Philip Randolph Papers, Library of Congress.

Testimony before the Committee on Education and Labor (1961)

Randolph believed that equal opportunity in apprenticeship programs was essential to achieving parity in employment. Recognizing the fact that African Americans were grossly underrepresented in the building and construction trades, he believed that eliminating discriminatory apprenticeship practices was essential to the opening of American workplaces. To address this, he called for an end to the nepotism of father-son apprenticeship programs and the relaxation of union standards that kept journeymen from equitably competing for jobs.

Mr. Chairman, my name is A. Philip Randolph, I am international president of the Brotherhood of Sleeping Car Porters and president of the Negro American Labor Council of 217 West 125th Street, New York.

I wish to take this opportunity to congratulate your committee upon holding hearings on the subject of apprenticeship training and to express my approval and support of H.R. 8219 which proposes to withdraw federal support and approval from apprenticeship programs that are conducted upon a basis of race bias. It is an understatement to observe that the elimination of racial discrimination from all apprenticeship training programs involves the economic life and death of the black laboring masses. This is so for the following reasons: One, the relatively small number of skilled Negro workers in the nation. Two, racial barriers to participation in apprenticeship programs. Three, the concentration of disproportionately large numbers of Negro workers in the categories of unskilled workers. Four, the phenomenal pace of the automation revolution which is changing the work force and the work tools, the result of which is the decrease in demand for the unskilled worker. Five, the slow, spotty and inadequate action on the part of organized labor effectively to grapple with this problem.

Now, relative to the first proposition, namely, the relatively small number of Negro artisans in American industry, may I say that it is a matter of common knowledge that there was a disproportionate and alarming decline in the number of Negroes in the skilled trades between 1920 and 1950, especially in the building trades where the Negro was once relatively fairly well represented in the South, and where the total number of mechanics has increased. Census reports—especially for 10 Southern States: Alabama, Arkansas, Florida, Georgia, Louisiana, Mississippi, North Carolina, Tennessee, and Virginia—the percentage of Negro carpenters enumerated in these states declined from 23.12 percent in 1920 to 10 percent in 1950. Painters declined from 25.3 percent in 1920 to 13.8 percent in 1950. Bricklayers decreased from 54.7 percent in 1920 to 37.5 percent in 1950. Plasterers, formerly heavily representative of the Negro, diminished from 66.5 percent in 1920 to 57.9 percent in 1950. It is useless to extend the list. The above-indicated status of the black skilled artisans is a fair sample of the changing position of the Negro in the building trades in the South. In this instance, the decline represents a grave threat to their economic progress and to the economic progress of the country as a whole.

It is because of this serious situation that the subject of apprenticeship training takes on such timely significance. Obviously, by the law of attrition, unless the decline of Negro skilled workers is arrested and newly trained Negro artisans in relatively large numbers enter the work force, it will be only a matter of a short time when the skilled Negro workers will disappear from the building construction occupations of the country.

What about a second issue, or racial barriers, to Negro worker participation is apprenticeship training programs? While it is a grave indictment of the building trades' unions, yet no one denies that less than 1 percent of the apprentices of the building trades are Negroes. Even in New York State, perhaps the most liberal, racially, in the country, only 2 percent of the apprentices are Negroes. The only local union which seems to be trying consistently to do something about this problem is Local 3 of the International Brotherhood of Electrical Workers, whose business manager is Harry Van Arsdale. Since he became the leader of the New York Central Labor Council some definite action is being taken, with a view to breaking down the racial barriers in the craft unions' apprenticeship training programs. I know of no other city central body which is doing a comparable job on this question. . . .

The answer is that one of the major reasons for the grim fact that the rate of unemployment of Negroes is twice, or more, the national rate of white workers is that unskilled workers are not only the first fired and the last hired but also the first to be liquidated by radical technological advances. Hence, the acquisition of skills by Negro workers are trapped in the no-man's-land of the unskilled, they constitute the hard core of joblessness, which means that these workers remain unemployed during depressions, recessions, booms, inflations, and deflations; during cyclical, seasonal, residual, technological, ethnic, and economic maladjustments of the economy.

Verily, there is a large segment of black slum proletariat, untrained, largely the product of race bias, caught up among the structured unemployment and unemployable and, probably untrainable. It is important to note that the phenomenal pace of the revolution of automation is not only changing the work force and the work tools that unskilled Negro workers cannot use, but it is also raising the productivity level and reducing the work force, which is certain to precipitate sharp and bitter competition not only between black and white workers and competition among black workers, as well as competition between women and men workers for the same jobs. And, of course, the automation revolution will bring about a decreasing demand for the unskilled blue-jean worker, which hits the black laboring masses.

Our fifth problem involves the slow, spotty, fragmentary, and woefully inadequate action which has been taken by trade unions effectively to grapple with the question of opening the doors of apprenticeship training to every worker, regardless of race, color, religion, national origin, or ancestry. Legislation as suggested by your committee is definitely essential to enable Negro workers to break through these well-nigh institutionalized racial barriers in apprenticeship training courses.

Projections of estimates by the U.S. Department of Labor and other economic, social-political agencies indicate that by 1970 the population of the country will range around 208 million. This, of course, will require a vast increase in the gross national product, the production of which can only be achieved by expanding the work force of skilled artisans. The New York State Department of Labor indicates, in a survey of jobs in 1960 to 1970, that 46,000 additional craftsman will be needed annually if the state's needs for skilled workers in the 1960's are to be satisfied. A comparable need of craftsmen exists in practically every state in the Union, but Negro workers will be practically completely excluded from apprenticeship training programs in the states of the South. Thus, apprenticeship training is a definite source of economic security for the workers.

Now, job entry is a letter of introduction to a craft or trade. Where job entry is dependent upon apprenticeship, and if the number of apprentices is artificially controlled to keep out or to limit the number admitted from certain ethnic groups, this means a denial or restriction of the number who may expect to get on-the-job training. The latter is tantamount to denial of craftsman's status. The closure, or circumscription of craftsman's status, forces persons refused apprenticeship training to seek job entry in low-occupational jobs. Ultimately, persons forced into jobs with low occupational and economic status are faced with little economic security. Vocational schooling, unless linked with on-the-job training, is time wasted in such trades as printing, building, cutters in the needle trades, and so forth.

One such group faced with this problem is the Negro, and that these problems are faced by Negroes in reality is succinctly delineated in the 1960 report of the U.S. Department of Labor entitled: "The Economic Situation of Negroes in the United States." In this covering letter to President Eisenhower, Secretary [of Labor, James P.] Mitchell states: "Negro skill rates remain disproportionately low, and as a result Negro unemployment rates are disproportionately high. The 1959 averages reveal a level of 4.6 percent for whites, but 11.5 percent for nonwhites. Negro participation in apprenticeship training is still far too low." The general picture outlined by Mr. Mitchell does not really go to the heart of the matter because in particular trades, as the building trades, not only has Negro participation in the apprenticeship training programs been almost nil, but the Negro has been losing ground in many of these trades, which have traditionally been his in the South. Thus, we are confronted with a dual problem. One, the Negro is losing ground in many trades where he has held high representation. Two, one avenue of replacement, the apprenticeship training program, is excluding him.

To deal with the question of apprenticeship we must first deal with the question: What is the employment outlook in the various trades? The total volume of employment at any particular time is related to the volume of spending, both private and public. We know that, regardless of the level of employment, our population is increasing, which means that the demand for housing will increase. When we add to the private sector's needs, redevelopment programs, slum clearance, and so forth, the need for skilled mechanics [will increase]. . . .

Of equal importance is the fact that construction occurs everywhere. This means that employment opportunities will be present everywhere, varying from city to city and from trade to trade. The number of workers to be hired will necessarily be greatest where the greatest amount of construction is going on—the larger cities and in those parts of the country in an active stage of industrial development and population growth. However, in the older sections of the country, where construction activity seems unlikely, new workers will be needed to replace those leaving the labor force. It should be noted that in the older sections of the country redevelopment programs have added a new spurt on construction activity. . . .

Various studies reveal that the trade is losing more workers than are being replaced. The most effective manner in which skilled manpower may be added is through the apprenticeship program. Thus, there should be thousands of opportunities for boys interested in the building trades, Negroes as well as whites. But we know that this is just not so. Discrimination and race prejudice have prevented the entrance of Negroes into the building trades. In many instances it has been through exclusion from unions, either by "white only" clauses, tacit consent, or preference given to white journeymen. In other instances, the Negro has been excluded from the job by the employer.

For the most part, opportunities for Negroes have been best in plastering and brick laying, and the poorest in the mechanical trades—electrical work, plumbing and pipe fitting, operating cranes, and other related work. Even where the Negro has acquired the necessary skill in one of the crafts, union exclusion presents a major handicap since most of the new construction is done under union contract. It is particularly severe for the applicant interested in apprenticeship training; but in spite of this and other handicaps a limited number of Negroes desiring to enter the building trades have been able to do so through informal on-the-job training for all the building trades. . . .

Let us try to answer the question, "What is apprenticeship?" Apprenticeship is a means of job entry into a craft. It is a job at which a worker learns while producing and earns an established proportionate wage of the journeyman. This worker has the definite objective of becoming a craftsman in his chosen trade. At the end of his apprenticeship period this worker should be eligible for journeyman's status. The apprenticeship agreement includes all the terms both parties [are required] to meet. The agreement is registered with the State Council on Apprenticeship. In many instances, advance apprenticeship standing is given for skill acquired in the Armed Forces or through vocational schools.

Since we have mentioned vocational training, it may be helpful to distinguish between vocational education and apprentice training. One essential difference is that on-the-job training involves some 40 hours per week in practical work. In the vocational course the student spends about 50 percent of his school time, or 15 hours a week, on practical shop work, which is less than half the amount of time an apprentice spends each week. The results are that while the vocational graduate may be granted advanced standing as an apprentice, he is by no means a fully qualified journeyman. Furthermore, it is the consensus of opinion that vocational training cannot and is not intended to produce full-fledged craftsmen. This can only be expected after on-the-job training has supplemented vocational training. . . .

Although we have established the fact that the outlook for the building trades is good and there is sufficient work for the available workforce, at least two other things should be mentioned. One is whether a sufficient number of replacements are being trained to replace both those dying and those retiring from the workforce. The second is whether or not there are Negroes available in the proper age groups with sufficient educational background to be qualified for apprenticeships. With respect to question one, a Joint Congressional Committee on Housing in 1947 found in one city alone that for every new worker entering the trade, the trade was losing nine old workers. This situation was typical. While numbers varied from city to city, there is no doubt that losses from the ranks of skilled labor were greater than the current rate of replacement. To answer the second question we need two types of statistics: (1) availability of Negro youth for apprenticeship programs, and (2) does this youth have the necessary educational background.

Availability can be noted in a negative manner since the male Negro youth in the 18 to 19 age group suffered 27.2 percent unemployment and the 20 to 24 age group had 16.3 percent unemployment, indicating the availability of potential apprentices. Now that we know there is available a group of Negro youth for apprenticeship programs, we ask, do they have the educational qualifications? As an example, we will take the youth in school between the ages 14 to 17 in 1956. These youths should be available for apprenticeship programs in 1959 since the 14-year group would be of age and the 17-year group will still be available because the apprenticeship ages are from 18 to 24. In 1956 those Negro youths in the 14 to 17 age group had some 81 to 82 percent in school, but still the number being accepted for apprenticeship programs was negligible as compared to [that for] white[s].

Proportionately, the Negro craftsman is declining in the building trades; this source is drying up and this is closing the likelihood of Negro craftsmen serving as teachers to Negro apprentices. Also, the number of Negro apprentices accepted is so small, assuming that they complete the course, that the future outlook is negligible. In addition, there are certain crafts which have barred the Negro entirely from their apprenticeship programs which, in combination, act to limit the Negro's economic security in the building trades.

There are several reasons why Negro youth don't clamor to get into building trades:

(a) Limitations suffered by capable Negro mechanics in many communities, such as denial of union membership or protection, refusal of employment at prevailing wages, marginal status of craftsmen, etcetera, often discourage Negro youth from choosing building trades as a vocation.

(b) The long-term effect of the above limitations in some communities has been to reduce the quality of Negro mechanics, the more promising and ambitious going into fields offering more attractive opportunities. Youth get the impression that all Negro mechanics are poorly trained and inefficient and hesitate to identify themselves with these trades.

(c) The apprentice training program operates principally through union channels, and as Negroes are often out of touch with these channels not too much is known among them as to the provisions and availability of the program. Since the organized labor movement is a basic factor in giving reality and integrity to an apprenticeship training program, I was pleased to note from the statement of George Meany, president of the AFL-CIO, which was presented to your committees, that he supported your bill.

Recommendations for achieving greater equality of employment opportunity and optimum utilization of minority manpower throughout the economy:

1. Federal fair employment practice legislation such as H.R. 262.

2. Reduction of indenturing term for the graduation of a journeyman craftsman. The present term of indenturing apprentices harks back to the old

medieval guilds that sharply restricted entry into the craft guilds. These restrictions are retained and maintained for job monopoly by the craft unions. This is not objectionable as long as the unions are open that, in turn, keep and maintain occupations and jobs open.

3. Abolish father and son system of designating candidates as apprentices for training programs.

SOURCE: House Committee on Education and Labor, *Equal Opportunity in Apprenticeship Programs: Hearings before the Special Subcommittee on Labor of the Committee on Education and Labor, House of Representatives,* 87th Cong., 1st sess., August 21, 22, and 23, 1961 (Washington, D.C.: GPO, 1961), 121–26.

The American Trade Union Movement at the Crossroads: Address at Brown University, Providence, Rhode Island (1962)

In this address, Randolph asserts that in the 1960s Americans were at a dividing line in history between the empowerment of humanism and the forces of regimentation wrought by massive institutions. He foresaw that the lack of union affiliation among white-collar and service industry workers was a major challenge facing the labor movement and warned of a coming totalitarianism if unions failed to check the power of "Big Business."

There are three great centers and sources of power, authority and responsibility in our democratic American society. They are Big Government, Big Business and Big Labor. These three forces developed as a result of three American revolutions. There was the nationalist revolution of 1776 which not only drove British colonialism from America, but cleared the way for the capitalist development of the United States. Old colonial feudal strictures on industry and trade were removed. Enterprise became free and business was no longer restricted by rigid prescriptions of the guilds concerning [the] prices and quality of products and services. The white laborer, too, was freed from bondage, a sort of hangover or remnant of colonial feudalism. He no longer was bound to his job for a specific period; he could quit when he wanted to and work where he pleased without being branded a vagrant.

The Revolution changed the whole face and life of America. A manufacturing industry began and commerce began to boom. Despite the common law of conspiracy, workers started to organize unions, though small and weak. The important historical fact here is that the same revolution which released business for growth and development released the workers, at least to sell their labor in a free market. Of course, it is a matter of common knowledge that the wage earners were never as free or as well organized as business.

The next revolution was the Civil War. While the central dramatic issue of this great historic event was the freedom of the Negro slave, the freedom of the slave also involved the future of America as an industrial nation. The Civil War, though a destructive, bloody conflict, was a vitalizing historical, political and economic event. The victory of the North over King Cotton was indispensable if America were to develop giant industry, corporate business and a flourishing nation-wide enterprise. The plantation slave economy was the halter around America's neck, preventing a mercantile nation from becoming an industrial power. If the old Slave South had maintained its grip on Congress and the [presidential] administration as in the pre–Civil War period, it would have been fatal to industry, as well as to labor.

Here, again, the Civil War revolution provided opportunity for growth of nascent American industry under tariff protection, mass markets and subsidies. Although employers, following the Civil War, unleashed warfare against the labor movement by crushing scores of strikes in blood and violence, and forced many unions out of business, especially during the depression of 1873–1878, the workers fought back through the Molly Maguires of the Coal Miners, railroad strikes of 1877, the Haymarket Riot in Chicago in 1886, Pullman in 1893, and other industrial and labor disorders. The foundation of business trade unionism was laid, which expressed itself in the organization of the American Federation of Labor in 1886.

The Roosevelt New Deal Era marked another revolution, affecting both business and labor through a series of far-reaching legislative acts, which served to bail business and labor out of the depression. The Roosevelt period strengthened American capitalism and business unionism and social unionism. This was inevitable since both were, and now are, creatures of the free enterprise economy, industrialism and political democracy.

The American trade union movement is at the crossroads, not only because of the damage to its image as a result of corruption in a few unions, and I emphasize the word *few* because the great majority of unions are honestly and well run by business unionists along with social unionists, but because of its lack of solidarity and its loss of evangelism.

Business trade union individualism, or the policy and practice of every union for itself (expressed in bitter jurisdictional disputes), tends to give the labor union the complexion of a mere business enterprise operated to extend its jurisdictional sovereignty to secure dues-paying members without concern about the basic purpose of the labor movement; namely, the organization of the organized worker and advancement of the welfare of the workers through struggle. This concept of the development of prosperity and power, for and by national and international unions, as a major objective emphasizes materials at the expense of sacrifice of humanism—the original rationale of the existence of trade unions.

Labor unions, like the early Christian movement, have their basic roots in the struggle to give honor and respect to the dignity of the personality of the common man, the worker. The labor movement, like the church movement, must be, and is, a moral movement concerned with the freedom and majesty of the human spirit, as well as the material well-being of the worker. When, and if, the free democratic trade unions lose their concern about the welfare and freedom of the worker as an individual and as a class, they will lose their spiritual and moral force.

Thus, though the business movement and the labor movement have their origin[s] in the free enterprise economy, they have different objectives and reasons for being. The former exists for profits and the latter exists to improve the life and living of man. Business is a profit-making movement while Labor is a non-profit movement. Hence, it is unsound and weakens the labor movement morally and spiritually to identify it with, and commit it to the support of the profit system, which is a system of the exploitation of Labor. . . .

A grave point of crisis of organized labor is its decline in membership, as a result of the contraction of various industries, such as railroads and coal mining. Probably one of the greatest challenges of organized labor is the unorganized non-manual workers, such as retail, wholesale, government, financial, insurance, real estate and service employment sectors. While the blue-collar workers are decreasing, the white-collar workers are increasing. With the evident apathy of this class of workers toward trade unions, together with the loss of the messianic fervor which characterized the labor movement at the turn of the century and during the decade of the 1930s, organized labor has failed to organize the unorganized. It takes union members to organize workers into unions. Union members must proselytize their fellow workers. This is not being done today.

Moreover, because of jurisdictional barriers and internal structural problems, the AFL-CIO is unable to rally its entire membership in a membership campaign. The high command of organized labor does not have the power, in the loose confederation of the AFL-CIO, to mount and command a massive campaign to organize the unorganized, even if it has the will. This fact is largely responsible for the fact that the organized labor movement is not moving . . . if the organized labor movement continues to fail to organize the unorganized workers, it is quite likely to prove to be a tragic blow to the working class and our democratic society, since Labor will be unable to serve as a countervailing power to the growing power of Big Business, which will tend to accumulate and amass a disproportionate concentration of power under its control.

A too great, disproportionate concentration of power in the hands of Big Business or Big Labor tends to corrupt Big Business or Big Labor; which may result in such power being used against the public's interests. Moreover, too great an imbalance between these two power structures could result in the destruction of our democratic society, which is founded upon the assumption of the existence of plural centers of power and authority. This is the basic assurance and defense against the development of a monolithic totalitarian state. Thus, the organized labor movement must grow to remain strong and free, if our American economy and political democratic order are to grow and remain strong and free.

Our American national labor policy must not tend to foster an imbalance between these two basic forces of our democratic society. To this end, free collective bargaining should be recognized and supported for all American workers. Therefore, "right-to-work" laws are not only not in the interest of the progress of free workers, but they are not in the interest of a free America. But while it is in the interest of our democratic society that Labor possess the right of free collective bargaining and be able to provide the crucial balance to the economic power of private enterprise, organized labor must never lose sight of the fact that it must be concerned about bargaining not only from a position of strength, but also from a position of truth, reason, integrity and dedication to the public's good.

SOURCE: Box 36, folder: Speeches, January 17, 1962–July 15, 1962, A. Philip Randolph Papers, Library of Congress.

Testimony before the Committee on Labor and Public Welfare (1963)

Randolph devoted nearly a quarter century to bringing about a federal statute outlawing employment discrimination. In this document, he testifies before Congress in support of a permanent fair employment practice committee. As Randolph put it, "economic and civil rights are inseparable," and he reasoned that abolishing segregation meant little if African Americans remained so economically disadvantaged that they could not enjoy their newly won freedoms. Although the national program of full employment for which Randolph advocated never materialized, his vision of a federal fair employment law become a centerpiece of the omnibus 1964 Civil Rights Act.

My name is A. Philip Randolph. I appreciate the opportunity to appear before your subcommittee on behalf of the Brotherhood of Sleeping Car Porters, AFL-CIO, and the Negro American Labor Council to testify in favor of the enactment of fair employment practices legislation.

If legislation for a permanent, federal FEPC had not been killed by filibuster in 1946 and again in 1950, our economy, our democracy and our internal peace would not be in the same crisis that confronts them today. If this renewed attempt should suffer a similar fate, no responsible Negro leader can

safely predict or control the ultimate consequences. Fair employment practices legislation would not, of course, have solved all of our crucial problems
of employment and civil rights, but it might have established a sound basis on
which steady progress toward equality could have been made.

The urgency of the accelerating pressures across the country for equality
now can best be understood against the background of such past defeats.
There is usually a time when gradual, if sustained, change is desirable and
possible. But there is also another time in which a vacuum created by the lack
of action explodes when needs which will no longer wait [to] press into it.
This summer we have reached that hour. A superficial look at the national
scene might indicate that the civil rights struggle has recently begun to move
from the area of intellectual needs—such as education and status in public
accommodations—to economic needs: jobs and a decent standard of living.

In actual fact, large masses of Negroes were first involved almost spontaneously in a political struggle for their own rights more than twenty years ago in
the initial drive for FEPC. Economic and civil rights are inseparable. The economic gains for the oppressed Negro workers made that time are the basis on
which the larger struggle for democracy was built. All of our minority groups
have benefited from [and] now support the executive orders and state legislation which partially embody the FEPC idea. But it is important to remember
that when the national drive toward fair employment practices began, it was
essentially . . . a movement of Negroes. The march on Washington movement
was a march of Negroes, of a Negro community united as never before around
a common goal. And the un[ful]filled hopes which filibusters could thwart
but could not kill are today the goal of a united Negro community.

History clarifies current events. As always, Negroes had been harder hit by
the depression of the thirties than their fellow white Americans. Still, all had
suffered together. It was with the beginning of the defense industry, when "No
Help Wanted" signs changed to "Help Wanted—White" that the indignant
organization of Negroes to gain a fairer share in the nation's reviving economy
spurted. It took the combination of a wartime manpower shortage and the
threat of a march on Washington to secure Executive Order 8802 on June 25,
1941, and the establishment of the President's Committee on Fair Employment
Practices. But as soon as the national war emergency was over—and democracy safe—the old, national pattern of "last hired, first fired" crept back. Fair
practices were filibustered away, and even the Korean emergency brought
no permanent change. Further executive orders, particularly in the field of
government contracts, have shown that the nation's conscience could never
again be completely quieted in the fact of discrimination; and party platforms
of both major parties have been better than the voting record of either in the
Congress.

But from the fifties until today, efforts to secure for Negroes and other minorities the same right to work as other Americans have progressed slowly and inadequately, state by state. In more than twenty years, twenty-three states, including Hawaii and Alaska, have adopted some form of fair employment legislation. But the long and arduous road of investigation of individual complaints has not been good enough; and a majority of states still lack even that. The result has been that, economically, the Negro appears to stand today in the same relative economic position he occupied in the depths of the depression. The unemployment relief census of October 1933 showed about twice as high a proportion of Negroes on public relief roles as of whites: 18 percent contrasted with 9.5 percent. The President's broadcast to the nation on June 11 indicated about twice the proportion of Negroes in the work force unemployed as of whites: 10 percent contrasted with 5 percent.

When momentum for the March on Washington Movement began to gather, in October 1940, statistics showed that after 8 years of the New Deal, one-fourth of the Negro work force was unemployed in contrast to 13 percent of the white. The 2-to-1 proportion seems a constant. But in some ways the relative position of Negroes is worsening, and there are discernible trends of a still worse future. Whites take home about twice as much in wages as Negroes do. The average American Negro income is $3,233, 54 percent of the white family's $5,835. But 10 years ago, it was 57 percent.

This has a great deal to do with FEPC. The percentage of Negroes in professional, clerical, sales, and skilled labor jobs has doubled in 20 years, and anyone who remembers the first Negro saleswomen in a famous department store and many other firsts know that state legislation has helped. But where does this enormous gain leave us? Government figures of 1955 have shown 12 percent of the Negro work force and 42 percent of the white in professional, technical, managerial, and white-collar, clerical, and sales positions. Forty-seven percent of the Negro work force is still in service and other unskilled and non-farm jobs.

Even though segregated and inferior education and lack of training opportunities have much to do with the lower earning capacities of Negro workers, the full responsibility does not rest there. A report of a conference sponsored by the President's Committee on Equal Employment Opportunity held [on] May 19, 1962, revealed that 22 percent of white college men were reported as becoming proprietors, managers, or officials, compared with 5 percent of Negro college men. Negroes with some college training were found in service and laborer jobs in numbers five times greater than whites with similar training. Of those who had not completed high school, 34 percent of the nonwhites were nonfarm workers, against 10 percent of the whites with similar training. The situation of women was similar. Ten percent of the Negro women who finish college end up as domestic workers, but [only] 1 percent of the whites [do]. Two-thirds of the Negro groups with some high school [education] are in domestic and other service jobs, but 17 percent of the white [are].

All this is bad enough. The changing nature of the economy is making it worse. The relatively high-wage heavy industries into which Negroes have been moving since World War I, where union organization has benefited them along with other workers, have failed to grow in the last five years. In some cases there are less employed today. In manufacturing industries, the shift of numbers from plant to office is displacing minority-group workers. It is estimated that 3 million jobs have been eliminated by automation since 1953, and various different estimates indicate about a 2-million-a-year displacement of lesser [skilled] and unskilled workers.

Because most Negro workers are still in unskilled and semiskilled trades, more of them will be displaced each year. A specific example out of many possibilities may bring this home: within four years, 30,000 elevator operators in New York City were displaced by self-service elevators. Within a very few years, this job category will have disappeared completely. Nearly all of these operators are Negroes and Puerto Ricans. But displacement is by no means confined to the cities. Mechanization of agriculture is adding to the changes that have driven millions of farm families off the land within a generation. The hardest hit in the last two years—and in the next two also—are southern Negro hired farm workers and tenants displaced by mechanization of the cotton harvest. This is unemployment concealed as underemployment, and unemployment normally not registered because workers are not covered by unemployment insurance. But the work time of a quarter of a million workers is no longer needed, and an equal number will be replaced in the near future.

Along with other rural pressures, this means a strong likelihood of an exodus from the land and into urban centers in search of work comparable only to that of the 1870's and the World War I period. Thus, as the great city minorities feel the pressures of increasing unemployment and poverty themselves, their numbers may well be swelled by other unskilled workers from the country.

For although the number of unskilled jobs is declining [and] the need of the nation for skilled workers is increasing, there is no single craft in which Negroes form even 2 percent of the total number of workers. And although figures on apprenticeship are hard to get, estimates place the number of Negro apprentices also as something under 2 percent. Unless action is taken at once, "no jobs today" will be perpetuated as "no jobs tomorrow." The Negro community rejects such a future for its children. It is easy, endless, and perhaps repetitious to belabor the meaning of poverty. It starts with birth. Four Negro women die in childbirth to each white [woman]; and in fact mortality is five times greater. It means childhood in slums—cultural deprivation is one way to say it; disproportional criminal statistics and the horror of dope addiction are a few of the byproducts. Inferior education, lack of incentive—or the closed door to those with better education and higher aspirations. The cycle must be broken. It must be broken now. And it must be broken at its start with the right to a decent livelihood.

All civil rights are built on this. It is not enough to outlaw discrimination in housing unless the Negro earns sufficient income to pay the rent or to buy the land. It is not enough to permit him to stay at a hotel or eat in a restaurant, to attend a movie or play on a golf course, unless he has the price of admission. Segregation and discrimination in education must go. But the child must have a break in environment so that he is ready for the school just as the school is ready for him.

The right to vote is inherent in democracy and depends on nothing but humanity. But citizens who participate as equals in the economic life of the country would vote more wisely than those whose just grievance against society begins with inability to support their families. The rising tide of discontent in both our northern cities and our southern cities is related to the number of adults without jobs and youth without futures. It is no accident that the greatest outburst in the civil rights struggle to date has taken place in an industrial city plagued with unemployment. It is no coincidence that in the large northern centers where civil rights legislation is on the books, demonstrations directed toward equal employment opportunity are growing daily in size and militancy. Yet, so long as we are trying to share more equally in jobs of which there are not enough to go around, we have not tackled a major problem.

We cannot have fair employment until we have full employment. Nor will we have full employment until we have fair employment. National planning for jobs for all Americans is an urgent need of the hour. Government must take leadership in investment policies, tax policies, public works policies. Management and labor have their part to play. I realize that a program for full employment is not the immediate focus of this subcommittee. But it would be dangerous and misleading to call for fair employment practices enforcement without at the same time calling attention to the declining number of employment opportunities in many fields. Our insistence upon jobs for Negroes and other minorities in accordance with ability is not a program to replace white workers, but rather for the opportunity to share equally with them in the building of the nation's future and in the fruits of that greater abundance which only the contribution of all can make possible.

SOURCE: House Subcommittee on Employment and Manpower of the Committee on Labor and Public Welfare, 88th Cong., 1st sess., S. 733, S. 1210, S. 1211, and S. 1937: *Bills Relating to Equal Employment Opportunities* (Washington, D.C.: GPO, 1963), 170–75.

Right-to-Work Laws Called Threat to Decent Wages (1966)

As a lifetime unionist, Randolph saw the right-to-work movement as a ruinous force that would drive down wages and erode existing job opportunities. As he argues in this article, the movement was especially dangerous for the working poor.

The Negro Labor Alliance won the fight a few years ago in Ohio to repeal the so-called "Right-to-Work" law and is waging a vigorous fight to break the Dirksen filibuster against the repeal of Section 14(b) of the Taft-Hartley Act. Why? The answer is that under Section 14(b) [the] "Right-to-Work" law cost the workers in Ohio 15,000 jobs as a result of runaway industries to "Right-to-Work" states.

The nineteen "Right-to-Work" states made possible by Section 14(b) of [the] Taft-Hartley Act, stand as a threat to wages and decent working conditions for the workers in the thirty-one "free" states, and the low wage levels are held out as lures to industries to move to the compulsory open-shop areas.

Not only do workers in states without the "Right-to-Work" laws lose jobs by industries moving to low-wage non-union states, but the black and white working poor in the "Right-to-Work" states of the South, noted for sweat-shop-starvation wages, are not free to organize bona-fide unions to fight for living wage.

SOURCE: *Chicago Defender*, February 26, 1966.

A Vision of Freedom (1969)

In 1969, leaders of the civil rights and labor movements and visiting dignitaries feted Randolph in celebration of his eightieth birthday. Randolph's remarks at this event include a review of his accomplishments and a message of encouragement to his colleagues who continued to carry on the struggle.

I need not tell you how happy I am that you all saw fit to come here, and how much I appreciate your attitude towards the work that I have tried to do. I want to salute our lovely friend, Mrs. Martin Luther King, a lady of grace and dignity and great dedication to the cause of the black worker, and to the cause of all other workers. I'm also happy to see Governor Rockefeller here, a man I have known for a long time. He and I worked together in developing the movement for a Fair Employment Practices Committee. I remember a luncheon we had at the Pierre Hotel at a time when no one thought the FEPC would ever be realized, and I recall that during the discussion Governor Rockefeller said, "No, No. It can be realized if we fight for it." And I am also very glad to see my good friend George Meany at this dinner. I know George Meany very well, and I have great admiration and respect for him. He's a man of his word who does not pretend to be for something when he isn't. But if he commits himself to a program, he will work at it and carry it through. We have worked together over a long period of time, and I think that we have made some progress in the field of Civil Rights. And of course, my good friend Bayard Rustin. He and I have been in this struggle together now for over twenty-five years, and he's still a young man. He has a genius for organization. I have asked him to work on various marches, and the March of 1963—the biggest ever given in this country—was under Bayard's direction. So I am very, very happy that you have all been kind enough to join me on this occasion.

Our gathering here tonight is an honoring, and for that I am deeply grateful and humbled. But in a more profound sense it is a rededication—to a cause to which I have contributed my energies, and to principles to which I have dedicated my life.

The cause has been the liberation of the Negro in America. I have seen fit in this endeavor to try to establish an alliance between the Negro and the American trade union movement. I have been guided by the belief that Negroes are a working people, and that because of their history on American soil—a history of suffering and tragedy, but also of struggle, endurance, dignity and, ultimately a history of human triumph—that because of this history they have been a dispossessed people who have often had to migrate thousands of miles in search of the means of subsistence. The labor movement has been the home of the working man, and traditionally it has been the only haven for the dispossessed. And, therefore, I have tried to build an alliance between the Negro and the American labor movement.

I have not been alone in my efforts. In 1925, almost half a century ago, I and my colleagues founded the Brotherhood of Sleeping Car Porters. In our struggle to build the union we faced destitution and continual harassment, but we did build it, and our struggle conferred upon us collectively a certain dignity. With this victory, my brothers and I in the union not only improved the conditions under which we lived and worked but we were enabled to reach beyond ourselves to our brothers and sisters on the plantations and in the ghettos. We were able to reach out and build a movement of the Negro masses struggling to realize, upon this American soil, the freedom and justice which they had so long been denied.

The Negro masses awakened in 1941. They challenged the President of the United States to integrate the defense industries and all other places of public employment. And they were victorious. The Negro masses were in motion. They were removing the mark of oppression from their brows and [the] burden of economic misery from their bodies. This struggle has continued down to the present day. Like a mountain stream that grows in size and momentum as it rushes downward, the struggle of the Negro masses for social and economic equality has become irrepressible. From Memphis, Tennessee, to Charleston, South Carolina, they cannot now be satisfied with anything less than total liberation.

Our ceremony of rededication tonight is to the cause of freedom, but it is also to principles governing the means by which freedom must be achieved. In my life I have tried to abide by the principles of democracy, nonviolence and integration, but there are some today, particularly among our black youth, who would question the validity of these principles in our on-going struggle. I urge them to reconsider their position and to engage with me [in] a reaffirmation of these fundamental principles. We must reject confrontationism and together reaffirm the necessity for democratic means of political protest. We must reject violence, and together, with the conviction that one day our nation can cease to be divided within itself, reaffirm our abiding faith in integration. We cannot reject these principles without also denying ourselves the possibility of freedom.

Salvation for the Negro masses must come from within. Freedom is never granted: it is won. Justice is never given: it is exacted. But in our struggle we must draw for strength upon something that far transcends the boundaries of race. We must draw upon the capacity of human beings to act with humanity towards one another. We must draw upon the human potential for kindness and decency. And we must have faith that this society, divided by race and by class, and subject to profound social pressures, can one day become a nation of equals, and banish white racism and black racism and anti-Semitism to the limbo of oblivion from which they shall never emerge.

SOURCE: *A. Philip Randolph at 80: Tributes and Recollections,* May 6, 1969 (New York: A. Philip Randolph Institute, 1969), 27–29.

A Labor Day Message (1978)

In what is likely his last public message, Randolph offers up no holiday platitudes. Militant as ever, he calls upon workers to think globally, to defend themselves from the onslaught of political and economic attacks, and to use the ballot box to affect change.

Labor Day, more than any other national holiday, has special significance for Black Americans. For on this day, we proclaim our steadfast solidarity with millions of other workers who share our deep commitment to racial equality, economic justice and democracy.

These values, we insist, are the sturdy and time-tested bonds which unite all workers—both Black and white—in a common struggle against common adversaries.

This unity, we believe, has acquired even greater importance today as we confront unprecedented attacks on the labor movement. Throughout the land, the forces opposed to labor—the same forces which opposed every advance in the civil rights movement—are on the offensive.

They share the same objectives so vigorously pursued by the business leaders of earlier times; they seek the destruction of the labor movement. This intensified assault on trade unions and collective bargaining, if successful, will have a devastating effect on Black people. As history has shown, it is only through trade unions that the great masses of Black workers can expect economic justice and the transcendence of poverty and indignity. In concert with their fellow workers Black people can take decisive control of their own destinies; with a union, they can approach their employers as proud and upright equals, not as trembling bowing slaves. Indeed, a solid union contract is, in a very real sense, another Emancipation Proclamation.

On the political front as well, Black people must strengthen and nourish their alliance with the labor movement. At a time when business and its New Right allies have emerged as powerful forces for privilege, inequality, and neglect of the poor and unemployed, the labor movement—almost alone among Americans institutions—has convincingly challenged the myths of the new aristocrats, those who would return us to the days of laissez-faire capitalism and all its brutality.

Because of its commitment to justice, the labor movement has become a champion of full employment. It has advanced programs which encompass all workers, not just union members. It has defended the minimum wage from those who call for poverty level wages. And it has become the leading force for a comprehensive national health insurance program, a program which would benefit all Americans, especially low and middle income workers.

While domestic concerns occupy much of our attention, we must constantly remember that the movement for freedom and democracy has an international dimension as well. Just as we oppose oppression and intolerance in America, we must also speak out in a loud voice on behalf of all threatened minorities, individuals and trade unionists throughout the world. Unfortunately, the violation of human rights seems to be escalating everywhere. In the Soviet Union, a newly formed trade union is being strangled before it can utter its first words. Soviet dissidents like [Anatoly] Shcharansky and [Yevgenia] Ginzburg are treated like common criminals and confined to the Gulag. And throughout Asia, Africa, and Latin America, free trade unions and political dissenters are being bludgeoned into abject submission by dictatorial regimes of both the right and left. For us, then, every assault on the workers and dissenters of other countries must be viewed as an assault on the freedom and security of American workers. Thus, our concern for universal human rights must be regarded as an integral component of our overall philosophy and strategy.

Freedom and democracy are not mere luxuries, they are absolute necessities for those who desire the true liberation of humanity. The values I have discussed here should not be regarded as treasures to be stored away and ignored. Rather, they must motivate our daily lives, and direct our every action: they demand our personal involvement and commitment.

As a first step toward living these values, Black Americans must boldly seize their birthright—the ballot. By registering and voting, Black people proudly proclaim their independence, their power, and their claim to full and equal citizenship. And by joining forces with their brothers and sisters in the labor movement, Black people become an indispensable element in the grand alliance for social progress in America.

SOURCE: *Amsterdam News*, September 2, 1978.

3

Randolph Speaks His Mind, 1919–1967

A. Philip Randolph made his mark as a union organizer and civil rights leader, but his accomplishments and insights as a public intellectual also made him a voice of conscience. From his early days of delivering speeches on soapboxes on Harlem street corners to the newspaper columns he wrote during his elderly years, Randolph constantly sought platforms from which to remind Americans about the ills that plagued them and offer radical solutions to the problems of the era.

The documents in this chapter reveal consistent themes in many of Randolph's public pronouncements. He was a stern critic of all forms of discrimination, and a champion of egalitarianism. He spoke out against social divisions that created disharmony. Putting an end to lynching was at the top of Randolph's agenda, but so was ending segregation in all aspects of life, from education to public accommodations. Randolph was also a critic of any institution that seemed to be allied with those who would oppress black Americans. Early in his *Messenger* days, he chastised churches and religious leaders who toed the capitalist line about workers' rights or who were silent on the subject of racial prejudice. This position is at the heart of "The Failure of the Negro Church," a polemic that earned Randolph the label of atheist. Though at his most radical he may have seemed to approach that position, Randolph did not stray far from his African Methodist Episcopal roots. In fact, as he grew older, his public words became increasingly laced with religious overtones. This is particularly evident in the 1962 address he delivered in Bermuda, wherein he demonstrates a comfortable familiarity with church history and teachings. In this noteworthy speech, Randolph also predicted that the flourishing of a militant spirit would someday lead to an African American serving on the Supreme Court and, given enough time, residing in the White House as president of the United States.

These documents also reveal Randolph's deep commitment to the American traditions of democratic action, radicalism, and freedom. He was a champion of free speech. Perhaps nothing demonstrates this more than the 1944 controversy with Boss Crump, wherein Randolph defied the notorious Memphis sheriff to deliver an address about the importance of civil rights and civil liberties in a democratic society.

Perhaps the most impressive document in this chapter is Randolph's speech at the third annual meeting of the Negro American Labor Council. In it, one can find most of the major themes of his public career. He speaks historically, drawing a line between the civil rights struggles of the nineteenth century and those of the twentieth; he appeals to progressive solutions; he criticizes violence; and he promotes unity, democracy, economic prosperity, and freedom. This is Randolph at his best, and it was one of the last times that the nation listened attentively to his words.

FOR FURTHER READING

Dray, Philip. *At The Hands of Persons Unknown: The Lynching of Black America.* New York: Random House, 2002.

Gilmore, Glenda Elizabeth. *Defying Dixie: The Radical Roots of the Civil Rights Movement.* New York: W. W. Norton & Company, 2009.

Honey, Michael. *Southern Labor and Black Civil Rights: Organizing Memphis Workers.* Urbana: University of Illinois Press, 1993.

Lichtenstein, Nelson. *Walther Reuther: The Most Dangerous Man in Detroit.* Urbana: University of Illinois Press, 1997.

Massey, Douglas, and Nancy A. Denton. *American Apartheid: Segregation and the Making of the Underclass.* Cambridge, Mass.: Harvard University Press, 1993.

Newman, Richard S. *Freedom's Prophet: Bishop Richard Allen, the AME Church, and the Black Founding Fathers.* New York: New York University Press, 2009.

Sugrue, Thomas J. *Sweet Land of Liberty: The Forgotten Struggle for Civil Rights in the North.* New York: Random House, 2006.

Walker, Randolph Meade. "The Role of the Black Clergy in Memphis during the Crump Era." *West Tennessee Historical Society Papers* 33 (January 1979): 29–47.

A. Philip Randolph, ca. 1911. (Library of Congress, Prints & Photographs Division, A. Philip Randolph Papers, LC-USZ62-97538)

Lynching: Capitalism Its Cause; Socialism Its Cure (1919)

Randolph applied a class analysis to the crisis of lynching in America. As he saw it, this form of racial violence was the result of a Jim Crow system that kept poor whites and blacks separate and in a subordinate position. Through socialism, Randolph believed, economic and political power would be fairly distributed, thus removing the fractures that were at the foundation of social animosity. A critique of the two-party system underlies Randolph's conclusions, and this position is one he held true to for the next five decades.

First, What is lynching? Lynching, historically speaking, is a loose term applied to various forms of executing popular justice, or what is thought to be justice. It is punishment of offenders or supposed offenders by a summary procedure without due process of law. In short, the essence of lynching is that it is extra-legal.

What Object Does It Achieve?

From the lynchers' point of view it avenges crime—and is calculated to prevent future crime. During the Reconstruction period the Ku Klux Klan applied the lynch law to intimidate the newly enfranchised Negro voter; to prevent him from voting the Republican carpetbaggers from the North into control of the Southern state governments. The competition was between the former slave-holding class and the carpetbaggers for the power to levy taxes, to issue paper money, to raise revenue, and to grant franchise to private individuals for the operation of public utilities. Today lynching is a practice which is used to foster and to engender race prejudice to prevent the lynchers and the lynched—the white and black workers—from organizing on the industrial and voting on the political fields to protect their labor-power. Why do I affirm this and how is it done? This brings me to the consideration of capitalism as the cause of lynching.

Now, just a word as to the reason for inquiring into the cause. All medical scientists are agreed that precedent to prescribing a remedy for a disease, a diagnosis should be made in order to ascertain its cause—because in order to remove the effects of a disease, physical or social, you must first remove the cause. To illustrate: Let us assume that a community is situated beside a swampy marsh where poisonous vapors hover over the putrid, pestiferous, standing waters, and where malarial germs and mosquitoes infest. Let us further assume that the people of this community suffer continually from malarial fever. Scientists have determined that mosquitoes are carriers of malarial germs. Now, is it not logical to assume that the swampy marsh is the cause of the malady and the mosquito but the occasion, and that in order to wipe out the effects, malarial fever, it is necessary to remove the cause of the occasion—the marsh? This, then, is no less true of lynching than of any other disease or social evil, such as child labor, white slavery, intemperance, poverty and criminal acts in general.

For clarity of exposition I shall divide the causes into two classes, and I shall treat them in the order of ultimate and immediate or occasional causes. But, before proceeding to build our structure of the real causes of lynching, we shall do the excavation work by clearing away the debris of alleged but fallacious causes. First, it is maintained by most superficial sociologists that "race prejudice" is the cause of lynching. But the fallacy of this contention is immediately apparent in view of the fact that out of 3,337 persons lynched between 1882 and 1903, there were 1,192 white persons. Leo Frank, Frank Little and Robert Prager, all white men, are instances of recent date. Second, it is held by some that "rape of white women" is the real cause. Again, this argument is untenable when it is known that out of the entire number of persons lynched during the above stated period, only 34 percent can be ascribed to rape as the cause. Third, still others contend that the "law's delay" is the controlling cause. This also is without force when the fact is known that men have had their day in court—[but they were] taken out and lynched, despite the fact that they (the accused) were convicted or acquitted; Leo Frank is an instance in proof. Thus much for what are some of the occasions but not the causes of lynching. We shall now consider the real and positive causes of this national evil.

As to the Meaning of Capitalism

Capitalism is a system under which a small class of private individuals make profits out of the labor of the masses by virtue of their ownership of the machinery and sources of production and exchange. For instance, the railroads of this country are owned by less than 600,000 stockholders who employ more than 3,000,000 persons. The ownership of the railroads by the 600,000 stockholders enables them to make billions of profits out of the labor of the 3,000,000 workers. Now there is the crux of the problem. A business is carried on for profits. Labor is the chief item in the expense of production. It is to the interest of the employer to work the laborer long hours and pay as low wages as possible. On the other hand, it is to the interest of the laborer to get as high wages and work as short hours as possible. Hence the conflict between the capitalists and the workers. The desire and power to make profits of the owner of the means of wealth production, which labor must use in order to make wages which to live, is at the basis of this conflict.

Let us see how it applies to our proposition in question. We will now review its economic aspects.

During the Civil War, one-third of the manpower of the South was killed off. The Civil War resulted in the abolition of property rights in Negroes. Free labor was abolished. For 250 years the slave-owning class had the right, sanctioned by government, to use a Negro as a horse, a machine. And the invention of the cotton gin had forced the market value of slaves up. Huge fortunes had been made and the slave-owners had lived in luxury, ease, comfort and splendor off the labor of Negroes. When the end of this came, the industry of the South was paralyzed. There was a shortage of white labor-power. The Negroes had been freed and they distrusted and suspected their former masters. In short, intoxicated with the new wine of freedom, they were disinclined to work.

But cotton must be picked; lumber must be cut; turpentine must be dipped; railroads must be built. In fact, profits must be made. Negroes must work or be made to work; besides, they must work cheaply. How can this be done? This is how it was and is done: Vagrancy laws are enacted which provide for the imprisonment of all Negroes who have no visible means of support. Of course, it is impossible for a Negro to show that he has any visible means of support. The result is that hordes of unemployed Negroes are hustled off to jail and the convict camps. Their fines are paid by employers of labor for lumber mills, cotton plantations, railroads, etcetera, [and] they are assigned into their custody, put to work at a wage of 30 and 40 cents a day. They are also compelled to trade at the company's store, which sells its wares at 100 percent higher than other stores. A debt for railroad fare to the works and for maintenance while at work 'til payday is made. Moreover, when the fines of imprisoned Negroes are paid, they are required to sign labor contracts, the non-performance of which is presumptive proof of fraudulent intent at the time of making it, which the state laws make a crime. And as a white planter himself tells the story: A planter can arrest a man upon the criminal charge of receiving money under false pretenses, which is equivalent to the charge of stealing; you get him convicted; he is fined, and being penniless, in lieu of the money to pay the fine he goes to jail; then you pay the fine and cost, the judge assigns him to you to work out the fine and you have him back on your plantation, backed up by the authority of the state. This is peonage. It is maintained for profits. This is capitalism. And this does not apply to Negroes only. It is the common fate of the servant class, black and white. But they must not [be allowed to] understand that their interests are common. Hence race prejudice is cultivated. Lynching, Jim-Crowism, and segregation are used to widen the chasm between the races.

This profit system of capitalism also applies to the farmer through the crop-lien system. This is a system whereby a lien mortgage is taken upon the crops of the poor white and black famers for a loan. It operates in this way: The poor farmer, being in need of provisions for his family until harvesting time, borrows money on his planted, and sometimes unplanted, crops from a big merchant or bank. The rate of interest is so high, sometimes as high as 1000 percent on the dollar, according to Comptroller of Currency John Skelton Williams, [that] the farmer is unable to pay the interest, to say nothing about the principal.

The farmer's inability to meet his note results in the loss of his farm. He then becomes a farm tenant and works up the Metayer system, or the plan of giving a part of the crop produced to the owner for the privilege of cultivating the land. This crop-lien system is profitable to the bankers of the South. Both white and black farmers are fleeced by this financial system. But white and black farmers won't combine against a common foe on account of race prejudice. Race antagonism, then, is profitable to those who own the farms, the mills, the railroads and the banks. This economic arrangement in the south is the fundamental cause of race prejudice, which is the fuse which causes the magazine of capitalism to explode into race conflicts—lynchings.

Prejudice is the chief weapon in the South [that] enables the capitalists to exploit both races. In the East, North and West, state militias, secret detective strike-breaking agencies, religion or nationality is used. The capitalists play Jewish against Irish Catholic workers. As we have our Waco, Memphis and East St. Louis lynching of Negroes, there are also Bayonne, West Virginia and Ludlow massacres of white workers and their families. The capitalists want profits, they don't care who makes them for them. In the South today over a million little white children are taken from school, put into factories and driven 10 and 12 hours a day until their little bodies are broken upon the wheels of industry; all because their labor is cheaper and more profits can be made out of them than out of grown-ups. They are competing with their fathers and brothers and they force the wage scale down by virtue of their increasing the labor supply.

This is how much the Southern white gentlemen capitalists care about white children [of] whom they prate so much. Capitalism knows no color line. It will coin the blood, sweat and suffering of white women and white children or black women and black children into dollars and dividends. So much for the economic aspects.

But this thing must be supported by law, and this brings us to the political cause of lynching. How does it operate? Vagrancy laws are enacted by politicians who are selected by political parties which are controlled by those who supply the campaign funds. These funds are contributed by the bankers, railroad directors, lumber mill and cotton plantation-owners whose large profits depend upon the low wages and long hours of work of the servant class. This has been the work of [James] Vardaman, [Ben] Tillman and the "lily white" Republicans. The laws making the nonperformance of a labor contract a crime are placed on the statute books by certain anti-labor and incidentally anti-Negro politicians. Sheriffs into whose custody Negroes charged with criminal acts are placed are nominated, elected or appointed by parties, which are responsible to powerful financial agencies which profit by fostering race prejudice and lynching, etcetera. This is why sheriffs don't protect their prisoners, not because they are afraid of the mob. So that when a mob demands a Negro in the custody of a sheriff nominated and elected by a political machine whose campaign funds are made up by banks and loan agencies, and by big employers of labor, which lend money to poor white and black farmers at usurious rates of interest and who hold labor in peonage, you can realize and appreciate how the sheriff will act. Self-interest will control his actions and he can always be expected to act in the interest of those who have the power to remove him.

The ruling class of the South has, through disfranchisement and the poll-tax, deprived the working class of the power to protect their interests. The electorate there is small. It is easier for the capitalists to control or to corrupt a small electorate than a large one. Politically, race feeling is also capitalized [on] by young ambitious politicians who make their campaigns on the slogan of "Negro domination." This is how politics fortifies and re-enforces lynch law in the South.

What are the social causes? There are three: the schools, church and press. An uneducated working class won't revolt, won't organize; hence, the meager sums of $2.22 and $4.92 are appropriated for the education of [a] black and white child, respectively, per year. The white church is paid to preach the Christianity of lynch law profits. The press is owned and controlled by the employing class, and it is used to influence the minds of the race; to foment race hatred; it gives wide circulation to that insidious doctrine of the Negroes being the hewers of wood and drawers of water for white men. It features in bold headlines such titles as "lynch the black brute," "young white girl raped by black burly fiend," etcetera. This produces a psychology which expresses itself through the mob. Anything may occasion a community to burn a Negro. It might be a well-dressed Negro; a Negro who speaks good English or a Negro who talks back to a white man.

To sum up, capitalism is at the basis of the economic, political and social arrangements of the South and it is defended, supported, promoted and upheld by the Republican and Democratic parties of the North, South, East and West. Neither the Republican nor the Democratic party has ever condemned peonage or lynching. They can not [because] they are owned by the capitalists.

What then is the cure? I hold . . . that Socialism is the only cure. Why? First, what is it? Briefly, it is the social ownership and democratic management of the means and sources of production and exchange for social use and not for private profit.

How Does This Effect Lynching?

Socialism would deprive individuals of the power to make fortunes out of the labor of other individuals by virtue of their ownership of the machinery which the worker must use in order to live. When an individual or class may make profits out of the labor of black and white workers, it is to his or to the interest of the class to use any means to keep them (the workers) from combining in order to raise wages, to lower their hours of work or to demand better working conditions. This is the only reason why prejudice is fostered in the South. Of course, it may not be possible to trace every lynching or act of prejudice to a direct economic cause, but the case may be explained by the law of habit. When social practices are once set, they act or recur with a dangerous accuracy. It is now a social habit to lynch Negroes. But when the motive for promoting race prejudice is removed, viz., profits, by the social ownership, control and operation of the machinery and sources of production through the government, the government being controlled by the workers; the effects of prejudice, race riots, lynching, etcetera, will also be removed.

For instance, if railroads were owned and democratically managed by the government, collective and social service function would not be prostituted to Jim Crow cars in order to pander and cater to race prejudice. No individuals would be making profits out of them and consequently there would be no interest in promoting race antagonisms. Lynchings, the product of capitalism, would pass as the burning of heretics and the Spanish Inquisition, the product of religious intolerance, passed. Besides, Socialism would arm every man and women with the ballot. Education would be compulsory and universal. The vagrancy law, child labor and peonage would no longer exist. Tenant-farming and the crop-lien system would be discarded. And every worker would receive the full product of his toil. This is the goal of Socialism. This is why every Negro should be a Socialist.

In conclusion, workingmen and -women of my race, don't allow Republican and Democratic leaders to deceive you. They are paid by Rockefeller, Morgan, Armour, Carnegie, owners of Southern railroads, coal mines, lumber mills, turpentine stills, cotton plantations, etcetera, who make millions out of your labor. Don't be deceived by the small increase in wages which you are receiving; the capitalists are taking it back by increasing the cost of food, fuel, clothing and rent. Don't be deceived by any capitalist bill to abolish lynching; if it became a law, it would never be enforced. Have you not the Fourteenth Amendment, which is supposed to protect your life, property, liberty and guarantee you the vote? Does it do it? No. Why? Because it is nullified through administration by capitalists, Republican and Democratic representatives, who profit from lynching and who want lynching to continue. Lynching will not stop until Socialism comes. You can strike a death blow to lynching by voting for Socialism. Black and white workers unite. You have nothing to lose but your chains; you have the world to gain.

SOURCE: *The Messenger* 2 (March 1919): 9–12.

A New Crowd—A New Negro (1919)

The Russian Revolution and other challenges to the hierarchies taking place throughout Europe inspired Randolph. Believing that these events signaled that the "Old Crowd"— those of the old ruling class—were being swept away, he believed that America was ripe for similar changes. In this essay from *The Messenger,* Randolph maintains that African Americans need to support a "New Crowd" of fresh leaders and cast aside the Republican cronies whose ineffectiveness at challenging racism was becoming glaringly obvious in the face of such injustices as lynchings and persistent inequality.

Throughout the world among all peoples and classes, the clock of social progress is striking the high noon of the Old Crowd. And why? The reason lies in the inability of the Old Crowd to adapt itself to the changed conditions, to recognize and accept the consequences of the sudden, rapid and violent social changes that are shaking the world. In wild desperation, consternation and despair, the proud scions of regal pomp and authority, the prophets and high-priests of the old order, view the steady and menacing rise of the great working class. Yes, the Old Crowd is passing, and with it, its false, corrupt and wicked institutions of oppression and cruelty; its ancient prejudices and beliefs and its pious, hypocritical and venerated idols.

It's all like a dream! In Russia, one-hundred and eighty million of peasants and workmen—disinherited, writhing under the ruthless heel of the Czar for over three hundred years, awoke and revolted and drove their hateful oppressors from power. Here a New Crowd arose—the Bolsheviks, and expropriated their expropriators. They fashioned and established a new social machinery, the Soviet, to express the growing class consciousness of teaming millions, disillusioned and disenchanted. They also chose new leaders—Lenin and Trotsky—to invent and adopt scientific methods of social control; to marshal, organize and direct the revolutionary forces in constructive channels to build a New Russia. . . .

And the natural question arises: what does it all mean to the Negro? First it means that he, too, must scrap the Old Crowd. For not only is the Old Crowd useless, but like the vermiform appendix, it is decidedly injurious, it prevents all real progress. Before it is possible for the Negro to prosecute successfully a formidable offense for [fighting] injustice and [establishing] fair play, he must tear down his false leaders, just as the people of Europe are tearing down their false leaders. Of course, some of the Old Crowd mean well. But what matter is it that poison be administered to the sick intentionally or out of ignorance? The result is the same—death. And our indictment of the Old Crowd is that: it lacks the knowledge of methods for the attainment of ends which it desires to achieve. For instance, the Old Crowd never counsels the Negro to organize and strike against low wages and long hours. It cannot see the advisability of the Negro, who is the most exploited of the American workers, supporting a workingman's political party.

The Old Crowd enjoins the Negro to be conservative, when he has nothing to conserve. Neither his life nor his property receives the protection of the government which conscripts his life to "make the world safe for democracy." The conservative in all lands are the wealthy and the ruling class. The Negro is in dire poverty, and he is no part of the ruling class.

But the question naturally arises: who is the Old Crowd? In the Negro schools and colleges the most typical reactionaries are Kelly Miller, [Robert Russa] Moton and William Pickens. In the press [W. E. B.] Du Bois, James Weldon Johnson, Fred R. Moore, T. Thomas Fortune, Roscoe Conkling Simmons and George Harris are compromising the case of the Negro. In politics Charles W. Anderson, W. H. Lewis, Ralph Tyler, Emmet Scott, George E. Haynes, and the entire old line palliating, me-to-boss gang of Negro Republican politicians, are hopelessly ignorant and distressingly unwilling of their way.

In the church the old crowd still preaches that "the meek will inherit the earth," "if the enemy strikes you on one side of the face, turn the other," and "you may take all this world but give me Jesus." "Dry Bones," "The Three Hebrew Children in the Fiery Furnace" and "Jonah in the Belly of the Whale," constitute the subjects of the Old Crowd, for black men and women who are overworked and under-paid, lynched, Jim Crowed and disfranchised—a people who are yet languishing in the dungeons of ignorance and superstition. Such then is the Old Crowd. And this is not strange to the student of history, economics, and sociology.

A man will not oppose his benefactor. The Old Crowd of Negro leaders had been and is subsidized by the Old Crowd of White Americans—a group which viciously opposes every demand made by organized labor for an opportunity to live a better life. Now, if the Old Crowd of white people opposes every demand of white labor for economic justice, how can the Negro expect to get that which is denied the white working class? And it is well nigh that economic justice is at the basis of social and political equality. For instance, there is no organization of national prominence which ostensibly is working in the interest of the Negro which is not dominated by the Old Crowd of white people. And they are controlled by the white people because they receive their funds—their revenue—from it. It is, of course, a matter of common knowledge that Du Bois does not determine the policy of the National Association for the Advancement of Colored People; nor does [Eugene] Kinkle Jones or George E. Haynes control the National Urban League. The organizations are not responsible to the Negroes because Negroes do not maintain them.

This brings us to the question as to who shall assume the reins of leadership when the Old Crowd falls. As among all other peoples, the New Crowd must be composed of young men who are educated, radical and fearless. Young Negro Radicals must control the press, church, schools, politics and labor. The conditions for joining the New Crowd are: ability, radicalism and sincerity. The New Crowd views with much expectancy the revolutions ushering in a New World. The New Crowd is uncompromising. Its tactics are not defensive, but offensive. It would not send notes after a Negro is lynched. It would not appeal to white leaders. It would appeal to the plain working people everywhere. The New Crowd sees that the war came and the Negro fought, bled and died; that the war has ended, and he is not yet free.

The New Crowd would have no armistice with lynch-law; no truce with jim-crowism, and disfranchisement; no peace until the Negro receives complete social, economic and political justice. To this end the New Crowd would form an alliance with white radicals such as [the] I.W.W. [Industrial Workers of the World, or "Wobblies"], the Socialists and the Non-Partisan League, to build a new society—a society of equals, without class, race, caste or religious distinctions.

SOURCE: *The Messenger* 2 (May–June 1919): 26–27.

The Failure of the Negro Church (1919)

Randolph's criticisms of the church early in his political career resulted in his being labeled an atheist for most of his life, but a close reading of this article suggests that what he really wanted was a transformation of the Christian churches in the African American community. Rather than eliminating religion, Randolph hoped that churches would assume a larger role in African American communities. In his view, the church could help workers by supporting unionization and sponsoring consumers' co-ops, taking a stand on civil rights issues, and empowering individuals so that they would have the wherewithal to work against the economic and political status quo.

Yes, the Negro church has failed. It has failed in a great crisis. Its failure is patent and apparent. The only question before us then is: why and how? The chief cause of the failure of the Negro church is economic. That is to say, the church has been converted into a business, and the ruling characteristic of a business is that it is run primarily for profits. The interest is focused upon debits and credits, deficits and surpluses. This has been the Scylla and Charybdis of the Negro church.

To the money power in the community and the country, the church has bowed. The trustee boards of the smallest and most humble are composed of the most prosperous of the church members, who are adjudged as competent to create a surplus by organizing rallies, and by devising other means that are effective in inducing the public to release the necessary moneys. Preachers break with denominations, and set up independent churches, on account of being removed from "fat charges." Collections occupy three-fourths of the time of most services. Sermons are usually selected with a view to impressing the members with the importance of the injunction that "it is more blessed to give than to receive."

Then there is that class of Negro churches that is directly dominated by white capitalists. These are the Episcopal, Congregational, Presbyterian and Methodist Episcopal. Their policies are molded [by] and handed down from the white ecclesiastical oligarchy. This ecclesiastical oligarchy, in turn, is controlled by the "money power" of the country. It is a matter of common knowledge that Trinity Church, situated at the head of Wall Street, is one of the biggest corporations in America. It controls a large number of apartment houses from which it reaps blood money in the form of extortionate rents from the working people. Now, since the "money power" of the country which consists of the masters of the railroads, mines, factories, land, etcetera, receive their power from rent, interest and profits, and since the great masses of the people depend upon wages for a living, which are low when profits, rent and interest are high, and high when profits, rent and interest are low, it is plain that the interests of the people and the interests of the "money power" which dominates the church are opposed.

Since it is beyond question that a servant will obey its master, that the power over a man's subsistence is the power over his will, one is not surprised at the church's obedience to the power that maintains it. The church split over the issue of slavery into the North and South. The Northern church, at the behest of the industrial power, condemned it; the Southern church, upon the order of the slave owners, blessed it. Thus, the church, now as then, is using its power to defend poverty, crime, prostitution, war, ignorance and superstition which are outgrowths of the system that allows one man to live off another's labor.

So much then for the cause of the failure. Now, how has it failed? Briefly, it has failed to educate the people. Ministers are leading Negroes who are below in intelligence the lowest member of their church. The Negro ministry is ignorant of the modern problems of capital and labor. It is disinterested in unionism as a means of securing higher wages, shorter hours and better working conditions for Negro workers. It regards the discussion of politics in the church as sacrilegious unless some good, old, Abraham Lincoln Republican desires the vote of the Negro and is willing to pay for educational propaganda. It has failed to use its power to rouse the Negro against disfranchisement and lynching. No conference of Negro churches has ever gone on record as endorsing the principle of unionism.

But you ask, what constructive program do we offer? First, the Negro ministry must be educated. It must get the education of information instead of the education of inspiration. It needs less Bible and more economics, history, sociology and physical science. Second, the Negro church must be put to different uses. It must become an open educational forum where problems of hygiene, labor, government, racial relationships, national and international questions are discussed by specialists. [Churches] might also be used as places for the beginning of co-operative stores that will enable the Negro workingman to reduce the high cost of living.

In conclusion, the world has moved a long way forward since 1914. Times have changed, and institutions, if they would survive, must adjust themselves to the changed conditions. The New Negro demands a new ministry—an educated fearless and radical ministry. The New Negro demands a new church—a church that is the center of his social, economic and political hopes and strivings. The church must become something more than a temple of prayer to a people who are lynched, disfranchised and Jim-Crowed. Prayer has been tried for over fifty years. In short, the church must set its face against a philosophy of profits to a philosophy of service.

SOURCE: *The Messenger* 2 (October 1919): 6.

Segregation in the Public Schools (1924)

Randolph looks to historical context in this attack on segregation, and he sees linkages between slavery and contemporary Jim Crow practices. He assails the logic of racial segregation, arguing that keeping white and black separate is about power relations, not social equality. As Randolph saw it, segregation was designed to give whites political and economic advantages over blacks and to keep the working class divided. Indeed, if he had looked back on this essay three decades later, Randolph would not have been surprised by the school integration crises in Little Rock and other cities.

If segregation is a menace, it ought to be condemned and rejected; if it is a promise, it ought to be accepted and advocated. Before accepting or rejecting it, however, it is well to inquire into its nature, cause and effects, in order to determine just what it is, and how it functions; obviously one is unwise to accept or reject that which he does not understand.

What Is Segregation?

The word "segregation" comes from the Latin word *segrego*—a compound of *se,* aside, and *grex* or *greg,* flock—to flock aside. The Latin root derivation or the dictionary definition, however, is not adequate to explain the present meaning and significance of the term. Words, like everything else, undergo an evolution—through this process they take on new meanings. A conspicuous instance in point is: manufacture. Etymologically it means to make by hand, derived from the Latin words *manus,* hand, plus *facio,* make. It is the outgrowth of the pre-capitalist period of production when all commodities were made by hand tools in the home of the artisan. But the industrial revolution which gave the world labor-saving machinery, changed the method of production, and consequently the denotation and connotation of certain words, such as the word "manufacture," which today, means to make by machine. Languages, like religions, ethics, education, law, literature and art, assume transformations in meaning in consequence of basic changes in the socio-economic modes of getting a living.

Historical Background of Segregation

From the beginning of the dawn of the systematic trade in Negro life and labor in 1517 [it] made possible, as well as profitable, by the cultivation of sugar, tobacco, cotton, rice, etcetera, in the Spanish, Portuguese, English and French possessions in North, Central and South America and the West Indies, the Negro was viewed as personal property, such as an ox, a plow or clock, subject to the whims of the owner. He was naturally set aside, at the convenience of his master, just as a hog or leper. The social attitude toward people of color in these United States, entrenched and fortified by profit and privilege, persisted with legal sanction and religious justification, for approximately half a thousand years.

Now upon the abolition of our slave economy in America in 1863, the legal sanction of coercive segregation of Negroes as chattel property passed; but the economic need for cheap labor increased as a result of the demands of industrial and agricultural reconstruction. But cheap labor can be exacted only from docile, subservient human beings, beings who will not protest, organize labor unions and strike for a living wage, decent hours and conditions of work. Exploiting the labor of the newly emancipated slave, drunk with the red wine of freedom, was a big and difficult task, especially [for] the old slave masters, who, having recently fought to maintain slavery, were viewed as the devil incarnate. Their mental attitude toward the white ruling class was hostility personified. Such a spirit was economically unprofitable to the owners of lumber mills, turpentine stills, railroads, cotton plantations and the banking and commercial interests generally. For if Negroes didn't work, there was no production of goods; if there was no production, there was no sale; no sale, no profits. But the issue was not merely to get Negroes to work, but to get them to work cheaply. Hence the will to loaf or to demand a wage of a civilized human being must be broken upon the wheel of persecution, such as lynching, mob law, vagrancy laws, segregation and grandfather clauses. Now it was perfectly all right to maim or kill a Negro, since he was not owned by anyone, and hence would constitute no economic loss to anyone save himself. Thus [with] the end of the perpetuating [of] the moral and mental slavery of the Negro recently relieved from his physical chains of bondage, a hellish and vicious engine of persecution and terrorism was devised and set in motion, beside which the hateful Inquisition of the Middle Ages [looks like] a benevolent institution. In the unspeakable whirlwind of hate rising during the period of Reconstruction, thousands of Negroes succumbed though that was incidental to the process of reducing the Negro to the status of a mental slave. For the objective of the white South was not to kill off all Negroes, because that would mean the destruction of the chief source of the labor supply, which would be virtual economic suicide, but to kill his manhood, his spirit to resist economic subjugation.

One of the most effective weapons in the hands of the white owning class of the South was segregation; the business of making the "niggers" know "their place." This policy of setting the negroes aside as a thing apart, an evil thing, an "untouchable," caused even the "white trash" to throw out its chest and look contemptuously upon the Negro as an inferior being, unfit to be admitted to the community of civilized society. The white working class assumed this arrogant attitude, despite their wretched and miserable poverty and ignorance, made possible by the same system of robbery practiced upon Negroes.

Hence the barrier of race prevented the unity of class. The god of segregation issued the commandment to both races: Thou shalt not commit the sin of contact, that is, in public where the equality of the races may be recognized. So insistent has been this decree of segregation that it has very largely secured the acquiescence of the victim—the Negro himself—who in many instances is wont to defend it as necessary and beneficent, an attitude which relieves the Lothrop Stoddards and the Ku Klux Klan of the necessity of continuing to use their time and energy in pressing segregation. In other words, the Negroes who defend segregation *ipso facto* become unconscious accessories to their own enslavement.

But this is the crux of the question. How do we know that segregation is a menace to the Negro?

The Reason for Segregation

From our survey of the social history of segregation, it is clear that it has now assumed an invidious connotation. Anyways, superiors segregate their inferiors, not inferiors their superiors. In the South, we never hear of Negroes segregating white people. It is explanatory of the social law that wherever two groups are in proximity, the stronger will subjugate or segregate the weaker group. The segregating, too, is usually done for the benefit of the segregator, not the segregated. Of course, the segregating group invariably suggests segregation presumable in the interest of the segregated, and then seeks, through subtle propaganda, to get the segregated to accept their lot as inevitable and just.

The Functioning of Segregation

Let us note how segregation functions. In our social life, the criminal is segregated, not the law-abiding citizens; the insane, not the sane; the diseased, not the healthy. In very truth the entire history of segregation carries with it the idea of people of social position, culture, wealth, power and refinement setting aside their alleged inferiors as outcasts, pariahs. I have only to mention the following instances in proof: The English segregate the Irish, not the Irish the English; the Japanese the Koreans, not the Koreans the Japanese; the white American the Indian, not the Indian the white American; the rich the poor, not the poor the rich.

Sociology and Psychology of Segregation

The social method of segregation which results in the deliberate perpetration of palpable injustices upon the weak by the strong, upon the ignorant by the educated, upon the laborer by the capitalist, grows out of the conception that mingling of groups savors of equality. It is as unnatural for equals to segregate each other as it is natural for them to mingle together. Equals demand equal privileges and rights; unequals demand unequal privileges and rights. If John feels that he is equal to Jim, he will accept no less than Jim. But if Jim feels that he is inferior to John, he will demand and accept less than John. The former develops the superiority complex, the later the inferiority complex.

Now, in every community, the dominant propertied group seeks to keep up the fiction of inherent, inescapable, eternal fundamental difference between, and the inferiority of the non-propertied element and themselves, by enforcing segregation. The psychology of this method is that anything affirmed and repeated sufficiently long will come to be believed. The segregator and segregated will grow to believe and defend the principle of segregation. Generally the policy of segregation emanates from the economic masters of a community, realizing that the slaves or exploited group will revolt immediately they come to feel and think themselves the equal of the self-appointed master class, and that this belief will develop through contact, for contact tends to strip one of his self-acclaimed, godlike, superior attributes, to expose his weaknesses, his commonplaceness and similarities to the so-called common people, unless he be, indeed, intrinsically superior. Such is the reason for the hierarchical organization of monarchies and empires. The plain people are permitted only periodically, on some august or state occasion, to view the person of the King. It is ever shrouded in the halo of mystery, thereby investing the ruler with the power, authority and aspect of the supernatural. In democracies and republics, too, those who own for a living struggle to be worshipped and obeyed as little uncrowned kings by those who work for a living. In order to be so regarded, they avoid contact with the despised common herd. True is the old adage: familiarity breeds contempt. It is a fact of common knowledge to all students of the history of the slave regime that the slave owners prevented, upon pain and severe punishment, the association of free Negroes with Negro slaves. Labor history is replete with the brutal methods, legal and illegal, employed by the capitalists in order to prevent contact between union and non-union labor. Contact invites examination. Examination dissipates unreal differences. Common people clamor for the rights and comforts of kings when they know and realize that they are all human beings of common mud. Sweated non-union men will fight for a union wage when they are educated through contact with their union brothers. Negroes will not continue to accept the deserts of half-men when they awake, through contact, to the fact that they are no less than white men in body and mind.

Who Benefits from Segregation

It is obvious from the foregoing that segregation never originates in the interest of the segregated, but in the interest of the segregator. For instance, it is not to the interest of criminals to be segregated. Assuming, for the sake of argument, that there are persons in society better than they, criminals undoubtedly could improve themselves through contact with the so-called "best people." Imitation in society, according to [Gabriel] Tarde, is one of the greatest forces for modern progress. Certainly the association of criminals with their betters could not make them worse. The old saying "show me the company you keep and I will tell you who you are," carries with it the idea that if one associates with criminals, he is a criminal; if he associates with respectable people, he is respectable. It goes further, and implies that if one is respectable and associates with bad people, he will become bad. But the reverse should also be true, viz.: that if the "no-good" associate with the good, they will become good. This principle of sociology is borne out by the entire body of literature on the subject of child psychology. Witness the institution for incorrigibles, the classes for mental defectives. No one without a sense of humor will contend that association between children of strong and weak minds will result in making the minds of the weak-minded children weaker, or that the insanity of the insane is accentuated by contact with the sane, or that the physically weak will be made weaker by contact with the physically strong, or that common people will be made more common by association with the kings and aristocrats, or that the ignorant will become more ignorant by contact with the educated. Now, granting that the theory of separating the bad from the good, the criminal from the law-abiding citizens, is sound, for the Negro or any other group to accept segregation is to acknowledge themselves inferiors and incompetents, and, therefore, entitled to inferior treatment. To illustrate: no one will maintain that a criminal ought to receive the same treatment as a law-abiding citizen, or that a diseased person should be allowed the same freedom as a healthy one. On the contrary, the current notion is that justice should punish the criminal in the interest of the law-abiding citizen. While this is a fallacy, it is, nevertheless, the custom.

Social Value

Upon close analysis, it will be found that the philosophy of social value arises out of certain conceptions of superiority and inferiority—with respect to persons and things. This element of relative worth is reflected in every aspect of our social life, especially the economic. Note the case of a Negro caught in a wreck. He will be awarded less damages than a white man similarly injured, of similar nature. Why? Because the social estimate of a Negro is that he is less valuable than a white man, even if certain Negroes, in material possessions and culture, are obviously greater than certain white men. As a worker, a Negro will be paid less wages than a white worker, because it is assumed that his standard of living is lower; that is, that he has less wants for higher good, not that he consumes less. This is based upon the fact that the Negro worker is recognized as being able to produce less of value. It is idle and futile to expect an inferior person to produce as much of value as a superior one. But you say that a Negro worker can produce as much of value as a white worker. Of course that's true, but the question is not what is true but what is generally believed and felt to be true. Human beings act more strongly upon belief and feeling than they do upon thought and reason. To accept the status of an inferior and then cry for being denied the recognition of a person of superior worth is as childish as it is useless. Thus, the social evaluation of a people has definite economic significance. A powerful reason for opposing any measure that affixes the stigma of inferiority to the Negro.

Evaluation of Other Species

Proceeding with our train of reasoning. Let us apply this principle of evaluation to other species. A robin will not bring the price or get the treatment of a canary, because it is thought to be worth less. Nor will a common cur dog receive the attention of or fetch the price of a Newfoundland or English Bulldog, because of the conception of relative values. There is no market for a backyard cat, while a Maltese is highly prized. An ordinary cow will not secure the consideration of a Holstein or Jersey cow. These conceptions of worth grow out of the belief that one yields a larger measure of service, the other, of pleasure. The inference is that, in proportion as one is believed to be valuable, superior, competent, or valueless, inferior, incompetent, he will be treated and recognized as such. Hence the importance of social esteem. It does not matter that one is [actually] more or less valuable than he is believed to be, he will be appraised and treated according to the prevailing social belief of his merit or demerit. Now, if the social treatment of a person or group is based upon the social estimate of his or its value, how he or the group ranks in the social scale, it logically follows that it is always to the interest of the person or group to fix, in the mind of society, the belief that he or the group is as socially valuable, and is socially [the] equal of any other person or group in the community. Because as community thinks and feels, so it acts. Men and women only mob their supposed inferiors. White, Protestant, Nordic Americans mob and lynch Jews, Negroes, Catholics, foreigners and unionized workmen.

But, you say, while it is true that the social treatment of individuals and groups reflects the social estimate of them, which in turn reacts on their ability to earn a living, still opposition to segregation is tantamount to a demand for social equality. True. We plead guilty. But what of it? If a demand for social equality is equivalent to a demand for the right to live, then there is no sensible and logical alternative to a demand for social equality. This brings us to the question: What is social equality? Suppose we listen to the definition of [its] most rabid Negro opponents. What say John Sharp Williams, Pat Harrison, Thomas Dixon and their ilk? With tongue and pen they cry out to the high heavens against the Negro aspiring to become educated, to vote, to do the most skilled work, work which they dub a "white man's job"! It is clear, then, that to the Negrophobists, political opportunity is social equality; that educational opportunity is social equality; that economic opportunity is social equality. Hence to deny that you want social equality is to admit that you don't want political, educational and economic opportunity. In other words, you admit you feel that you should apologize for living, for without the above-named opportunities, life is impossible. The logic of Cole Blease and the Ku Klux Klan is sound. You cannot educate a person or race in the same things in which you are educated and continue to convince him or it that he or it is inferior to you.

Social Contact

But it is further argued by our friendly enemies that educational, political and economic opportunity can only be achieved through contact, and contact is the essence of social equality. Here again our industrious detractors are on sound ground. But is contact, per se, objected to? No, not at all. Social contact is objected to—that is, contact with Negroes as ladies and gentlemen. There is contact a-plenty after dark. Witness the six million mulattoes in this country. They were not brought into being through the mystic magic of some Aladdin. Besides, the results of this twilight contact have progressively increased. Note that in 1850, there were 405,751 mulattoes in these United States. In 1910, there were 2,050,686, an increase of 9.8 percent. So much for biological contact.

Now as to the Social Manifestations of Social Equality

It is a matter of common experience that contact between Negro bellmen, waiters, Pullman porters, ushers in theatres, chauffeurs, cooks and nurses and their white employers as servants, obtains generally and daily. Contact in the capacity of a servant is not objected to. But there is objection to a Negro appearing in the same Pullman coach, theatre or hotel as a guest, as a gentleman or lady, being served as others are served. Still, there is obviously less contact with the white patrons when the Negro is in a dining room, a Pullman car or a theatre as a guest than when he is there as a servant. Because as a guest he occupies his own particular seat or berth as the other white guests do; whereas as a servant, he moves freely among all of the white patrons constantly. Again, the Negro may live under the same roof with the rankest Bourbon Southern Negro hater as a servant, but no Negro must buy a house beside him and live [there] as a neighbor, as an owner.

Nor is it a question of economic status here. The Negro who purchases a house in a white neighborhood would be objected to were he a millionaire doctor or a plain ash-cart driver. A white common workman who was able to buy in an exclusive neighborhood would not be objected to, however. Why? Because there is always a desire to see an evidence of inferiority on the part of the Negro, and the capacity of a menial servant is reckoned as such evidence. But again, why? The answer is simple. If the great laboring masses of people, black and white, are kept forever snarling over the question as to who is superior or inferior, they will never combine or they will take a long time to combine for the achievement of a common benefit: more wages, a shorter work-day and better working conditions. Combination between black and white working people in the South would mean the loss of millions in profits to railroads, cotton magnates, lumber barons and bankers. White railroad workers fear the Negro as a strikebreaker, but still refuse to take him into their unions because of the social pressure that decrees that Negroes are inferior to white men, and hence should be religiously denied contact. This is an instance of a direct blow at the very life of the race as a result of the mandate of segregation.

SOURCE: *The Messenger* 6 (June 1924): 185–88.

Randolph Defies Boss Crump (1944)

In November 1943, a group of African American residents of Memphis, Tennessee, invited Randolph to give a talk at a local Baptist church. City officials led by Edward Hull "Boss" Crump forced them to cancel the event. When the president of the American Federation of Labor, William Green, learned of the incident, he used the aegis of the AFL to reinvite Randolph in March 1944. In his speech, which was reprinted in *The Black Worker,* Randolph argues for the centrality of free speech to a democratic society. The context of World War II was important, and Randolph identified First Amendment freedoms as a defining difference between the United States and its totalitarian enemies.

Mr. Chairman and Fellow Citizens of Memphis, Tennessee:

I have returned to Memphis because I consider it my Constitutional right, my democratic privilege and my moral duty. I am not here because of any belief that Memphis must hear me speak in order to be saved. I do not consider that I possess any unusual, extraordinary or cosmic wisdom that anybody else lacks. I am just a humble official of a trade union, The Brotherhood of Sleeping Car Porters, affiliated with the American Federation of Labor, which is doing its best to improve the standards of wages and working conditions of its members, and to help advance the general cause of the Negro people, and all of the workers, regardless of race, color, religion or national origin.

Now, let me at this point express on behalf of myself, personally, and of the officials and members of my organization, the Brotherhood, and I think that I can also say on behalf of the Negro workers generally, our very great appreciation for the fine, forthright, timely and courageous position Brother William Green, President of the American Federation of Labor has taken on this controversial question of free speech and free assembly in Memphis.

I hail President Green because under tremendous pressure he remained firm, insisting upon the holding of this meeting without reservations or equivocation. He concurred with my opinion that the A. F. of L. was morally obligated to take a definite stand on the right of free speech for free men of labor in this city, and promptly appointed Brother George Googe, able, fearless and aggressive Southern organizer for the Federation, to plan a public mass meeting under the auspice of the American Federation of Labor and the Brotherhood of Sleeping Car Porters and other sister unions of the city of the Federation, and invited me to address it. . . .

Hence, it is quite proper that such a meeting as this should be sponsored by labor, organized labor, under the banner of the American Federation of Labor, for it is labor which has waged the battles of the front-line trenches in every important historical period to uphold the Bill of Rights, guaranteeing these fundamental constitutional principles, namely, freedom of speech, freedom of the press, freedom of assembly, trial by jury, right of petition, right of habeas corpus and freedom of worship. Labor has led the fight for free public schools and also took its stand against the sinister institution of chattel slavery.

It is because the American Federation of Labor is unalterably committed to free speech, free assembly and free press, the cornerstones of our democratic system and traditions, that the Federation rejects the totalitarian doctrines of Germany's Nazism, Russia's Communism, Italy's Fascism and Japan's Militarism. All of these systems of state power have banned and destroyed the freedom of the press, speech and assembly. Thus, the avowed purpose of this war by the United Nations is to uphold, preserve and maintain the democratic principles, ideals, heritages, values, and faiths expressed and symbolized in the right of free speech and free assembly. Labor is conscious of the fact that its cause involving wage levels that insure decency, comfort, health, and a cultural development, the right of self organization, collective bargaining and the selection and designation of representatives of its own choosing, could never have been attained if labor had been denied the right of free speech and free assembly. It is a matter of common knowledge that public opinion is the most powerful force in the world today, and this force is primarily molded and shaped through the freedoms of speech, press and assembly.

But, men must not only have the right to say that which may be right, but also the right to say that which may be wrong. It is only through the interplay of different, varied and opposed opinions and ideas in the arena of public discussion that truth emerges. Some opinions that were accepted as wrong yesterday are regarded as right today, and some ideas that were looked upon as right yesterday are rejected as wrong today. Who is to serve as the infallible judge of right or wrong opinions? There is none so wise or so just to serve in this role. The history of the progress of civilization is the story of the clash of opinions. Wherever anyone sets himself up as possessing a monopoly on truth, he stands across the path of human advancement. This has been true from the days of Caesar to Hitler. A government of law and free men could not either come into existence or long endure were men not free freely to express their convictions concerning men and measures. Washington, Jefferson, Jackson, and Lincoln upheld the freedoms of free expression in speech and press. . . .

Needless to say, the idea of a speech of mine provoking a race riot is unthinkable in my own mind, but I am not going to permit Crump or anybody else to curb my right of free speech or tell me what to say merely because he predicts all sorts of dire and dreadful happenings from it. If E. H. Crump's policy on free speech was permitted to prevail, one could only exercise the right of free speech when he said what Crump wanted him to say. This is dictatorship with a vengeance. Indeed, the Memphis political boss out-Hitlers Hitler.

Because of the great gravity of this issue of free speech in Memphis and the attitude of the city officials and Boss Crump on the question, I want to discuss some basic fallacies of thought that are responsible for this anti-free speech position, and also the stake of labor in this issue. To begin with, all is not well in Memphis so far as the races are concerned, or so far as organized labor is concerned. If all were well, white people would not have called up the police commissioner stating that they were buying guns to start a race riot if the meeting was held. No such thing has occurred in any other Southern city where I have spoken or in any other section of the country. . . .

SOURCE: *The Black Worker* 16 (April 1944): 4; (May 1944): 4; and (July 1944): 4.

Keynote Address at Negro American Labor Council Convention (1962)

This address before the 3rd Annual Convention of the Negro American Labor Council was one of Randolph's longest. It ranges from the history of the labor movement to an analysis of the schisms between the modern labor and civil rights movements. One can see how the latter issue, combined with the growing disconnect between established leaders like Roy Wilkins and younger militant leaders, troubled Randolph. He envisioned the NALC as a kind of glue that would hold these movements together.

Black America has been thrust into a job rights and civil rights struggle. It is not an accident or an incident; it is a massive event. It bodes danger and opportunity. There is danger that black America may be blocked and thrown back[ward] in the fight for job rights and civil rights, and there is opportunity to accelerate the struggle for the conquest of job rights and civil rights and human dignity. Which of the two paths it takes depends upon the principles, programs and practices it adopts. But the principles, programs and practices considered will only have reality in relation to the nature and origin of the crisis.

Thus, while Negro workers have made progress their economic status is still low. They exist within the shadow of poverty. Yes, they are virtually locked up in a socio-economic, poverty-structured system. Not only are Negro workers a hundred years behind their white brothers but their relative pace of progress is stretching the distance between them, with black workers, under the advance of radical technology, falling further and further behind with no visible prospects, given the continuance of present policies and attitudes of trade unions, industry and government, of ever catching up.

The Negro's struggle for equal employment opportunities over the past one hundred years is of more than historical or commemorative interest. The crises of the present are rooted in the failures of the past, and lessons unlearned are tragedies prolonged. In our own time the prolonged tragedy of black labor weighs heavily upon all Americans. It is becoming increasingly clear that no lasting political freedom or social equality is conceivable without the integration of the Negro into the economic life of the nation. How far have we come, and how far have we to go?

The Emancipation Proclamation not only freed the slaves but, in doing so, made the question of equal job opportunities a major social problem. Even before the Civil War the question had arisen, though in less pressing form, with regard to the half million free Negroes. Generally, those free Negroes who lived in Southern cities, where Negroes often had a monopoly on mechanical skills, fared better economically than those who lived in the

Northern cities, where they faced competition from skilled immigrant labor. So serious was the economic discrimination against free Northern Negroes that in Philadelphia, for example, Negroes in 1837 comprised 14 percent of the poorhouse population, though only 7 percent of the population at large. This dusty statistic is an early example of a 2-to-1 relationship that has shown remarkable persistence down to the present.

During the 1830's many free Negroes organized the so-called Conventions Movement, of which Frederick Douglass was eventually elected president. It is of immense interest that this movement, in 1855, adopted an economic program calling for the establishment of an industrial college and for a type of apprenticeship training program for Negroes. Thus, even before the Civil War, Negroes, feeling the squeeze of job discrimination and segregation, organized to fight for economic security and advanced programs that have a familiar ring today.

The slaves freed on January 1, 1863 were liberated not only from their masters but from their livelihood as well. Thaddeus Stevens, looking toward the transformation of the former slaves into a class of small independent farmers, advocated the government's giving them "forty acres and a mule." The Northern industrialists, however, who had gained control of the Republican Party, could not countenance the confiscation and division of large plantations. Many of the Negroes who did secure homesteads were driven off under President Johnson's program of restoring the land to white planters. Homeless and property-less, the great mass of Southern Negroes had no alternative but to return to the plantations, this time as tenant farmers and sharecroppers.

The failure of Reconstruction to provide Negroes with an economic base—the tragedy of the period—foredoomed all efforts at [achieving] political democracy in the South. Even as the Negro was enjoying the fullest participation in political life, helping to maintain Republican power in the South, the stage had been set for the time when, a score [of] years after Reconstruction, his landlord would march him to the polls with voting instructions, and later disfranchise him altogether. Few examples in history so vividly illustrate the fragility of political freedom unmoored in economic security.

Thus the Negro found himself cut adrift into the Gilded Age, the nadir of Big Business morality, the pinnacle of its speculative and exploitative irresponsibility. From the industrial revolution that was sweeping the country the Negro was excluded North and South. In the South the Negro had never really competed with the poor white for land, having been reduced almost immediately to sharecropping, but he had offered competition in mechanical skills. In fact, at the end of the Civil War, 100,000 of the 120,000 artisans in the South were Negroes. By 1890 the skilled Negro worker had virtually ceased to exist. The mania for textile mills and tobacco factories . . . gripped the South in the last decades of the nineteenth century . . . plant managers promised poor whites industrial salvation in the new white-only enterprises. In the North, which claimed 10 percent of the Negro population in this period, Negroes were systematically barred from all but the most menial tasks in the burgeoning mass industries.

To what extent the denial of equal job opportunities to Negroes in both the North and South "stemmed from interlocking control or management" is "difficult to determine," as the historian Rayford W. Logan points out in *The Negro in American Life and Thought*. Nonetheless, after the famous Compromise of 1877, "Big Business continued to constitute the principal force for peace at almost any price, for 'leaving the South alone.' Further investigation may reveal close links between Northern capital and management and the supposedly predominantly Southern enterprises of cotton and tobacco factories." In any case, the Southerners had their own reasons for keeping these factories white. Whatever the motives of the Northerners, their policy was deliberate, and it is clear that Northern capital made ample and profitable use of Negroes as strikebreakers.

Not only the federal government (through its Reconstruction and post-Reconstruction policies) and Northern and Southern capitalists were responsible for the deterioration of the Negro's economic condition; the unions were also to blame. It is not entirely coincidental that the surge of American capitalism, the freeing of the slaves, and the formation of the first national labor organization should occur almost simultaneously. Yet the confluence of these events was significant for the future of the Negro. The National Labor Union, formed in 1866, was a weak counter-weight to the power and influence being wielded by the industrialists [who were] backed up by the Supreme Court and other agencies of government. Before its destruction following the panic of 1873, the National Labor Union had recognized the danger posed by Negro strikebreakers and decided to organize black workers, but into separate locals. The reaction of Negro workers was the formation, in 1869, of the National Negro Labor Union.

The fate of the National Negro Labor Union was predictable. Although Negroes had successfully established independent churches in the eighteenth century, inexorable economic laws militated, then as now, against the organization of workers along racial lines. Efforts of the National Negro Labor Union to affiliate with white labor were unsuccessful. Negro workers remained isolated and were increasingly used as strikebreakers.

The Knights of Labor, founded in 1869, was more anxious to recruit Negroes. Aiming at unskilled as well as skilled workers, the Knights brought Negroes into some all-black locals and also some mixed ones. In 1887 it may have had as many as 90,000 Negroes out of a total membership of a half million.

Many of its organizers played courageous roles in the South, braving terrorist anti-labor tactics of a sort all too familiar to students of the CIO drives in the Thirties. The decline of the Knights following the Haymarket Riot of 1886 was paralleled by the rise of a new union and a new labor philosophy.

Unlike the Knights, the American Federation of Labor, founded in 1886, had a decentralized structure consisting of essentially autonomous craft locals. Because of its disinterest in unskilled workers, the AFL could attract few Negroes; at the same time, various unions that constitutionally excluded Negroes from membership could not be curbed because of the federation structure of the national body. Structural questions aside, however, the AFL lacked the broad idealistic spirit of the Knights of Labor, and for the latter's crusading spirit substituted a more narrowly economic and "practical" program. Still, the Federation's 1893 and 1894 conventions stated: "We here and now reaffirm as one of the cardinal principles of the labor movement that the working people must unite and organize, irrespective of creed, color, sex, nationality, or politics." The resolution was not binding, only a request. But consistent discrimination by its affiliates whittled away at even this principle, so that by 1901 the federation gave ground on the issue of social equality and approved the organization of separate locals. It also scolded Negro workers for strikebreaking, as if the AFL's exclusive policies were unrelated to that practice....

Whoever was most to blame—government, management or labor—the results were clear. Despite the march of the nation from agrarianism to industrialism in the second half of the eighteenth century, 88 percent of all Negroes in 1890 remained in agriculture and domestic service. By 1900 the figure had dropped only to 86.7 percent. To describe this phenomenon as a pattern of unequal employment opportunities is euphemistic. Only when viewed as an almost total exclusion from the national revolution in technology and economic organization can the Negro's experience prior to World War I be understood in terms of the lack of skills with which he met the Twentieth Century. This economic alienation of the Negro was of course paralleled by his deepening social and political alienation....

In withdrawing its support of the equal opportunities principle, Congress paved the way for the inevitable decline of skilled Negro craftsmen and foremen. Having won the war against racism abroad [during World War II], with the help of her thirteen million Negroes, the nation apparently no longer felt constrained to continue that war at home. Once again the federal government had abandoned the Negro to economic oppression.

Certainly recent years have seen progress in the Negro's struggle for equal opportunities. In the absence of federal legislation, a score of states and numerous cities have enacted their own Fair Employment Practices programs, varying in scope and enforceability. Direct action by Negroes at the 1948 Democratic Party convention was largely responsible for President Truman's Executive Order 9981 ending segregation in the armed forces. President Kennedy's Committee on Equal Employment Opportunities, established in March 1961, is a considerable improvement over its phlegmatic predecessor, though it still lacks some of the powers of Roosevelt's FEPC. That discrimination persists in employment created by federal grant-in-aid and loan programs, as in National Guard and reserve units, is documented in the 1961 Civil Rights Commission Report. Moreover, the Commission has reported that: "Efforts of the federal government to promote nondiscriminatory employment by government contractors and federal agencies have not generally been effective in overcoming resistance to hiring Negroes in any but the lower categories."

The labor movement has made welcome advances. During the forties, there were still twenty-six AFL affiliates whose constitutions barred Negroes from membership—and thus from fruitful employment. Today only the Brotherhood of Locomotive Firemen and Enginemen explicitly excludes Negroes. Twenty-six international unions and seventeen state central bodies have established civil rights committees. One and a half million Negroes now reside in the house of labor and they have won increasing representation in labor's governing councils, even in the South. The 1961 AFL-CIO Civil Rights Resolution forthrightly proclaimed: "The AFL-CIO is in the forefront of the civil rights revolution in our land. It is a foremost force in the drive to eliminate and prevent every form of race discrimination and race injustice in the American community." It is not without interest that no comparable statement has come from any national manufacturing organization.

Still, resolutions are not enough. In apprenticeship training, hiring policies, seniority lists, pay scales, job assignments and the like, discrimination persists in too many locals, especially in the building trades. Negroes continue to be barred from some unions, segregated in others. To combat these evils, hundreds of Negro trade unionists banded together in 1959 to found the Negro American Labor Council. Loyal to the labor movement and recognizing it as the most progressive institution in our society, the NALC has fought vigorously to cleanse the trade unions of every vestige of Jim Crow. Racism, we have insisted, is uniquely incompatible with labor's needs and aspirations; it is no less an evil than Communism and corruption and must be met with equal severity. . . .

The crisis confronting the Negro worker today can be summed up in one word: Automation. The displacement of men by machines hits the unskilled and semiskilled workers first and hardest, and these are the jobs to which Negroes have been relegated. As late as 1955, only 12 percent of the Negro workforce had risen into professional, technical, managerial, and white-collar clerical and sales jobs (as opposed to 42 percent of the whites). 47 percent of the Negroes were in service and other unskilled (nonfarm) jobs. Another 15 percent were in agriculture. At present there is no single skilled craft in which Negroes constitute even 2 percent of the total! More ominous than the figures themselves is the fact that the elevation rate of the Negro into more skilled occupations has fallen behind the rate of automation displacement.

Nowhere is the crisis more starkly revealed than in the unemployment figures. Far from indicating progress, they point to an almost steady deterioration in the position of the black worker. Whereas the unemployment rate during the years 1947–1955 did not exceed 8.9 percent for Negroes and 4.6 percent for whites, the rate in 1958 was 12.6 percent and 6.1 percent respectively. The Bureau of Labor statistics for August 1962 show 11.4 percent of the Negro workforce unemployed as against 4.6 percent of the white. Thus, despite all progress, the black unemployment rate has remained double that of whites for decades, and at the moment is two and one-half times that of whites. A recession for white workers is a depression for black workers. The extent to which the Negro unemployment rate is due to automation is suggested in the statistic on chronic unemployment. Most of the chronically unemployed are victims of technological displacement. At present, among those unemployed for more than fifteen weeks, 2.8 percent are nonwhite. Statistics can be endlessly elaborated. Their meaning is plain: the relative position of the Negro in the economy has remained astonishingly static over the years and the future threatens even that woeful position. The Negro is not the only loser. Automation is likely to create more skilled jobs than men to fill them, according to the U.S. Civil Rights Commission. Yet, as a nation we passively observe the languishing of untapped talent in stagnant pools of unskilled labor continuously drained by automation into the sewers of unemployment. . . .

What Is To Be Done?

The first step is to awaken, inform, arouse and mobilize Negro workers in and out of the unions, and transform them into a militant and massive movement, since history is full of lessons to the effect that it is virtually impossible to move the labor movement, or the business movement, or the government without a movement. Moreover, our pluralistic democratic society, with [its] many varied and various segments of the population, with their specific interests and concerns, invariably encounters, if not provokes, opposition from a particular group or groups of the population with adverse interests and concerns. Such is the case with such major groups as capital and labor, as represented by the National Association of Manufacturers and the AFL-CIO; the Negro and the South, as represented by the NAACP and the White Citizens Councils and its allies. There are also numerous sub-groups of citizens that organize to protect their interests, such as the senior citizens movement that fights for legislation for medical care within the framework of Social Security, which was bitterly attacked and defeated by the American Medical Association. And in the long run, the group wins out and achieves its goals, not always because its cause is right, but because it possesses the more effective leverage and can bring the more pressure to bear upon, and constitutes the greater threat to, the power and stability of the government. Of course, it is an advantage when a group can claim moral grounds for its cause, which, interestingly enough, no group is willing to admit is not the case. Thus the awakened oppressed ever disturbs their oppressors.

Note the long struggle against slavery in the United States. It was the insurrections led by black revolutionists under the valiant Toussaint L'Ouverture in Santo Domingo in 1793, the slave revolts led by Gabriel that alarmed the masters of slavery in South Carolina in 1800, the uprisings in Virginia by Denmark Vesey in 1822 and Nat Turner in 1831 that shook, shocked and frightened the daylights out of the pompous slave masters. Such are the mechanics and dynamics of the struggle of the oppressed against their oppressors, not only in the United States but also in Africa and Asia against Western colonial tyranny and terror, as well as revolts in Eastern Europe under Communist savage oppression and violence.

Many proposals have been made. Perhaps the most pretentious is the President's Committee on Equal Employment Opportunity "Plans for Progress" program, the purpose of which is to secure the large employers and the national and international trade unions of the AFL-CIO to sign with Vice President Johnson, at the White House, a "Plans for Progress" for equal employment opportunity. This strategy may be immensely helpful only if the government does not leave compliance upon a voluntary and permissive basis, but takes firm positive action to compel some 38,000, more or less, contractors operating 50,000 or more facilities and 100 national and international unions to abolish race bias or accept the penalty of the cancellation of contracts and the elimination of jobs. . . .

Before we in the Negro American Labor Council ask ourselves whether there will be jobs for all, black and white, and what kind of jobs will be available, let us take a look into the future, or as early as 1965—three years from today. According to estimates of population projections, the 1.9 million graduates of 1962 will become 2.5 million, an increase of 600,000, 60,000 of which will be Negroes, by 1965. If the ratio remains constant, practically 800,000 will seek college training while 1,500,000 will enter the labor force. Their dropout counterparts will increase this number to approximately 2.3 million new workers. The large number of youth reaching the age of 18 will increase from 2.6 million in 1962 to 3.8 million in 1965, approximately a half million of whom will be blacks. These youth will enter a rapidly changing world, with technological improvements in industry making it possible to produce more units of goods and services in less time, and liquidating, as it were, some two million unskilled and semiskilled jobs annually.

The question might well be raised: can our black youth survive and move ahead in a highly competitive, racially prejudiced labor market, in view of an increasing demand for skilled, technical, professional training which they possess but sparingly? This question must be met.

Moreover, without access to unlimited areas of vocational and scientific education, reinforced by on-the-job apprenticeship training (which is only possible in industry), schools and trade unions completely free from race bias, Negro youth will be trapped in a dilemma of job impermanency, a trade or skill acquired today becoming obsolete tomorrow as a result of the bewildering sweep of change incident to the revolution of automation. This is why, my dear brothers and sisters, the presence and role of the Negro American Labor Council is so grave, urgent and imperative.

Youth of minority groups, and especially Negro youth, have particular problems that must be realistically met. They include:

1. Development of a creative and constructive self-image which is in consonance with the universal image of forward-moving youth of America.

2. Identification of the needs, responses, aspirations, yearnings and rising expectations with the militant march of disadvantaged youth under the yoke of colonialism and imperialism of world capitalism and Communism in Africa, Asia and Eastern Europe.

3. Inspiration and motivation from status symbols of accomplishment of black leadership in the skilled trades, technical, professional and scientific fields.

4. Development of adequate personality mechanisms to deal with hostility and rejection on ethnic grounds.

5. Development of constructive personal attitudes towards work and achievement.

6. Belief in his personal worth as a human being, regardless of race or color.

The Negro American Labor Council must formulate and evolve ways and means of helping black youth find their way, not only to economic success, but to moral and spiritual service to the black community in particular, and the entire city, state and nation in general. Breaking through ethnic marginal economic opportunities cannot occur in a vacuum, it can only develop in a community context in which indigenous community leaders and institutions play a key role. Many significant jobs are not filled or even found on the basis of merit, but on the basis of a complicated system of community and personal connections and pressures. The opportunity available to a Negro youth must be construed as the function of the total community and not the sole personal responsibility of the individual youth or of his parents. The use of all the devices for breaking down barriers to employment and job mobility and progression upward in wage rates and status is a personal responsibility that falls on the leaders of community institutions and movements—religious, labor, business, educational, fraternal, political and civic.

I am sure the leaders and members of NALC share with me a sense of the tremendous magnitude of the problem of the job and skill training crisis of Negro youth, as well as a sense of the great inadequacy which now exists in our general efforts to cope effectively with the dimension of the issue of job insecurity. Whether it is the part-time and occasional effect of private agencies and voluntary groups, or the more systematic programs of public schools and public institutions which have direct contact with large numbers of Negro youth, I think there is little doubt but that these programs fall desperately short of filling the vacuum which exists in this area. The problem increases both in magnitude and complexity year after year and with each generation of Negro youth. We have only to show on the favorable side of the ledger a few individual success stories which circumstance has accidentally placed in our hands, and on the negative side the mounting delinquency and jobless rate, with their attendant psychological costs to the youth involved and the staggering social losses that cannot be reclaimed. . . .

What Is NALC?

First of all, let it be understood that NALC is not a trade union. It is a labor organization committed to fighting for equality and civil rights for black workers in the house of labor, and also to the philosophy of free, democratic trade unionism. Therefore, it negotiates no contracts concerning rates of pay or rules governing working conditions, nor does it seek to adjust grievances or claims. Nor is NALC a civil rights movement, although it supports civil rights movements like the National Association for the Advancement of Colored People, the Southern Christian Leadership Conference, the Congress of Racial Equality, and the Non-violent Student Movement, as well as other bona fide civil rights organizations. . . . We are a specialized movement with a clear objective; namely, the abolition of race bias against black workers in trade unions, industry and government. It is a big enough task for any one movement. In very truth, it is big and difficult enough to engage the interest and concern of every Negro, labor, and liberal movement in the country if we hope to win our goal in time for it to be meaningful to the black laboring masses. Moreover, NALC is not equipped with the requisite training personnel and experience to enter into the civil rights field. Nor is it equipped with the requisite training, personnel and experience to negotiate or evaluate contracts. This is the function of a trade union. We are only concerned with inquiring into the nature of a contract of a union when it involves race bias. NALC is non-partisan, but not non-political. It is primarily concerned about increasing registration among Negro workers, and the use of political action to secure executive and legislative measures for labor's rights and civil rights. NALC is not anti-white, but it is pro-Negro. NALC is not anti–AFL-CIO or any bona fide trade union. It is pro–AFL-CIO.

NALC Objectives

1. The complete abolition of race bias in trade unions, industry and government.

2. Integration of Negro trade unionists into the policy-making bodies of unions, local, national and international, city central labor councils and state AFL-CIO federations.

3. Integration of Negroes into the staff structure of unions.

4. Desegregation of southern city central labor bodies and state AFL-CIO federations.

5. Establishment of civil rights committees in national and international unions, city central labor councils and state AFL-CIO federations.

6. Negotiation of non-discriminatory clauses in union contracts.

7. Abolition of Jim Crow local unions.

8. Elimination of exclusionary membership clauses, based upon race or color, or by tacit consent. . . .

NALC is the only area of dialogue, though quite inadequate, between Negro and white trade unionists, upon a basis of equality, in the country today. While a Negro staff person for a union may, and does, have dialogue with his boss, it is an employer-employee sort of thing, which is hardly the same as when Negro and white trade unionists have dialogue upon a basis of quality. But, in order for Negro and white trade unionists to have fruitful dialogue there must be an area of consensus. What could this be? It could be:

1. Common commitment to free, democratic trade unionism.

2. Commitment to a democratic form of society within the framework of which alone can free democratic trade unionism survive and develop.

3. Opposition to the totalitarian Communist or Fascist form of society under which the trade union is an organ of the state without the right to bargain collectively on a basis of equality with management, and without the right to strike.

4. Commitment to civil rights, which is an attribute of a free and independent citizen.

5. Commitment to the spiritual and moral values of the Judeo-Christian tradition that emphasize the worth of every human being and the sacredness of the dignity of the human personality.

6. Commitment to first-class citizenship in the house of labor of all workers, regardless of race, religion, color, national origin or ancestry.

7. Commitment to the principle of any worker, white or black, Jew or Gentile, Protestant or Catholic, to equality of opportunity to learn in order to earn.

8. Commitment to union and ethnic democracy.

If we fight and faint not, we shall win.

SOURCE: Box 36, folder: Speeches, January 17, 1962–July 15, 1962, A. Philip Randolph Papers, Library of Congress.

African Methodism and the Negro in the Western World (1962)

In this speech commemorating the Diamond Jubilee of the Bermuda African Methodist Episcopal Conference, Randolph expresses his appreciation for the importance of religion in black life. He places the audacity of Richard Allen, a Revolutionary-era African American religious leader, in the context of Martin Luther and other Christian heroes. Randolph grew up in the AME tradition, and his reverence resonates throughout these remarks. His familiarity with religious doctrines is equally impressive, as he shows a mastery of both church history and biblical scriptures.

Being one of the sons of African Methodism I am honored to share in the fine fellowship spirit of this celebration of the 75th anniversary of this great church in Bermuda. Many periods of history bear a distinguishing imprint of some dominant idea, philosophy, personalities, movement or event. One such period was the age of the Hebrew prophets, thirteen centuries before the Christian era. These mighty men of Israel—Isaiah, Amos, Hosea and Micah—preached the supremacy of moral values and the importance of social righteousness, and thundered their wrath against rituals and sacrifices as substitutes for right and justice. Thus spake Amos to the wealthy and nobility: "I hate and despise your feast days and I will not delight in your solemn assemblies. Though ye offer me burnt offerings and your meat offerings, I will not accept them; neither will I regard the peace offerings of your fat beasts . . . but let judgment run down as waters, and righteousness as a mighty stream."

Five thousand years ago the image of the ancient world was largely determined by two giant empires, Egypt and Babylon. Egypt, with its Nile Valley, the cradle of human culture, enslaved the Children of Israel, while the Babylonian kings crushed the Kingdom of Judah. Twenty-five hundred years after the ancient nations of despotism had perished and had been swept away, and five hundred years before Christ, Athens, described by anthropologists and archeologists as a veritable miracle, moved upon the stage of history with its unexampled passion for truth, beauty, simplicity and freedom, developed in a rocky little seaport in the midst of barbarian superstition, despotism and splendor. There a light was lit that will never go out. In those brief centuries Athens reached its summit in the few years of the Golden Age of Pericles of literature, science, philosophy, art, democracy, religion, the main achievement of the modern world, with the greatest constellation of luminaries of the book, the mind and the spirit yet known to mankind. The magnificent flowering of the genius of Athens is reflected in her honored sons: In philosophy, Socrates, Plato and Aristotle; in drama, Aeschylus, Sophocles and Euripides; in history, Herodotus, Thucydides and Xenophon; and the odes of Pindar, the epic Iliad of Homer, and the sculpture of Phidias.

In the upward climb of man to higher levels of ethical and spiritual consciousness, God sent his son, Jesus Christ, who became the leader of a little band of Christians in Judea in the first century, to become the Messiah of mankind under the banner of the One and the True and the Living God, which was in sharp conflict with the polytheism of the Roman Empire of the Caesars and the religions of the ancient world.

In the ancient world (except Athens) where only the kings, the priestcraft and the great warriors were free, where dreadful human wretchedness and unspeakable fear and cruelty tended to transform the great laboring masses into cringing and hideous mindless human beings, Jesus, the lowly Nazarene, in perhaps the most revolutionary declaration made in those days of darkness and damnation, said to the multitude: "Come unto me all ye that labor and are heavy laden, and I will give thee rest; take my yoke upon you and think of me for my yoke is easy and my burden is light, and ye shall find peace unto your soul."

And in reaffirming his deep concern about the people, Jesus said: "I have compassion on the multitude because they have now been with me three days and have nothing to eat. And if I sent them away fasting to their own houses they will faint by the way, for divers of them came from far." And he blessed a few loaves of bread and fishes and fed them. This strange witness of the will of God startled his followers, when he observed: "For whosoever will save his life shall lose it, but whosoever shall lose his life for my sake and the gospel's, the same shall save it." He shocked the Pharisees, Sadducees and scribes, as well as his own disciples, when he declared: "It is easier for a camel to go through the eye of a needle than for a rich man to enter the Kingdom of God."

Jesus continued to confound his followers and the high priests. It is written (Luke 4:16–18): "And he came to Nazareth, where he had been brought up and, as his custom was, he went into the synagogue on the Sabbath day and stood up for to read. And there was delivered unto him the book of the prophet Esaias. And when he had opened the book, He found the place where it was written: The Spirit of the Lord is upon me, because he hath anointed me to preach the gospel to the poor; he hath sent me to heal the brokenhearted, to preach deliverance to the captives and recovering of sight to the blind, to set at liberty them that are bruised."

The revolutionary ministry of the brotherhood of man of Jesus Christ was made increasingly challengingly dramatic when he said: "woe unto you, scribes and Pharisees, hypocrites! For ye devour widows' houses, and for a pretense make long prayer; therefore ye shall receive the greater damnation." And with a universal injunction of Christian humanism, he gives this injunction: "But I say unto you, love your enemies, bless them that curse you, do good to them that hate you, and pray for them which despitefully use you and persecute you."

Jesus Christ, unlike the religious leaders of Egypt, India and China, brought hope to the multitudes with the things of the body, as well as the things of the spirit. The priests of Buddhism and Hinduism found strength to endure by denying any meaning and any importance to what they could not escape. The Egyptian world, where dead men walked and slept and feasted, was transmuted into what had always been implicit in its symbolism, the world of the spirit. In India, for centuries the leader of thought to the East, the world of reason and the world of the spirit were divorced and the universe was handed over to the latter. Reality—that which we have heard, which we have seen with our eyes—was construed as vague and unsubstantial and forever passing, the shadow of a dream. Only that was real which was of the spirit. This is always man's way out when the facts of life are too bitter and too black to be borne, and where there is little faith.

When conditions are such that life offers no earthly hope, somewhere, somehow, men must find refuge. Then they fly from the terror without to the citadel within, which famine, pestilence, fire and sword cannot shake. What Goethe calls "the inner universe" can live by its own laws, create its own security, be sufficient unto itself, when once reality is denied to the turmoil of the world without. . . .

Richard Allen, a black slave, aroused, angered and awakened by the manifestation of racial discrimination while at worship in Old St. George Methodist Church in Philadelphia, rejected, resented and resisted the affront, and walked out of the Jim Crow gallery on the Lord's Day, to breathe the air of religious freedom. By this expression of his wrath against religious Jim Crow he, like Crispus Attucks (a black man, and the first to fall in 1770 in the Revolutionary War of Independence for the thirteen American colonies), struck a blow for civil rights and first-class citizenship. Inspired by the sacred soil of Independence Square, where stood the Hall in which the Liberty Bell sounded the call to freedom and equality for all mankind, he purchased an abandoned blacksmith shop nearby and hauled it with his team to Sixth and Lombard Streets and established the first African Methodist Episcopal Church.

During these eventful times the fires of freedom and independence were burning down the rotten temple of British colonial tyranny which had been denounced and condemned in the Declaration of Independence by Thomas Jefferson. These struggles on the part of Samuel Adams, George Washington, Jefferson, Alexander Hamilton, [James] Madison, Benjamin Franklin and Tom Paine against colonial slavery stirred the Negro, slaves and free Negroes to strike a blow against chattel and religious slavery. Verily, this was the beginning of the independent church movement. And it was essentially a blow struck for racial church integration, not separation or segregation.

The growth of the A.M.E. Church is a significant and glorious tribute to the Negro's genius. It has given him a sense of his potentiality and promise. Its institutions and laws, its distinguished bishops and ministers, are the result of Negro initiative, courage and venture, wisdom and vision. African Methodism was a religious reflection of the deep revolutionary currents set in motion by the French Revolution which had given rise to the doctrine of the Rights of Man. African Methodism struck at white religious royalty and aristocracy and unfurled and held aloft the banner of *Liberté, Egalité* and *Fraternité*. . . .

Richard Allen was one of those rare spirits which opposition cannot quell. When the attempt was made to pull Absalom Jones from his knees, Allen and his friends walked out of the church, then and there. This action had greater nobility of spirit and entailed more personal sacrifice than that of Martin Luther who nailed his ninety-five theses to the church door at Wittenberg or when he stood before the Diet of Worms. On that day, and by that deed, Richard Allen broke down the iniquitous partition wall of racial proscription and segregation in the Christian Church, not only in the United States but throughout the world. Verily, the test of Christianity is the test of the color line, as the test of democracy is the test of the color line. Well might Richard Allen have exclaimed, "I called to the Eternal in my plight, I cried to my God for aid. . . . He heard my voice."

Richard Allen died in 1831, the year of the insurrection of the slaves of Virginia under the leadership of the slave, Nat Turner. The manifestation of a burning passion of Negro slaves for freedom shook the American white society to its very foundation. Stringent laws against the slaves followed, but slave insurrections continued in every colony and, finally, in every state in the Union. Millions of slaves preferred to die on their feet fighting for freedom than to exist on their knees begging for life. Thus, the refrain of the slaves:

Before I'd be a slave
I'd be buried in my grave
And go home to my God
And be free. . . .

African Methodism inspired and stimulated Negro leadership to action for abolition and to fight for political progress. During the twelve Reconstruction years, 1865 to 1877, two Negro senators from Mississippi were seated in the Congress, and fourteen Representatives in the House. Some of these men came out of the African Methodist Church. And let us not forget Abraham Grant, Benjamin W. Arnett, Benjamin Tucker Tanner, Wesley J. Gaines. And there were Bishops Lee, L. J. Coffin, Parks, Heard Flipper, John Albert Johnson, Carey Becket, Tyree, Ransom, Fountain, Gaines, and Green. These great leaders of African Methodism might well exclaim: "Upon this rock we have built this Church, and the gates of hell shall not prevail against [it]."

Today, Negroes in the United States represent twenty billion dollars in wealth annually. They lose thirty billions because of race bias. Their economic problems are grave because they are the first fired and the last hired and their rate of unemployment is twice as high as the unemployment rate of white workers. Their average annual median wage is 58 percent of the annual average median wage of white workers. Because Negroes, on account of race bias, have been deprived of opportunity to acquire craft skills, they are disproportionately concentrated in unskilled and semi-skilled categories of industry. They are the hardest hit by the revolution of automation.

But Negroes are awakened and aroused to the realization of the fact that "he who would be free must himself strike the first blow," and hence young college Negro boys and girls are demonstrating against race bias by "sit-ins" and "freedom rides" and, when arrested, they express their desire to go to jail and not accept bail, which is in the great tradition of lovers of liberty all over the world. With this militant spirit the future of Negro citizens' fight for first-class citizenship is promising and they will, undoubtedly, eventually get a Negro on the Supreme Court and there is a possibility and probability that a Negro will some day sit in the White House as the President of the United States, but only if Negroes continue to fight for their rights.

SOURCE: Box 36, folder: Speeches, January 17, 1962–July 15, 1962, A. Philip Randolph Papers, Library of Congress.

Lincoln University Commencement Address (1967)

A. Philip Randolph's address to graduates at Lincoln University, the flagship of the Historically Black Colleges and Universities in Missouri, hints at the fissures that were threatening the civil rights movement in the mid-1960s. Ideological differences about the wisdom of Black Power, local squabbles over control of schools, and the ongoing war in Vietnam all generated intense debate within the ranks of civil rights movement organizers and tacticians. In this speech Randolph argues that conservatives would be elected in 1968 if the progressive coalition continued to splinter, and he warns that the gains made by the movement thus far would disappear, just as they had during the collapse of Reconstruction nearly one hundred years earlier.

Permit me to express my pleasure and delight to have been honored with the opportunity to share in the fine fellowship spirit of this Commencement of this great institution of learning. It has given us some of the distinguished leaders of our country. I have come to reflect, with the faculty and students, upon the rise, struggle and promise of the Negro Freedom Movement.

We live in an age of revolutions. There is the revolution of science, technology and industrialism, revealing the new and bewildering phenomena of special explorations and nuclear fission; and the revolutions of civil rights and nationalism, with the restless and challenging mood of rising expectations, the fires of which have swept over the great continents of Asia and Africa, and the areas of Latin America and the Caribbean, leaving in their wake the ashes of the old hated and hateful empires of colonialism.

Nor is the Church and religion, as shown by the spread of the spirit of ecumenism initiated by Pope John XXIII, Protestant and Jewish religious leaders, untouched by the winds of revolutionary change.

After nearly 300 years of exploitation and humiliation, the thunder of the protest of the Black Revolt has shaken America to its very foundations. Perhaps the most stirring and dramatic event of modern times is the great world of color, two-thirds of mankind, on the march to freedom and human dignity.

This manifestation of unrest and discontent, if not wrath, of the peoples of color against rejection, oppression, alienation and apartheid is a dynamic upward thrust of the so-called undeveloped areas in an essentially new and potentially revolutionary attack upon the decadent and mythical concept of white supremacy. Having stepped out of the long night of slavery and serfdom of the past into the bright light of the present struggle for nationalist independence and racial justice, millions of men of color, with heads bloody but unbowed, souls uncurbed, are marching into the future for a better tomorrow and the fellowship of man.

But while colonialism has been swept from the continents of Africa and Asia, the baffling socio-economic problems of poverty, illiteracy and disease remain. The fact is, lessons of history teach that economic and political democracy and social well-being do not automatically follow nationalist or civil rights revolutions. More profound social change is imperative to lift the people to higher levels of life and living. Social revolutions must inevitably follow hard upon the heels of the development of a self-governing state and the triumph of a revolution for civil rights. A self-governing state has the task of developing a viable economy which must rest upon the modernization of agriculture and advancing industrialization. Such has been the behavior pattern of the transition of a colony from a sort of imperialistic mercantilist status to an independent nation-state. And American Negroes, while members of a free, powerful nation-state, are far from free. Of course this political and social change is not simple or easy, for the developing countries never had a chance, under the mercantilism of colonialism, to achieve any considerable capital formation, mechanical or social technology. This is understandable, since the colonial powers were fearful lest too much self-development of colonial subjects might encourage the spirit of independence and threaten continued colonial rule. In the South, Negroes have been and even are now brutally subjugated by white rule which stems partially from fear of a black revolt.

In fact, the rise and development of world racism is contemporaneous with the rise and development of world colonialism and imperialism. The reason being that subjugation, domination and exploitation of peoples of color in Africa and Asia, the United States, the Caribbean and Latin American countries, required pseudo-moral justification and social and political explanation for the material gain or economic profit out of the human misery of colonialism. Hence, racism had to be invented.

With a profound sense of prophecy the late and lamented William Edward Burghardt Du Bois, in his *Souls of Black Folk,* stated: "Herein lie buried many things which if read with patience may show the strange meaning of being black here at the dawning of the Twentieth Century. This meaning is not without interest to you, gentle reader, for the problem of the Twentieth Century is the problem of the color line. Verily, the history of the American Negro is the history of this color line."

Of the black slaves' fighting faith in freedom, Du Bois continues: "Away back in the days of bondage they thought to see in one divine event the end of all doubt and disappointment; few men ever worshipped Freedom with such unquestioning faith as did the American Negro for two centuries. To him, so far as he thought and dreamed, slavery was indeed the sum of all villainies, the cause of all sorrow, the root of all prejudices; emancipation was the key to a promised land of sweeter beauty than ever before the eyes of wearied Israelites.

"In song and exhortation swelled one refrain, Liberty; in his tears and curses the God he implored had freedom in his right hand. At last it came—suddenly, fearfully, like a dream. With one wild carnival of blood and passion came the message, in his own plaintive cadences:

Shout, o children!
Shout, you're free!
For God has bought your liberty!"

But had the dawn of the morning of freedom really come? While the Reconstruction Revolution was celebrated by the enactment of the famous War Amendments—the Thirteenth of 1865 abolished slavery; the Fourteenth of 1868 made the Negro a citizen; and the Fifteenth of 1870 gave him the right to vote—reinforced by the Civil Rights Act of 1876, it is a notorious fact that neither of these measures was ever fully enforced.

Why? There were four major reasons:

One, the reconciliation of the old ruling slave oligarchy with former liberals, with some prominent abolitionists. Even such former anti-slavery publications as the *Atlantic Monthly, Harper's, The Nation, North American Review,* resorted to the use of such myths as the hereditary racial inferiority of the Negro.

Two, the desertion of the Republican Party. This was evident when following the Hayes-Tilden election of 1876, President Hayes, Republican, who won as a result of highly questionable political maneuvering, withdrew the federal army forces from the South, leaving the Black Freedmen to the tender mercies of their former slave masters. Of course, this deal was mutually beneficial to the North and South. The former needed control of the federal government power of taxation to protect and advance rising industrial capitalism, and the latter, completely bankrupt, needed cheap labor to rebuild the cotton plantations.

Three, the rise of the Confederate Counterrevolution following the end of the war. Mounted by the terror and violence of the Ku Klux Klan and the U.S. Supreme Court decision of *Plessy vs. Ferguson* in 1896, which propounded the doctrine of separate but equal, the legal foundation for the American system of racial segregation and discrimination—the Confederate forces drove the Freedmen from the ballot box, and with the poll tax, white primaries, grand-father clauses and literacy tests, banished the Negro from the political and civic life of the South.

Fourth, labor and farmers' revolts. And, finally, the Freedmen were soon forgotten by the American public. This was due largely to violent nation-wide strikes and farmers' rebellion against the Gilded Age, which denied the work-ers decent wages and the right of union organization, and the farmers prof-itable prices for their products. This upheaval resulted in pushing the Black Freedmen from the center of the stage of American history.

Negroes emerged from this dreadful crisis landless, voteless, moneyless and friendless, if not hopeless. Though the march of the Black Americans to Canaan, the Promised Land, was stopped dead in its tracks by the fires of hate and terror, there was no turning back. The seeds of the Civil Rights Revolu-tion had been planted by the slave insurrections of Cato in 1739, Gabriel in 1800, Vesey in 1822 and Nat Turner in 1831. Black slaves were striking hard to break the system of slavery itself through violent group insurrections, flight from the land of Pharaoh and suicide. Thus, Hugh McCall, one of the earli-est historians of Georgia, remarked that "the Negro could not be supposed to be content in slavery, and would grasp with avidity at the most desperate attempts which promised freedom."

In 1910, Dr. W. E. B. Du Bois, together with a few dedicated white liberals, formed the National Association for the Advancement of Colored People. A long chain of battles have been fought, won and lost for Negro freedom. In 1954 the U.S. Supreme Court handed down the momentous *Brown* decision for the desegregation and integration of public schools, as a result of legal action of the NAACP. In 1955 there was the famous boycott of Jim Crow buses in Montgomery, headed by Dr. Martin Luther King, followed by a rash of demonstrations in the form of lunch counter sit-ins, freedom rides, the fight against segregation and police-dog brutality in Birmingham, Alabama, the Big March on Washington of August 28, 1963, the Montgomery-Selma, Alabama march; school boycotts, marches for jobs, marches against ghettos, marches to strengthen the war on poverty, and highlighted by the racial explosions in Watts, Harlem, Chicago, Cleveland, Philadelphia, and many other areas.

With the vigorous leadership by President Johnson of civil rights legisla-tion in the Congress, the Civil Rights Act of 1964 and the Voting Rights Act of 1965 were enacted into law. This was a major victory of Civil Rights Revolu-tion because it enabled Negroes to enjoy public accommodations in southern cities hitherto denied them, and made possible widespread and extensive voter registration in the South. The first impression in many areas was that the battles of the Negro freedom movement were over.

While federal civil rights legislation had established the illegality of discrimination and segregation based upon race or color, in public schools, industry, and labor unions, the big problem, yet unsolved, was implementation. Because of the obvious progress of the Civil Rights Revolution, Negroes today, as they did at the end of the Civil War, paradoxically face an uncertain future. When emancipation was proclaimed in 1863, Negroes were no longer slaves, but they were not yet citizens legally. So, today, Negroes are legally free American citizens, but they cannot yet completely act like it because the legality is still questioned by the diehard segregationists. But while the implementation of existing civil rights legislation and the enactment of a Federal Fair Housing Act are not less difficult than enactment of primary civil rights legislation, the basic fulfillment of the mission of the Civil Rights revolution has been achieved.

Thus, Negroes face the challenge of effecting a transition from, or a transformation of, the Civil Rights Revolution into a Social Revolution, which alone can solve the problem of joblessness and poverty, slum housing, ignorance and disease for the black and white working poor. This will require a struggle to achieve profound social change in the institutions of our American society, involving a more equitable redistribution of the abundant wealth of our affluent economic order, the National Gross Product of which today is some seven hundred billion, five hundred million dollars, and in the Seventies will no doubt reach a trillion dollars. Thus, the Social Revolution requires a base for an effective powerful thrust toward economic and social objectives wider than the Civil Rights Revolution of black Americans can provide.

Since the Social Revolution envisions new and different goals from the conventional civil rights objectives, new tactics and strategies, or tools with which to build and advance social change, must be developed. This will be the task of the workers in the trade unions, the black and white unemployed, brutally exploited migrant farm laborers, and the enlightened and liberally oriented members of the religious faiths—Jews, Catholics and Protestants—and the intellectual, liberal and student forces, committed to a free, democratic society.

Apostles of Black Power (a more dramatic term for Black Nationalism or Black Garveyism) and White Power (another term for Nazism and apartheid), magnificent delusions of racial grandeur, are committed to a reversal of an irreversible world view and trend of science and technology toward integration and cooperation. It represents a futile hope for and belief in racial salvation through isolation and separation, a policy long advocated by segregationists in the United States and propagandists of apartheid in South Africa.

But this is not to suggest that Negroes should not work to develop power. They need to build political power through the ballot; economic power through labor unions and all forms of business enterprises, cooperatives and credit unions; and social power through community organizations. Practically all ethnic groups—Jews, Irish and Italians—and trade union workers have proceeded along this path. But the doctrine of black power or white power has overtones of racism which tends to propel the poor of ethnic groups into confrontation[s] of violent conflict instead of mutual cooperation for social progress.

But while I reject the implications of black power, its advocates must be free to be heard in a free society. The right to be wrong is as sacred as the right to be right. Any ideology or schism should be permitted to stand or fall in the free market of discussion. However, black or white racism, or anti-Semitism, is a menace to a free community and a free world, and it must be opposed.

While Negro youth can secure inspiration and motivation from the identification with the glorious ancient aboriginal African cultural endowment and heritage, the deification of a race tends to become antisocial and eventuates into racial extremism such as white supremacy, Nazism, anti-Semitism and black nationalism, which can become a danger to freedom, democracy, racial and social justice.

Fearful and disturbing adumbrations of a racist doctrine are already manifesting themselves in the increasing well-meaning, but misguided, demand of some Negroes in some communities for Boards of Education to surrender to them the right to determine curricula and select principals and teachers of public schools, on the grounds that Negro youth need the inspiration of Negro educational leadership. Though Negro youth can benefit from Negro symbols of educational progress, it is unwise and a distinct disservice to Negro youth for their parents to possess such power, since most of the Negro parents, like white parents, lack the professional education to equip them to evaluate, for instance, a prospective teacher of mathematics or physics, chemistry or languages. Some agitation has developed against white teachers, per se, in Negro communities, and even the ugly head of anti-Semitism has been raised. No teacher should be assigned to teach in any public school on a basis of race. While, no doubt, this has been done, such a policy must not be supported.

Relative to the Civil Rights Revolution and the Peace Movement, permit me to observe that I, too, am committed to the Peace Movement although I am not a pacifist. I opposed the First World War because of its hypocritical slogan of "making the world safe for democracy" while Negroes were being mobbed and lynched and denied the right to vote though they were fighting and dying overseas. However, I supported the Second World War because of Nazi racism and anti-Semitism. I also supported the Korean War, which was waged to arrest the expansion of communism. Of course I should like to see the United States stop the bombing of North Vietnam and avoid further escalation of the war, and effect a disengagement of its military force's involvement in Southeast Asia at the earliest possible date, which I feel certain President Johnson also wants and seeks to achieve. But I would not advocate the unilateral withdrawal of the United States Army, nor do I place all the blame for the continuance of the war on the United States, for there is no doubt about the repeated efforts of the President to take the war from the battlefield to the conference table.

I am not for or against the war in Vietnam, since taking sides would only serve to help plunge the Civil Rights Freedom Movement into the raging war–peace controversy. But this is not to suggest that Negro boys should refuse to answer the call of their country to serve along with white boys in this war. And, of course, I am unequivocally opposed to the burning of draft cards, and especially do I condemn burning the flag of our country. In relation to the civil rights and peace movements, I consider it tactically unsound for a civil rights leader, or a leader of the peace movement, to attempt to assume a position of leadership in both movements at the same time.

Either the civil rights Alabama-Mississippi front or the Vietnam War front will receive primary consideration. Up to this day, the Vietnam War has received national focus and has practically pushed the Civil Rights Revolution off the center of the stage of contemporary American history. The white liberals and students, while no doubt are still for civil rights, are marching for peace in Vietnam, not for civil rights in Alabama and Mississippi, where Negroes are still exposed to the propaganda fire power of the segregationists and civil rights workers are still victims of violence and murder.

Because of the crisis in the Civil Rights Revolution which has been deepened by the peace movement against the war in Vietnam, civil rights leaders need to come together oftener for consultation on tactics and strategy, and even goals. There is practically no consultation among civil rights leaders during this crisis. Since tactics and strategy are the tools with which movements are advanced, they must be developed and evaluated in response to existing social and racial realities, with relevance to time and locale, from time to time. I raise this question because probably the most costly of political casualties to the Civil Rights Revolution was the defeat of Senator Paul H. Douglas of Illinois, a liberal of towering moral and political strength in the Senate. Consultation by civil rights leaders on tactics and strategy, involving the marches in Chicago and Cicero during his campaign for his political life, might have saved this champion of racial and social justice.

Now, one of the most vital and significant Presidential elections ever held in the United States is coming in 1968. Civil rights leaders face an urgent call, implicit in the rapidly shifting political spectrum, to foregather in a closed conference for consultation on political trends toward the approaching Presidential election. Even without proclaiming collectively any choice of a candidate, they should ponder the future fortunes of the Civil Rights Revolution and the fate of the black and white working poor which will inevitably be involved in the question: which American shall direct the political destinies of our nation from the White House? If Negro Americans lose this election it may result in their losing not only the Civil Rights Freedom Movement, but they may be alienated from the center of federal power for a generation; a situation comparable to the collapse of the Reconstruction movement following the withdrawal of the federal army from the South by President Rutherford B. Hayes in 1877. Hence, the time is rapidly approaching when civil rights leaders will be expected to tell the Negro masses where they stand.

To the graduates and students, may God give you the courage, strength and faith to serve, with your knowledge and understanding, as a mighty fortress of moral commitment and dedication to the sacredness of the dignity of the human personality, democracy and freedom, racial, social justice and peace for all men everywhere, and may you never falter.

Let me close with a priceless gem from the great American poet, the lamented Langston Hughes:

Hold fast to dreams
For if dreams die
Life is a broken winged bird
That cannot fly.

SOURCE: Box 37, folder: Speeches, 1967, A. Philip Randolph Papers, Library of Congress.

4

Randolph's Views on Politics in the United States

A. Philip Randolph was a radical, but he was not a revolutionary. The purpose of his life's work was to reform and improve, not overthrow, existing structures. He had great faith in America's public and private institutions and thought that they had the capacity to become ever more democratic. Time and again, the documents in this chapter illustrate his relentless efforts to reshape and reform existing social, political, and economic structures. They also point to another aspect of Randolph's character: he was intensely political. Despite this, although some wanted him to run for office, being a politician never held much appeal for him. This is well illustrated by an episode that took place in the 1940s, when Randolph refused to run for office in a race that was ultimately won by another iconic New Yorker, Adam Clayton Powell Jr. As Randolph saw it, the best way he could serve the struggle was not as a politico who crafted legislation.

The first document in his chapter suggests that Randolph's interest in politics came naturally. In this unpublished piece, "My Father's Politics," he draws a direct line tracing his own positions back to those of his father. Both men dedicated their lives to creating better opportunities for African Americans and to widening democracy. A major difference between father and son were their party allegiances. Asa's father was a member of the Republican Party, the political home of most African Americans in the late nineteenth century. Unlike his father, who inherited the "party of Lincoln" and grew to realize that it never "lived up to its mission," A. Philip Randolph struggled to find any political party compatible with his ideas. Early on he was a Socialist, but he distanced himself from this affiliation in the 1930s. Although he was ambivalent about aligning himself with any political party, he endorsed the Socialist candidate, Norman Thomas, in 1948. In the 1960s, however, Randolph fell in line behind Lyndon B. Johnson and became an ardent Democrat. To him, the alternative, Barry Goldwater, was a nightmare that had to be stopped.

Randolph's quest to establish a third major political party in the United States was connected to his desire to pressure American politicians to implement policies that benefited those on the bottom rungs of their society. Behind this tactic was a belief that an outside force could make the existing parties more liberal, if not more progressive. His most succinct statement on these topics came immediately after the Second World War. This call for a new party, published in the *Antioch Review,* came at a time when a vibrant and meaningful third party seemed possible. Randolph's ideas on politics evolved through the many years he was involved in public life, and the documents contained in this chapter trace aspects of his political thought.

FOR FURTHER READING

Ali, Omar H. *In the Balance of Power: Independent Black Politics and Third-Party Movements in the United States.* Columbus: Ohio State University Press, 2008.

Arnesen, Eric. "A. Philip Randolph: Labor and the New Black Politics," in *The Human Tradition in American Labor History,* edited by Eric Arnesen, 173–91. Wilmington, Del.: Scholarly Resources, 2003.

Foner, Eric. *Reconstruction: America's Unfinished Revolution.* New York: Harper and Row, 1988.

Lawson, Steven F. *Running for Freedom: Civil Rights and Black Politics in America since 1941,* 3rd ed. Malden, Mass.: Wiley-Blackwell, 2009.

Mann, Robert. *The Walls of Jericho: Lyndon Johnson, Hubert Humphrey, and Richard Russell and the Struggle for Civil Rights.* New York: Harcourt, 1996.

Ogbar, Jeffrey O. G. *Black Power: Radical Politics and African American Identity.* Baltimore: Johns Hopkins University Press, 2005.

Smith, John David, and J. Vincent Lowery, eds. *The Dunning School: Historians, Race, and the Meaning of Reconstruction.* Lexington: University of Kentucky Press, 2013.

Solomon, Mark. *The Cry Was Unity: Communists and African Americans, 1917–36.* Jackson: University Press of Mississippi, 1998.

Swanberg, W. A. *Norman Thomas: The Last Idealist.* New York: Scribner, 1976.

Unger, Nancy C. *Fighting Bob La Follette: The Righteous Reformer.* Chapel Hill: University of North Carolina Press, 2000.

My Father's Politics (n.d.)

Although a Socialist as a young man, Randolph eventually became a strong supporter of the Democratic Party. That said, throughout his life he believed that a third party was what was needed to pressure both mainline parties not to take the black vote for granted. Although he appreciated the historical support for racial equality demonstrated by the Republican Party in the past, he also understood that his father's politics had been formed at a time when the GOP stood firmly behind black political participation.

My father was strongly committed to the Republican Party. The first political meeting I attended in Jacksonville, I was carried there by him. It was one of the most interesting and unique assemblages I ever witnessed. It was an open-air meeting and was held at the intersection of two of the main streets of the city. A black man sat in the middle of the platform and served as the chairman of the meeting although every other person on the platform was white. This Negro leader was the Rev. Joseph E. Lee. He was also a distinguished minister in the African Methodist Episcopal Church and as a pastor of the Mount Olive Church in Jacksonville, which my mother, my brother and myself attended. He opened this meeting with a statement on the importance of developing the political strength of the Republican Party in Florida. At this time, the Republican Party was a significant factor in the South although it was not in power. The white politicians on the platform were Republicans who were looking to build up political fences for patronage, in the form of important federal offices. They supported Joseph E. Lee.

At this period in the history of the South, the winds of racism were blowing hard against Negro progress. The Ku Klux Klan, organized in 1867, was rampant and sought to drive and keep Negroes out of public office. Joseph E. Lee, in addition to being a minister of the church, was a prominent lawyer with an office in the federal post office building. Father took James and myself there to meet him in his office because he wanted us to see a Negro in command of an important federal post. I recall that he had a white secretary, and we asked Father how could he retain a white woman as secretary in a southern city like Jacksonville. Father said that the politicians and business leaders of Jacksonville and Florida knew that Mr. Lee was a federal appointee and they were not disposed to challenge his position. He was probably one of the last of the Negro politicians to hold a federal post in the South.

Following the Civil War, the ravages of the Ku Klux Klan sought to sweep Negro political office holders into political oblivion. Thousands of Negroes were lynched, and some burned alive, as a method of intimidation of the so-called "smart" Negro politicians. The conditions became so unspeakably bad that the Congress, with Charles Sumner of Massachusetts in the Senate and Thaddeus Stevens of Pennsylvania in the House, demanded that there be federal examination of the plight of the Negroes in the South. This was done. Even General Grant made a trip, together with other prominent Republican leaders, through the South to determine what could be done to protect the black freedmen from persecution by their former slavemasters who were backing the depredations of the Klan. Of course this was a natural outcome of a condition where the old slaveocracy, having been stripped of their political ascendancy and economic power as a result of the Civil War, were bent upon two things: regaining control of black labor and winning back their place in the Congress. For two generations the old slave Bourbons had dominated the Congress. During that period they benefited from the fact that while the slaves didn't vote, they were counted. A slave was considered to be three-fifths of a man.

But with the progress of the country, slavery became an uneconomic system. It became obvious that the reign of the system of slavery was reaching its end. The industrial and financial interests of the country became fully aware of the fact that the growth of capitalism involved the eventual supremacy of the bourgeoisie. There could be no basic progress in America under the banner of the old slave-ruling class which represented social and economic decadence. Negroes were able to sense this important change in the life of a nation; they could see that their future destiny was bound up with a growing capitalist class and labor union movement in the nation. In fact, America was witnessing a type of bourgeois revolution comparable to the bourgeois revolutions of the latter part of the eighteenth, and beginning of the nineteenth centuries in Europe.

The institution of slavery was a stopgap upon the economic progress of the nation. Moreover, it was an instrument of suppression and repression of the working class, both slave and free workers. There were three major forces that resisted this trend: expansion of the power of capital, the growth of a working class, and the resistance of slaves. The progress of this social and economic change was inevitable. It was a sparkplug of the Civil War.

Thus, the Civil War was not merely for the emancipation of the slave. It was a great, powerful social force for the emancipation of capital and labor from the incubus of the system of slavery. Thus, the victory of the Civil War was inevitable. Although the labor movement was an infant institution at that time, the workers became conscious of the fact that their hope[s] and future were dismal were they forced into competition with slaves for their economic life. They, therefore, as a class, joined hands with the bourgeoisie, not only to halt the progress of slavery but to destroy the system. It was evident that there was no future for either the black or white proletariat where one man was owned by another and whose labor was not his own. Despite that fact, there were riots in New York among some sections of the working class against being conscripted to fight in the Civil War. Of course, they were not conscious of the nature of the forces at work in this great social drama. But the great masses of the laboring classes together with ex-slaves constituted the army of the Union forces. Nor did the leaders of industry and finance take their stand against slavery out of any ethical compunction. They knew that slavery did not only split the nation in half, but excluded a vast area of the American market from the consumption of commodities produced by the growing industrial system.

Negro slaves who were accounted as being ignorant and unaware of the reasons for their plight were not only wide awake, but united with the Union forces when the armies were marching through the South. Around 200,000 fought for the victory of the Civil War. Frederick Douglass, Wendell Phillips, and a host of liberals waged an unforgettable crusade throughout the nation to awaken the people to the menace of a possible victory for the South.

When the old Confederate states were readmitted to the Union, the forces of southern slaveocracy sought to break the spirit of the former slaves through raging violence at the polls and the Black Codes. Even after the 13th Amendment was enacted for the abolition of slavery in 1863, Negroes, who had a right to participate in the election of representatives to state legislatures and to the Congress, were the victims of unspeakable repression and oppression. However, dauntless and unafraid, and with an iron will to assert their new citizenship, black freedmen challenged this wave of terror and voted in the elections. Throughout the nation, the forces of the abolitionist movement, under the leadership of the dauntless William Lloyd Garrison and the intrepid Frederick Douglass, denounced not only the assault of the old Bourbon forces of the South against the freedmen, but also exposed the weakened and indefinite position of the leaders of the federal government in not waging effective opposition to this anti-freedmen movement.

When the dark clouds of racism were lifted as a result of the defiance of the emancipated slaves, Negroes stood for election themselves to the new state legislatures of the South and to the Congress. The record shows that all of the state legislatures in the South had Negro representatives. In South Carolina, Negroes constituted a majority of the members of the legislature. One prominent Negro political leader became the Secretary of State of Mississippi and another Negro became Lieutenant Governor and, for a brief period, a Negro served as Governor of the State of Louisiana. In Louisiana, this Negro leader was [P. B. S.] Pinchback. Two senators sat in the Senate of the federal government and a fair number of Negro freedmen were elected to the Congress. Practically all of them were Republicans.

With the terrorism of the Ku Klux Klan, the Black Codes, and the growing indifference of the so-called "Republican friends of the Negro," this era of Negro participation in the political life of the state legislatures of the South came to an end. But the record of the Negro political leaders in this Reconstruction era constitutes an inspiration to black people in America and all the peoples of color of the world. They reflected courage, intelligence and integrity comparable to that of white legislators. The period is not distinguished for any great number of shining leaders of light. But when it is considered that these black men of politics who had just emerged from slavery wrote some of the most liberal and progressive legislation for public education of the youth of the country, they ought to be honored. Black legislators were responsible for the creation of free public schools in the South.

My father was cognizant with this history, both because he was a part of it, though not a leader, and because he had the soul of a fighting revolutionist. He told James and myself that Rev. Joseph E. Lee could not [have] serve[d] as a chairman of a political meeting, as he did in Jacksonville, had it not been for the fact that Negroes fought, bled and died for the right to vote and to be voted for. At that time, a Negro Democrat was unheard of. It would have been difficult for one to survive in a Negro community because Democrats were associated with the South and oppression of the Negro.

While my father didn't believe that the Republican Party had lived up to its mission or reflected the courage to stand up for the former slaves, it was politically the ship, and all else the sea, for the Negro freedmen. He knew that it was not tactically and strategically sound for Negroes to put all of their political apples in one basket. He was not aware of the fact that the social forces of that period created the Republican Party and the Democratic Party and arrayed one against the other. This was so because they reflected opposing economic philosophies. But since all of the leaders of both parties were white, it was the belief of our father that it was not difficult for them to get together against black Americans.

I recall that he religiously voted in the federal elections, that is, for the president of the United States. Few Negroes presented themselves for the ballot in the state and municipal elections until this dreadful era of political, economic and social white supremacy and persecution was partially ended.

SOURCE: Box 37, folder: Speeches, Undated, A. Philip Randolph Papers, Library of Congress.

The Negro in Politics (1919)

Randolph's overview of the relationship between America's two major political parties and African Americans reveals, at best, an unhealthy one. As Randolph saw it, the Democratic Party explicitly supported racial oppression and sought to repress black voters. Little better, the Republican Party took African American voters for granted and offered them little substantive legislation in return. This left African American voters with few visible focuses for their political energies. Recognizing the inadequacy of these two options, Randolph saw the Socialist Party as a legitimate means to advance the black working class. The time for "my father's politics" (see previous document) had clearly passed.

Also of interest in this document is how strongly Dunning School historiography influenced Randolph's view of African American politicians during Reconstruction. This perspective was not seriously challenged until the publication of W. E. B. Du Bois's *Black Reconstruction* (1935).

The Negro has had a pathetic and unpromising history in American politics. His eventful and hapless career began under the shadow of the institution of slavery, from which he had just emerged. He was played upon by two forces, viz., the open opposition from his former masters, on the one hand, and the fraud and deception of the white carpetbaggers who swarmed South like vultures to prey upon his ignorance and credulity.

We have but to take a glimpse into the history of the Reconstruction period to witness his tragical fight wrought by a paradoxical combination of his Northern Republican friends and his Southern Democratic enemies. During this period the Negro was a political football between his former slave masters and Northern political adventurers. The economic basis of this contest was the power to tax, to float bonds, to award franchises, [and] in short, to gain control over the financial resources of the newly organized states. These were big stakes for which to contend. Hence, the carpetbaggers used the enfranchised Negro to assist them in securing control over the Southern state governments, and the Southern politicians fought the Negro viciously to prevent this Carpetbagger-Negro political ascendency.

This period of storm and stress gave birth to two significant social organizations, the Union of Loyal League of Negroes and the Ku Klux Klan, which attempted to protect the political interests of the Negroes and Southern whites, respectively. They only served, however, to engender bitterness, to breed and to foster suspicion and hate between the races, which resulted in lawlessness, crime and general social anarchy. These, too, were natural, political and social consequences of the Reconstruction policy. The inordinate lust for power, overwhelming ambition to rule, the instinct to secure an advantage, impel individuals and social groups to adopt the policy of force, the policy of fraud, or the method of education: whichever policy is available, and is recognized as likely to secure the more permanent results.

Such were the political vicissitudes of the Negro in the South. The Ku Klux Klan and the tissue ballot were social and political inventions of intimidation to discourage the Negroes' participation in politics. The Thirteenth, Fourteenth and Fifteenth Amendments to the federal Constitution, the federal army and the Carpetbaggers were designed to protect the Negroes' suffrage in order that the Negro might entrench, reinforce and fortify the Republican Party's control over Congress. The lessons of this period had been hard, bitter, and disappointing to the Negro. The army, the arm of protection of the federal government, had been withdrawn. The Negro office holders and their Republican supporters had been hurled from power. The Reconstruction legislation had been emasculated from the statute books. The Southern states had begun a systematic and organized campaign of nullification of the freedom and enfranchisement of the Negro. In fact, the Negro had been reduced to serfdom. [By] 1876, the last vestige of Reconstruction governments had disappeared, and it cannot be maintained by the sober and dispassionate historian that the Negro had legislated and administered the state governments wisely and well. As he had ignorantly fought with and tilled the fields for his former masters to maintain slavery, he had also voted to strengthen his Republican political masters to dominate the government, only to be forsaken, neglected, naked to his enemies. No Negro with a genius for leadership had arisen in this period. So much for our Reconstruction history.

What has been the subsequent political course of the Negro? The complete scheme of the Negroes' disfranchisement was in [the] process of development in the South. The South had resented and ignored the fourteenth amendment, which had demanded a reduction in representation in Congress if the Negroes' suffrage was restricted. Intermittent cries against this political brigandage were heard but finally subsided. The South continued to weave a fabric of law, the grandfather clauses, which gave legal sanction to an already general custom of Negro disfranchisement. The Republican Party, pretended friend and defender, had assented. Yet the Negro remained a Republican. Why? First, the Reconstruction legislation of the Republican Party had forged the "Solid South." The Solid South was dominated by the Democratic Party. The Democratic Party had striven to maintain slavery. It had been the father of the fugitive slave law, the nullification of the Missouri Compromise of 1820, and Chief Justice Taney had handed down the famous *Dred Scott* decision, which gave constitutional sanction to the extension of slavery into new territory.

On the other hand, the Republican Party [that] had been the party of the North, the refuge of the fugitive slave, the home of the abolitionists, Wendell Philips, [William Lloyd] Garrison, [Elijah] Lovejoy and [Charles] Sumner, was in power when freedom came. It had used the Negro as an office holder and continued to distribute political crumbs in the form of collectors of internal revenue, deputy collectors, registrars of the treasury, ministers to Haiti, Liberia and such places that required no legislative ability, no intelligent understanding of the methods, objects and principles of government. In truth, the Negro office holders were mainly of the "rubber stamp" variety. But it was sufficient that the Republican Party had awarded jobs to secure the undiscriminating and unquestioning devotion of the Negro. Thus, the Negro became as staunch a Republican as the Irish[man] a Democrat. It was considered race treason for a Negro to profess any other political faith. Here and there an eccentric Negro had claimed to be a Democrat, but his claim was considered lightly. It is true that in New York City a tiny fraction of Negroes had bolted the Republican ranks and joined Tammany Hall, seeking political jobs.

There had also arisen among the Negroes a political schism, namely a belief in the virtue of dividing the vote. In support of this political heresy, it was maintained that by dividing the vote the Negro would be able to secure the good will of both parties: it was further maintained that it would create fear in the Republican Party, which would result in its giving the Negro a fairer consideration, and that the Negro would be sure of political preferment, regardless of which party was in power. And in 1912 and 1916 a few Negro leaders had professed sympathy for Woodrow Wilson as the Democratic presidential nominee.

The formation of the Progressive Party of 1912 had marked another important rift in the Negro Republican voters. The love for Roosevelt, the expectation of jobs and the general dissatisfaction with President Taft's attitude towards Negro job holders in the South, had produced this alienation. In the mayoralty election of New York City in 1917 occurred another change in the Negroes' political course. This change resulted in 25 percent of the Negroes voting the Socialist ticket. This vote, too, it might be observed, was achieved despite the fact that heretofore there had been no Socialist vote among Negroes of New York State.

These movements have had their leaders. Who were they and what did they stand for? During the Reconstruction period the Negro leaders were unschooled, credulous, gullible. They had been led by the Republican agents from the North, the carpetbaggers. Ex-Governor [P. B. S.] Pinchback, [John R.] Lynch, [Franklin] Moses, etcetera, had been accomplices of the most shameless raids upon the funds of the states' destructive legislation and issuance of spurious, inflamed paper. In Congress [George H.] White and [Blanche K.] Bruce had done one thing, they had been loyal to the Republican Party. During the long years from the passing of Negro representatives in Congress, no Negro of large vision and intelligent grasp of the forces in politics had arisen.

Booker T. Washington had become prominent in the industrial development of the Negro but had counseled the "let-alone policy." Bishop Walters, W. E. B. Du Bois, James Monroe Trotter and Rev. James Milton Waldron—Negroes of national standing and prominence—had turned Democratic. Their object was to make the Republican Party repentant. These men had a vision of the rise of a radical Negro; they had recognized the failure of the Republican Party; [but] they had not caught the message of Socialism and they were still ruled by the belief that the test of the political progress of the Negroes was the number of jobs he held. They had not realized that out of 12,000,000 Negroes but a tiny fraction could become job holders. The value of workmen's compensation legislation, widow's pensions, social insurance legislation, measures reducing the cost of living, shortening hours of toil and increasing the wages of the masses, had escaped them.

In the Republican Party, Charles W. Anderson, Ralph Tyler, W. T. Vernon and W. H. Lewis are figures of national proportions. These are men of the old school who make much over what they style as "playing the game of politics," which in other words simply means getting next to "campaign slush funds" and landing a rubber stamp job. Their positions rest upon their ability to echo the will of the masters through flamboyant oratory and their unquestioning obedience to the Republican machine. Even the generous student of politics cannot accord to them any fundamental understanding of the relation between politics and the business of getting a living, the social purpose and economic basis of modern legislation and the scientific methods of administrative government. They, with the ward-heeler-politician, identify their personal prosperity with that of the race and insist that their holding of a government job is an unmistakable sign of the Negroes' political progress.

Negro leaders, generally, have been creatures of the Republican or Democratic parties, which hold them in leash and prevent them from initiating anything fundamental in the interest of the Negroes. This brings us to the consideration of the appointment policy. Aptly, and truly too, has it been said that the "power over a man's subsistence is the power over his will" or expressed more popularly "he who pays the fiddler will call the tune."

Since Negro leaders have been the appointees of the Republican and Democratic bosses it is but natural that they would obey the voice of their masters. And the Republican and Democratic bosses are servants of the employing or capitalist class which thrives upon low wages and high prices, the ignorance and degradation of the workers of which 12 percent are Negroes. This principle, however, of appointing members of the servant class to positions in the government or to places of race leadership, has been uniformly adopted by the ruling class in all parts of the world. The social experience is that a member of an oppressed class, invested with power by the master-class, becomes the brutal oppressor and exploiter of his class. Note the vicious class of foremen [and] headwaiters, who are recruited from the working class. Great Britain employs 250,000 natives of India to hold in subjection 300,000,000. She has also applied this same rule in Ireland and successfully exploited these people for 800 years. Hence, it is apparent that the Negro leaders, the hirelings of the Republican and Democratic bosses, who are in turn the agents of anti-labor forces, are the worst enemies of the race.

The movement is conceived in the idea that those whom the people elect will represent them. But, in the light of the history of government, it cannot logically be maintained that all persons elected by the people will represent the people. For instance, during the Reconstruction period the Negro office-holders and legislators represented the carpetbaggers and not the people. Today, all legislators are elected by the people but [it is] the people [who] suffer most from poverty and ignorance, hence it cannot be maintained that the present government represents the people, if by representation we mean the enactment of legislation for the relief of human suffering and the improvement of social conditions. The people elect, but the capitalists select.

There are three main conditions to a representative's representing those by whom he is elected. First, his chief interests must be identical with those by whom he is elected; second, he must be the member of a party organization which is controlled by his constituents; and third, he must be sufficiently intelligent to understand his class interests. To illustrate: if a real estate owner is elected to the legislature from a district composed largely of working people, his tenants, his chief interests would lie with the members of his class—the real estate owners—and in opposition to those who elected him—the tenant class. If a measure was raised to abolish the "law of dispossess," who would wonder as to how the real estate owners would vote, despite the fact the measure would be palpably in the interests of those whom he was presumed to represent. Again, suppose the representative's chief interests are identical with those of his constituents and is also the member of a political organization which is controlled by forces which are opposed to the chief interests of his district. Is it not plain as to how he would vote? The history of politics is clear on this point. The lack of regularity would result in his political death. Note the fate of ex-Governor [William] Sulzer of New York, who opposed the Tammany machine which created him. Note the Roosevelt's plight who bolted the Republican machine in 1912. Lastly, given that the two foregoing conditions are satisfied, if the representative was not sufficiently intelligent he might be used as the most effective opponent of his own and his constituents' interests.

Thus, it is apparent that the election of a Negro by Negroes is not enough and does not guarantee Negroes, of whom 99 per cent are working people, that their chief interests as working people will be represented. Just as the election of a woman by women does not guarantee that their chief interests will be represented. Witness Jeannette Rankin, woman representative from Montana, lining up with the Republican and Democratic parties in unquestioning support of the capitalists, despite the fact women and their children are the chief sufferers from long hours and low wages in factories and mines. Witness the election of the Negro Assemblyman, E. A. Johnson, from the 21st Assembly District of New York City, introducing a bill to permit children of the tender age of 12 when they are out of school to be exploited at work. Note, too, that he cites as his main reason for his bill the recent exodus of Negroes from the South and the likelihood of idle Negro children getting into mischief in the streets of New York. This bill was condemned by the educators and union leaders, on the ground that children are in need of play and recreation as much as they are in need of book learning. Work stunts the bodies and arrests the mental growth of children.

Here, two facts are evident: first, that the Assemblyman was ignorant of the fundamental recreational and educational needs of children; second, that he is part of the Republican machine, which represents the factories' and canneries' interests which makes millions out of child labor. Here then is the clear case of a Negro being the father of a measure from which Negro children will be the chief sufferers, being as they are in more need of education and wholesome recreation. However, I might observe that I am simply predicting of the Negro representatives what is true of all white representatives of the capitalists parties, Republican and Democratic.

Will the entrance of Negro women into politics change the general tenor of things? My answer is no. The history of women in public affairs, black and white, warrants me in taking this position. Their traditions, education and environment, are similar to those of the men and they may be expected to follow the same course of political thinking. They will also be influenced by their male companions. However, I might observe here that Negro women especially may profit from the political blunders of Negro men. It is admitted by both white and black that the Negro men have made a mess of politics. It is further admitted that during his entire political career he has been nothing else but a Republican, so that the logical deduction is that . . . Negro women [will] make a similar mess of politics.

The political radicalism of the Negro has been marked by three definite movements: first, the entrance of the Negro into the Democratic Party; second, the transition to the elective idea of representation; third, and the most fundamental and significant of all, is the change from the old parties to Socialism. The last of these changes has been the result of the rise of a new type of leaders. The old Negro leaders have had the intent to serve the interests of the Negroes, but they have lacked the knowledge as to how they could best serve them. It is recognized today that the possession of an intent to do good without knowledge is more fatal than the possession of knowledge without the intent. To illustrate: history attests that during the early Christian era, Marcus Aurelius was the most savage persecutor of the Christians, yet he was one of the [most] upright of men and it is maintained that he persecuted them on the ground that he was saving them from the consequences of their folly. His intent was to do good. Even Protestant historians accord to those who maintained the Spanish Inquisition honest intentions while they murdered, massacred and outraged the heretics of their day. The suppression of free speech, the freedom of the press and the lynching of Negroes and I.W.W. are based upon the intent to serve the country's interests. The system which produces these conditions determines the social consequences of the policies, adopted by both good and bad men. Thus, it is apparent that an individual's power to do social and personal mischief is in proportion to the intensity of his belief in the rightness of his act and the absence of knowledge as to its social consequences. An ignorant man may [mis]take bi-chloride of mercury for quinine; the result is death, though his intent and desire was to live.

Thus it is obvious that the hope of the Negro lies first in the development of Negro leaders with the knowledge of the science of government and economics, scientific history and sociology; and second, in the relegation to the political scrap heap of those Negro leaders whose only qualifications are the desire to lead and the intent to do good. The old Negro leaders have been factors in producing and perpetuating a patent contradiction in American politics: the alliance of a race of poverty, the Negro, with a party of wealth, the Republican Party. The Republican Party has been the instrumentality in American politics of abolishing [the] agricultural feudalism of the South for the establishment of industrial capitalism of the North. Industrial slavery has been substituted for human slavery.

But how is the Negro to know which party to support? Before answering this question may I observe that a party is a body of individuals who agree upon a political program and who strive to gain control of the government in order to secure its adoption. Its campaigns are made possible by a fund created by those persons who desire the adoption of its program. It is natural and plain, then, that those who supply the funds will control and direct the party. . . .

But since neither [of] the Republican and Democratic parties represent[s] the Negroes' interests, the question logically arises as to which party in American politics does? I maintain that since the Socialist Party is supported financially by working men and working women, and since its platform is a demand for the abolition of this class struggle between the employer and the worker, by taking over and democratically managing the sources and machinery of wealth production and exchange to be operated for social service and not for private profits; and further, since the Socialist Party has always both in the United States and Europe opposed all forms of race prejudice, that the Negro should no longer look upon voting the Republican ticket as accepting the lesser of two evils, but that it is politically, economically, historically and socially logical and sound for him to reject both evils, the Republican and Democratic parties, and select a positive good—Socialism.

The Negro, like any other class, should support that party which represents his chief interests. Who could imagine a brewer or saloonkeeper supporting the Prohibition party? It is like an undertaker seeking the adoption of a law, if possible, to abolish death. Such is not less ludicrous, however, than that of a Negro living in virtual poverty, children without education, wife driven to the kitchen or wash-tub, continually dispossessed on account of high rents, eating poor food on account of [the] high cost of food, working 10, 12, and 14 hours a day, and sometimes compelled to become sycophant[ic] and clownish for a favor—a "tip"—supporting the party of Rockefeller, the party of his employer, whose chief interests are to overwork and underpay him. Let us abolish these contradictions and support our logical party—the Socialist Party.

SOURCE: *The Messenger* 2 (July 1919): 16–21.

The Issues—The Negro and the Parties (1924)

African American voters became increasingly important in electoral politics during the 1920s. They gained suffrage through the Great Migration by fleeing the South's repressive Jim Crow and used their newly accorded voting rights to influence all levels of government. Randolph reached out to this newly enfranchised group, arguing that Republicans and Democrats had poor records on important civil rights issues. Only the Progressives, he said, seemed to offer a difference. This third party fared well in the 1924 presidential election. Republican candidate Calvin Coolidge won in a landslide against the Democratic challenger, John Davis, while Robert La Follette, the Progressive candidate, took home 17 percent of the popular vote.

Issues are those questions, controversial in character, which arise in the life of a community and vitally affect its future. They vary in degree of interest. They come and go. In each campaign each party stresses certain particular issues. An attempt always is made to hit upon a question which has an emotional appeal, regardless of its relation to the well-being of the people. Thus, each oppressed minority must be careful to see whether or not the so-called issues trumped up by scheming political demagogues are really vital to their lives. Especially should Negroes be ever vigilant on the matter of issues, for having themselves an unpopular cause no party will willingly champion it. For with the Negro and labor, an attempt is always made to make it appear that the issues that affect their interests are not interests at all. Gradually all national American political parties are abandoning the Negro problem because of its unpopularity with the masses of the American people. Less and less will the problem of the Negro be an issue in political campaigns.

Why? Because the chief source of this problem, the South, bitterly objects, and all political parties, Radical, Liberal, Socialist, Labor and Conservative, hope to break the "Solid South." And in the not distant future, the "Solid South" will break. It will break because of economic changes that will reflect themselves in the politics of the South. Already it is obvious to the casual observer that the South is gradually, and in some parts, rapidly becoming industrialized. Urbanization proceeds apace. Seaports are fast developing. New cities are growing up. Old cities are growing larger. It is all the result of the penetration of industrial and financial capital into the South. . . .

It is but recent political history that the Democrats, under the Wilson administration, put a tariff of one cent a pound on rice, a Southern product. The Republicans, under this administration, raised the tariff to two cents a pound. The Democrats under the Wilson administration put a tariff of three-quarters of a cent a pound on peanuts. The Republicans, under this administration, raised the tariff to four cents a pound. When President Harding came to appoint a Democrat on the Tariff Commission, he appointed Mr. [Henry] Glassie on the recommendation of the political representatives of the protected cane sugar industry of Louisiana. The South produces immense quantities of vegetable oils. The Republicans, under this administration, gave a solid protection to vegetable oils.

What does it prove? It proves that the protectionist sentiment is on the upgrade in the South and that the Republican Party, with a view to breaking the Solid South, is nourishing it. Nor is this new policy of the Republican Party toward the South alone the product of the desire of a few skillful Republican politicians to secure additional power. Not at all. The Republican Party is obeying the mandate of its Northern industrial and financial masters who are steadily investing extensive capital in the South. Note the huge automobile plants which Henry Ford has already begun in Jacksonville, Florida.

Only recently in the early summer, the Southern cotton manufacturers joined the Northern mill owners in a demand for a high protection on cotton goods. In volume of cotton manufacture, North Carolina is now second only to Massachusetts, South Carolina is third, and Georgia is fifth. These three States, together with Alabama, Virginia and Tennessee, turned out in 1921 over 41 per cent of the total value of cotton goods produced in the United States. They are expanding much more rapidly than the North, and operations are extending into Oklahoma, Texas and other cotton growing States. This sets up two opposing currents: an alliance of the propertied interests of the South with Northern capital and an alliance of Southern mill, mine and factory labor, which is chiefly white and therefore can vote with the Northern and Western labor organizations and forces of social reform.

Under such vital industrial changes, the South cannot remain united politically. Besides, the cotton industry is not the only field of such realignment. Alabama and West Virginia have extensive coal mines. These two states produced in 1921 over $35,000,000 worth of steel, or nearly 8.5 percent of the nation's total. West Virginia is the second State in the manufacture of glass. Missouri is the third in the making of explosives. It also produces shoes. In the manufacture of turpentine and resin, the South leads; in fertilizing, Georgia is second; Virginia is third; North Carolina and South Carolina are sixth; chemicals are also made. Oil refineries in Texas and cane sugar refineries in Louisiana employ many workers. And [commercial fishing] shoals promise a further and effective enhancement of the importance of the industrialization of the South.

Such is the economic basis for the Republican Party's bid for Southern support. The La Follette Progressives are also bent upon cutting into the Solid South. They are appealing to this new industrial proletariat which is the product of the mills, mines and factories; and also to the farmers. They are also cognizant of the fact that the National Farmers' and Industrial Union, the basis of the Populist Party, which was a revolt against the Democratic and Republican Parties' subservience to the Wall Street Bankers, had its rise in Texas. In 1892 the Populist candidate for President, General James B. Weaver, polled a million votes. Hence, the Progressives hope to profit from the impending economic cleavage which will reflect itself politically below the Mason and Dixon Line. . . .

The most chronic and disastrous of our economic maladjustments is unemployment. It is a product of our capitalist plan-less method of production and distribution, upheld by both old parties. Much of the acute social suffering among the workers could be eliminated were the government to initiate the construction of large and extensive public works during periods of widespread unemployment. This would absorb the over-supply of labor. But Republican and Democratic politicians, the servants of the big employers of labor, dare not attempt to do anything to eliminate unemployment. For the trusts can more effectively beat down wages when there is a large army of unemployed who may take the jobs of the employed. The [Robert] La Follette Progressives are committed to a plan of social legislation which is calculated to meet the problems of unemployment. Negroes will benefit from any policy which will bring a solution of unemployment, for they are the first fired and the last hired. Until we reach a more rational organization of society, the most effective methods of decreasing unemployment are a short workday, the government construction of public works in periods of industrial depression and the extension of seasonal work such as the building industry over the entire year. The Progressives recognize and approve these methods.

Without the railroads American society would wither and die. Were they to stop for a day, our industrial system [and] our social life would become paralyzed. Thus, their social importance. Still, they are in the hands of a small group of capitalists who run them not for the public good but for private gain. The Progressives are opposed to this. The Democrats and Republicans uphold it. The railroad owners are demanding that the Inter-state Commerce Commission over-value the railroads; to set it at $30,000,000,000, about ten billions too much. What does this mean? It means that the railroads will thereby be permitted to increase their freight rates and passenger rates to a frightful point in order to realize their legal rate of return on their capital. This means an intolerable increase in the cost of living, which of course will injure Negroes most because their income is the lowest. The nationalization of the railroads will insure also a larger measure of protection to the Negro workers on them. It is quite unlikely that any Negro postal employees would advocate turning over the post office into private hands to be run for profit.

No other group of people in any country is more important and necessary to the welfare of a country than the farmers. But under our present system the middlemen, such as the bankers, the mill and elevator owners, keep the farmers bankrupt and upon the threshold of starvation. It is estimated that out of every dollar spent by the consumers for the products of the farmers that they (the farmers) receive only 25 cents. The Progressives would abolish the parasitic middlemen and establish cooperatives to market the farmers' products, which will both insure a legitimate profit to the farmers and also reduce the cost of living for the worker-consumer. The disastrous policies of the Republican and Democratic parties were the cause of the bankruptcy of over 600,000 farmers in 1920, and the failure of over 2,000 banks holding farmers' notes.

Nearly 50 percent of the working-class Negroes' income goes to rent. Some Negroes pay more in rent than they receive in wages. High rent is due to the scarcity of houses and the high cost of building materials. The remedy for the excessive cost of building materials, due to price fixing by the building materials monopolies, is more effective government regulation and control of monopolies, together with the building of homes for the people by the government. The Progressives favor this plan. The Democrats and Republicans oppose it. Enough said for Negroes.

For every worker and consumer, taxation is a serious issue. For ultimately the burden of taxation falls upon the consumer. What is the remedy? The answer is the abolition of the indirect tax, and the increase of a progressive income tax, of the inheritance tax, of the excess profits tax, etcetera. This will shift the incidence of taxation from the shoulders of the poor to the shoulders of the rich, its proper place. Only the Progressives favor this policy. Its benefits to Negroes [are] obvious.

A word as to the political issues. Some Negroes maintain that the Supreme Court is the chief bulwark of their liberties. Strange reasoning this when it is remembered that the Dred Scott decision of the Supreme Court declared that "a Negro has no rights which a white man is bound to respect" [and] that the Supreme Court also declared the Sumner Civil Rights Bill unconstitutional. On social legislation, which is of as much benefit to Negroes as whites, the Supreme Court is backward and reactionary. Note that it declared the Federal Child Labor Law, the Income Tax and Minimum Wage laws unconstitutional. The Progressives would limit this power, the Democrats and Republicans would preserve it. As to the Constitution. Some political demagogues would make it appear that to change the Constitution is a sin. But the Constitution is not sacred. Read it and one will find that it sanctioned and protected chattel slavery until 1808. Besides, Republicans and Democrats don't object to the nullification of the 14th Amendment to the Constitution, that is, as it applies to the Negro. . . .

The Progressives oppose war. They would abolish it by taking the profits out of war; internationalizing the sea routes, the economic sources of national rivalry, the democratic cooperation of nations and the institution of open diplomacy; the abolition of great armies and navies; and the holding of a referendum on war. Only bankers and munitions makers profit from war. The people suffer.

Such are the issues before the American people in general and the Negro in particular.

What will YOU do?

SOURCE: *The Messenger* 6 (November 1924): 345–47.

Testimony before House Committee to Investigate Communist Activities in the United States (1930)

In 1930, Randolph testified before the House Committee to Investigate Communist Activities in the United States. In his testimony he complained about the Communist threat to the Brotherhood of Sleeping Car Porters and complied with the interrogation, but he did not give the committee much more information than they already knew. Taking this anti-Communist position put the BSCP and its leader within the mainstream of American political thought, and as such, gave the fledgling union an appearance of legitimacy as the voice of black labor.

Testimony of Asa P. Randolph (colored)
(*The witness was duly sworn in by the chairman.*)

The Chairman. What is your full name?
Mr. Randolph. Asa P. Randolph.
Mr. Bachmann. What is your occupation, Mr. Randolph?
Mr. Randolph. I am president of the Brotherhood of Sleeping Car Porters.
Mr. Bachmann. How long have you been president of that organization?
Mr. Randolph. About five years.
Mr. Bachmann. And what was your occupation prior to that time?
Mr. Randolph. Editor of the *Messenger Magazine.*
Mr. Bachmann. How long did you edit that magazine?
Mr. Randolph. About 10 years.
Mr. Bachmann. You live in New York City?
Mr. Randolph. I live in New York City.
The Chairman. Now, will you proceed in your own way and give us any information at your disposal in regard to the activities of communists among your group of people. You are not a communist yourself?
Mr. Randolph. No.
The Chairman. Will you give us what information you may have of the activities of the communists, whether it is of recent origin, whether it is increasing, how it is affecting your people, and so on. Just take your time.
Mr. Randolph. Well, I would say that the communist activities among negroes began about the same time that they began among the whites; not on as large a scale, however. The beginning of the communist movement was not as aggressive, probably, as it now is. In the last year and a half, I should say that the activities have increased among the negroes throughout the country. As to the number of negro communists, I can not speak with any certainty. I think you have but a very small number of negroes who are actually in the communist movement. I should say that probably there has been an increase

in sympathy and sentiment among negroes for the communist movement in the last year and a half or more.

The Chairman. Do you know the reason for that? Is it the fact that orders have come over from Russia to intensify the campaign among negroes within the last year?

Mr. Randolph. I think that the communists in America among negroes are acting under orders from Moscow.

The Chairman. Do you know specifically whether orders have come recently to that effect—that it must be accentuated among the negroes?

Mr. Randolph. I read in the papers to that effect, that specific orders have come recently and that the activities have increased and they have become more aggressive. Now, I want to state specifically about my organization and the activities of communists in relation to our group. The Brotherhood of Sleeping Car Porters was organized in August 1925, in New York, for the purpose of getting more wages and shorter hours of work for the Pullman porters. At that time the Pullman porters received $67 a month and were working about 400 hours a month, and the sentiment among the men was to have an organization affiliated with the American Federation of Labor.

Mr. Bachmann. You are affiliated with the American Federation of Labor?

Mr. Randolph. We are affiliated with the American Federation of Labor.

The Chairman. Are you secretary of that organization?

Mr. Randolph. President. The Pullman porters now receive $77.50 a month. Now, in 1928 we projected a strike maneuver. On June 8 we planned to execute a strike among the Pullman porters in the interest of getting the demands that we had set forth. When this strike program was initiated, the communists attempted to penetrate the various divisions of our organization throughout the country, with a view to either capturing the organization or wrecking it.

Mr. Bachmann. Now, let me ask you right there: When you say they endeavored to penetrate your organization throughout the country, the points of their penetration were only in New York and Chicago; is not that true?

Mr. Randolph. What do you mean, points of penetration?

Mr. Bachmann. Well, you said the communists were trying to penetrate your organization through the country.

Mr. Randolph. Yes. Well, in most of the districts they were active.

Mr. Bachmann. Well, were there any other places outside of Chicago and New York?

Mr. Randolph. Oh, yes. In Kansas City, Oakland, Los Angeles, Portland, Seattle, Washington—

Mr. Bachmann. Detroit?

Mr. Randolph. Washington D. C.; so that there were many points where they were active. Now, they went to our various organizations in various districts and attempted to make them feel that they had the power to win the strike and they were going to set up relief stations when the strike occurred; they were going to collect money in the interests of the strike, and, of course, our various organizers did not know about the communists. They did not know who they were and what their program was, and it was only due to the fact I knew something about their activities, knew the nature of their activities, their strategy, motives, and technique, that I was able to warn our various organizers against them, through telegrams, and immediately ordered the various organizers to drive them out and have absolutely nothing to do with them.

The Chairman. Is it not a fact you have had some association in the past with the radical movement?

Mr. Randolph. Yes.

The Chairman. And that is how you happen to have this knowledge?

Mr. Randolph. Yes, that is how I happen to have this knowledge.

The Chairman. Did you used to be a communist yourself?

Mr. Randolph. No; I used to be a socialist.

The Chairman. A socialist?

Mr. Randolph. Yes. They attempted to establish their connection with the group, but by taking the matter in hand immediately, we were able to cast them out; although recently, here in New York, they have made attacks on our movement. I have some exhibits here of their activities in the various meetings that we have held. They have come into the meetings and, at certain times, they would have members of their group stationed in different parts of the hall and, when the program proceeded to certain point, why, they would rise and proceed to introduce confusion [*handing papers to the chairman*]. So that our organization is practically the only organization among the negroes which is attacked by the communists. They have sought to break up the Brotherhood of Sleeping Car Porters because they [know] we are part of the American Federation of Labor and because they were not able to capture the movement.

The Chairman. How many Pullman-car porters have you in your organization?

Mr. Randolph. We have about 8,000 members in our organization. We are not yet recognized by the Pullman Company, but that is the fight of the movement—to secure recognition form the Pullman Company.

The Chairman. What can you tell the committee about the American Negro Congress?

Mr. Randolph. The American Negro Labor Congress is the official organization of communists among the negroes for propaganda of the organization of the communist doctrines. It was organized a few years ago and it is headed by very capable and aggressive young negro men; on the average, I should say they are about as capable as the whites and they are very, very aggressive.

Mr. Bachmann. Do you know what is the membership of that organization?

Mr. Randolph. I think the membership is very small. I doubt if it runs into, oh, say a couple hundred—

The Chairman. Do you know where the money comes from?

Mr. Randolph (*continuing*). But, of course, the membership does not represent the extent of the organization, you know.

Mr. Bachmann. I understand.

Mr. Randolph. Because they have a sort of closed membership, as Mr. Leary pointed out, as a dues-paying group; but, as a matter of fact, the group is much stronger and much more extensive than the membership implies.

Mr. Nelson. How many Pullman porters have refused to join your order?

Mr. Randolph. Well, there are about 12,000 Pullman porters in the service.

Mr. Nelson. And you have about 8,000?

Mr. Randolph. We have about 8,000—the large majority.

The Chairman. This American Negro Labor Congress has a letterhead and the names of the officers are given, and the board of directors or organizing committee of about 60. Are you familiar with them? I will present it to you, with the names of these men who are on that committee, and ask whether the most of them are here in New York [*handing paper to witness*]?

Mr. Randolph (*after examining paper*). I am familiar with some of them. Cyril Briggs is of New York; Otto Hall is not of New York—I think he is of the West; Otto Huiswoud is of New York; Richard B. Moore is of New York; James W. Ford, I think, is of Chicago.

Mr. Bachmann. Was Ford a Pullman porter?

Mr. Randolph. No. These are not Pullman porters.

Mr. Bachmann. I was asking whether he was. Do you know what his occupation was before he got involved in this movement?

Mr. Randolph. I think he was in the Post Office; I think he was in the Postal Service. Sol Harper is of New York, formerly of Schenectady and Syracuse, I think. Those are all of the negroes I know.

Mr. Nelson. You must have talked with a good many of these fellows. What do they say and what is the appeal to them in this?

Mr. Randolph. Well, I might say, as a general thing, there is discontent and unrest among the negroes as a whole throughout the country, and that unrest and discontent arises as a result of the existence, I believe, of a recrudescence in lynchings at the present time. Then you have, also, the existence of widespread peonage in the South. . . .

Mr. Nelson. Now, as regards those grievances of the colored people (and many of them are very real), the communist agitator promises to do away with all of them?

Mr. Randolph. The communist agitator capitalizes [on] those conditions.

Mr. Nelson. And they promise, with the inauguration of their regime, that all man shall stand equal?

Mr. Randolph. Right, sir; that is, there is that program. And I might say that the communists have a paper known as the *Negro Champion.*

The Chairman. When is that issued?

Mr. Randolph. You must have a sample of that there.

The Chairman. Where is that published?

Mr. Randolph. I think that is published in New York. I am not so sure, but I know it was published in New York.

The Chairman. Is that the only one you have?

Mr. Randolph. The only one among negroes.

The Chairman. Do you know where the money comes from that keeps up a paper of that kind and also keeps up the American Negro Labor Congress.

Mr. Randolph. Well, I think they get the money from the same source as the whites, whatever that is—I think from Russian Government, from Moscow.

The Chairman. Do you know anything about the colored American citizens being sent to Moscow to study over there?

Mr. Randolph. Yes; I know of a number of instances where young negro men and women have been sent to Moscow to study and then they have to come back as agitators to propagate the communist philosophy.

The Chairman. Do you know whether any of them have been sent from New York City—any that you know personally?

Mr. Randolph. Yes; I do. There is one man by the name of [William] Patterson, who is a lawyer, who has gone over and he has not returned; and, from Chicago, there have been a number of young men and women sent to Russia.

The Chairman. I want to take occasion to state that, acting in the capacity of chairman of this committee, I have issued subpoenas for about 20 of those members of the board of directors of the American Negro Labor Congress.

Mr. Randolph. Yes.

The Chairman. Assuming that they were all communists, and wanting to have them appear here.

Mr. Randolph. Yes.

The Chairman. We were unable to serve the subpoenas. We want to give those men an opportunity to express their views before this committee; we are not seeking to persecute or to prosecute them but are seeking to have the views of the negro communists before the committee; but, so far, we have been unable to locate them.

Mr. Nelson. How many colored people are there in New York City?

Mr. Randolph. Well, it is variously estimated. I suppose the next census will definitely show, but they say there are from two hundred to two hundred and fifty thousand.

Mr. Nelson. How many of those would you say are communists?

Mr. Randolph. Oh, I should say, in the Communist Party, I doubt that you would have 50 who are members of the communist organization.

Mr. Nelson. And how many are active as propagandists?

Mr. Randolph. That is just an estimate. I should say that you would have about half a dozen or a dozen active propagandists.

Mr. Nelson. Where were you educated?

Mr. Randolph. New York City; the City College of New York.

The Chairman. Are you a native American?

Mr. Randolph. Yes; I was born in Florida.

The Chairman. Is there more activity among the West Indian negroes than among the native American negroes?

Mr. Randolph. Well, I do not know. I think that you have about an equal split. For instance, this man Patterson was an American negro, who has gone over to Russia. He is a lawyer, and some of the most prominent of the negro communists are American negroes, and they about equal up.

Mr. Nelson. Did you ever live in Boston?

Mr. Randolph. No; I never lived in Boston.

Mr. Nelson. You have the accent of Boston East Beacon Hill.

The Chairman. You say there are about 50 in the Communist Party. Here are the names, I think, of 65 right here.

Mr. Randolph. Well, all of those are not negroes, I do not think.

The Chairman. Can you show any white men on that list? I think it is called the American Negro Labor Congress.

Mr. Randolph. Yes; they call it the American Negro Labor Congress.

The Chairman. You do not know of any white men on that list?

Mr. Randolph. I do not know; but those I mentioned are negroes.

The Chairman. You do not know the name of any white man on that list?

Mr. Randolph. Well, I do not know the name of any white man on that list.

The Chairman. I do not think you will find any on it. I think there are 65 names, and I think they are all negroes and most of them of New York.

Mr. Randolph. It is quite possible, though, that there would be white men on this list with the negroes for the purpose of helping them to carry on the movement. I doubt if all of those are negroes.

Mr. Bachmann. What is the procedure followed by the communists to attract your group to this movement?

Mr. Randolph. Well, they employ meetings in halls and they have street meetings and they disseminate literature among the negroes, especially where situations arise such as strikes. Now you will take, for instance, in Sunny Side and Mott Haven yards, of the Pullman Company, the communists stand out near the gates and give the Pullman porters the *Daily Worker* and sometimes the *Negro Champion.*

Mr. Bachmann. Now, after they attract them to the movement, what is that procedure?

Mr. Randolph. Well, after they are attracted to the meetings, why the communists proceed to tell them that the present order of society is unsound and present generally the communist philosophy, and also proceed to exploit the various grievances of the negroes—for instance, the present condition, such as lynching and things of that sort, and exposing the negro leaders and denouncing various representatives of other political organizations affiliated with the American Federation of Labor that is active.

Mr. Bachmann. Can you say whether you have information where they have some of the white women who assist them in a way to attract negroes at those meetings?

Mr. Randolph. Well, I do not know about that. Of course, you have the communist men and women coming to these meetings, and I have simply stopped at these meetings and listened to them; I have not gone to any of their hall meetings; I have not had the time; but I know generally just what they do and the methods they employ. In Atlanta, now, they have a little communist group there, which was quite a surprise to me; when I went down there to lecture to some colleges I found the communists.

Mr. Bachmann. Where was that?

Mr. Randolph. Atlanta, Georgia. I found there was a little communist group in Atlanta; not very large, but apparently quite active.

Mr. Nelson. On what subjects do you lecture?

Mr. Randolph. Why, in the colleges, on economics, history, sociology, psychology, and things of that sort, especially presenting the labor angle of the question of the negro worker, and also setting forth the work of the Brotherhood of Sleeping Car Porters.

The Chairman. Who is the actual head of the communists among your group here in the city of New York?

Mr. Randolph. Well, I think that probably Richardson B. Moore is the most prominent here in New York. . . .

Mr. Bachmann. There is no question, is there, Mr. Randolph, that those of you who understand this movement, through your organization are well able to combat it?

Mr. Randolph. Oh, yes. The Brotherhood of Sleeping Car Porters has grappled with the communists, and we routed them and practically destroyed their movement so far as it relates to the Brotherhood of Sleeping Car Porters. They do not molest us any more now in the way of coming to our meetings.

Mr. Bachmann. You do not feel, do you, they are making much of an inroad into your organization?

Mr. Randolph. Oh, no; they are not making any inroads into our organization.

Mr. Bachmann. The movement is on the decrease there rather than on the increase at the present time?

Mr. Randolph. Oh, yes. We had our struggle with them, don't you see; our struggle was rather intense at the time; but we were able to overcome them and to rout them.

The Chairman. Now, can you tell the committee anything about Mr. Cyril Briggs?

Mr. Eslick. Let me ask one question first: The representatives of the Communist Party approaching your organization, are they negroes, white men, or both?

Mr. Randolph. They are both.

Mr. Eslick. Both?

Mr. Randolph. Yes.

The Chairman. Can you tell the committee anything about Mr. Cyril Briggs, who is the national secretary of the American Negro Labor Congress?

Mr. Randolph. Yes; I know Mr. Briggs. He is a writer; he does not do very much speaking, but he is a very capable writer and has been quite active in the communist movement from the very beginning, I think, and is located here in New York.

The Chairman. Is he associated with the paper you referred to as being a communist paper?

Mr. Randolph. *The Negro Champion*—yes; I think he is.

The Chairman. Is he the editor of that?

Mr. Randolph. I think he is the editor of that. You will see it in the heading there.

The Chairman. Therefore he must have an office here in New York?

Mr. Randolph. Yes; he has an office here in New York.

The Chairman. And could he be reached and a subpoena served on him?

Mr. Randolph. Yes. He has an office somewhere here.

The Chairman. And what does Mr. Otto Huiswoud do?

Mr. Randolph. Mr. Otto Huiswoud is one of the beginners of the communist movement in the country.

The Chairman. Has he an office here?

Mr. Randolph. Well, I think he has some place where they do their work; but they have no real office where you have—

The Chairman. There are no negro communists' general headquarters where they hold their meetings—rooms?

Mr. Randolph. Well, they hold their meetings here in certain places. They were located on One Hundred and Thirty-Fifth and Seventh Avenue, in the new building right above the Chelsea Bank.

The Chairman. Is that the Rockefeller Building up there?

Mr. Randolph. No; it is a place of the Chelsea Bank. They were there; I do not know whether they are there still or not. They go from place to place and usually operate on the street corners.

The Chairman. What does Mr. Richard B. Moore do?

Mr. Randolph. Mr. Richard B. Moore, I think, is the leading spirit in the communist movement here now. He was nominated for one of the city offices on the communist ticket, recently.

The Chairman. Has he any profession or vocation?

Mr. Randolph. Well, I do not know of any profession that he has. He gives all the time, I think, to communist activities.

The Chairman. Do you know whether Herbert Newton comes from New York or not; do you know him?

Mr. Randolph. I do not know where he comes from; I never heard of him before . . .

SOURCE: *House Hearings before A Special Committee to Investigate Communist Activities in the United States,* 71st Cong., 2nd sess. (Washington, D. C.: GPO, 1930), 242–51.

Why I Would Not Stand for Re-Election for President of the National Negro Congress (1940)

The National Negro Congress was formed in 1935 as an umbrella organization for those involved in civil rights struggles during the Great Depression. It was initially a united-front group that welcomed everyone, especially those on the political left. A. Philip Randolph, a Socialist, was its first president, and its national secretary was John P. Davis, who had ties with the Communist Party. This uneasy partnership ruptured in 1940, resulting in Randolph's resignation from the presidency and loudly renouncing the NNC.

I am convinced that the Third National Negro Congress has not succeeded in removing from the mindful of the public that the idea that the charge of the Dies Committee, that the National Negro Congress is a Communist Front and a transmission belt for Communist propaganda, is not true. In fact, the Congress has brilliantly succeeded in giving the charge every appearance of the truth and validity. I am convinced also, that until the stigma of the Communist Front is wiped from Congress it will never rally the masses of the Negro people.

The procedure, conduct and policies of the Negro Congress as set up in this third national meeting will make its influence in the affairs of the American Negroes short lived. The American Negroes will not long follow any organization which accepts dictation and control from the Communist Party. The American Negro will not long follow any organization which accepts dictation and control from any white organization. In the last national Executive Committee meeting in New York City, Brother John P. Davis was authorized to go out and borrow $1,000 to help put the third congress over. He informed me that he had borrowed it and mentioned the name of a man. I was given no specific identity of the man. What was the source of this money? The delegates to the Congress should know. Because whatever is the source of the money with which the Congress is run will also be the source of its ideas, policies and control. It is a well known fact that most of the contributions to this Congress expressed by the Secretary, Mr. Davis, are from CIO unions. Is this the reason why the Congress is taking the CIO line? In an Executive Committee meeting in New York City, Mr. Davis informed it that the Communist Party contributed $100 a month to the Congress. . . .

When the National Negro Congress loses its independence, it loses its soul and has no further reason for being. It also forfeits and betrays the faith and confidence of the Negro masses. It will shatter the hopes and aspirations of the Negro people, who yearn and pray for the Negro Congress not to sell out either to labor or capital, Communists or Republicans or Democrats. Since the trend of the National Negro Congress is obviously toward domination by the Communists and the CIO, I would not stand for reelection for President. I do not oppose the domination of the Congress by the CIO because I am opposed to the CIO. I would be opposed to domination of the Congress by the A.F. of L. or any other white organization. With respect to the domination by the Communists, I am not only opposed to domination of the Congress by them, but I consider the Communists a definite menace and a danger to the Negro people and labor, because of rule or ruin and disruptive tactics in the interest of the Soviet Union. . . .

The third National Negro Congress was a miserable failure, so far as representing the sentiment of the American Negro people is concerned. Uproarious applause greeted every favorable reference in the Congress to Soviet Russia. The statement was even made that the Negro people would not fight in an imperialist war against the Soviet Union. But this is far from the truth. If the United States declared war upon Communist Russia tomorrow, the Negro would fight Russia with all of the fervor and patriotism of any other 100 percent American. Anyone who believes to the contrary is living in a fool's paradise. Soviet Russia was hailed as the land without poverty or race prejudice. But the fact is there are no Negroes in Soviet Russia that would occasion any manifestations of race discrimination. However, it is significant to note that the Bolshevik Russia freely sold oil to Fascist Italy to assist the murderous war of invasion of the peace-loving and ancient kingdom of Ethiopia.

I quit the Congress because I was opposed to linking it up with Labor's Non-Partisan League, the political mouthpiece of the CIO, since this was a departure from the original minimum program upon which there could be general agreement and a sound basis for rallying the Negro masses. It seems axiomatic and as simple as one, two, three, that the Congress could not rally the Negroes in the A.F. of L., if it were tied up with the CIO, and it could not rally the Negroes in the CIO, if it were allied with A.F. of L.

I quit the Congress because I was opposed to it, or its officials, expressing sympathy for the Soviet Union, which is the death prison where democracy and liberty have walked their "last mile" and where shocking "blood purges" wipe out any and all persons who express any dissenting opinions from dictator Stalin.

I quit the Congress because I saw that the Communists were firmly in the saddle and the delegates were not subject to the influence of facts and reason. Their minds were already made up when they came there by Communist manipulations, caucuses and propaganda. Nothing could shake them. Even poor old men and women from the deep South and from some parts up North, who didn't have the slightest idea of what it was all about, parrot fashion, went down the Communist line, like bleating sheep led to slaughter.

I quit the Congress because it is not truly a Negro Congress. Out of some 1,200 or more delegates, over 300 were white, which made the Congress look like a joke. It is unthinkable that the Jewish Congress would have Gentiles in it, or that a Catholic Congress would have Protestants in it, or that the famous All India Congress would have in it as members natives of Africa. Why should a Negro Congress have white people in it?

SOURCE: *The Black Worker* 6 (May 1940): 1.

Why I Did Not Elect to Run for Congress (ca. 1944)

Randolph was intensely political, but he preferred to act from outside the system. Early in his public career, however, he ran for office on the Socialist ticket—in 1920 for New York state comptroller and in 1922 for New York secretary of state. In 1944, he was asked to run again, this time for Congress from the Twenty-Second Congressional District, which included Harlem. Randolph declined, and his friend Adam Clayton Powell Jr. ran instead. Randolph's explanation reveals the complexity and nuance of his reasoning, as well as underscores the fact that he devoted his professional career to advancing the cause of working-class African Americans.

I wish to express my profound appreciation for the interest and fine spirit of cooperation that my friends have shown in attempting to get me to stand for election for Congress in the Twenty-Second Congressional District of New York City. After giving this matter my serious thought, I have come to the conclusion that I do not elect to run for Congress. My reasons are as follows:

One: I do not wish to become involved in the entanglements of politics and politicians, although I have the highest respect and admiration for the race pride, integrity and spirit of independence of such men as Herbert Bruce, Democratic Leader, and Harold C. Burton, Republican Leader, and a number of others in our community.

Two: I am unconvinced that I cannot render useful service to the cause of the Negro people, the workers of our community, outside, as well as inside, Congress. In fact, I believe that a Negro should be elected for Congress for New York, and of course, one will as a result of the new reapportionment, but I do not share the opinion that it will achieve the results in terms of Negro advancement apparently generally expected by the people unless the composition of the House were such as to render the position of the Negro Congressman unusually strategic in voting on various issues. His work would be largely propagandist through the presentation of speeches on the floor of the House and the sponsoring of certain bills. Of course, I do not suggest that this is not an important and valuable service to render the Negro people.

Three: I do not believe that any one man is indispensable to the representation of the Harlem community and the Negro people of this country in Congress.

Fourth: I want to remain free and independent to pursue the course I think best in doing my humble bit in the interest of winning freedom, justice and democracy for the Negro people in America and the world. While I have been assured that I would have no partisan alliances that would tie my hands, I am constrained to believe that the law of compensation demands and requires that there be a pay-off somewhere down the road in some form or other. In politics, as in other things, there is no such thing as one getting something for nothing. The pay-off may involve compromises of various types that may strike at the basic convictions and ideals and principles that one has held dear all of his life.

Fifth: Moreover, I do not consider that the domestic and foreign policies of the Republican or Democratic parties are such that I could support them, since in my opinion, they are not calculated to extend, preserve or consolidate the forces of democracy at home or abroad. Thus, it is difficult for me to see how one could do an effective job in Congress for an oppressed group and the workers, and all of the people, if he was not a part of one of the two major political organizations, or a liberal-labor block, which could rally forces back of the measures initiated and introduced by him. I would not accept the designation from the Left-Wing American Labor Party, because it is Communist dominated.

Finally, the officials of the Brotherhood of Sleeping Car Porters are divided as to whether I should or should not run for Congress. While none of them would oppose my running for Congress, I, having worked with them for eighteen or twenty years, have the utmost respect for the opinions of all of them because of the struggle and price they have paid to build a great economic movement such as the Brotherhood of Sleeping Car Porters, which has raised the wage bill of this class of workers from seven and a half million, when the union began in 1925, to over twenty million at this time, and also achieved security on the job for them.

May I say to the people in my community, and the Negroes and workers generally, that there is no price that I would not be willing to pay to carry on a battle to break down the barriers of Jim Crowism and beat back the rising tide of anti-Semitism and fascism that threaten our democratic institutions in this country, but I am not certain that my going to Congress is the only way I can serve this cause. I believe that the talent, genius and ability, and the moral, spiritual and intellectual resources of every member of an oppressed group should be subject to the command and placed at the disposal of the well-being of the minority groups, the workers and the country, but he should be permitted to stand fast by the basic convictions and principles and values and faiths to which he has dedicated and consecrated his life.

SOURCE: Box 38, folder: Speeches, Undated, A. Philip Randolph Papers, Library of Congress.

For Political Reorientation (1946)

Randolph frequently argued for a third political party, and he was particularly optimistic about this prospect in the months that immediately followed the Second World War. In this essay, he argues that the present time was especially ripe for "a complete break with the old political order."

A canvass of American political opinion, as found in various strata of our industrial and social life, would seem to reveal that the American people voted in the last Congressional election more against something, than for something.

There are many reasons for this attitude, one of which was the absence of a program and actions from the Democrats to improve the economic and social well-being of the American people, as well as no presentation of a plan to improve the socio-economic conditions by the GOP. It was a vote of political frustration on the part of the American people.

Liberals have provided no guiding star for the peoples' political thinking in the past few years. Following the death of former President Franklin D. Roosevelt, the so-called progressives have been distressingly unwitting of their way in politics, government and economics; having held on to the apron strings of FDR so long, when finally thrown upon their feet, they could not stand firmly and their political knees buckled under them, indicating a probable fall to the canvas under the blows of reaction.

Not only have liberals failed to move with political sureness, faith and vision, but the American labor movement, too, hedged in and controlled largely by the psychology of a short-ranged, day-to-day program of improvisation and opportunism, was caught in a fog of economic and political contradictions without the Messiah of the New Deal to point the way.

At this hour, a call for ideas to effect a political reorientation is becoming increasingly audible. The National Educational Committee for a New Party, whose Declaration envisages a program of exploration and education to assess political sentiment for a new mass political movement throughout the country, and also to organize the idea, came into being as a result of the interest of a few labor and liberal individuals.

Through the storm and stress of the coming economic depression, together with a national educational campaign on the basic meaning, possibility, and necessity of a new party, the National Educational Committee for a New Party has hope and faith that organized labor eventually, if not now, will see the wisdom and necessity of taking the long-range view of co-operating with the other liberal forces to build a basic national people's political party. Verily, this party must be a complete break with the old political order as represented by the Democratic and Republican parties. A third political movement envisaged by the NECNP, must be done by trading with the old parties for patronage, advantage, and election expediency. It must be committed to a program of planned economy within the framework of political liberty. Cognizant of the baneful influence of monopoly capitalism, this new party must set its face against the evil of monopoly control of the economic life of America and seek the socialization of the key and crucial property of our national community. Adherence must be maintained to the basic principle of industrial democracy with a view to developing and strengthening the machinery of collective bargaining and fostering co-operative labor-management.

One of its basic tenets should be the achievement of ethnic democracy through the enactment of legislation and the development of educational forces designed to eliminate discrimination based upon color, creed or country, in labor unions, business and industry, education and civil relationships.

On the international front, a new party must support international control and inspection of atomic energy, and should be committed to the abolition of colonialism and world imperialism and the exemplification on the part of the United States of a sound leadership of the moral forces of the world.

This national people's political movement of a third party, must, of course, be non-Communist, without being anti–Soviet Russia or pro-British, although a third party should recognize its kinship with the British Labor Party and support democratic socialism throughout Europe, South America and Asia to prevent the spread of totalitarian fascism on the right and totalitarian communism on the left.

Albeit, this third party must unequivocally fight for disarmament, the outlawing of war and the elimination of the war system, as well as its fundamental economic-root causes, and uncompromisingly oppose peacetime conscription.

SOURCE: *Antioch Review* 6, no. 4 (December 1946): 602–4. Reprinted by permission of the Editors.

Why I Voted for Norman Thomas (1948)

Despite the fact that President Truman had come around on civil rights and issued two meaningful executive orders that directly benefited African Americans, Randolph endorsed Norman Thomas in the 1948 presidential election. Randolph acknowledges that endorsing a third party was essentially throwing his vote away, but he was hopeful that a good showing for the Socialist ticket would nudge the Democrats and Republicans closer to ideals that progressives like himself could comfortably support.

A citizen faced with the problem of casting his vote in the presidential election should have made up his mind to vote for either [Harry] Truman, [Thomas] Dewey, [Henry] Wallace, Norman Thomas or J. Strom Thurmond upon a basis of three considerations:

1. Record of candidate on the issues which the citizen thinks are vital
2. Program of the candidate
3. Control of the candidate.

Analyzing the records of the candidates on the Democratic, Republican, Progressive, Socialist and Dixiecrat tickets, the following facts meet the citizen:

With respect to President Truman on civil rights, his record involves the issuance of the famous Civil Rights Report and the submission of a ten-point program to the Congress for legislative action. While this was commendable, he failed to fight for the translation of the report into basic legislation.

The civil rights platform adopted by the Democratic Convention, as a result of the memorable leadership of Mayor [Hubert] Humphrey of Minneapolis, Minnesota, and other delegates of the Americans for Democratic Action, although not repudiated by President Truman, was far too drastic for his temper and liking, since it is a well-known fact that he counseled a colorless plank on civil rights comparable to the one adopted by the 1944 Democratic Convention. However, under the pressure of the civil disobedience campaign he issued two Executive Orders; one, against Jim Crow in the armed services, which also provided for a committee to carry out the purpose of the order; and, two, an Executive Order for a FEPC in government with the purpose of eliminating discrimination based upon color, religion, nationality and ancestry. Those Executive Orders are praiseworthy and valuable.

On labor, President Truman made the grave blunder in 1946 of calling upon the Congress to adopt legislation to break strikes in the crucial industries by putting workers in uniform. However, when the infamous slave labor measure known as the Taft-Hartley Law was passed by both houses and presented to him, he vetoed it. In relation to housing, President Truman has done more noble talking than acting. He has roundly condemned the action of the 80th Congress for its failure to do anything to relieve the housing shortage in the interest of GIs and other citizens. But what about the 78th Congress which was criminally negligent in seeking an effective solution to the problem of housing in this country?

One notable credit which President Truman may claim is the appointment of Negroes to some of the distinctively important places in American government. As far as his dealings with high prices and the problems of inflation, the President recommends price control, although he is responsible, together with the Republicans, for the emasculation of the OPA [Office of Price Administration], which upon the occasion of its dismantling, he styled as a phase of a police state. Regarding the basic question of monopoly and the problem of achieving a greater measure of equality and the distribution of wealth in America among the population, both President Truman and the Democratic Party have taken no position. As long as our fundamental natural resources and big monopolies are exploited for the profit of a few people in the country, democracy is in peril.

In terms of the foreign policy of President Truman and the Democratic Party, there is a lack of definite outline and a program which would have merit and value. There is such vacillation and indecision on vital questions such as Palestine and Germany that people at home and abroad are at sea as to where the U.S.A. stands. So far as control of the President and the Democratic Party is concerned, it is in the hands of politicians without vision or idealism, and who think in terms of politics, patronage and power.

Although it was claimed that Governor Dewey of New York had better chances of election over President Truman, it is doubtful that the people would have fared any better under him than they have under President Truman. His civil rights program consists of the New York State FEPC, which was wrung from his grudging hands under pressure, and his education bill for FEPC was enacted without his leadership or special sympathy. But he used these measures as evidence of his civil rights records. On the whole, there is nothing in the political career of Governor Dewey which will get him down as a warm champion of civil rights. In fairness to the Governor, however, it must be admitted that he has been outstanding in giving Negroes high and responsible positions. He does not, however, exceed President Truman in this respect.

So far as labor is concerned, while he has not sponsored any anti-labor legislation during his regime in Albany, he has, as the titular head of the Republican Party, gone on record as giving the Taft-Hartley Law his blessing, a position which naturally earns the suspicion and distrust of organized labor. In the field of housing, Governor Dewey's record is no better or worse than President Truman's. For the correction of high prices and inflation he has the typical big business remedy [of] free enterprise, normal and natural competition in a free market. The only thing wrong with this remedy is that it is not a remedy, in the first place because it is based on assumptions that are highly questionable, namely, the existence of a free market and natural competition. In the domain of foreign policy, Governor Dewey did not dissent from the position of President Truman but only claimed that he would do the job better. On domestic issues involving monopoly and the more equal distribution of goods and services among the people of the nation, Governor Dewey reflected the philosophy of the National Manufacturers' Association, which stands for monopoly without government interference. In terms of control of Governor Dewey and the Republican Party, it is a matter of common knowledge that the Republican Party is the political voice of big business in America—although it may be said in deference to Governor Dewey that he would have been perhaps more independent of big business control than Hoover, Harding or Coolidge, whatever that means.

Perhaps the most sensational campaign which was made for the presidency must be credited to Henry A. Wallace. At least he had huge crowds that paid cash to hear him. On civil rights, Henry A. Wallace may be truly styled as a "Johnny Come Lately," for although his challenge to Jim Crow in the deep South is commendable, when the fight was being waged for Odell Waller, Negro farm boy accused and framed of the slaying of his farm employer; and when Marian Anderson was rebuffed when she sought to sing in Constitution Hall; and during the struggle of Negroes, liberals and labor to unseat Jim Crow in the nation's capitol and various departments of the federal government, although Mr. Wallace was at one time Vice-President, at another time Secretary of Agriculture and finally Secretary of Commerce, he was as silent as the sphinx, neither giving aid or comfort to the struggle against Jim Crow in the interests of civil rights for all people regardless of race, creed, color or national origin. I can authoritatively speak on the question since I led the committee in the interest of Odell Waller in Washington to seek the support of President Roosevelt, Henry A. Wallace and other leaders of the government.

The housing program of Henry A. Wallace is sounder than that of President Truman and Governor Dewey. He promises to deal effectively with the elimination of the housing shortage and sets up a plan which has merit. On labor his pronouncements are far more fundamental than the positions of either President Truman or Dewey. But in the field of foreign policy he is extremely vulnerable from the point of view of our national security and the struggle of democracy against Communism. His opposition to the Marshall Plan is as indefensible as it is unsound. This brings me to the question of control of Mr. Wallace and the Progressive Party, for the position of Mr. Wallace on the Marshall Plan stems from the control over him and the Progressive Party. It is a

A. Philip Randolph at the White House with President Lyndon B. Johnson, ca. 1966. (Library of Congress, Prints & Photographs Division, A. Philip Randolph Papers, LC-USZ62-104210)

matter of common knowledge that the Progressive Party was organized by the Communists, and the Communists have resolutely prevented any measures from being included in the platform of the Progressive Party that are objectionable to the Kremlin. Whenever Wallace decides to oppose the plans of the Kremlin, the brethren of the Comintern will start a whispering campaign which will result in his complete elimination and repudiation, as they have with others for the slightest deviation from the Moscow line. Wallace is the wrongest good man in the presidential campaign.

J. Strom Thurmond, former governor of South Carolina and candidate for the presidency on the Dixiecrat ticket, has the clearest program of Truman, Dewey or Wallace. He simply wants to set back the clock of civil rights to the days before the Civil War, and that is that.

Norman Thomas, candidate on the Socialist ticket for the presidency, is by long odds, in moral and intellectual stature, head and shoulders above Truman, Dewey, Wallace or Thurmond. I voted for Norman Thomas because he has been a consistent champion of civil rights, though never possessing public office to put his ideals into practice. No cause for freedom, justice or democracy for the oppressed minorities has failed to receive his support and cooperation. If there is a struggle on the picket line against open-shop autocracy, he is there. If sharecroppers are victimized by ruthless exponents on the farms of the South or the far West, he is there. If Japanese-Americans are denied their human rights, Norman Thomas gives them aid. If the fight for the poll tax, the abolition of lynching and the establishment of an FEPC is on Thomas is with it.

His program and the program of the Socialist Party strikes at the roots of social injustice and maladjustment by seeking the socialization of natural resources, natural monopolies and the introduction of the policy of production for use and service instead of profit. While Thomas cannot be elected president, I would rather vote for him on the Socialist ticket, whose principles and ideals I believe in, than to vote for Truman, Dewey, Wallace or Thurmond, whose programs and parties I don't believe in. I am for Norman Thomas because a strong Socialist vote may serve as the basis for the organization of a national third party based upon sound socialist principles which will make for peace, plenty and freedom.

SOURCE: *The Black Worker* 20 (November 1948): 2, 6.

Randolph Hits Barry Goldwater (1964)

Randolph perceived the rise of Barry Goldwater in national politics as a major development in American history and saw it as a threat to the civil rights movement. To combat the reactionary forces Goldwater represented, Randolph maintained that mass political participation such as door-to-door voter registration drives was necessary.

While Senator Goldwater may not openly call for the impeachment of Supreme Court Justice Earl Warren, he preaches the doctrine of a sterile individualism and the weakening or reversal of the evolution of the American government's constitutional order by opposing the centralization of political power in a strong federal system. While the American constitutional system provides for both federal rights and states' rights, wherever states' rights invade the domain of the civil rights of citizens, it is construed to constitute states' wrongs, which must be set right in the interest of racial and social justice by the intervention of federal power to protect the citizens' federal rights as set forth in the 14th and 15th Amendments to the Constitution.

Verily, it is passing strange that a candidate for nomination by the Republican Party who professes to be opposed to racial bias could make a major speech before the Platform Committee and discuss Communism, war in Southeast Asia and foreign policy but fail to mention Civil Rights, the dominant domestic issue of the century. Besides, the Senator bemoans the alleged failure of President Johnson's administration to mobilize its maximum federal power to protect the interests of the country from enemies from without, but decries the use of federal law to help stop the enemies from within from violating the civil rights and civil liberties of American citizens, the most dangerous of which is racial bigotry, naively suggesting that the latter be left to the dubious business of the eventual participation of the heart.

The law is not expected to change the hearts of men, but to serve as a deterrent to the commission of overt harmful acts by an individual or organization or even the state against an individual or individuals. As a result of the influence of the law on human behavior it is conceivable that ultimately it may tend to alter and eliminate human hate in the minds and hearts of some men, even in Mississippi. While it is no doubt true that the law cannot compel klansmen to love a black man, it can prevent klansmen from lynching a black man. In fact, the hope of mankind for a better tomorrow is based upon the assumption that man can and does change toward man. If, according to Senator Goldwater, the law is useless in the fight of Negro for first-class citizenship, why enact and maintain laws against murder, burglary or arson?

But regardless of the opinion of Negroes, Liberals, and Labor about Senator Goldwater and his limitations with respect to labor, civil rights and civil liberties, the fact remains that he is now the nominee for the presidency. In light of the powerful forces of reaction back of him and his Eighteenth Century concept of government and economic progress, together with his lack of moral commitment to the cause of human rights, it is possible for him to become the next president of the United States. Therefore, he constitutes a grave danger to the struggle of Negroes for the realization of equality, freedom and first-class citizenship.

Despite the fight of modern Republicans and Negro agitation against Goldwater's nomination at the Republican Party Convention in San Francisco, he won. But if Negroes will initiate a nationwide campaign on a house-to-house basis to secure the registration and voting of Negroes, Senator Goldwater can be stopped at the polls in November. Therefore, the battle for Civil Rights has shifted. Now the task is to methodically and systemically and unrelentingly work to increase the registration of Negroes in the big cities such as New York City, Philadelphia, St. Louis, and Detroit. The forces of political rightism as represented by Senator Goldwater can be routed and driven into political oblivion.

Finally, it is self-evident that in view of the utter contempt Senator Goldwater has shown for Negroes by voting against civil rights, no self-respecting Negro can cast a vote for Goldwater.

SOURCE: *Amsterdam News,* August 1, 1964.

5

The March on Washington Movement and the Fair Employment Practice Committee

In the 1940s, Randolph came into his own as a leading voice both in the labor movement and in struggles against segregation and discrimination. Beginning in 1941 with the call to march on Washington, Randolph sought to apply labor's tactics of mass demonstrations to civil rights campaigns. Toward that end, he founded the March on Washington Movement (MOWM), an organization that sustained steady grassroots protests in several cities during World War II. As Randolph's correspondence with Walter White indicates, preparations for the original march necessitated collaboration with a number of preexisting groups, especially the NAACP. Although MOWM failed to achieve most of its stated goals as outlined in its Eight Point Program, this organization proved effective in helping implement the nondiscrimination order mandated by Executive Order 8802. To enforce this mandate, President Franklin D. Roosevelt created the Fair Employment Practice Committee (FEPC). This federal agency had little legal authority, but its presence during the war is correlated with a noticeable rise in the number of African Americans employed in defense industries. These gains were worth preserving, and Randolph pushed hard to make the FEPC a permanent federal agency.

Of the documents in this chapter, Randolph's 1944 essay "March on Washington Movement Presents Program for the Negro" is his most cogent explanation of how MOWM and the campaign for a permanent FEPC fit within the broader aims of the "Double V" impulse for victory against Hitler's fascism abroad and Jim Crow's racism in the United States. This essay first appeared in *What the Negro Wants* (1944), a volume edited by Rayford Logan that also included pieces by luminaries such as W. E. B. Du Bois, Mary McLeod

Bethune, and Langston Hughes—clearly Randolph was in good company. In it, Randolph compares America's racial tensions to the challenges against the color line occurring throughout the world, and he grounds MOWM's foreign-sounding tactics of "non-violent goodwill direct action" within the context of African American freedom struggles such as the abolitionist movement and the Great Migration. He hails the securing of Executive Order 8802 as an important gain, but realizes that this single mandate is far from sufficient. To achieve MOWM's ends, Randolph calls for the creation of a "national non-partisan Negro political bloc" whose efforts would be politically aided by a rise in African American voters and a massive direct-action campaign that attacked segregation and discrimination in public accommodations and at job sites.

The FEPC ultimately disbanded after the war, but Randolph, along with a coalition of labor and organizations representing various ethnic and religious minorities, fought for the enactment of a federal fair employment law. From 1944 to 1955, the National Council for a Permanent FEPC sought to unite groups such as the NAACP, the National Urban League, and the CIO into an organized push to affect change through a single-issue campaign. Fair employment legislation could not get through a Congress dominated by pro-segregation Southern Democrats, but states such as New York and New Mexico implemented their own smaller-scale versions of this law. By 1964, when Title VII of the Civil Rights Act created the Equal Employment Opportunity Commission, more than two dozen states already had laws of this kind on the books. MOWM had disbanded long before, but its impact clearly resonated. Indeed, the FEPC itself was created to appease Randolph for calling off the threat to march in 1941, and the long fight to save that agency resulted in the various states implementing its aims within their jurisdictions.

FOR FURTHER READING

Chen, Anthony S. *The Fifth Freedom: Jobs, Politics, and Civil Rights in the United States, 1941–1972.* Princeton, N.J.: Princeton University Press, 2009.

Garfinkel, Herbert. *When Negroes March: The March on Washington Movement in the Organizational Politics for FEPC.* New York: Atheneum, 1973; first published by the Free Press, 1959.

Kersten, Andrew E. *Race, Jobs, and the War: The FEPC in the Midwest, 1941–1946.* Urbana: University of Illinois Press, 2000.

Kruse, Kevin M., and Stephen Tuck, eds. *Fog of War: The Second World War and the Civil Rights Movement.* New York: Oxford University Press, 2012.

Kryder, Daniel. *Divided Arsenal: Race and the American State during World War II.* New York: Cambridge University Press, 2000.

Lucander, David. *Winning the War for Democracy: The March on Washington Movement, 1941–1946*. Urbana: University of Illinois Press, 2014.

MacLean, Nancy. *Freedom Is Not Enough: The Opening of the American Workplace*. Cambridge, Mass.: Harvard University Press, 2006.

Moreno, Paul D. *From Direct Action to Affirmative Action: Fair Employment Law and Policy in America, 1933–1972*. Baton Rouge: Louisiana State University Press, 1997.

Reed, Merl E. *Seedtime for the Modern Civil Rights Movement: The President's Committee on Fair Employment Practice, 1941–1946*. Baton Rouge: Louisiana State University Press, 1991.

Welky, David. *Marching across the Color Line: A. Philip Randolph and Civil Rights in the World War II Era*. New York: Oxford University Press, 2013.

Let's March on Capital 10,000 Strong, Urges Leader of Porters (1941)

Known for its wartime "Double V" campaign—victory against fascism abroad and racism in America—the *Pittsburgh Courier* carried news of the march on Washington and reprinted many of Randolph's announcements. In this early call to march, Randolph lays out a program for a 10,000-person rally in Washington to "shake up" the government and open publicly funded jobs to Depression-stricken African American workers. Masses need to be organized, he argues, in order for their power to materialize.

Negroes are not getting anywhere with national defense. The whole national defense setup reeks and stinks with race prejudice, hatred, and discrimination. It is obvious to anyone who is not deaf, dumb and blind that the south, with its attitude that the Negro is inferior, worthless, and just simply don't count, is in the saddle. It is a matter of common knowledge that the Army, Navy, and Air Corps are dominated and virtually controlled by southerners. But the southerners are not alone responsible for the fact that Negroes are being brutally pushed around. The north, east and west are also to blame, because they wink, connive at and acquiesce in this practice of discriminating against Negroes. But regardless of who is responsible for the raw deal Negroes are getting, the big bald fact is they are getting it.

Responsible committees of Negroes who seek to intercede in behalf of the Negro being accorded the simple right to work in industries and on jobs serving national defense and to serve in the Army, Navy and Air Corps are being given polite assurances that Negroes will be given a fair deal. But it all ends there. Nothing is actually done to stop discriminations.

It seems to be apparent that even when well-meaning, responsible, top government officials agree upon fair and favorable policy, there are loopholes, and subordinate officers in the Army, Navy, and Air Corps, full of race hatred, who seek its contravention, nullification, evasion. This is why upstanding, independent, able and intelligent Negroes should be in responsible posts of every department of the government. They must be there to stimulate, suggest, and initiate the formulation of certain polices favorable to the Negro, and they must be there to help police these policies in the interest of their fair and consistent execution.

Now, fortunately, Negroes have good, able, and sound people in Dr. Channing H. Tobias in the Draft Board, Judge William H. Hastie in the War Department, Dr. Robert Weaver in the National Defense Commission, Frances Williams in the Consumers' Section, and a few others, but they are helpless without the collective mass support of the Negro people. Aggressive, articulate, determined, mass support will strengthen their hands. It is not enough for Negroes to want jobs in the factories, mills, mines, and offices, they must diplomatically and undiplomatically, ceremoniously and unceremoniously, cry out in no uncertain terms their demand for work and their rightful places in every department of the Army, Navy, and Air Corps, based, of course, upon recognized qualifications.

Evidently, the regular, normal and respectable method of conferences and petitions, while proper and ought to be continued as conditions may warrant, certainly don't work. They don't do the job. However, they are necessary preliminary, advance-guard work, for only a small committee can intelligently formulate a program. But the few people of ability who may develop a program may not possess the power to enforce or secure its adoption.

Just a casual analysis and survey of the dynamics and mechanics of modern movements, legislation, administration and execution show that only power can effect the enforcement and adoption of a given policy, however meritorious it may be. The virtue and rightness of a cause are not alone the condition and cause of its progress and acceptance.

Power and pressure do not reside in the few, the intelligentsia, they lie in and flow from the masses. Power does not even rest with the masses as such. Power is the active principle of only the organized masses, the masses united for a definite purpose. Hence, Negro America must bring its power and pressure to bear upon the agencies and representatives of the federal government to exact their rights in national defense employment and the armed forces of the country. No real, actual, bona fide, definite and positive pressure of the Negro masses has ever been brought to bear upon the executive and legislative branches of the city, state, and national governments.

Now, as to a practical program:

I suggest that 10,000 Negroes march on Washington, D.C.[,] the capitol of the nation, with the slogan: *We Loyal Negro-Americans Demand the Right to Work and Fight for Our Country.* Negroes could join this march from various sections of the country from all trades, professions and callings, such as laborers, doctors, nurses, lawyers, teachers, preachers, mechanics, soldiers, women, and youth groups. Our demand would be simple, single and central; namely, jobs in national defense and placement as soldiers and officers of all ranks we are qualified for in the armed forces.

No propaganda could be whipped up and spread to the effect that Negroes seek to hamper defense. No charge could be made that Negroes are attempting to mar national unity. They want to do none of these things. On the contrary, we seek the right to play our part in advancing the cause of national defense and national unity. But certainly, there can be no true national unity where one-tenth of the population are denied their basic rights as American citizens.

Committees of the marchers could be planned to meet and confer with various government officials about the needs, demands and rights of the Negro. Such a pilgrimage of 10,000 Negroes would wake up and shock official Washington as it has never been shocked before. Why? The answer is clear. Nobody expects 10,000 Negroes to get together and march anywhere for anything at any time. Negroes are supposed not to have sufficient iron in their blood for this type of struggle. In common parlance, they are supposed to be just scared and unorganizable. Is this true? I contend it is not.

What an impressive sight 10,000 Negroes would make marching down Pennsylvania Avenue in Washington, D.C., with banners preaching their cause for justice, freedom and equality.

One thing is certain, and that is if Negroes are going to get anything out of this National Defense which will cost the nation 30 or 40 billions of dollars that we Negroes must help pay in taxes as property owners and workers and consumers, WE MUST FIGHT FOR IT AND FIGHT FOR IT WITH GLOVES OFF.

SOURCE: *Pittsburgh Courier,* January 25, 1941.

Letters to Walter White (1941)

Although the relationship between the NAACP and MOWM would eventually sour, these organizations collaborated closely in the months leading up to the threatened march. In these two letters, Randolph reaches out to Walter White of the NAACP for support for the march on Washington. At least in the early months of the March on Washington campaign, the partnership was fruitful. In addition to throwing the elder organization's weight behind Randolph's efforts, White personally contributed hundreds of dollars to the cause.

March 18, 1941

Dear Walter,

Just a word of remembrance and good hope that you are feeling fine.

Now I have been thinking about the Negro and national defense and have come to the conclusion that something drastic has got to be done to shake official Washington and the white industrialists and labor forces of America to the realization of the fact that Negroes mean business about getting their rights as American citizens under national defense. To this end I have decided to undertake the organization of a march of ten thousand Negroes or more upon Washington. When I come back east I want to talk with you about it.

I hope it may be convenient for you to join with me and a few other persons in the issuance of a call to the Negro people for such a march.

If we are able to mobilize Negroes on such a program it is certain to have a favorable effect upon your splendid plan to get the whole question of national defense and the Negro proved by the Senate.

It is my hope that we may be able to plan the march to take place either before or directly after the conference of the NAACP in Houston.

Cordially yours,
A. Philip Randolph

June 2, 1941

Dear Walter,

Permit me to thank you for your arranging to send an additional $100.00 to help in the initial expenses to the March on Washington Committee.

If the returns from the buttons and certificates are sufficient, it may be possible to reimburse the NAACP and the Brotherhood for the advances they have made, with the exception of the first $100.00. If the returns are not adequate, they will have to be considered as contributions. However, I think that we will be able to secure sufficient funds to meet the needs of the March.

Now, I am sure it will be quite possible for you to reach Washington in time for the demonstration.

I have planned that you make the principal speech setting forth the whole question of national defense and the Negro, outlining the facts, etcetera. It is my thought that your speech should be first so that the representatives of the government would benefit therefrom.

Very Sincerely Yours,
A. Philip Randolph

SOURCE: Group II, box A-417, The Papers of the NAACP, Library of Congress.

Letter to Franklin D. Roosevelt (1941)

In this letter to Franklin D. Roosevelt, Randolph writes of the multiplicity of organizations supporting the impending march on Washington and invites him to address the crowd. In doing so, Randolph is careful to characterize the protest as being in accordance with widely held American principles of fair play and equality. His measured tone is decidedly formal, some might even say obsequious, a fact that illustrates the level of respect Roosevelt and other presidents of his generation evoked from the general public.

May 29, 1941

My Dear Mr. President:

Because the Negro people have not received their just share of jobs in national defense, and our young men have not been integrated into the armed forces of the nation, including the Army, Navy, Air Corps and Marines, on a basis of equality, some of the Negro leaders have formulated plans and set up the necessary machinery in the various sections of the country for the purpose of mobilizing from ten to fifty thousand Negroes to march on Washington in the interest for securing jobs and justice in national defense and fair participation and equal integration into the Nation's military and naval forces.

This movement has been initiated by the officers of the National Association for the Advancement of Colored People, the National Urban League, the Brotherhood of Sleeping Car Porters, the Young Men's Christian Association's branch of the Harlem Community, the Negro Labor Committee of New York, the Elks and a number of other groups.

A call for the march, to take place July 1st, is signed by Walter White of the National Association for the Advancement of Colored People, Reverend William Lloyd Imes of the Presbyterian Church of Harlem, Frank R. Crosswaith, Chairman of the Negro Labor Committee of New York, Layle Lane, Vice-President of the American Federation of Teachers, Dr. Rayford Logan, Chairman of the National and State Committees for the Participation of Negroes in National Defense, Henry K. Craft, Secretary of the 135th Street branch of the YMCA, J. Finley Wilson, Grand Exalted Ruler of the Independent Benevolent Order of Elks of the World, Reverend Adam C. Powell, Jr. of the Abyssinian Baptist Church of Harlem and the undersigned.

March-on-Washington local committees are being set up throughout the country with a view to recruiting the marchers and carrying out the general program in the interest of developing an all-out total demonstration of the Negro people for full participation in the national defense program.

A week prior to the march on Washington, plans have been developed to stage marches in various cities in the interest of urging the Mayors and City

Councils to memorialize you, as President of the United States, to issue an executive order to abolish discrimination in national defense and all departments of the Federal Government.

Following the march in Washington, the program includes a great rally at the Monument of Abraham Lincoln, because of its historical symbolism in relation to the issuance of the Emancipation Proclamation for the liberation of the Negroes from chattel slavery.

As a humanitarian and idealist who has captured the hearts of the peoples of the world for your constructive vision and matchless statesmanship, and as the greatest living champion of the cause of democracy and liberty, I, in the name of the aforementioned committee, wish to request Your Excellency to address the Negroes who will be assembled at this rally in person and the Negroes of America who will be listening to the program and waiting for your voice on this occasion.

I want to assure you, Mr. President, that the Negroes of America are deeply stirred over the question of their receiving equal opportunity to share in the benefits and responsibilities and duties and sacrifices incident to this great and tremendous national effort to build a defense machinery for the protection of our own country and to safeguard the cause of democracy.

I am sure that nothing has arisen in the life of the Negro since Emancipation which has gripped their heart and caught their interest and quickened their imagination more than the girding of our country for national defense without according them the recognition and opportunity as citizens, consumers and workers they feel justified in expecting.

I, therefore, cannot too strongly stress and urge you, as a leader of the American people, to honor this occasion with your presence and message.

Kindly accept assurances of my high personal esteem and appreciation for your interest and cooperation for the cause of the advancement of the Negro people of America and the historic role you are playing to create a better world for all mankind.

Very Sincerely Yours,
A. Phillip Randolph, Director

SOURCE: Official File 391: Marches on Washington, Franklin D. Roosevelt Presidential Library.

A. Philip Randolph addresses a rally for the Fair Employment Practice Committee in St. Louis, Missouri, in 1942. (State Historical Society of Missouri, Arthur Witman Photographic Prints, 836.265)

8 Point Program—March on Washington Movement (1942–1943)

These two documents outline Randolph's expansive vision for the March on Washington Movement during World War II. As seen below, the fight against racism occurred on many fronts.

"Winning Democracy for the Negro Is Winning the War for Democracy"

The war in which our country is engaged not only involves a major share of its resources, but also every one of its citizens both white and black. The Negro citizen, therefore, who is part of the warp and woof of these United States, is vitally concerned not only in a military victory of his country but also of the expressed aims of the war.

Every statement of war aims by responsible leaders in all walks of life, the principles of the Four Freedoms, the eight point program of the Atlantic Charter and, it is to be hoped, the prospectus of a much needed Pacific Charter, express the desire that the outcome of this vast and terrible conflict will be the triumph of democracy and its establishment on a wider and firmer basis. To ensure such a result the preservation and extension of our democratic principles must be an essential part of winning the war.

For the masses of people, abstract principles have vitality only in concrete expression: Freedom from want is real only when it means a chance to work for sufficient food, clothing and shelter. Likewise for the Negro, and for all oppressed people everywhere, the fight for democracy has meaning only when it grants to them the full measure of every right as well as of every obligation for which democracy stands.

We Negroes do not enjoy these rights in the country to which we have given fully of our labor, our talents and of our blood. To ensure that national unity so essential for victory, it is imperative that the Negro be given an equal chance with every other American to enjoy the privileges of American citizenship.

The source of our disabilities lies in the caste system maintained by the Southern states, where segregation and discrimination in social, economic and political life spread [their] vicious influence everywhere. Only an all-out attack by the national government on this caste system at its source will destroy its danger to our national unity.

(1) We demand in the interest of national unity, the abrogation of every law which makes a distinction in treatment between citizens based on religion, creed, color, or national origin. This means an end to Jim Crow in education, in housing, in transportation and in every other social, economic, and political privilege; and especially we demand, in the capital of the nation, an end to all segregation in public places and public institutions.

(2) We demand legislation to enforce the 5th and 14th amendments guaranteeing that no person shall be deprived of life, liberty or property without due process of law so that the full weight of the national government may be used for the protection of life and thereby may end the disgrace of lynching.

(3) We demand the enforcement [of the] 14th and 15th amendments and the enactment of the Pepper Poll Tax Bill so that all barriers in the exercise of the suffrage are eliminated.

(4) We demand the abolition of segregation and discrimination in the Army, Navy, Marine Corps, Air Corps, and all other branches of national defense.

(5) We demand an end to discrimination in jobs and job training. Further, we demand that the F.E.P.C. be made a permanent administration agency of the U.S. Government and that it be given power to enforce its decisions based on its findings.

(6) We demand that federal funds be withheld from any agency which practices discrimination in the use of such funds.

(7) We demand Negro and minority group representation in all administrative agencies so that these groups may have recognition of their democratic right to participate in formulating policies.

(8) We demand representation for the Negro and minority racial groups on all missions, political and technical, which will be sent to the peace conference so that the interests of all people everywhere may be fully recognized and justly provided for in the post-war settlement.

Nothing less than this program will afford Negroes their constitutional rights; nothing less will be evidence of America's devotion to the democratic way of life.

Additional Points on 8 Point Program

The Program and Strategy Committee recommends the addition of the following points to the 8 Point Program, bearing in mind that the original eight points are primarily aimed at the National Government:

(9) We demand the end of discrimination and anti-Negro propaganda wherever it exists throughout the national press, radio, and other channels of public information; we demand fair and full coverage of Negro news by the national press and the use of Negro reporters on white papers to implement such fair coverage.

(10) We demand the fair and equal treatment of Negroes by department stores, hotels, restaurants, busses and all other agencies which serve the public, both as to treatment of Negro patrons and as to employment opportunities for Negroes.

(11) We demand the employment of Negroes in more equitable numbers, and on the basis of equal merit by all private industries and public utilities;

and that Negroes be permitted to rise in the employment scale within these industries in accordance with their merit. We further demand that Negro women be given full and free opportunities to enter industries as women labor is further coordinated into the defense effort.

(12) We demand the passage of Civil Rights Laws, and their enforcement by the state legislatures where such laws do not now exist.

SOURCES: "March on Washington Movement Action Conference, Harlem Y.M.C.A., February 13, 1943" (program), and "Report of Committee on Program and Strategy," in Proceedings of Conference Held in Detroit, September 26–27, 1942, p. 34; March on Washington Movement, 1941–1945, FSN Sc 002, 968-3, Schomburg Clipping File, New York Public Library.

March on Washington Movement Presents Program for the Negro (1944)

Written for Rayford Logan's anthology *What the Negro Wants,* this essay is Randolph's clearest and most comprehensive statement about the tactics and aims of the March on Washington Movement. Critical and patriotic, bold and conciliatory, militant and pragmatic, Randolph's explanation of MOWM's program is a highlight of this chapter. A justification for excluding Communists, an explanation for maintaining an all-black membership policy, and a plan to distance African American voters from partisan loyalty are some of Randolph's most salient points. Also of significance are his articulation of nonviolent direct action and his interpretation of how that technique is squarely within the fabric of African American history.

This statement is being presented at an hour when the lamps of civilization are burning low. If the Axis powers win, the lamps may go out, and if they do, they may not be relighted in a thousand years. The lamps of enlightenment have gone out before. They may go out again. Thus, the Nazism of Hitler, the Militarism of Hirohito, and the Fascism of Mussolini and now Badoglio must be destroyed. The cause of the United Nations must prevail. But the colored peoples know from a tragic experience that it is not enough for the arms of the United Nations to win.

AIMS OF THE NEGRO

The oppressed darker races want something more.
They want much more.
They want the cause of true democracy to march forward.
They want the Brotherhood of man to triumph.
They want a durable and just peace.

They want security and plenty with freedom.

They want to put an end to the vile and sinister doctrine of the Master Race.

They want ethnic equality.

They want economic, political and social equality.

They want to abolish the racism and colonialism of the Anglo-American empire systems.

"Will this ever come?" ask the Negro bootblack, jitterbug, and Ph.D.

DARKER RACES MUST FIGHT FOR FREEDOM

It will not come if the Axis powers win.

It may not come if the United Nations win.

Albeit, it will not come automatically.

It will come only if the downtrodden peoples fight for it.

The darker races can get no solace from the proclamations of Prime Minister Churchill or President Roosevelt. With inept Machiavellian diplomacy, the Atlantic Charter states its concern only for the European countries under the Nazi yoke. And Mr. Churchill observes, in the unvarnished language of the "brass hat" imperialists, that he has not become the first minister of the King to preside over the liquidation of the British Empire. He also adds in a note of somber and sullen militant imperialism, that they will hold their own.

Thus the Negro, labor and liberals might well demand to know: Are we fighting this global war to restore Singapore, Malaya, and Burma to Great Britain? Will the peace reestablish the ill-fated Italian Empire, and give back to notorious Belgium the African Congo? Are the "natives" of Africa to continue to live in slavery of the mandated colonialism of white powers?

FREE AFRICA

The March on Washington Movement proclaims the slogan of a free Africa. It joins the cry of a "Fight for a Free India and China." It hails the struggle for the freedom of the common man everywhere—the common man, whether black, white, brown, yellow, red, Protestant, Catholic, Jewish, native or foreign, worker, storekeeper, artist, teacher, minister.

NOT A WAR FOR FREEDOM

But be not deceived. This is not a war for freedom.

It is not a war for democracy.

It is not a war to usher in the Century of the Common Man.

It is not a Peoples' Revolution.

It is a war to maintain the old imperialistic systems. It is a war to continue "white supremacy," the theory of *Herrenvolk,* and the subjugation, domination, and exploitation of the peoples of color. It is a war between the imperialism of Fascism and Nazism and the imperialism of monopoly capitalistic democracy. Under neither are the colored peoples free.

But this war need not be a world movement of reaction. The people can make it a People's Revolution—a Revolution whose dynamism against Axis tyranny will be greater and more powerful because it will possess the fighting faith and crusading confidence of the masses of all colors and races. The people can cause this war to usher in the Century of the Common Man. This is the meaning of the call of Gandhi for an independent and free India. It is the reason for the stirrings of the "natives" of Africa, the war by the Chinese against the dominion of Nippon, the rebellion of the blacks in the Caribbean Islands against a bare subsistence wage, and the fight of the Negro people of the United States for equality.

CAUSE OF FREEDOM IN RETREAT

Let no Negro, in the pattern of the ostrich, bury his head in the sand and assert the denial of a raging storm of reaction that is now setting in against the Negro people. The Negro must face stark reality in all of its forbidding aspects. The fact is, the cause of freedom and democracy is already in full retreat everywhere. Fascism and reaction are on the offensive. It is obvious to the casual observer that the arms of the United Nations may win and democracy lose. Note that in England, the "Cradle to Grave Security Plan" of Sir William Beveridge has been practically turned down, and the National Resources Planning Board has met rebuffs with its post-war program of security and plenty for all in the United States of America.

The defeat of Senator Norris, the liberal of Nebraska; the expulsion of Leon Henderson, foe of inflation, from OPA; the lost fight to save Odell Waller; the vile and vicious attacks upon the First Lady, Mrs. Roosevelt, by die-hard Tories; the continuance of the infamous Dies Committee which had sought to smear, discredit and destroy Negro, labor and liberal leadership; and the enactment of the Smith-Connally Anti-Labor Fascist Bill over President Roosevelt's veto, are significant signs of the times. Yes, it is also important to add the torpedoing of the scheduled railroad hearings on racial discrimination by FEPC. Indeed the future looks dark. Developments point to the revival of the cry "back to normalcy," or the conservatism of Coolidge and the rugged individualism of Hoover, or maybe an era of furious Fascism with the Negro playing the chief role of the victim in America as did the Jews in Germany. This is why the Negro must seek, discover and devise a program of liberation.

NEGRO MAY BEAR THE TORCH OF DEMOCRACY

A militant fight of the Negro for equality may save the day for the democratic way of life. But before a program of any oppressed minority or majority can be formulated, it ought to be determined what the group needs and wants. A discussion of needs and wants is timely because a group may need what it does not want and it may want what it does not need.

Since Negroes in the United States of America live under a democracy—of a sort—yes, a sharply limited democracy, especially in terms of race, where public opinion, the most powerful single force in society, is created, or rather ought to be created by the free inter-play and free competition of ideas in the arena of public discussion, they, the Negroes, need and must have the status of free and equal citizenship. They must be free and equal to participate in and help shape and determine constructive and creative human action and human institutions for the advancement of the common good.

However, Negroes must be free in order to be equal and they must be equal in order to be free. These are complementary and supplementary rights and conditions. The existence of the one is a condition to the existence of the other. Under the terms of our liberal democratic traditions, the absence of freedom or equality means the absence of democracy. Men cannot win freedom unless they win equality. They cannot win equality unless they win freedom. By the same token men cannot remain free unless they remain equal. And they cannot remain equal unless they remain free. These are the axioms of a democratic progressive society. Their validity and verity are as unquestionable as the mathematical proposition, two plus two equals four.

This is why the historical experience of the modern world shows that political democracy can never be truly attained until it rests upon the underpinnings and is the correlative of industrial and economic democracy. There can be no true political democracy where equality is the ascendant note until there is a comparable dispersal of economic equality in our social order. Now, the principle of the indivisibility of political, industrial, economic, and social democracy is a condition of total equality, political, industrial, economic, and social for all of the citizens of a given community. Just as a nation cannot survive half free and half slave, it cannot survive half equal and half unequal in terms of political, industrial, economic and social opportunity. . . .

MEETING THE PROBLEM

How can this problem be met?
Naturally this question suggests methods.
Around methods invariably revolve multiple opinions.

Now the basic phase of the Negro problem is economic.

Why?

The origin of the Negro problem was economic, for it had its seat in the slave trade.

The reason for subjecting Negroes to slavery was economic.

It had residence in cheap labor.

The reason for the abolition of slavery was economic.

It rests upon the rise of capitalist industrialism and the growing uneconomic character of slave labor in the production of cotton, rice, sugar and tobacco.

Verily, the biggest problem confronting Negroes today is economic, that is, getting work and wages to buy food, clothing and shelter.

Thus the March on Washington Movement sets forth as the cardinal and primary cornerstone of its program: economic action.

Economic

LABOR UNION

The major and paramount form of economic action by the Negro people must necessarily be the building of trade and industrial unions and the employment of the technique of collective bargaining. This is so because well-nigh 99 and 9/10 percent of the Negro people are workers of hand and brain who earn their living in the sweat of their brow by selling their labor in the market for wages. Hence, the biggest business of the Negro consists in his selling at the highest price that which he has the most of, namely his ability to work. But this business of the Negro worker selling his labor is not as simple as it sounds. For immediately he enters the market for jobs, he is met with a color bar in some of the trade unions, or prejudice on the part of some employers. Not only is he the last hired and first fired, but he meets this vicious cycle when applying for work or a union card. The employer rejects him because he hasn't got a job.

Thus, the progress of the Negro in the modern industrial system will depend in a large measure upon cleansing the labor unions and personnel manager systems of the sins of race prejudice. This is one fight Negro and white workers must wage which they cannot afford to lose since trade unions are the main bulwark of democracy. But this bulwark cannot stand if part of the workers possess[es] economic citizenship and another part is economically disfranchised because of color and race.

The March on Washington Movement sets its face resolutely toward the complete integration of the Negro workers into the organized labor movement.

If an industry in which Negroes work is controlled by the A.F. of L., they are urged to affiliate with this body. On the other hand, if an industry is under the control of the CIO, in which Negroes work, they are urged to affiliate with the CIO. If Negroes are employed in an industry which is not organized by either the A.F. of L. or CIO, they are urged to organized and become a part of one of these federated labor bodies.

EMPLOYMENT FOR NEGROES

No greater wrong has been committed against the Negro than the denial to him of the right to work. This question of the right to work is tied up with the right to live. But Negroes are not only denied the right to work on certain jobs but they are sentenced in some industries to a sort of blind alley position. For instance, the Negro may be employed as a Pullman porter but not as a Pullman conductor, although he demonstrates his ability to perform this service by running-in-charge, at a slight differential in pay. A Negro may be employed as a waiter on the dining cars but not as a steward, although here, too, he demonstrates his ability to perform the services of a steward, in which event he receives a slight differential in pay. The Negro may operate as a brakeman or flagman[,] but, because of custom, practice and tradition resulting from racial discrimination, he is not promotable to the job of train conductor, although all train conductors were former brakemen or flagmen. It is a matter of common knowledge that Negro train porters teach hundreds of white brakemen how to operate as train conductors. And Negro waiters break in white stewards, and Negro Pullman porters instruct white Pullman conductors how to make out their diagrams.

The March on Washington Movement rejects this economic discrimination and segregation of the Negro worker and calls for the abolition of the racial blind alley job. The March on Washington Movement maintains that Negroes should be upgraded and assigned positions in industry, in the interest of industrial justice and efficiency, upon the basis of their merit and ability. It contends for the right of the Negro worker to break through the barrier of non-promotability so that a Negro Pullman porter may become a conductor; a Negro waiter, a steward or a head waiter; a Negro brakeman or flagman, a conductor; and a Negro fireman, an engineer.

While the shortage of manpower, economic necessity, and the President's Committee on Fair Employment Practices have provided jobs in defense industries and the Government for Negro workers, practically over 75 percent are still victims of discrimination when they seek upgrading in skill[s] and wages. Negro women, too, who are being put into war industries[,] are suffering from all types of discrimination that are visited upon Negro men. For instance, Negro women are employed as porters in the terminal stations, but they are not allowed to perform responsible work in the railroad yards, such as white women are employed to perform. White women are being used as trainmen, but this privilege is denied to Negro women.

GOVERNMENT ALSO GUILTY

But private industry is not the only agency which sins against the Negro worker. The federal government is the chief offender. Hence, the March on Washington Movement fights for employment of Negroes in every part of the government, municipal, state and federal, from a porter or janitor to the highest form of technical, skilled, and professional service, upon a basis, naturally, of merit and ability. Since Negroes, as workers and consumers, are tax-makers and tax-payers, they have a right to fight for placement in all types of employment in public utilities. Public utilities in every city should have their Negro motormen, conductors, bus drivers, mechanics, ticket agents, telephone girls, gas-meter readers, bookkeepers, stenographers, and foremen[,] and also places in the higher supervisory and managerial brackets.

TECHNIQUE OF ACTION

But it is one thing to want a thing and another thing to get it. The whole world wants peace but how shall we get it? The workers want industrial democracy but how shall they get it?

Hence, there is nothing more important than method, technique, [and] strategy in planning the solution of a problem. MOWM employs the following pattern:

1. Negotiation
2. Inter-racial, inter-faith pressures
3. Mass marches
4. Picketing
5. Boycott
6. Seeking and developing trade union co-operation
7. Public relations
8. Membership in trade unions, the natural ally of the Negro.

The March on Washington Movement, in seeking to secure employment for Negroes in industries hitherto excluding them, resorts first to the method of negotiation with the industrial management. Failing in this procedure, it seeks to coordinate inter-racial and inter-faith pressures to secure the consideration of personnel managers and the heads of industrial enterprises. When the aforementioned pressure proves ineffective, MOWM employs the nonviolent direct action technique of mass marches. These marches are then reinforced by the relatively permanent picket line until some form of favorable action is secured.

Supplementing the technique of direct mass action is sometimes developed a boycott. The most basic and effective form of action consists in well directed and organized public relations to keep the public advised and informed that the reason for the campaign against a given enterprise and trade union is employment opportunities for Negroes. Because of the progress of the closed and union shops and the maintenance of membership clauses for the benefit of trade unions, the fight for membership in all of the trade unions must and will be relentlessly waged by the Negro worker.

The March on Washington Movement assigns economic ignorance on the part of the white workers as a primary reason for the victimization of the Negro worker. Being in the main without knowledge of the far-reaching implications of monopoly capitalism and how all workers regardless of race, religion, color or national origin are the objects of exploitation, the white worker picks out the Negro as the scapegoat. But the white workers will change in their attitude towards the Negro as the forces of Fascism turn upon them and workers' education and economic pressure become more widespread.

EXECUTIVE ORDER 8802

Because the workers must eat, the March on Washington Movement made the fight for jobs in the early stages of the national defense program its cardinal plan of action. It was the coordination of the National Association for the Advancement of Colored People, National Urban League, civic, church, trade union, and educational movements into a formidable program to march on Washington that was largely responsible for the issuance of Executive Order 8802 and the establishment by the President of the Committee on Fair Employment Practices. Here, the technique of non-violent direct action in the form of a March on Washington bore fruit. It was the continuous pressure of the March on Washington and the above mentioned group of organizations that rescued the Fair Employment Practices Committee from the War Manpower Commission and brought about the rescheduling of the railroad hearings that had been postponed indefinitely by the Chairman of the War Manpower Commission, Mr. Paul V. McNutt.

Political

But economics is only one arm with which the Negro people may fight for their liberation. The struggle[s] of all oppressed peoples show that economic action requires the supplementation of political action. To this end, the March on Washington Movement suggests as a major strategy for the effective employment of the political power of the Negro, the building of a national non-partisan Negro political bloc, with branches in the various local communities in the country. This does not require that Negroes come out of the Republican, Democratic, Socialist or Communist parties. But it does require that, when a crucial question of universal concern and importance to the Negro arises, Negroes will express their united political strength regardless of party politics. When this is done, it will strengthen the position of Negro leaders in the Republican and Democratic parties and make the white boss politicians more disposed to give serious consideration to all questions affecting the interest of the Negro. It will prove that Negroes are not so died-in-the-wool Republicans or Democrats that they will not ignore political labels when a crisis comes, for the benefit and advancement of the Negro. It goes without saying that any form of political action which favorably serves the interest of the Negro people also favorably serves the interest of our country. It is a matter of common knowledge that Negroes as Democrats do not amount to much. They can get but little done for Negroes. Similarly, Negroes as Republicans are not very strong and their voice is seldom heeded. Negroes as Socialists or Communists are helpless, but when Negro Republicans and Democrats step forward in a united front expressed in a powerful non-partisan political bloc, they will be heard and heeded by political boss or mayor, governor, president, Senate or House Committees. The value of a non-partisan political Negro bloc consists in the fact that it represents power. It is well-nigh the law of the life of the politician that he respects nothing but votes. Politicians are seldom, if ever, moved by questions of principles, ideals or human justice. Politicians are hungry for power and jobs. This is true of [both] white and black politicians. They fear votes and the righteous wrath of the people. They will only do the right thing for the people when they are made to do so by pressure, public opinion and votes.

Therefore, upwards of 15 millions of Negroes need not forever play the role of political mendicants. They have power if they will mobilize by registering in mass for non-partisan political action. Such a political bloc should be financed by Negroes entirely. It is still true that the power over man's subsistence is the power of his will, and he who pays the fiddler calls the tune. Therefore, such a non-partisan political bloc should not accept any money from Republican,

Democratic, Socialist or Communist party. It should be entirely free. It cannot be free if it is subsidized by any politicians.

HOW POLITICAL BLOC MAY FUNCTION

This piece of political machinery, during campaigns, could send speakers into districts to oppose the enemies of the Negro and support their friends on a basis of their record in office and public life. Literature on the issues and candidates could be prepared and distributed widely throughout the country, expressing the position of the Negro on them. Whole[-]page advertisements setting forth the position and demands of the Negro people should be carried in strategic papers, dailies and weeklies, during a campaign to let the world know that Negroes are not asleep or weak. If such a powerful non-partisan political bloc is honestly, courageously and intelligently directed, it could transform the political status of the Negro people in our American community, put a Negro on the United States Supreme Court, Negroes on federal courts, a Negro in the Cabinet, Negroes on policy making commissions, get Negroes their rightful share of jobs in government agencies, elect them to municipal and state legislatures as well as to the Senate and the House of Congress, abolish anti-Negro legislation, reverse anti-Negro court decisions, eliminate racial bias in administrative agencies, and secure for Negroes the respect enjoyed by other citizens. It could aid effectively in passing anti-poll tax legislation, put a federal anti-lynching law on the statute books and enable the Negroes to have their voice heard above the ranting and raving of the Bilbos and Rankins.

HOW BLOC CAN BE BUILT

A non-partisan Negro political bloc is not unprecedented. Already because of anti-labor legislation, the A.F. of L. and CIO, the Big Four Railroad Brotherhoods, and the National Farmers Union are seeking a common ground of political unity. They realize that as individual groups they are practically hopeless politically, [b]ut united they become a formidable power.

The technique of setting up such a bloc is simple, and consists in the federation of religious, fraternal, civic, labor, educational, women, business, and various political groups upon a minimum political program. This organization would be similarly constructed in local communities. It would mobilize its forces to operate the door-bell-ringing plan to reach every man, woman and child to get them to register and vote against a given political menace and to put literature into the hands of all citizens of the community. It would also conduct public forums to keep the interest and issues alive and focus attention upon the public evils.

This powerful non-partisan political bloc of Negroes would also serve the cause of labor, progressive, liberal and social legislation. It is pretty generally a matter of fact that the enemies of the Negro are the enemies of labor and progress[,] and the enemies of labor are the enemies of the Negro. Note that the poll-tax congressmen and senators who filibuster against legislation to free the Negro from mob violence and lynching and white primaries are the same leaders that pilot the fight to enact fascist legislation such as the Smith-Connally bill.

Such a bloc would necessarily use its force against reaction and on the side of progress. Why? The answer is Negroes are the victims of reaction and the beneficiaries of progress.

Nor is it difficult to see that the strategy of a non-partisan political bloc has its validity in the experience of the struggle of groups to achieve certain objectives. Big business has the most powerful non-partisan political bloc in America. It has been built and is directed by the National Manufacturers Association. This bloc assails and opposes all liberal and social legislation. Farmers, too, have a non-partisan political bloc. It is represented by the American Farm Bureau Federation and the National Farmers Grange.

EXCLUDING THE COMMUNISTS

While Democrat, Republicans, and Socialists may be coordinated in such a non-partisan political bloc, Communists must be excluded. The reason is simple. It is silly and suicidal for Negroes to add to the handicap of being *Black,* another handicap of being *Red.* Moreover, the Communist Party seeks only to rule or ruin a movement. It has one objective. It seeks to use the Negro and labor or any group which may be at hand for the purpose of consolidating the foreign policies and fortunes of Soviet Russia. They have their feet in America but heads and hearts in Moscow. For this reason the Communists constitute a pestilence, menace and nuisance to the Negro people as well as to organized labor. It would be an eminently unsound and destructive strategy for Negroes to tie up with Communists[,] since the primary and fundamental interest[s] of the Negro and labor are common and the same, but labor has long since recognized the danger of the Communist movement, and thus the A.F. of L. and CIO have condemned and repudiated the Communist Party, its policies, program, tactics, and so forth, and have adopted the policy of throwing Communists out of the unions whenever they are discovered. Hence, Negroes cannot logically and with sound wisdom tie up with a movement such as the Communist, which organized labor in America condemns and rejects. The history and record of this political cult shows that it conforms with rigid fidelity to the rapidly changing, unpredictable climate of Soviet Russia, without regard to the national interests of any other group. When the war broke, the Communists who had posed as the savior[s] of the Negro promptly dropped him like a hot potato. This was not the first time the Communists deserted the Negro. When Soviet Russia was seeking recognition from the United States government, Joe Stalin suddenly and unceremoniously halted the plans for the making of the well[-]advertised, grandiose pro-Negro film, exposing the sins of America against the colored people, when he saw that such action would help Soviet Russia win the approbation of Southern politicians that might advance his interest in securing the said recognition. . . .

NON-VIOLENT GOOD WILL ACTION

Discrimination against Negroes in restaurants, dance halls, theatres, and other public places of amusement and entertainment above the Mason-Dixon line are alarmingly quite general. There are few hotels in the big cities that freely admit Negro patrons. When approached for accommodations by Negroes, all sorts of ruses are resorted to. The well known excuse is that no rooms are available. It is difficult to meet this situation. But the March on Washington Movement has proclaimed its dedication to and advocacy of non-violent good will direct action as a method of meeting this discrimination. It works in this way: White friends who believe in the right of the Negroes to exercise their civil liberties are organized, trained and disciplined with Negroes.

The technique works as follows: The white friends who precede the Negro patrons to a table in a given restaurant or hotel or place of amusement, upon seeing the Negro citizens denied service, will thereupon join the Negroes in requesting conference with the management to discuss the reason for the anti-Negro policy. If the manager agrees to a conference, efforts are made by the Negro and white persons to convince the manager that he is violating the Constitutional rights of the Negro citizens, and if there is a civil rights law in the state, a copy of same is presented to the manager in proof of the state. If a conference is denied, civil rights action against the place in question may be filed, or another visit may be made to the place with a larger number of Negro and white friends and picketing may ensue, or the white and colored friends may decide to stage a sit[-]down strike in the place to bring the issue to a head.

Before any form of direct action is engaged in, all the resources of negotiation are exhausted. If in the process of attempting to exercise the right of Negroes to receive service in a given enterprise, the Negro and white friends are violently ejected from the place, the policy of the March on Washington Movement is not to fight back. Every individual who participates in such a project is pledged to non-violent action, to the extent of not even using violent language against the management or the employees. If a Negro or white friend seeking to break down the discriminatory barriers is physically injured, no effort will be made to secure financial damages for same, for it is considered as a part of the price which must be paid, in sacrifice and suffering, to eliminate an evil which has been acquiesced in and permitted to exist by the inaction and fear of the Negro people.

NON-VIOLENT ACTION IN THE SOUTH

The areas in which Non-Violent Good Will Direct Action will be initiated will be carefully studied and selected with a view to the avoidance of any unnecessary violent and destructive social explosions. MOWM recognizes that the barriers of racial discrimination in the Southern section of the country cannot be abolished overnight and that they must be approached in terms of the conditions of the racial climate of the community. But it also insists that a policy of do-nothing is also dangerous and provocative. Therefore, MOWM plans a series of Non-Violent Good Will Direct Action institutes throughout the country where techniques and strategy will be carefully evaluated and appraised with a view to their utilization in various fields of social interest. Thus, all persons who participate in these non-violent projects are required to go through a rigid training and discipline to develop self control and the requisite moral and spiritual resources and armament with which to meet the most trying ordeal that the principles of MOWM may not be compromised.

The March on Washington Movement takes the position that Negroes in the South can make an effective gesture against Jim Crow by setting aside a day when they refuse to send their children to a Jim Crow school. This will have a psychological value of focusing the attention of the South upon this social cancer. The Jim Crow railroad coach in the South for Negroes can be scrupulously avoided as a leper on some given day set aside for that purpose. Street cars and buses in the South could also be boycotted on a given day. But these forms of social discipline and response can only follow well-planned educational programs.

Contrary to many hysterical and intemperate attacks upon Non-Violent Good Will Direct Action by some of the Negro intelligentsia and petty bourgeoisie that [claim] Negroes cannot comprehend and execute such a principle, this form of social protest and revolt was used by Harriet Tubman in her underground railroad for the escape of Negroes from slavery to the east and eastern Canada before and after the Civil War. Migration movements of Negroes from the South are instances of Non-Violent Good Will Direct Action. Upon the introduction of the Jim Crow car in the South following Reconstruction, thousands of Negroes refused to ride on them. They rode in hacks and wagons and sometimes walked in protest against this insult. Instead of the strategy of Non-Violent Good Will Direct Action instigating and promoting violence and bloodshed, rioting and mob action, racial hatred and ill will, it is designed and will tend to eliminate these forms of racial irritation and conflict. Of course, the MOWM does not contend that Non-Violent Good Will Direct Action is the final and complete answer to Jim Crow. It is only one method of attack.

MARCH ON WASHINGTON

Pivotal and central to the whole struggle in the Negro liberation movement at this time is the abolition of Jim Crow in the armed forces. Many and varied opinions have been expressed about the merits and the danger of the March on Washington. The *Pittsburgh Courier,* the journalistic spokesman of the petty black bourgeoisie, with bitter attacks, shrieks its condemnation of the March on Washington Movement because of the proposed march upon the nation's capital, viewing with alarm and a mortal, chronic fear the imagined consequence of such an adventure. It wants results without risks, achievement without action. Resting upon the feather bed of deluxe material comfort, it winces and cringes before the gathering forces of the Negro masses for direct action, [even] though non-violent.

The MOWM is not unaware of the significance and value of every form of agitation and organization in the fight for Negro rights, including news articles and editorials in the press and magazines, sermons in the pulpit, orations on the public platform, programs on the radio, dramas and the movies, but it is committed to the thesis that none of these agencies can and will project the cause of the Negro into the main stream of public opinion as effectively as direct action, mass action, and, of course, always, non-violent action.

The immediate, positive and direct value of mass action pressure consists of two things: One, it places human beings in physical motion which can be felt, seen and heard. Nothing stirs and shapes public sentiment like physical action. Organized labor and organized capital have long since recognized this. This is why the major weapon of labor is the STRIKE. It is why the major weapon of business is the lock-out and the shut-down. All people feel, think and talk about a physical formation of people, whoever they may be. This is why wars grip the imagination of man. Mass demonstrations against Jim Crow are worth a million editorials and orations in anybody's paper and on any platform. Editorials and orations are only worthwhile and effective when they are built around some actual human struggle for specific social and racial rights and against definite wrongs.

Mass social pressure in the form of marches and picketing will not only touch and arrest the attention of the powerful public officials but also the "little man" in the street. And, before this problem of Jim Crow can be successfully attacked, all of America must be shocked and awakened. This has never been done, except by race riots that are dangerous socio-racial explosions. Moreover, mass efforts are a form of struggle for Negro rights in which all Negroes can participate, including the educated and the so-called uneducated, the rich and the poor. It is a technique and strategy which the "little Negro" in the tavern, pool-room, on the streets, jitterbug, store-front preacher, and share-cropper, can use to help free the race.

ALL NEGRO MOVEMENT

Now, the March on Washington Movement is an all Negro movement, but it is not anti-white, anti-American, anti-labor, anti-Catholic or anti-Semitic. It's simply pro-Negro. It does not rest so much upon race as upon the social problem of Jim Crow. It does not oppose inter-racial organizations. It cooperates with such mixed organizations as the National Association for the Advancement of Colored People and the National Urban League, and churches, trade unions. Its validity lies in the fact that no one will fight as hard to remove and relieve pain as he who suffers from it. Negroes are the only people who are the victims of Jim Crow, and it is they who must take the initiative and assume the responsibility to abolish it. Jews must and do lead the fight against anti-Semitism, Catholics must lead the fight against anti-Catholicism, labor must battle against anti-labor laws and practices. This does not mean that Negroes should not invite Catholic, Jewish, Protestant, labor and liberal business groups of white people to help them win this fight. Labor unions are composed only of workers, but they seek the help of clergymen, housewives and liberals who may be non-workers. During strikes, unions form citizens' committees to help them, but they do not take the citizens into the unions. It is well-nigh axiomatic that while white and Negro citizens may sympathize with the cause of striking miners or auto-workers or lumber-jacks, the fact remains that the miners, auto-workers and lumber-jacks must take the initiative and assume the responsibility and take the risks themselves to win higher wages and shorter hours. By the same token, white liberals and labor may sympathize with the Negro's fight against Jim Crow, but they are not going to lead the fight. They never have and they never will. The fight to annihilate Jim Crow in America must be led by Negroes[,] with the cooperation and collaboration of white liberals and labor. And the fight against Jim Crow is the fight against fascism.

The petty black bourgeoisie are always hunting for some white angel at whose feet they may place the Negroes' problems. This provides a middle of the road or lofty, professional, neutral, so-called scientific objectivity or a severely critical but do-nothing attitude. At one time they unloaded their troubles on the GOP on the grounds that it was the party of "Father" Abraham Lincoln. Then when the political pickings became slight they fled to the

Democratic Jackass. Ere long they will learn that there is no fundamental difference between Democrats and Republicans, either with respect to Negroes or labor, that they are like two peas in a pod, two souls with a single thought—tweedledee and tweedledum.

RACE RIOTS

Now, what of the race riots that now bedevil the Negro and the country? The March on Washington Movement urges Negroes to hold public meetings to discuss the epidemic of race riots now sweeping the country to bring the issue intelligently and boldly into the open.

People's committees should be picked in the meetings from the floor by the people and given the mandate to go to see the mayors of the cities, and to join with other committees of similar cities in a state to see the governor to urge and demand that commissions on race relations be appointed to study the labor, economic, housing, recreational and law enforcement agencies and policies and forces with a view to making recommendations to the mayor and governor to take measures to prevent riots, and to stop them promptly and effectively when they start.

These public meetings should also call upon President Roosevelt to appoint a National Commission on Race to perform the aforementioned task on a national scale. They should call upon Congressman Sam Rayburn, Democratic Speaker of the House of Representatives, and Congressman [Joseph W.] Martin, Republican Minority Leader, to set up machinery for a Congressional investigation of the Detroit race riot and the riots in Beaumont, Texas; Mobile, Alabama; Los Angeles, California; New York City and other places. The public meetings should also plan the formation of city-wide inter-racial inter-faith committees, composed of trade unionists, business, educational, [and] political representatives which will serve as a public group of citizens to cooperate in the study and maintenance of law and order. Such meetings should also call upon the President to send Negro and white troops into riot areas and to keep them there to ensure the right and opportunity of the Negro workers to continue on the jobs with the white workers in the production of war materials, ships and planes to enable the United Nations to win the war and destroy Axis tyranny.

NEGRO SOLDIER VOTE

What of the vote of the 400,000 or more Negro soldiers in the South? Because of recent legislation removing the obligation to pay a poll-tax by soldiers from the poll-tax states, Negroes have the opportunity to exercise considerable influence upon national political affairs in the coming presidential campaign. They can practically wipe out the menace of lily-white Republicans who are no better than Dixie Democrats. Because of superior numbers, the Negro soldier can be used to stage separate state Republican conventions and wield the balance of power in the selection of the next Republican candidate for President. This would enable the Negro to bargain for substantial concessions in the form of the Republican Party support of a national civil rights bill, anti–poll-tax bill, an anti-lynching bill and equal consideration of jobs in all categories in the government.

Negroes should also present themselves to register and vote in the Democratic primaries. But they should not appear as individuals. They should appear in groups of ten or more. Where there is more than one Negro appearing to exercise his constitutional right to vote, there is less likelihood for attempts at intimidation and fraud. Negroes must also attack the rotten borough political system in the South. It can and must be destroyed. This fight will help save democracy in America. Both major parties, Democratic and Republican, must answer for the fact that Negroes are deprived of the right to vote in direct violation of the Fourteenth Amendment. A flagrant evidence of the unwarranted power this disfranchisement gives the South is shown by the following figures from the 1940 census:

State	Total Population	Citizens over 21	Voters	Rep. in House
South Carolina	1,899,804	989,841	99,830	6
Washington	1,736,191	1,123,725	793,833	6
Arkansas	1,949,387	1,198,986	200,743	7
Connecticut	1,709,242	1,011,658	781,502	5
Georgia	3,123,723	1,768,869	312,539	10
Wisconsin	3,137,587	1,941,603	1,405,522	10

The national government does nothing in this situation to enforce that provision of the Fourteenth Amendment which directly states [that] the representation of any state will be cut down in the proportion that it discriminates. Negroes are denied an equal share of federal money appropriated under the Smith-Hughes and the George-Deen Acts for vocational education. The national government does nothing to see that this money is spent equitably.

Negroes are discriminated against in every aspect of life—in housing, transportation, health facilities, recreation, education and employment. This treatment has made the Negro bitter and determined that if Negroes have to serve in a Jim Crow army and risk their lives overseas for freedom, they are going to enjoy that freedom here. They wish to avoid race tension and conflict, but the major responsibility for avoiding conflict rests with those who refuse to change their thinking and practices in a period when great social changes are taking place. The Republican and Democratic parties cannot escape responsibility for these conditions; therefore the March on Washington Movement, representing thousands of Negroes throughout the country, wants specific answers to the following questions:

1. What will the Republican Party and its representatives in Congress do to enforce that provision of the Constitution that reads: "No person shall be . . . deprived of life, liberty, or property without due process of law?"

2. What will the Republican Party and its representatives in Congress do to cut down the representation in Congress of those states which discriminate against Negroes in voting?

3. What will the Republican and Democratic Parties and their representatives in Congress do to abolish Jim Crow in housing, transportation, education, recreation and other social services?

4. What will the Republican and Democratic Parties and their representatives in Congress do to ensure the permanency of the Fair Employment Practices Committee as an administrative agency to bring the techniques of intelligence, of fact and of justice, to the problems of breaking down discrimination in employment?

5. What will the Republican and Democratic Parties and their representatives in Congress do to break down discrimination in the armed forces?

Finally, let me pose this challenging issue of the War.

Fellow Citizens!

ARE NEGRO AMERICANS CITIZENS?

Right here in our own country is one of the great issues of the war: SHALL WE HAVE DEMOCRACY FOR ALL OF THE PEOPLE OR FOR SOME OF THE PEOPLE?

This is a great moral issue since a war for democracy against Nazi racialism cannot consistently be prosecuted on a Jim Crow basis. This is also a great practical issue since racial antagonisms are grave handicaps in the national effort to win the war and plan the peace.

THE AMERICAN PEOPLE HAVE NOT MET THIS ISSUE.

THE ANSWER CAN NO LONGER BE POSTPONED TO THE QUESTION: ARE NEGROES AMERICAN CITIZENS WITH THE SAME RIGHTS AND OBLIGATIONS AS WHITE CITIZENS?

The Constitution states:

All persons born or naturalized in the United States and subject to the jurisdiction thereof, are citizens of the United States and of the State wherein they
reside. No State shall make or enforce any law which shall abridge the privilege
or immunities of citizens of the United States; nor shall any State deprive any
person of life, liberty or property without due process of law; nor deny to any
person within its jurisdiction the equal protection of the laws.

In these explicit words the Congress of the United States intended to help
the newly freed people progress from slavery to free citizenship. But the
promise of the Fourteenth Amendment, written into the Constitution itself,
was never fulfilled. An undemocratic pattern of "white supremacy" and Jim
Crow was evolved in the Southern states to take the place of chattel slavery.
The shameful pattern has spread beyond the Mason-Dixon line and has
infected racial relations throughout the country.

There are more than 13,000,000 Negroes in this country. Among them are
laborers, labor leaders, tradesmen, poets, musicians, scientists, doctors, lawyers, social workers, teachers, ministers, writers and philosophers. The overwhelming majority are working people, whose toil and struggle have for more
than 300 years helped build America. Negroes are loyal to America and to the
democratic principles for which our country stands. Though only 10 percent
of the population, Negroes, in 1940–41, furnished 16 percent of all volunteers
in the United States Army. They love their native land and have fought for it
from Bunker Hill to North Africa.

BUT HOW HAVE THEY BEEN REQUITED?

They are discriminated against in the very armed forces which summon
them to shed their blood for their country. They are drafted in Jim Crow
quotas, trained in Jim Crow regiments, segregated in every possible way from
their white comrades in arms. And all this despite the fact that Section 4A of
the 1940 Draft Act states:

In the selection and training of men under this Act, and in the interpretation
and execution of the provisions of this Act, there shall be no discrimination
against any person on account of race or color.

We in the March on Washington Movement are disturbed by these things. We
call on our fellow Americans to fight with us to wipe out these practices which
violate both in spirit and in letter the Declaration of Independence and the
Constitution.

We demand a democratic army and call upon the President as Commander-
in-Chief to enforce the Draft Law which forbids discrimination.

We demand that Negroes be employed on the basis of their skill and intelligence in all branches of our federal service in every public and private industry. This means a functioning FEPC with power to end discrimination in training, in placement, in wages, in promotions and in membership in labor organizations.

We demand equal education opportunities with equal access for the Negro student to all public tax-supported institutions.

We demand the democratic right to vote without poll-taxes, white primaries and other devices which keep the majority of Southern Negroes a voteless group with no voice either in the selection of their representatives or [as] a check on unjust public policies.

We demand an end to segregation in transportation, in housing, in health and recreational facilities and in all other social service.

We demand the enforcement of that provision of the Constitution which provides "No person . . . shall be deprived of life, liberty, or property, without due process of law."

We demand the abrogation of every law which makes a distinction in treatment between citizens based on religion, creed, color or national origin.

We demand Negro and minority group representation on all administrative agencies so that these groups may help to determine policies for all people.

These demands are issues which concern all of us, both white and black, for every American has a stake in the fight against racial discrimination. For the rise of Hitler to power shows us racial prejudice is one of the most effective and dangerous tools of fascism. Just as the great mass of German people, their trade unions, their political parties and other organizations were crushed along with the Jews, so over here, reactionary forces will also strike down the trade unions, free religious and liberal institutions and the common people of America. The colored people of Asia, Africa, and Latin America will measure the genuineness of our declarations about a free world to the extent that we create a free world within our own borders.

In the name of America, past and future, in the name of the common interest of humanity, of the tenets of democracy, of those who now are dying and of those who live for freedom, we call upon all in the nation and the Christian Church to join in this struggle for human dignity and for the equality of all men and women.

In conclusion, let me add that the March on Washington Movement holds the following position[s]:

1. It does not seek to overthrow the American government. We shall uphold and defend it, but seek to purge it of its sins and make it better, and true to its ideals.

2. It does not seek to change the economic, political and social status of the Negro through bloodshed and violence.

3. It is determined to fight to abolish Jim Crow through non-violent, good will, direct action or constitutional obedience.

4. It does not seek to provoke race riots and increase race tensions and conflicts.

5. But[,] on the contrary, it works to prevent race riots and decrease racial tensions by bringing the cause of race riots through the medium of public mass meetings, marches and public relations, into the open with frank and truthful discussion.

6. It is the general belief of the March on Washington Movement that the Negro would sooner or later be compelled to march on Washington to strike our heaviest blow against second-class citizenship, and the issuance of a national Proclamation to abolish Jim Crow in the armed forces by the President, just as Abraham Lincoln issued a Proclamation to abolish slavery during the Civil War.

7. The MOWM does not approach this problem with rancor, hatreds or fears. We approach it with the spirit of brotherhood and good will. We believe in the essential decency of the great majority of the American people. We believe they will respond to a continuous challenge of the moral law of human unity and cooperation.

Statement at U.S. Senate Fair Employment Act Hearings (1945)

Black America's "labor leader at large" lives up to his name in this U.S. Senate hearing. Equipped with facts such as employment statistics and public opinion polls, Randolph makes a cogent argument for pending legislation known as S. 101 that would make a permanent FEPC. He appeals to the ideals of the Atlantic Charter and points to fair employment laws as a way to make "democracy a reality in New York and Alabama." Coming near the end of the war, this hearing represented one of Randolph's last chances to preserve the gains made by the March on Washington Movement.

S. 101 is a bill designed to enact legislation in the interest of fair employment opportunities for all workers, regardless of race, color, religion, national origin, or ancestry. The tragic display of racial discrimination in the various industries throughout the country has seriously hampered war production, and has provided an opportunity for a false cry on manpower shortage. The so-called manpower shortage would soon vanish were workers accepted without regard to race or color, and their labor and skills fully utilized in every phase of war production. For instance, in the railroad industry alone, according to the United States Railroad Retirement Board's report, setting forth some of the personnel needs of railroads as of February 1, 1945, [the numbers] were as follows: Baggagemen, 49; boilermakers, 977; brakeman, 2,457; Carmen, 3,131; electricians, 558; locomotive engineers, 70; locomotive firemen, 851; machinists, 3,356; telegraphers, 1,392; switch men, 2,994.

Now, while the railroad industry needs the aforementioned number of employees in the various classifications named to do with war jobs, Negro workers competent to fill a number of these vacancies were not allowed to do so because of racial discrimination. In fact, according to the hearings of the President's Committee on Fair Employment Practice in the case of the Negro railroad employees, held in Washington D.C., September 15 to the 18th, 1944, a Southeastern Carrier's agreement was signed, February 18, 1941. This agreement was concluded between The Brotherhood of Locomotive Firemen and engine men and 22 southern railroads, in order to reserve "featherbed jobs" for the whites. These jobs meant firing locomotives with mechanical stokers or diesel engines. By stipulating that only "promotable" men should be employed on diesels—"promotable" meaning white—and by other clauses, this agreement meant that Negroes on all but two southern railroads were restricted to the ancient steam power, hand stoke engine, and the lowest paid and least desirable runs. . . .

Some of the undisputed facts established by the evidence at the hearings were: That the present shortage of skilled white railroad labor has caused a delay in the transportation of troops and war material, damage to the rolling stock, and death or mutilation of young, inexperienced workers.

A. Philip Randolph receives a donation from Oren Root Jr. from the proceeds of the March 6, 1948, FEPC testimonial dinner. *Standing left to right:* Roy Wilkins, Henry Epstein, Max Delson, and Jules Cohen. (Library of Congress, Prints & Photographs Division, Visual Materials from the National Association for the Advancement of Colored People Records, LC-USZ62-137743)

That racial discrimination has been practiced by the white brotherhoods over a period of thirty years as a definite attempt to drive colored workers from the desirable jobs; that close union collaboration with certain carriers permitted the development of intricate systems of employment and promotion control.

That evasions, chicanery, and intimidation have been and are today being used against Negroes on the job by unions and management.

That during depression in 1921 and 1931–34, there were outbreaks of violence in the lower Mississippi region and Negro firemen were literally shot out of their cabs; fifteen were killed and twenty-nine wounded.

That though the white brotherhoods bar Negroes from membership, they assumed to represent them in making contracts with the companies, and in dealing with government agencies. The evidence showed that the unions would handle no grievances for Negro workers if they involved more than routine matters between them and the management.

That the campaign to eliminate the skilled Negro from the roads has been so successful that between 1930 and 1940 the percentage of Negro firemen on the southern roads dropped from 41.2 to 29.5; and since 1910, the percentage of colored trainmen from 29.8 to 15 percent.

The Railroad Retirement Board reports show the personal needs of individual railroads that are a bit enlightening. For instance, as of February 1, 1945, the Alton Railway Co. needed 13 locomotive firemen, 14 machinists, 10 brakemen. The Atchison, Topeka and Santa Fe Railroad Co. needed 56 boilermakers, 28 electricians, eight locomotive firemen, and 146 machinists. The Atlantic Coast Line Railway Co. needed 11 boilermakers, 63 brakemen, 104 car men, 68 locomotive firemen, 35 switchmen, 54 machinists. The Baltimore and Ohio Railway Co. needed 325 brakemen, 33 boilermakers, 92 car men, and 75 locomotive firemen. The Central Georgia Railway Co. needed 12 boilermakers, 19 machinists, and 9 switchmen. The Illinois Railway Co. needed 29 locomotive firemen, 40 boilermakers, 39 brakemen, and 96 machinists. The New York Central Railroad Co. needed 97 boilermakers, 295 machinists, and 95 locomotive firemen. The Seaboard Air Line Railway Co. needed 19 boilermakers, 50 brakemen, 16 locomotive firemen, 74 machinists, and 30 switchmen.

These are but a few railroads that are in need of additional personnel in the aforementioned classifications. Of course, there are a large number of other skilled jobs that are unfilled on the railroads, but it must be remembered that Negro workers are only acceptable in these jobs under pressure, and on some jobs even pressure, that is, the request type of pressure, has failed to open the doors.

Yet, let me emphasize the fact that there are Negro firemen, switchmen, brakemen, machinists, automakers, electricians, and so forth, throughout the country now looking for work. But discriminations on account of race and color, which is permitted to do business as usual, step between the Negro workers and these jobs, and the consequence is [that] our war effort is hindered.

Now, if it is difficult to get Negroes into jobs for which they have the skills under the pressure of war needs, how much more difficult it will be for Negroes to get fair employment opportunities when the country moves from a war to a peace economy. But this problem of discrimination against minorities in employment relations in peace will not be any less challenging than it is during these times of war.

The same type of discrimination which prevails in the railroads also pertains in the public utilities and many other industries throughout the country.

The policy of some employers not to employ Negroes is justified by the claim that the Negro workers don't have union cards. Upon receiving this information, some of the Negro workers probably go to the unions and request the opportunity to join in order to receive union cards to work in a plan under a closed-shop agreement, and they are politely advised that they cannot get union cards until they get union jobs. Thus, they are caught between the two forces of union evasion and employer discrimination. May I say that this is not true of all unions or all employers, but it is sadly true of far too many. Obviously, the Negro workers are victimized when both the shops and unions are closed. But may I observe here that I am by no means opposed to the principle of the closed shop, if the union is open to all workers, regardless of race, color, religion, or national origin.

But objection is raised to this bill, S. 101, on the grounds that it is coercive and that it is an attempt to eliminate race prejudice out of the hearts of employers and the workers; and hence S. 459, stressing education and legislation, without enforcement powers, is urged. The fallacy of the Taft bill is to pose education as the opposite of legislation with enforcement powers. This is an example of setting up a straw man to knock down.

Legislation, in fact, is part of the process of popular education. Legislation provides the arena in which opportunity is afforded for the people in schools, barber shops, churches, trade unions, chambers of commerce, and fraternal lodges to discuss, debate, and explore all aspects of vital social issues so as to develop sound social thinking for the welfare of the country. But the people cannot discuss that which is not brought before them. The fight to secure the enactment of bills into law dramatically presents social questions to the people and helps to awaken and inform public opinion as to the significance of these questions.

This bill, S. 101, is not concerned with race or religious or nationality prejudice. It deals with only one thing, and that is the practice of discrimination on the grounds of color, religion, national origin, or ancestry, which deprives a worker of a job, or rather, his right to live, because on the job the worker receives wages, and with the wages he buys food, clothing, and shelter, the basis of his life. Therefore, whoever seeks to prevent a worker from securing a job, because of any reason, is seeking to deny him the right to live, which is a very definite nullification of the basic principles of the Declaration of Independence and the federal Constitution. It is a fallacy to construe race prejudice as synonymous with racial discrimination. They are two different things. Race prejudice is an emotion or feeling. Racial discrimination is a practice. While we cannot by law make a white worker love Negro worker, or Protestant worker love a Jewish worker, or a worker in Boston love a worker in Atlanta, Georgia, we can stop the workers from closing the shops and the unions at the same time. Laws can stop hoodlums from smearing synagogues and cathedrals with swastikas. Laws can stop mobs from lynching people for any reason.

I do not condemn the trade unions, workers who discriminate against Negro workers and other minorities fundamentally. Black and white workers do not fight each other because they hate each other, but they hate each other because they fight each other, and they fight each other because they do not understand each other. But if they work together, they will understand each other.

Now, the fair employment practice bill, S. 101, does not seek to make white workers, black workers, or Jewish, or Catholic workers love each other, but to respect each other's rights to work and to live. If laws are an ineffective to prevent discrimination, why maintain them to continue discrimination, such as the Jim Crow car, and so forth?

It is well-nigh axiomatic that the instinct to live as human beings, regardless of race or color, religion or national origin, is so strong that they will fight for the right to work in order to live.

Hence, it is apparent that color wars may be set and played by our country in the postwar period, as a result of increased tensions incident to discriminat[ory] employment relations, unless the Congress shows the social vision and wisdom to enact S. 101. For this reason, the enactment of this bill will play an effective and constructive role in achieving social peace in our various communities in the postwar era.

Without fair employment to supplement and to complement full employment, the poison of Hitler's fascism may get into the bloodstream of our country and run to the heart of our Nation. In very truth, there cannot be full employment unless there is fair employment. This is true not only with respect to numbers, but also in relation to the utilization of the skills of the minorities, and it is apparent that there cannot be fair employment without an FEPC law with enforcement powers.

This question of increased racial tensions in the area of employment is not an imaginary, but a real danger. Now, the Taft bill cannot serve any useful purpose, because it has no enforcement powers and fails to make economic discrimination unlawful. Today, the twenty-two southern railroads and the Brotherhood of Locomotive Engine Men and Firemen have flouted the directives of the President's Committee on Fair Employment Practice. The Stacy Committee, appointed by the president to attempt to unravel this problem, has been without effect and force. Why? Precisely because the President's Executive Order 8802 has no enforcement powers.

If this is true in wartime, how much more true will it be in peacetime, when we do not have a war emergency with which to appeal to the patriotic spirit of employers and unions? The argument that a law with enforcement powers cannot achieve its objective will not bear examination. Witness the National Labor Relations Act, which has served the nation usefully by providing an opportunity for workers to choose their bargaining agent without coercion, interference, or intimidation. Therefore, this act was on our federal statute books as employers discriminated against union workers, just as some of them now discriminate against minorities. The workers were free to join unions, lest they be fired or not hired. The company union held sway, and the "yellow dog" contract was jammed down the throats of the wage earners. This is not so today. But twenty-five years ago, violent abuses and recriminations were heaped upon the heads of the American workers who sought to organize. Union men were damned and secret detective agencies were employed to frame union men to destroy the unions. This is largely history now. The National Labor Relations Act is chiefly responsible for this change. Now we have a considerable measure of labor-management cooperation. Employers no longer look upon labor leaders as some dreadful monsters with horns on their heads, daggers in their teeth, and torches in their hands, bent upon the destruction of industry. The War Labor Board will attest that the war effort has been greatly advanced by labor-management committees in industries from one end of the country to the other.

If we enact this fair employment practice measure, S. 101, it will serve as a legislative educational force that will someday make it a matter of history, when workers, on account of race or color, national origin or religion, were the victims of the abuses and violence and mis-representation that are now their unhappy lot. The present FEPC ends in June 1945. Unless further funds are appropriated, the problem affecting employment practices, however, will not end. It goes right on through the war and the reconversion and the peace. What is urgently needed now is a permanent FEPC, with its own enforcement provisions, with the same status as the SEC and the NLRB and other government regulatory commissions.

I feel that the FEPC is not a Negro question—there are many Jews, Mexicans, Catholics and other minority groups. It is an American question. It is the four freedoms at home, where we and the rest of the world can see that the Atlantic Charter is not globaloney and helped to make democracy a reality in New York and Alabama for our black and white, Jewish, Catholic, Protestant, Mexican, and Filipino boys, when they return from the foxholes in the Southwest Pacific and other battlefields and the seven seas of this war. . . .

SOURCE: Senate Committee on Education and Labor. *Fair Employment Practice Act Subcommittee of the Committee on Education and Labor,* 79th Cong., 1st sess., March 12, 13, and 14 (Washington, D.C.: GPO, 1945), 44–49.

6

Making and Witnessing History in the Civil Rights Movement

A. Philip Randolph's longtime vision of organizing the masses and using protest politics to attack Jim Crow came to fruition in the outpouring of mass demonstrations that characterized the civil rights movement. Randolph was a respected elder in his seventies by the time that sit-ins and Freedom Rides captured national attention, and he did not participate in these or other high-profile campaigns. His absence from direct action, however, does not mean that he sat silently by. During the "golden age" of the civil rights movement, Randolph collected the political capital he had accrued through five decades of involvement in the struggle and used his clout to help the cause. Perhaps most famously, he and longtime associate Bayard Rustin took a lead in organizing the March on Washington for Jobs and Freedom. In addition to overseeing the 1963 march that solidified Martin Luther King Jr.'s international prominence as a symbol of human rights, Randolph also planned and participated in three other marches on Washington during the 1950s. These underappreciated events sought gains in general civil rights and the implementation of Supreme Court rulings such as *Brown v. Board of Education* that mandated school integration.

Unlike at other periods of his life, in the 1960s Randolph functioned more as a theorist of change and less as an organizer. Still, he remained a vital link between labor unions and various civil rights organizations. Railroad travel was becoming a thing of the past and the Brotherhood of Sleeping Car Porters was on its last legs, but Randolph's tireless dedication to serving the working class made him a consummate insider alongside labor leaders like Walter Reuther and George Meany. As seen in Randolph's "Crisis of Victory" essay for the *Amsterdam News* and other documents in this chapter, this longtime involvement made Randolph a sought-after commentator on college campuses and in the news media. The 1966 Freedom Budget for All Americans, which called for massive federal spending aimed at eliminating unemployment and eradicating poverty, was Randolph's last significant contribution to the movement. Like President Lyndon Johnson's promise of a "Great Society," the Freedom Budget went unfulfilled. Nevertheless, it represented an important theoretical position about the possible direction various popular mass movements might take upon attaining desired legislative reforms.

The primary sources in this chapter outline major national events during the civil rights era, speak to debates within the movement, and exemplify Randolph's lifelong commitment to the causes he served. Marching on Washington, of course, is a theme connecting the 1940s with the 1957 Prayer Pilgrimage and subsequent marches. As his commencement address at Morgan State College and other speeches indicate, Randolph thought historically and in a very big picture. To him, strivings for human equality dated back to antiquity, and he saw the "Civil Rights Revolution" as yet another chapter in the long struggle of humanity to achieve greater freedom. The backdrop of cold war politics is evident in many of Randolph's remarks during this period, but it is especially pronounced in his denunciation of the not-guilty verdict rendered in the Emmett Till murder trial. The documents in this chapter also illuminate fissures within the African American freedom struggle. As is evident in a 1960 piece written for *The Black Worker*, Randolph tried bridging the gap between African American and Jewish leaders within the labor movement. Later in that decade, during the Ocean Hill–Brownsville controversy, this fault line became a chasm. In "Black Power—A Promise or a Menace" and a letter to longtime correspondent Layle Lane, Randolph's opposition to the black nationalist sentiments of the 1960s was ideologically and pragmatically grounded. Of course, he believed that there was something exceptional about the African American experience, and he addressed this issue in his opening remarks at the White House Conference, "To Fulfill These Rights." Still, taking positions that were out of step with popular discourse hinted that Randolph's time had passed and suggested he was no longer a leading voice of protest in touch with the masses of African Americans.

FOR FURTHER READING

Branch, Taylor. *Parting the Waters: America in the King Years, 1954–1963.* New York: Simon and Schuster, 1988.

Horton, James Oliver, and Lois E. Horton. *Hard Road to Freedom, Volume 2: From Civil War to the Millennium.* New Brunswick, N.J.: Rutgers University Press, 2002.

Jones, William P. *The March on Washington: Jobs, Freedom, and the Forgotten History of Civil Rights.* New York: W. W. Norton, 2013.

Joseph, Peniel E. *Waiting 'Til the Midnight Hour: A Narrative History of Black Power in America.* New York: Henry Holt, 2006.

King, Martin Luther, Jr. *Why We Can't Wait.* New York: Harper and Rowe, 1964.

Kluger, Richard. *Simple Justice: The History of* Brown v. Board of Education *and Black America's Struggle for Equality.* New York: Knopf, 1976.

Podair, Jerald. *The Strike That Changed New York: Blacks, Whites, and the Ocean Hill-Brownsville Crisis.* New Haven, Conn.: Yale University Press, 2002.

Sitkoff, Harvard. *The Struggle for Black Equality.* New York: Hill and Wang, 1981.

Sugrue, Thomas J. *Sweet Land of Liberty: The Forgotten Struggle for Civil Rights in the North.* New York: Random House, 2008.

Protest against Mississippi Lynching of Emmett Louis Till (1955)

Speaking at a New York City rally sponsored by the Brotherhood of Sleeping Car Porters, A. Philip Randolph added his voice to the chorus of outrage raised in response to Emmett Till's murder on August 28 of that year. Coming just two days after a not-guilty verdict was rendered in the Bryant-Milan trial, this September 25, 1955, rally was indicative of the national disapproval of Till's brutal death and the judicial system's failure to dispense justice appropriately. Randolph's awareness of America's position in the global community is of note in this speech, as is his appreciation for the context of cold war politics.

We have met today in this great outpouring of Negro and White, Jew and Gentile and Catholic and Protestant citizens for the higher purpose of making a massive, monumental, momentous and meaningful protest and demonstration against the Mississippi lynching of 14-year-old Emmett Louis Till of Chicago. Nothing in the darkest days of human tyranny of Attila and Genghis Khan exceeds this Mississippi exhibition of human bestiality, brutality and barbarism against Master Emmett Louis Till—just a lad in his tender teens, and all because of race and color.

Believing in the basic sense of fair-play and good-will of the common people of this country which, when touched, awakened, informed and aroused, expresses itself as public opinion before which even the wild, fanatical forces of white supremacy, Dixiecrat Ku Kluxism and racial hatreds must bow, the New York Division of the Brotherhood of Sleeping Car Porters was moved by this Mississippi lynching outrage, national disgrace and crime against humanity, to stage this protest rally to help the mobilization of the moral resentment and indignation of Negro and white New York in particular and America in general, to the end that the culprits may be brought to justice and that a similar manifestation of inhumanity may never happen again in this land.

Only the righteous revolt of the people, North and South, against racism mad with the mythology of white supremacy, can halt this wave of terrorism and tragedy, fear and frustration, desperation and disaster that hangs like a storm cloud over the heads of the people in certain areas of the South.

The dreadful death of little Emmett Louis Till, though unspeakably terrifying, is but a piece of a pattern of a cruel, systematic, organized cold warfare against citizens of color who insist upon securing the status of first-class citizenship and, especially, the implementation of the U.S. Supreme Court decision of May 17, 1954, requiring the desegregation of public schools. Hysterical with fear of the rise and progress of Negro Americans toward full freedom and equality, little men in politics, press and pulpit in Mississippi and some other sections of the deep South, would use the primitive weapons of discrimination, hatreds, mob violence and lynch-law to block the path of advancement of the Negro, fearing lest competition in the arena of the book, spirit and the mind may expose their pretentious preachments about the white man's superiority to be a hollow farce.

Such is the reason for the outcry and machinations against desegregation of public schools and the use of devious efforts, as well as the shotgun, to drive Negroes from the ballot box in the South. But Mississippi, like other white supremacy–minded states, will miss the boat. The march of the Negro toward first-class citizenship, freedom and justice in these United States and Africa may be set back but will never be stopped.

While Negroes are plagued, beset and harassed by racial violence, fired from jobs and shot down because of ignorance and fear on the part of the ruling politicians, farm owners and misguided workers, this is the last gasp of the Old South in its death throes. Enlightened white and Negro youth will build a new South with a heart and head of humanity. There are four great forces that are standing at the deathbed of the Old South. They are industrialism, trade unionism, extension of the ballot to the Negro and poor whites, and the democratization of education. These social forces are creating new white men and new black men. These new white men and new black men have no fear.

One only has to look at the trial of two white men in the court in Money, Mississippi, for the lynching of Emmett Louis Till. Watch Negroes in the courthouse. Especially observe the great uncle of Emmett Louis Till, Mr. Moses Wright. He has a noble and majestic posture, free from fear. Emmett Louis Till's mother shows no sense of timidity. It is this unconquerable spirit to resist and resent wrong and fight for freedom and for that which is right and just and fair for all the children of men which will usher in the dawn of a new South.

Thus, be not dismayed, desegregation will win even in Mississippi and Georgia. It will win not only because it is right but also because the Negro will fight to make it win. It is well to recognize that there are white citizens of the South, yes, even in Mississippi, who oppose justice and law by the rope and faggot. But, the decent people of the United States, North and South, white and black, must be stirred to action by this abomination in Mississippi and against God and man and help win the fight for desegregation of schools, [and to] enact federal and state civil rights legislation by joining the National Association for the Advancement of Colored People, which is ably leading the struggle against racism. It needs members. It needs money. It needs morale. Every person at this rally, black and white, should join it today.

Our Brotherhood, with its membership on the far-flung railroads of these United States, is pledged and committed to the struggle for complete, full-fledged and first-class citizenship. The rank and file members demanded that this protest rally be staged without fee or collection, because they have been schooled and educated in their struggle to fight for their rights.

And let me warn you against accepting help in this fight from communist forces, for their support is a kiss of death. They must not be permitted to smile their way into the liberation movements of the Negro and other minorities which they seek to control and destroy. Let me also warn the United States against a do-nothing policy about efforts for the suppression of the Negro, for such a policy will tend to cause this country to lose the confidence, faith and good-will of the whole world of color in Africa and Asia, representing two-thirds of the population of the world.

Source: Box 35, folder: Speeches, 1955, A. Philip Randolph Papers, Library of Congress.

Statement at Prayer Pilgrimage for Freedom at the Lincoln Memorial (1957)

Held on May 17, 1957, to commemorate the third anniversary of the *Brown v. Board of Education* decision, the Prayer Pilgrimage for Freedom was the first of three marches on Washington that Randolph participated in during the 1950s. In a time when dissent was seen as subversive, the prayer pilgrimage emphasized solemnity, piety, and devotion to the best of America's national ideals. Although Martin Luther King Jr. had been actively involved in public life for only about two years, Randolph praises him as a "prophet of our times."

My honored colleagues and co-workers, the Rev. Dr. King and the Hon. Mr. Wilkins, Ministers of the Church and fellow Prayer Pilgrims for Freedom:

In the pattern of good American traditions, Negroes and whites, Jews and Gentiles, Protestants and Catholics, trade unionists, professional and educational leaders have assembled here in a great pilgrimage of prayer for freedom at the monument of Abraham Lincoln, the Great Emancipator, to tell the story of our long night of trial and trouble and our renewal of faith in and consecration to the sacred cause of a rebirth of freedom and human dignity.

Thus, we have to memorialize the third anniversary of the historic United States Supreme Court decision for the desegregation of public schools, a veritable Emancipation Proclamation of the mind and spirit.

We have come to demonstrate the unity of the Negroes and their allies, labor, liberals and the Church, behind the civil rights bills now before Congress, in order that they might not be strangled to death by committee maneuverings and the filibuster.

We have gathered to proclaim our uncompromising support of the fight of the National Association for the Advancement of Colored People for civil rights and democracy under the able, resourceful and constructive leadership

A. Philip Randolph is seated with Roy Wilkins, Rev. Thomas Kilgore Jr., and Rev. Martin Luther King Jr. at the May 17, 1957, Prayer Pilgrimage. (Library of Congress, Prints & Photographs Division, A. Philip Randolph Papers, LC-USZ62-125026)

of Roy Wilkins, Executive Secretary. This is the agency which has been chiefly responsible for civil rights decisions in the courts of our land to eliminate second-class citizenship based upon race or color.

We are here to tell those who worship the false gods of white supremacy in the South to keep their evil hands off the National Association for the Advancement of Colored People. And we have come to warn the liberal, religious, educational, labor and business forces of the North of the grave danger of a spreading sentiment in some sections of the South to deny the right of existence to the National Association for the Advancement of Colored People. It is a matter of common historical knowledge that the denial of free, voluntary association for the advancement of lawful, social, political and economic objectives of a particular group in our national community will, like the contagion of disease, spread to other associations which, for the present, may not be the objects of persecution. In very truth it may be the NAACP which is banned by irrational racial legislation today, but the ban may come to the Knights of Columbus, B'nai B'rith, the AFL-CIO, and some sections of the National Council of the Churches of Christ in the USA, tomorrow.

We are here to make known our unqualified sanction of and cooperation with the magnificent, challenging and successful struggle against segregated buses in Montgomery, Alabama, the cradle of the old Confederacy, under the inspired leadership of a great church leader and prophet of our times, the Rev. Mr. Martin Luther King. This is one of the great sagas of the struggle for human decency and freedom, made effective by a veritable miracle of unity of some fifty thousand Negroes under the spiritual banner of love, non-cooperation with evil, and non-violence.

We are assembled here to express our righteous indignation against, and condemnation of, the notorious Ku Klux Klan and the White Citizens Councils. The revival of these agencies of hate and violence constitute a grave threat, not only to law and order in the South but to the democracy of our country, as well as a shock to the faith and confidence of peoples everywhere in the integrity of our moral leadership of the free world.

We have come to call upon President Eisenhower, our great national and world leader, who undoubtedly possesses a high sense of humanity, to speak out against lawlessness, terror and fears that hang like a pall over the hearts of citizens of color in the South as a result of devastating bombings of their homes and churches, shooting and killing of citizens who have the courage to assert their constitutional rights, and the intimidation of white and colored people by cross burnings and parades of hooded men and women.

As the highest expression of the moral and political authority of our country, we urge the President to help rebuild the shaken and shattered hopes of millions of Negroes and white peoples of the South, by raising his voice of counsel to the people to obey the laws of the land.

We have come to state our unshakable belief in the principles of human solidarity and the worth, value and dignity of the personality of every human being, regardless of race, color, religion, national origin or ancestry, and to point out the fallacy and mythology of the doctrine of white supremacy.

It is written in the Declaration of Independence of our country that all men are created equal and possess the inalienable right to life, liberty and the pursuit of happiness. These are natural human rights. They are God-given, not man-made. Every organ of government and official of state is required by constitutional fiat and the moral law to uphold these rights, not to conspire with anti-democratic forces to deny, nullify, and destroy them. Thus, civil rights have a moral and spiritual basis, for they are designed to implement and give reality and force to our human rights that exist as a result of our being human, and we are human because we have been created human beings by God. Since all men are the children of God, they are equal before God and should be equal before the laws of the state.

We are here to assert that the issue in the crisis of civil rights in our nation today does not involve opposition of Negroes to whites or whites to Negroes.

There are leaders in certain circles who would like to make this the issue, but the real issue involves conflict between certain basic social and moral values, such as freedom against slavery, truth against terror, justice against injustice, equality against inequality, love against hate, good against evil, the right to vote against disenfranchisement, law and order against mob rule. One has only to witness this great demonstration of prayer pilgrims for freedom to note that they have come from various creeds, colors, countries, classes, callings and crafts.

We like to think that God is on the side of our American way of life, but this will only be true to the extent that our American way of life is on the side of God, who said: "I am the way, the truth and the light." Hence, in the eyes of God there is neither black nor white, nor red nor yellow, nor Jew nor Gentile, nor barbarian nor Scythian, but all are brothers in Christ Jesus. "By this will all men know that you are my disciples if you love one another."

We reject the support and cooperation of communists in the fight for civil rights because we are opposed to the use of immoral means to attain moral ends. Further, we know that communists have no genuine interest in the solution of problems of racial discrimination but seek only to use this issue to strengthen the foreign policy of the Soviet Union.

We have come to assert our rejection of the promise and pattern and path to freedom by communists and communism as an illusion and a snare; a fraud and a menace, which can only lead to the dead end of chaos and confusion, frustration and fear, dictatorship, slavery and despair.

Finally, we have come to reaffirm our belief in, and devotion and allegiance to, the American constitutional system of government, within which citizens, though not fully free, are possessed of the priceless right to fight for their rights.

But, to the end of achieving these civil rights and giving strength and integrity to our democratic order of government, it is the obligation and responsibility of every citizen of color, wage earner and lover of liberty to exercise his constitutional right to register and vote. We suggest no party or person to vote for, but we call upon every Negro especially, not only to register and vote himself, but to serve as a missionary to get his neighbors in every house, in every block, in every hamlet, village, city and state of our country to register and vote, that we may build the power to help save the soul of America and extend and maintain the free world for free men.

Be not dismayed by the frightful wave of violence and persecution against persons of color now sweeping the South. It is written in the stars that the old order of southern feudalism, with its remnants and vestiges of lynching, peonage, vagrancy laws, mob violence, Ku Klux Klan, anti-labor union practices expressed in right-to-work laws, widespread illiteracy, and low wages, is dying; its death will come as a result of the emergence of the dynamic impulse for freedom surging in the hearts of Negroes, together with the march on industrialization, urbanization, labor union organization, extension of education and the modernization of government through the spread of the ballot. These new forces will create and build a new South, free for white and black masses to pursue a life of dignity and decency.

In conclusion, in the words of David, "I will lift up mine eyes unto the hills from whence cometh my help." Yes, we have set our hands to the cause of a better and happier tomorrow for all men, and though we be beset by setbacks, persecution and trouble, the lot of all peoples who have won liberty and justice, may God grant that we may never falter.

SOURCE: Box 35, folder: Speeches, 1957, A. Philip Randolph Papers, Library of Congress.

Why the Interracial Youth March for Integrated Schools? (1958)

The 1958 Youth March for Integrated Schools was one of several marches on Washington that Randolph planned and participated in prior to the 1963 March on Washington for Jobs and Freedom. The Youth March sought to address the defiantly slow pace of implementing the Brown decision and to chastise the obstructionism exemplified by school districts in Little Rock, Arkansas, and Prince Edward County, Virginia. Randolph released this statement to the press on October 25, 1958, the date of the event. He grounded his appeal on the principle of judicial review and the affirmation of presidential authority. By framing his argument on federalist grounds, he deftly affirmed the protest's intentions and nipped criticisms of Communist-directed rabble rousing in the bud.

The nature of the problem we seek to resolve is largely emotional, with roots deep in a morass of fears, frustrations, desperation and a guilt complex, born of a long history of conflict, contradiction and confusion over the irreconcilability of moral and religious professions and the practice on the part of some Southern politicians in the field of human and racial relations. Therefore, not only are federal law and court decisions needed, but federal power is indispensable to back and enforce the law and court decisions to avoid social chaos, troubles, tensions and turmoil.

This Youth March for Integrated Schools in Washington, D.C., was planned because it is apparent that despite the notable, monumental victories in the United States Supreme Court and the lower courts by the NAACP for the desegregation and integration of public schools, the civil rights revolution is heading for a grave crisis of roadblocks. Negroes are passing through an hour of trial of faith by fire. The hot winds of persecution are rising. Only the tried, true to the cause of human dignity will stand.

It is clear to him who runs and reads the Supreme Court decisions of 1954, 1955 and 1958 that striking down segregated schools has precipitated a raging controversy. The country has been virtually split wide open into two major camps. One camp stands for, and the other against, the public school policy of desegregation and integration. Though the South accepted the U.S. Supreme Court decision of *Plessy v. Ferguson* of 1896, which handed down the notorious concept of "separate but equal"—the doctrinal foundation of the system of segregation—it not only rejects the aforementioned decisions of the federal courts but recklessly denounces them as communist-influenced and brands them as unconstitutional and illegal. Thus, Governor [Orville] Faubus of Arkansas and Governor Almond of Virginia, slapped down by decision after decision by the Supreme Court and the district and circuit federal courts, in utter frustration and desperation, have projected a massive resistance movement of state power against federal power. Schools have closed down. Demagogic and inflammatory appeals by southern state officials, press and pulpit, to the passions and prejudices of illiterate southern masses have provoked explosive outbursts of violence in the form of bombings of schools, churches and synagogues, and homes of civil rights leaders. A veritable reign of terror in the form of mob rule, shootings and killings of Negroes, is sweeping the South.

Not only federal court decisions, but the moderate and firm injunctions of our great President Eisenhower to the South to obey and conform to the decisions of the federal courts as the law of the land have been arrogantly flouted. It has been estimated that 196 laws have been enacted by southern state legislatures since the Supreme Court decisions for evasion, if not nullification, of the court orders for desegregation and integration.

We must remember that the Supreme Court has reversed itself on great social issues before. Why? Because of the change and pressure of public opinion. Note the strange, amazing and incredible spectacle of a governor of a state appealing through a nationwide letter-writing campaign for public sympathy and money to establish and maintain segregated private schools for white children. Thus, it is obvious that while the court decisions for civil rights are clear and forthright, they may not be final. Southern white supremacy leaders will not readily let up in their plots and conspiracies to subvert and evade decisions of the courts favorable to the abolition of segregation. In light of this fact, the country needs to be alerted to the fact that, not only is integration of schools at stake, but our whole democratic governmental order, which rests upon the Constitution and the principles of the Declaration of Independence. If the court decisions for integration can be discounted, ignored and repudiated by any group in the national community, then a court order concerning any other social, economic or political issue can be ignored and disregarded. So it is evident that the attitude of the South toward court decisions on civil rights may lead to inevitable chaos and confusion and, perhaps, even civil strife.

But the only way to mobilize public opinion back of the great decisions on civil rights is to dramatize the question of integrated schools. This requires action. It must be action in the form of putting people into motion. No events in human history more deeply stir and capture the imagination of men and women than the marching of men. The marching of men is the basis of the grip of war upon man. Abolish the tread of the soldier down the streets of a city or village and the romance in war will pass. Just as marches of citizens may be utilized sometimes for anti-social purposes, they may also be employed to advance constructive ideas. The basic ideal of our March for Integrated Schools is the unity of Negro and white youth in participation in this common enterprise for a great moral issue; namely, democracy in education through integration.

Purpose of the March

First of all, because of some disquiet in the nation's capital concerning the purpose of the march by intimating its partisan character to embarrass President Eisenhower, let me state definitely and positively that this Youth March is wholly non-partisan and is absolutely free from any form of control or influence from communists or communism. It is our interest not to weaken but to strengthen the hands of the President, since we wish him to uphold the school decisions as the law of the land. Moreover, efforts to embarrass the President would only mar the moral grandeur of our noble cause and brand us unworthy of its advocacy. Our Youth March is designed neither to help nor harm Republicans or Democrats in the campaign. . . .

What then, is its purpose? The central and dominant purposes of the Interracial Youth March for Integrated Schools in Washington, D.C., are as follows:

1. To give dramatization to the God-given right of every child, regardless of race or color, religion or national origin or ancestry, to receive an education in the public schools, free from the insult of discrimination.

2. To build and demonstrate the unity of Negro and white youth in this historic struggle for the great moral issue of democracy in education through integration.

3. To help awaken, inform, arouse and mobilize the people to the realization of the patriotic duty of every American citizen to support the Supreme Court decisions for the desegregation and integration of public schools as the law of the land.

4. To point out and highlight the American way of life through democracy and Christianity, which seek to give every boy and girl an equal chance to build character and manhood.

5. To alert public opinion to the grave danger of the poison of Little Rock Faubusism infecting the bloodstream of American life.

6. To warn the American people of the peril of a growing trend, symbolized by Virginia's massive resistance to undermine, if not destroy, the confidence of the public in the role and integrity of the United States Supreme Court in our system of government.

7. To indicate that the disease germs of Little Rock Faubusism, like the disease germs of tuberculosis, know no color line. Little Rock Faubusism must be curbed and cured lest it infect the entire nation with its sinister germ of human hate, violence, anarchy and terrorism.

8. To meet the cold war of half-truths, whole lies, incitement to violence and racial hate of Little Rock Faubusism, which is attempting to brainwash the American people into rejecting and nullifying the Supreme Court decisions for the desegregation and integration of public schools, with the cold war of truth, righteousness, non-violence, goodwill, love and Americanism.

9. To point out and emphasize that children are not born with, nor do they inherit, racial or religious hatreds—but learn and acquire them in some homes, schools, churches, and from some books, newspapers, magazines, radio and television.

10. To indicate that children can learn to unlearn to hate other children and adults, solely because of race, religion, national origin or ancestry, by contact in the schools, by sound science, education and Christian teachings, for contact between children of different races will help children to know the truth; namely, that all human beings are created by God and are children of God and are, therefore, fundamentally alike, which will help to make them free from, and immune to, the sickness of human hate.

11. To emphasize that the so-called massive resistance movement of Virginia and Little Rock Faubusism against the Supreme Court decisions is the last stand of the dying order of the old slave-plantation Bourbon South.

The reign of terror, violence and hatred now sweeping over the South in the form of bombings of public schools, churches and homes, police brutality against Reverend Martin Luther King and the outrageous killings of Negro civil rights leaders is flush of the death, not life, of the old Bourbon Confederate South of white supremacy. In the grip of death throes, it is fighting hard not to die though it is impossible to live. These violent outbursts of savage physical attacks of the bomb and the gun and poisonous racial propaganda, together with judicial and legislative illegality against Negroes and labor unions and their organizers, is but a pathological manifestation of the fears, frustration and desperation of the old South before the onward march of urbanization, industrialization, widening education, labor unionization of the workers, white and black, and the conflict [with] and contradiction between the American creed and American dream of equality of opportunity [and the] empty rationalizations of the southern social system of segregation. . . .

SOURCE: Box 35, folder: Speeches, 1958, A. Philip Randolph Papers, Library of Congress.

Commencement Address at Morgan State College (1959)

In this June 1, 1959, address given at Morgan State College in Baltimore, Maryland, Randolph urges graduates to register and vote because that "represents power, and power is the only thing a politician, Democrat or Republican, can understand." Rallying for civil rights was a major component of Randolph's remarks, but, as classically trained audience members would notice, regular references were made to ancient Greek civilization, Enlightenment thinkers, and ruminations on what constitutes a life well lived. Randolph's underlying message in this graduation speech was clear: black college graduates should be well read, worldly, and committed to fighting injustice wherever it appeared.

America has brought the world to an awe-inspiring threshold of the future. Nuclear energy physicists are delving into the mysteries of the creation of matter. Automation has designed machines which operate and repair themselves. Our prosperity is unprecedented. Our arsenals bulge with fearful weapons. Our material wealth astounds the world. In a political sense, we have become the most powerful nation on earth. This is a dazzling picture of the USA in 1959. Yet, there is a bleak side. The nation is poisoned by the plague of racial conflict. Negro children, merely seeking an equal education, have been brutally driven from their classrooms. The legal apparatus of several states, mobilized as if for war, bars children from integrated schools. The right to vote is arrogantly denied to millions. Violence, terror, and murder have been unleashed to hold down a long-suffering and patient people. While the Constitution and our free traditions are thus violated, the federal government is gripped by paralysis. Millions of citizens remain confused and apathetic.

This is a moral and political crisis. We have created machines that think and people who fear to think. These are a complex of issues collectively termed civil rights. Basically, civil rights are attributes of citizenship. Without them, there can be no citizenship. I refer to the right to vote and to be voted for; right to trial by jury; right to habeas corpus; right of petition; right to freedom from seizure or search; right to freedom of speech, press, assembly, and association; right to freedom of contract; right to own, buy, and sell property; right to equality of opportunity to employment, education, recreation. Now, civil rights stem from human rights. Human rights are God-given, not man-made. I allude to the right to life, liberty, and the pursuit of happiness. These human rights exist, not as a result of laws of the state, decision of the Court or the Constitution, but primarily because of one's being human. But while human rights exist prior to the state, the exercise of human rights may be abridged or denied by the state or interfered with by extra-governmental agencies and forces. Thus, the raison d'être for civil rights is to prevent even the state, such as Mississippi, from interfering with the privilege of individuals to exercise their human rights.

Since God, as Father, created all men—all men are brothers. Since all men are brothers—all men are equal. They are equal before God and should be equal under law in the state. If all men are brothers and are equal before God, they are entitled to equal treatment in our democratic society. But this can only be assured and guaranteed by law, the state, decision of the Court. In short, by civil rights. However, Negroes do not possess their civil rights. Thus, Negroes are not fully free. They are not fully free because the Civil War Revolution was never fully completed. The Civil War Revolution was never fully completed because the new industrial and financial circles of America no longer needed to complete the Revolution in order to consolidate their forces as the economic masters of the new nation.

It must be remembered that the Civil War Revolution was comparable to the bourgeois democratic revolutions of England of 1688 and of France of 1789. These revolutions had certain basic objectives; the achievement of which was a desideratum to the coming into being of the new order. . . .

While the Civil War Revolution abolished chattel slavery, destroyed the Confederacy at Appomattox, liberated the slaves, centralized political power in a federal system, and effected the economic unification of the country, it failed to transform the former slaves into free workers. It failed to give them land. Instead, freedmen were transformed into tenant, sharecrop, and debt farmers, or veritable peons. This was possible because the old plantation remained; the old masters remained, and the need and greed to rebuild the old plantation economy on cheap labor were ever present.

The Civil War Revolution never established free public schools. Instead, the freedmen were cursed with a segregated school system. There was no free ballot. When the southern states returned to the Union they promptly established Black Codes, which tended to nullify the 13th Amendment of 1865, the 14th Amendment of 1868, and the 15th Amendment of 1870. The poll tax, white primaries, grandfather clauses—designed to make a mockery of suffrage and the so-called citizenship of the freedmen—were enacted into law.

Hence, the central struggle of the Negro today is not just securing the right to vote in Alabama; the right to sit in a park in Pensacola; ride in a seat in a bus in Montgomery or Tallahassee; become a stewardess on an airplane; or secure a house in Levittown, but it involves a civil rights revolution—the historical mission of which is to sweep away all of the vestiges, remnants and survivals of the old slave order, the elimination of the old system of color caste, and the complete annihilation of the sinister structure of segregation in every area of American life. This, alone, will constitute the completion of the uncompleted Civil War Revolution.

One organization resolutely pursuing these ends is the National Association for the Advancement of Colored People. It is significant that it is currently under heavy and vicious attack. Some equate it with the White Citizens Councils as extremist and trouble-maker. This misconstrues the aim and method of the NAACP. Its purpose is to realize the rights guaranteed in the Constitution. In a democracy, such a purpose cannot be extremist. Recognition will eventually come that the NAACP has made an imperishable contribution to America by insistently struggling for equal justice and thereby enlarging all the horizons of democracy. In your supreme bid for manhood rights, the NAACP is your most effective champion. Give of your time and talent to help build its membership to make it strong. Stand up and defend it when attacked.

If our moral complacency and preoccupation with gaudy products of our time are not transformed into a real demonstration for constructive action, not we alone, but also future generations, will inherit a weaker nation and a less than honorable past. America can meet its challenges with strong courage and a relentless steadfastness. To this end, we summon support for this minimum program:

1. Use of full powers and influence of the federal government to obtain prompt and full compliance with the decision of the United States Supreme Court condemning state-imposed racial segregation.

2. Application by all branches of the federal government—executive, legislative and judicial—of the policy that federal funds should be used in that manner as to encourage and secure compliance with the Supreme Court decisions condemning racial segregation.

3. Amendment of the rules of the Senate and House of Representatives to eliminate the filibuster and all other devices that thwart the will of the majority.

4. Vigorous support by the President and adoption by the United States Congress of effective federal laws prohibiting discrimination in employment, giving greater protection to personal security and the right to vote, and strengthening the civil rights activities of the Department of Justice.

Today, we are in the midst of a vast atomic, technological and scientific revolution. The whole basis of modern production and exchange of goods and services is in the process of change. Probably the biggest task confronting the Negro today is the transformation of a body of unskilled workers into highly skilled, technical craftsmen and technological experts. It is a matter of common knowledge that the large majority of Negro workers are unskilled and, unless trained and re-trained through apprenticeship courses and schools of science, they may be unable to participate in the operation of the vast machine of production in this age of automation.

Upon securing employment, it is to the best interest of Negro workers to join the unions that hold the contracts in the crafts, classes, or industries in which they are employed. It would not be sound strategy to stay out of trade unions because racial discrimination is in some of them. Were they consistently and logically to follow this policy it would compel Negroes to stay out of practically every institution and movement in this country, including the church, industry, schools, sports, government, politics, social service, and the professions. Moreover, while there is a long road ahead in eliminating discrimination in trade unions, as in other institutions in the country, some substantial progress is being made. One basic asset consists in the fact that the leadership—George Meany, president, and Walter Reuther, vice president—of the AFL-CIO are unreservedly committed to the policy of eliminating discrimination in the trade unions. . . .

One other basic force you must employ in the Negro liberation movement is the ballot, and the use of the ballot requires registration of the citizen. Thus, Negro youth should develop a veritable crusade in precinct after precinct, ward after ward, in every village and city, to get every eligible Negro to register and vote. Now, you need not be disturbed about whether Negro citizens register or vote as Republicans or Democrats, since there is no material difference between them. Your major concern should be that millions of Negroes register and vote throughout the nation. This represents power, and power is the only thing a politician, Democrat or Republican, can understand. To this task, my fellow graduates, you must set your hand, head, and heart. Yours is the responsibility to achieve the status of free men in a free democratic society. The essence of the Civil Rights Revolution is a struggle for individual liberty. . . .

Think of the fact that almost uniformly in human history, the great benefactors of the human race have had to live in exile because they have given humanity new truths and have dared to challenge old beliefs. Many of us have forgotten what liberty has cost, if not what it means. Men have had two things in mind when they have talked of liberty. The concern was concrete issues, and the attainment of concrete rights. The men of the Renaissance, when they spoke of liberty, meant freedom of the human spirit; freedom to ponder classical literature in contrast to religious obscurantism. To the men of the Protestant Reformation, liberty meant the right of private interpretation as opposed to the existing hierarchy. In the English Revolution, it meant the immunities of the subject in opposition to the aggrandizement of an overreaching monarch.

But you must take courage and renew your faith in the long march of man toward freedom, justice, plenty, and peace, in the life and history of some of the outstanding champions of human liberty, such as Locke and Hume, Voltaire and Diderot, Gibbon and Paine, Ingersoll and Jefferson, Spencer and John Stuart Mill. Your challenge is not only to acquire knowledge, but to use it in the fight in the interest of the advancement of a truly democratic society. The achievement of this goal may entail suffering, hardship, sacrifice, the loss of liberty and, sometimes, life.

Albeit, liberty must be won. It is never given by oppressors to the oppressed. Thus, the history of liberty has always consisted in warfare against oppression, persecution, intolerance, bigotry, racism, chauvinism, totalitarianism. From the days of the Athens of Pericles, when the first lamp of liberty was held aloft to light the path of man, to the revolt of Negroes in Montgomery against insult in bus transportation, under the matchless leadership of the Reverend Martin Luther King and the Pullman porter E. D. Nixon, and the uprising of the masses in Hungary, Nyasaland and Tibet, men have fought, bled, and died for the right to be free, or the right to act in accordance with their desires.

Indeed, the struggle of man for a free world has been enriched and inspired by the history and philosophy of Greece. While the Magna Carta of England dates from the thirteenth century, it would be difficult to overestimate the liberalizing influence of the Greek classics on British thinkers of the seventeenth and eighteenth centuries. If the Renaissance was primarily an artistic movement in Italy, it resulted in a civil and political movement in England. Even the Reformation in England was subordinated to the bourgeois revolution for individual liberty.

No one can gainsay that the influence of Aristotle was especially strong in the early stirrings of men against despotism. Moore, Hobbes, Bacon—all wrestled with questions of human liberty that were first raised by the Athenians. Milton, in the *Areopagitica,* cites the examples of the ancients for the struggle for intellectual liberty. But I beseech you to set your sights beyond the horizon of Athens, with all its dreams, its doctrine of human excellence, its grace and beauty of art, its reaches and challenge of philosophy, for even Plato had no concept of the principle of the universal unity of mankind and the dignity of the human personality of every human being—the gift of the Judeo-Christian tradition, since even the culture of Athens rested upon a pillow of flesh of human slaves.

Stake your faith in the great moral values of truth, honesty, love, freedom and justice. While material goods of this world are necessary, they are not a *sine qua non* for the good life. Verily, what profiteth [it] a man to gain this world and lose his soul? Though the Negro, in his fight for first-class citizenship, needs to develop allies such as labor, church, and business, it is well to realize that, in the final analysis, salvation must come from within. History attests to the fact that while your friends may help you, they cannot save you; you must save yourself. But you will be ill-equipped to save yourself unless you have built the character, granite-like in pattern, which can stand up for that which is right, though unpopular, under sharp test and trial.

In every age of human history, those who would be free had to bear the cross. It was the lot of labor, and still is. It was the lot of the early Christians. It is the lot of Africa and Asia. It is the lot of the Negro in our own land.

The night, however dark, is never endless. The star of the break of dawn is not far. The hour of decision and action is now. In the words of the Psalmist, "I will lift mine eyes unto the hills from whence cometh my strength."

SOURCE: Box 35, folder: Speeches, February 7, 1959–September 6, 1959, A. Philip Randolph Papers, Library of Congress.

There Is No War between Negro and Jewish Labor Leaders over Civil Rights (1960)

Randolph takes a clear stand against anti-Semitism, calling it a "dangerous and poisonous doctrine." The labor movement, he argues, has no room for provincialism of any stripe. Differences in perspective will inevitably lead to disagreement within a national organization like the AFL-CIO, but Randolph reminds readers that this diversity of viewpoints is not evidence of disunity. The Ocean Hill–Brownsville controversy remained several years away (see letter to Layle Lane in this chapter), but this document hints at fissures within progressive circles that widened during the next decade.

The headlines of an article appearing in the December 12, 1959 issue of the *Pittsburgh Courier,* "Will Negro, Jewish Labor Leaders War Over Civil Rights?" are unfortunate and misleading, if not anti-Semitic. This is not to suggest that the *Courier* is anti-Semitic. Far from it. Your readers know better. Let me emphatically affirm there is no war over civil rights between Negro and Jewish labor leaders and, in my opinion, such a thing is utterly unthinkable. This does not mean that differences of opinions may not arise from time to time, not only with Jewish leaders, but also Catholic and Protestant labor leaders, on matters of strategy, method and approach involving the fight against discrimination and segregation in the labor movement. In fact, this is well-nigh inevitable, but it is not to be construed as warfare or feuding among the aforementioned labor leaders. For instance, some differences of opinion arose over a report on discrimination in trade unions by Herbert Hill, Labor Secretary of the NAACP. Some labor leaders, Jewish, Catholic and Protestant, condemned it as not entirely factual or constructive. I, on the contrary, approved of the report. I considered it timely, factual and constructive.

There was also a difference of opinion on the resolutions presented to the AFL-CIO Convention in San Francisco by the delegates of the Brotherhood of Locomotive Firemen and Enginemen and the Brotherhood of Railroad Trainmen. Only the Negro delegates at the convention spoke and voted for this resolution, but this does not mean that there is warfare between the Negro and white delegates. In fact, following the debate on the resolution, there was no manifestation of ill will on either side because of this difference of opinion with respect to the resolution. The following statement appeared in the aforementioned article in the *Courier:* "Deeply involved in the conflict which threatens to break out into open warfare within the next two weeks are the NAACP, the newly formed American Negro Labor Committee and the Jewish Labor Committee." This is purely fantastic; it is not true.

It is a matter of record that the leaders of these movements work closely together for civil rights within and without the labor movement. The Youth Marches on Washington, D.C. for integrated schools and Prayer Pilgrimage for civil rights were projects initiated, supported and developed by an ad hoc committee of interracial and inter-faith composition, the Brotherhood of Sleeping Car Porters, the NAACP and the Jewish Labor Committee. Active in the leadership of the Jewish Labor Committee were Manny Muravchick and Charles Zimmerman, Vice President of the International Ladies' Garment Workers' Union and Chairman of the Civil Rights Committee of the AFL-CIO, who never failed to lend cooperation morally and financially, and whose anti-racial discrimination position cannot be questioned.

There is truth in your statement: "Officials of both the NAACP and the American Negro Labor Committee have complained bitterly about the AFL-CIO Civil Rights Committee's 'failure to deal effectively' with a memorandum filed in 1958 by Mr. Hill which cited 'specific instances' of union jim crow practices." But it must be remembered that these complaints about discrimination in unions have been made by the delegates of the Brotherhood of Sleeping Car Porters on the floor of the AFL Convention for well-nigh a generation. Resolutions against racial discrimination were adopted, but they were, on the whole, a meaningless gesture.

But even if Jewish labor leaders were not active in opposition to racial bias, Negro labor leaders would be indulging in suicidal folly to foster or countenance the dangerous and poisonous doctrine and propaganda of anti-Semitism, the infamous altar upon which Hitler sentenced six million Jews to torture and death. If I know the Negro trade unionists well, they will never dishonor their name and calling by playing the ignoble role of lending their energy and influence to a suggestion or promotion of any form of anti-Semitism.

I note the statement in the fourth paragraph of the article: "Already concerned are Roy Wilkins, NAACP executive secretary, and A. Philip Randolph, AFL-CIO international vice president, and one of the founders of the American Negro Labor Committee." I think I can definitely say for Roy Wilkins, able executive secretary of the NAACP, and myself is that the AFL-CIO get on with the business of cleaning out the house of labor of all forms of racism not only in the interest of Negro workers but for the strength and integrity of trade union democracy. The article pointed out: "Another charge leveled at Jewish labor leaders asserts that some of them have adopted a 'paternalistic and missionary' attitude toward Negroes. These 'missionaries' have, in turn, accused Negroes of being Negroes first and trade unionists second, which is not denied by Negro leadership."

My comment on this observation is that I have not recognized such an attitude among Jewish labor leaders. While I hold no brief for Jewish labor leaders who have a long, distinguished history in the American labor movement beginning with Samuel Gompers, an English Jew, who was the President of the AFL, certainly the characteristic paternalism toward Negroes is not peculiar to Jews. Without a doubt, there is labor paternalism toward Negro workers in some circles of petty trade union leaders. While this is a manifestation of the weakness of organized labor, it is primarily a sickness of our American culture. I am inclined to think that this paternalistic attitude towards Negroes is more general in non-trade union circles such as the press, church, business, government, sports, education and the stage. Now, while it is a fact of common knowledge that some progress has been made in the fight against discrimination and segregation in the AFL-CIO, it is not enough, and the pace of progress is entirely too slow. In this atomic age, racial discrimination is a socio-economic anachronism. It must be eliminated; not tomorrow, but today.

Negro trade unionists also know that success in the fight for civil rights in the labor movement, in Congress, in state legislatures and city bodies largely depends upon maintaining unity between the AFL-CIO and independent unions representing some sixteen million or more workers, and the NAACP and other movements that fight for civil rights. Because of the reality of the indivisibility of liberty, I am convinced and confident that the powerful American labor movement can be brought around to understand that civil rights are tied up with labor's rights and that enemies of organized labor are the enemies of the Negro, and that labor has no logical alternative than to join its forces with the forces of the Negro in the fight for racial equality, social justice and human dignity. White labor can never know freedom so long as black labor is in bondage. It is for this purpose that the Negro American Labor Council is being developed.

SOURCE: *The Black Worker* 32 (January 1960): 4.

Filibuster of the People (1963)

The following article published in the *New York Times Magazine* is noticeably different from the original draft submitted by Randolph weeks earlier (in A. Philip Randolph Papers). Gone is his call to interpret the March on Washington for Jobs and Freedom as a public mandate, as well as his advice to "determine where do you go from here and what are the next steps." Still, this is a unique document for the fact that it was one of few by Randolph published in a widely read mainstream white-owned newspaper or magazine. Cognizant of the diverse terrains covered by various civil rights groups, Randolph called for "unity without uniformity" in the movement and warned of growing animosity on both sides of the color line if segregation and inequality continued to persist.

The objective of Aug. 28 was more than civil rights legislation. The full march was a challenge to the conscience of the country; it was a creative dialogue between Negroes and their white allies, on the one hand, and the President, the Congress and our American democratic society, on the other. Its aim was to achieve a national consensus not only for civil rights legislation—but for its implementation.

Historically, the social forces of revolutions have been expressed through human beings. Hence, the leadership of the civil rights revolution cannot escape the moral responsibility for the maintenance of the highest order of unselfish, courageous and uncompromising fidelity to the ideals, values, hopes and faith of this sacred crusade for the recognition of, and respect for, the God-given human rights of Americans of color.

What then, is to be done?

First, Negro civil rights leadership must maintain unity without uniformity. Second, the coalition of the Negro community with the labor and church communities that supported the march must be preserved, broadened and deepened. If freedom is indivisible, then the fight for freedom by those forces devoted to freedom should be indivisible. Negroes—like other minority groups—cannot win their rights alone. The coalition of moral forces represented by civil rights, labor and church groups is unquestionably one of the most powerful instrumentalities yet devised to help create the ethical basis for interracial brotherhood which is imperative to give meaningfulness to civil rights laws.

Third, demonstrations in the streets—a recognized American tradition—by Negroes and their white allies must continue without relaxation until basic, tangible progress in the acquisition of jobs and apprenticeship training for jobs in industry, unions and government, and the abolition of race bias in public accommodations, schools and housing is made. Had it not been for demonstrations in the streets of Birmingham, Alabama, and other cities in the North and South, it is quite unlikely that President Kennedy would have submitted his package of proposals for civil rights legislation to the Congress. If street demonstrations were necessary to secure this action by the President, it is reasonable to assume that further street demonstrations will be indispensible to bring about the enactment of the proposals into laws, without emasculation.

Fourth, major emphasis should be placed upon building the unity of Negro leadership together with a coalition of the Negro, labor and church communities. This, of course, is the job of existing civil rights organizations. No new movement is necessary.

The Birmingham tragedy—a wanton bombing of a church and the murder of four little girls—marked not only a breakdown of law and order but also has shaken and weakened the faith and confidence of Negroes and, no doubt, of numerous liberal-minded white people in constitutional government and our free, democratic, Christian society. It damages the image of the United States in Africa in particular, and the world of color in general.

It is a matter of record that no white person or mob in the South responsible for the murder of a Negro has ever been brought to justice. However, Negroes, despite this unspeakable crime, must not forsake or abandon the nonviolent philosophy as a framework within which they should carry on their relentless struggle for the abolition of race bias.

We have no choice but to fight ceaselessly for civil rights legislation. If it should be killed, joblessness will continue to worsen, and humiliation in places of accommodation will go unabated. Then frustration—even desperation—may burst into fires of violent interracial conflict. Indeed, if the civil rights revolution is aborted by a counter-revolution, symbolized by the filibuster, it may not only turn against white America but move to devour its own children.

SOURCE: *New York Times Magazine*, September 29, 1963.

Address of A. Philip Randolph at the March on Washington for Jobs and Freedom (1963)

Like those of nearly everybody else who delivered an address at the 1963 March on Washington, Randolph's remarks have been lost in the long shadow cast by Martin Luther King Jr.'s oratorical masterpiece that day. This surely did not dampen the pride that Randolph must have felt as he looked out at the crowd of more than two hundred thousand who assembled on that hot August day to "Let the nation and the world know the meaning of our numbers." Civil rights are important, Randolph argues, but it must not be forgotten that freedom without opportunity is a pyrrhic victory. In this speech before what was undoubtedly the largest audience of his career, Randolph emphasizes that fair employment laws and access to education are just as important as desegregating public accommodations.

Fellow Americans, we are gathered here in the largest demonstration in the history of this nation. Let the nation and the world know the meaning of our numbers. We are not a pressure group. We are not an organization or a group of organizations. We are not a mob. We are the advance guard of a massive moral revolution for jobs and freedom.

This revolution reverberates throughout the land touching every city, every town, every village where black men are segregated, oppressed and exploited. But this Civil Rights Revolution is not confined to the Negro nor is it confined to civil rights, for our white allies know that they cannot be free while we are not, and we know that we have no future in a society in which six million black and white people are unemployed and millions more live in poverty. Nor is the goal of our Civil Rights Revolution merely the passage of civil rights legislation.

Yes, we want all public accommodations open to all citizens, but these accommodations will mean little to those who cannot afford to use them. Yes, we want a Fair Employment Practices Act, but what good will it do if profit-geared automation destroys the jobs of millions of workers, black and white? We want integrated public schools, but that means we also want federal

A. Philip Randolph meeting with the leaders of the 1963 March on Washington Movement: John Lewis, Whitney Young, A. Philip Randolph, Rev. Martin Luther King Jr., James Farmer, and Roy Wilkins. (Library of Congress, Prints & Photographs Division, U.S. News & World Report Magazine Collection, LC-DIG-ppmsca-31579)

aid to education—all forms of education. We want a free democratic society dedicated to the political, economic and social advancement of man along moral lines.

Now, we know that real freedom will require many changes in the nation's political and social philosophies and institutions. For one thing we must destroy the notion that Mrs. Murphy's property rights include the right to humiliate me because of the color of my skin. The sanctity of private property takes second place to the sanctity of the human personality.

It falls to the Negro to reassert this profit priority of values because our ancestors were transformed from human personalities into private property. It falls to us to demand new forms of social planning, to create full employment and to put automation at the service of human needs, not at the service of profits—for we are the worst victims of unemployment. Negroes are in the forefront of today's movement for social and racial justice because we know we cannot expect the realization of our aspirations through the same old anti-democratic social institutions and philosophies that have all along frustrated our aspirations.

And so we have taken our struggle into the streets as the labor movement took its struggle into the streets, as Jesus Christ led the multitudes through the streets of Judea. The plain and simple fact is that until we went into the streets, the federal government was indifferent to our demands. It was not until the streets and jails of Birmingham were filled that Congress began to think about civil rights legislation. It was not until thousands demonstrated in the South that lunch counters and other public accommodations were integrated. It was not until the Freedom Riders were brutalized in Alabama that the 1946 Supreme Court decision banning discrimination in interstate travel was enforced, and it was not until construction sites were picketed in the North that Negro workers were hired.

Those who deplore our militancy, who exhort patience in the name of a false peace, are in fact supporting segregation and exploitation. They would have social peace at the expense of social and racial justice. They are more concerned with easing racial tensions than enforcing racial democracy. The months and years ahead will bring new evidence of masses in motion for freedom. The March on Washington is not the climax of our struggle, but a new beginning not only for the Negro but for all Americans who thirst for freedom and a better life.

Look for the enemies of Medicare, of higher minimum wages, of social security, of federal aid to education and there you will find the enemy of the Negro—the coalition of Dixiecrats and reactionary Republicans that seeks to

A. Philip Randolph at the 1963 March on Washington. (Library of Congress, Prints & Photographs Division, New York World-Telegram and the Sun Newspaper Photograph Collection, LC-USZ62-126838)

dominate the Congress. We must develop strength in order that we may be able to back and support the civil rights program of President Kennedy. In the struggle against these forces all of us should be prepared to take to the streets. The spirit and technique that built the labor movement, founded churches and now guide the Civil Rights Revolution must be a massive crusade, must be launched against the unholy coalition of Dixiecrats and the racists that seek to strangle Congress.

We here today are only the first wave. When we leave it will be to carry the Civil Rights Revolution home with us into every nook and cranny of the land, and we shall return again and again to Washington in ever growing numbers until total freedom is ours. We shall settle for nothing less[,] and may God grant that we may have the courage, the strength and faith in this hour of trial by fire never to falter.

SOURCE: Box 36, folder: Speeches, 1963, A. Philip Randolph Papers, Library of Congress.

The Civil Rights Revolution—Origin and Mission (1964)

Randolph's worldly perspective shines in this 1964 address to the North Jersey Chapter of Jack and Jill of America, Inc., an African American organization founded in the Depression to better nurture and instill values in children. In this speech delivered at East Orange High School in New Jersey, he placed the "Civil Rights Revolution" in the context of other revolutionary moments in human history such as the storming of the Bastille in France and the securing of the Magna Carta at the Battle of Runnymede. Randolph believed that he was witnessing the culmination of an African American–led multigenerational struggle dating back to the nineteenth century, and that its success would represent the true attainment of freedom promised in the American Revolution and the Civil War.

On the fourteenth day of July, 1789, in Paris, when Louis XVI heard from the Duc de la Rochefoucauld-Liancourt of the fall of the Bastille, the liberation of a few prisoners, and the defection of the Royal Troop under popular arrack, the famous dialogue that took place between the King and his messenger is revealing. The King, we are told, exclaimed: "It's a revolt!" Liancourt corrected him: "No, sire. It's a revolution!" When the King declared that the storming of the Bastille was a revolt, he asserted his power to deal with conspiracy and defiance of authority. But his messenger replied that what had happened there was irresistible and irrevocable, and beyond the power even of the King. Behind these ominous words a mighty multitude of the poor and downtrodden, whom every century before had hidden in darkness and shame, poured like torrents of molten lava of an erupting volcano into the streets of Paris, which was not only the capital of France but of the entire civilized world. It was not long following this historic dialogue before this Bourbon King of France lost his head by the judgment of history in the raging reign of terror.

When the gathering storm clouds of the Civil Rights Revolution broke over the country it startled and stunned the nation. In a worsening mood of anger, resentment and frustration, if not desperation, over the snail-like pace of the desegregation and integration of public schools following the momentous decision of the United States Supreme Court in 1954, Negroes have initiated and developed waves of demonstrations against racial bias, North and South.

These demonstrations have taken varied forms: Sit-ins, lie-ins, lie-downs at construction sites, bus boycotts, freedom rides against Jim Crow bus and airline terminals, efforts at prayer-ins in white churches, school boycotts, and marches against city halls, state capitals and the nation's Capital. The black mass protest and petition under the leadership of Rev. Martin Luther King against white oppression in Birmingham, Alabama, where the police turned savage dogs upon Negro citizens and used electric cattle prods and fire hoses to frighten them into silence, have shaken and shocked America. In Raleigh, North Carolina, five hundred college students launched a drive for total integration by a demonstration at the Governor's mansion. In this same city, one thousand Negroes attempted to sit in at two movie houses and a public cafeteria. Verily, the storm winds of the Back Revolt raged against the white world through Selma, Alabama; Jackson, Mississippi; Jacksonville, Tallahassee and St. Augustine, Florida; Little Rock and New Orleans, and in the ghettoes of New York City, Philadelphia, Chicago, Detroit, Cleveland, San Francisco and Englewood, New Jersey. And the end is not yet! . . .

Civil Rights Revolution

Truly, these demonstrations are the manifestations of a revolution—a civil rights revolution, and a full-dress one at that. What is its historic mission? It is to effect a transition from the status of second-class citizenship to first-class citizenship, or a reversal of the relationship between the Negro and white America. This means the liquidation and elimination of the old racial habit systems that provide for and perpetuate the concept of the hereditary racial inferiority of the Negro. Upon this concept the entire structure of segregation and discrimination was erected and justified, with a body of weird racial myths, fictions, fantasies, eccentricities and idiosyncrasies.

Thus, the basic Civil Rights Revolution consists not in the current demonstrations, though [they are] valuable and indispensible, but in the complete orientation of the Negro from an old slave psychology to that of a free man, and the knowledge that his status of the "underclass," or social, economic and political substratum of the American society, is not inherent and an inevitable part of his human condition but can be changed and, further, that it is his responsibility to change it.

American Revolution

Verily, the behavior patterns of the Civil Rights Revolution are not drastically unlike the behavior patterns of the American Revolution, which resulted in the overthrow of British colonial rule and the achievement of independence. The Boston Tea Party of 1773 and the Boston Massacre of 1768 did not constitute the Revolution; they were manifestations of it. Its roots extended back to 1215 when, at the Battle of Runnymede, the Magna Carta was exacted from King John, and to 1265 when the common people of England won the right to elect representatives to Parliament, which was the background of a rich heritage of struggle for liberty which the Pilgrim Fathers brought to the New World. The cry of "taxation without representation is tyranny" was raised by Samuel and John Adams, Patrick Henry and James Otis, against the Stamp Act in 1765, long before Lexington and Concord in 1775. Besides, Samuel Adams had initiated and employed the Committee of Correspondence, and the Sons and Daughters of Liberty, to break down the loyalty of the people to British colonial rule, advocated and aroused the unity of the colonies and prepared the way for the formation of the First Continental Congress in 1774, culminating in the Declaration of Independence in 1776.

Origin of the Black Revolution

Now, the Civil Rights Revolution had its birth in the fact that, while the Civil War Revolution emancipated the slaves from chattel slavery, it failed to transform them into free workers, independent peasant proprietors with a government grant of acres of land, and into full-fledged, first-class citizens. The reason for this was that the new capitalism, under the Republican leadership of Abraham Lincoln, which waged the Civil War, had completed its major objective when it saved the Union. It had also overthrown the cotton plantation order, centralized political power in a strong federal system and effected the national economic unification of the country. Thus, the Union federal forces no longer needed the black freedmen, two hundred thousand of whom had helped win the war, and, during the Reconstruction period voted to keep the Republican Party in power in the former slave states, thereby enabling it to control the federal power of taxation to be used to levy and maintain a protective tariff for the bolstering and advancement of the growing capitalist economy.

Therefore, although the Civil War Revolution had achieved important civil rights gains, such as the 13th Amendment of 1865, the 14th Amendment of 1868, and the 15th Amendment of 1870, together with the Congressional Reconstruction Acts of 1867 and the Civil Rights Act of 1875 for the protection of the freedmen, they were soon swept into political oblivion by the wild fury of the Confederate Counterrevolution. When the eloquent voices of the "Great Commoner," Thaddeus Stevens, in the House of Representatives, and Charles Sumner, uncompromising leader of the anti-slavery movement in the Senate, were no longer heard in defense of the rights of the freedmen, the Reconstruction democracy came to an ignoble end. It was the year of the Hayes-Tilden election, 1876. Samuel J. Tilden, Democratic candidate for President of the United States, was far in the lead of Rutherford B. Hayes, Republican, with both popular and electoral votes. But historical necessity, in the interest of the national destiny, had virtually decreed that the power of the federal government should reside in the hands of the Republican Party, the political voice of nascent capitalism, the dominant force in the nation. Hence, a deal was made. It involved a shift of the electoral votes of Florida, Louisiana, South Carolina and Oregon over to Hayes, with the provision that he, when elected, would withdraw the federal Army—sole protection of the freedmen—from the South. Then, with the United States Supreme Court decision of *Plessy vs. Ferguson* in 1896, the doctrine of "separate but equal" was handed down, which has formed the foundation of the structure of racial segregation for practically a hundred years.

Add to these attacks upon the ex-slaves the anti-Negro legislative devices of grandfather clauses, white primaries and the poll tax, along with the rise of the Ku Klux Klan with its cross burnings and midnight terror accompanied by a wave of lynchings that, according to Tuskegee Institute, reached 4,733 persons who died from mob action from 1882 to 1901, and anyone can understand how the Confederate Counterrevolution, with prejudicial courts and hostile police, drove the freedmen from civil life back upon the cotton plantations to be robbed of his labor and made prisoner of black serfdom for virtually a hundred years. As a result, the freedmen entered the twentieth century, not as first-class citizens and free workers, but as debt peons, sharecroppers and farm laborers. They were voteless, moneyless, landless, jobless and friendless, with no status in the civic life as citizens or the free labor market as workers.

Awakening of the Negro

Negro slaves never meekly accepted their lot; they have ever rejected, resisted and resented human bondage. This was attested to by some 250 recorded slave revolts that frightened the slave power structure, though the leader of each revolt was put to death. This tragic story was written in blood and tears in a continuing exodus of slaves on the famous Underground Railroad, under the brave black woman conductor Harriet Tubman.

Under the leadership of three black giants, Frederick Douglass, eloquent orator; Booker T. Washington, noted educator; and William Edward Burghardt Du Bois, brilliant agitator, Negroes resorted to the federal courts and education. They had set their feet upon the path of a long journey to complete an incompleted Civil War Revolution. To this end, Dr. Du Bois and a few genuine white liberals—Mary White Ovington, Oswald Garrison Villard and John Haynes Holmes—organized the National Association for the Advancement of Colored People in 1910. Being increasingly subjected to fraud and violence and anti-Negro legislation in the former slave states by such demagogic politicians as [James] Vardaman of Mississippi, Hoke Smith of Georgia, and "Pitchfork" Ben Tillman of South Carolina, the NAACP went into the federal courts to establish the illegality of racial segregation and discrimination. The strategy worked! Grandfather clauses in the constitutions of southern states, lily-white primaries, the poll tax and restricted covenants were declared unconstitutional. Finally came the memorable decision of the United States Supreme Court for the desegregation and integration of public schools in 1954 which, on account of the snail-like pace of implementation, caused widespread frustration.

Baffled, impatient and angry, Negroes, by the hundreds and thousands, took to the streets and staged nonviolent, direct mass action with various forms of civil disobedience in protest against race bias and petitioned for direct and immediate remedy. Be it understood that it was not the leaders who surged into the streets, but masses of Negroes. Nor is the remedy sought only for the leaders, but for all Negroes. Nor is the remedy based upon merit, knowledge and ability, but upon need, justice and rights. The problem is all-inclusive, relating to the entire Negro community—and the remedy must be all-inclusive, affecting, as it were, all Negroes. No handful of Negroes can solve the problem of race bias, and no handful of Negroes should benefit by the solution of the problem.

Progress in our modern world can only be made by collective man in relation to individual man, and by individual man to collective man. Wars are won by vast armies not by individual generals, though they are necessary. Strikes for the benefit of workers are won by workers in a whole plant, railroad, hotel or factory, not by lonely leaders. Thus, Negroes, like the Italians, Irish, Jews, and southern whites, must use their mass power to win recognition of their mass interests and power as a means of providing opportunities for the gifted, talented, and the specially professionally, scientifically and artistically trained among us.

The order of Negro–white relations was to stress the importance and status of one or two Negroes, usually picked out by the white power structure for the Negro community. But this is no more. With the rate of unemployment of Negroes being two and a half times higher than [for] whites, the demand today is for jobs and training for all Negroes, not for only the talented. The desegregation of segregated schools, whether by law or custom, is for all children, Negro and other minorities and, for that matter, white children too— and not for just a few. The desegregation of housing and abolition of slums are for all Negro and white citizens, not only for the so-called elect.

The New Awakening

One of the unmistakable signs of a new awakening of Negro Americans was the great exodus of black Americans from the Egypt of southern bondage in the early part of the twentieth century, upon the call of the First and Second World Wars, in quest of the Promised Land of the milk and honey of jobs and freedom. Hundreds of thousands swarmed North; they went into the automobile factories, steel mills, meatpacking industries, shipyards and hotels. Many of these Negro workers joined unions and walked with their white brothers in the picket lines for higher wages and better job conditions. They were learning their lessons for the struggle for fair employment practice. Moreover, hundreds of thousands were drafted into the armed forces under practices of racial bias to fight with American white men against white men in Europe, Asia and Africa to make the world safe for democracy.

Meanwhile, a blaze of illumination in novels and poetry came from the hearts and minds of black writers that gave birth to the Negro Renaissance, centered principally in Harlem in New York City and in other metropolitan areas such as Chicago, St. Louis, San Francisco and Washington. Along with the flowering of the artistic life of the New Negro was heard the challenge of the strident voices of a new Negro radicalism, led by the *Messenger Magazine,* which opposed the Negro joining the Army to fight for a democracy abroad that he could not enjoy at home. Following the end of World War I and the return of Negro soldiers with a new spirit for their rights, race riots swept over the land from Chicago to Longview, Texas.

Verily, the lamps of freedom that had been lighted by the black leaders Frederick Douglass, W. E. B. Du Bois, Booker T. Washington, James Weldon Johnson, Monroe Trotter, Mary McLeod Bethune, Mary Church Terrell, are still burning. May they never go out. If they do, they may not be relighted for a hundred years. . . .

SOURCE: Box 36, folder: Speeches, January 30, 1965–September 17, 1965, A. Philip Randolph Papers, Library of Congress.

Crisis of Victory (1965)

This *Amsterdam News* column is noteworthy because it demonstrates Randolph's belief that knowledge of the past illuminates issues of the present. In this example, he takes a long view of history, placing decolonization and automation in the context of the American Civil War and the collapse of Reconstruction. Two major themes of his analysis are the presence of the color line and the persistence of exploitation as a method of controlling labor.

The civil rights revolution has been caught up in a crisis of victory: a crisis which may involve great opportunity or great danger to its future fulfillment. This victory consists in the winning of civil rights through the enactment of the civil rights act of 1964, for which Negroes have struggled over a hundred years. There is, therefore, opportunity for the civil rights movement to mount and carry out a vigorous program of implementation of the act, and also to look beyond civil rights to the larger goal of human freedom—political, social, industrial and economic. While civil rights is a phase of freedom, it is not to be equated with basic freedoms. Negroes enjoy civil rights in the north but they do not possess basic freedoms.

The socio-ethnic dynamism generated by the struggle for civil rights may be made available to help attain the goal of full freedom as a way of life—namely, freedom from poverty, freedom from ignorance, freedom from disease and freedom from fear, freedom from racial bias, religious bigotry, freedom from war—freedoms [that] the attainment of which will involve basic structural changes in our society and institutions. But let me hasten to add: the achievement of those freedoms is far beyond the power of any single segment of our society, for it is a fundamental challenge to the American establishment.

However, unless the fight is waged and won for the larger freedoms, [then] civil rights, like civil liberties in times of war, may not be permanently secure. It is difficult to find a social group which has been in possession of civil rights and civil liberties over a long period of history without economic rights, economic freedom, economic citizenship and public power. Thus, Negroes have no alternative except to seek as a major objective the enlargement and broadening of the base of civil rights to involve the basic freedoms.

Moreover, there is danger [that] the crisis of victory may plunge Negroes into a debilitating state of psychological and emotional relaxation which may not only undermine the morale of the civil rights activists and the rank and file civil rights workers, but weaken the entire organizational structure of the civil rights movement. Already, the membership of every civil rights organization has begun to decline. This is probably as inevitable as the night following the day.

But this behavior pattern of weakness following a showing of strength is not peculiar to the civil rights movement. Let us take a look at the behavior patterns of labor, organized labor. During the early Roosevelt era in the 1930's, a veritable second labor revolution broke upon the country in a blitz of sit-down strikes in the automobile industry and a paralyzing wave of strikes in the mass production industries, resulting in a bloody massacre in south Chicago in the Republic Steel plant [that was] sparked and directed by the CIO, a group composed of unions which had split from the AFL. The year 1937 brought the Wagner Labor Disputes Act, hailed by labor and liberals as the Magna Carta of the workers. Next came the Fair Labor Standards Act of 1938, which gave recognition, for the first time in federal law, to the principle of the minimum wage and the shorter work week.

Within the frame of reference of this pro-labor climate of the new deal, union membership grew into big labor, for confrontation with big business and big government. But it lost its evangelism and could no longer claim to be the conscience of the country, fighting the battles of the unskilled workmen, neglected migrant farm laborers, and the Jim Crow, underclass black laboring masses. And, withal, the American labor movement became richer in body but poorer in spirit.

Thus, in the years following the winning of the historic Wagner Labor Disputes Act organized labor became the victim of the Taft-Hartley Act, which included Section 14(b) under which "right-to-work" laws limiting the right of collective bargaining were enacted in some twenty states, more or less. In 1959 the anti-labor Landrum-Griffin Bill, with its varied restrictions and regulations, became federal law. While increased union membership has brought affluence and strength to labor, the growth of membership has been practically arrested by the spread of right-to-work laws, especially in the south and middle west. Without compulsory union membership required by federal law, big labor might not be so big. My point is that labor, too, has been caught up in the crisis of the victory of federal legislation, which provoked a sense of relaxation and weakened the will to struggle and resulted in the loss of much of its freedom.

A counterrevolution, which follows a revolution as reaction follows action, is already underway, as shown by the defeat of a California fair public housing act and the victory of Proposition 14, with a vote of 2 to 1. Fair housing ordinances have also been struck down in Detroit and Akron. These developments may be a signal of the beginning of an erosion of the national consensus for the Civil Rights Revolution which was chiefly responsible for the enactment of the Civil Rights Act of 1964. Any severe loss of public approval of the cause of the Negro freedom movement can constitute a grave threat, not only to the implementation of the Civil Rights Act of 1964 but to the struggle to improve and strengthen it . . . indeed, even to its maintenance without emasculating amendments.

Look at the black freedmen! Though the Union forces won the war and the slaves were emancipated, when the roaring thunder of the revolution of abolitionism was no longer heard[,] virtually every vestige of freedom and citizenship status of the Freedmen, including the 13th, 14th and 15th Amendments and the Civil Rights Act of 1875, were swept into political oblivion by the angry winds of the Confederate counterrevolution. The brief period of the Reconstruction democracy came to an ignoble end. The federal government withdrew its support of the cause of the freedmen and they became the victims of a new plantation feudalism as sharecroppers, peons and tenant farmers—landless, voteless, moneyless and friendless, if not hopeless and helpless.

Black freedmen no longer held the center of the stage of American history. The Farmers' Revolt of the 1870's, 80's and 90's, reflected by the Populist political movement, and the workers' revolution, marked by bloody and devastating strikes by the Knights of Labor, together with the glittering tinsel of the gilded age of American capitalism, tended to make the ex-slave the forgotten man of the period. He continued thus until the rise of the National Association of the Advancement of Colored People in 1910, the U.S. Supreme Court decision on the desegregation and the integration of public schools in 1954, and the coming of the Civil Rights Revolution.

First, the physiological and social gulf between the Negro masses and Negro classes—the professionals and intelligentsia such as teachers, students, doctors, lawyers, preachers, businessmen—must and can be bridged. This gulf is here . . . it is widening instead of narrowing. It is marked by a sense of skepticism and cynicism, by many employed and unemployed, skilled and unskilled and unemployable Negro workers and some of the so-called middle class, when approached by Negroes of the leadership class, unless the leaders are rabbleyers [sic], preachers, businessmen—rousers spitting fire and brimstone of Black Nationalism and anti-whiteism.

This climate of black racism, which is created by white racism, presents a major problem.

SOURCE: *Amsterdam News*, March 27 and April 3, 1965.

Address at Pilgrim Baptist Church (1965)

As the son of a rural Florida minister, Randolph appreciated the importance of religion to sustaining movements for social change. Although he rarely attended services, Randolph's knowledge of Christian scriptures and the frequency with which they appeared in his speeches suggests that he opened the Bible regularly. This 1965 speech he gave at Pilgrim Baptist Church, an institution founded by former slaves and still standing as the oldest African American church in Minnesota, illustrates Randolph's increasing willingness to work through the church for civil rights causes. Of particular salience in this speech is his linkage of Christian teachings about helping the poor to the necessity for civil rights forces to help repeal "right-to-work" laws.

And Jesus spake unto his disciples: "I have compassion upon the multitude because they continue with me three days and have nothing to eat; I will not send them away fasting for they may fall by the wayside, for divers come from afar." Jesus Christ was concerned about the poor, the forgotten man, the worker, the disinherited, the propertyless and the oppressed. When the lowly Nazarene said, "Come unto me all ye that labor and are heavy laden and I will give you rest. Take my yoke upon you and learn of me, for I am meek and lowly in heart; and ye shall find rest unto your souls; for my yoke is easy and my burden is light," and followed this declaration with this admonition to his disciples, "And again I say unto you, it is easier for a camel to go through the eye of a needle than for a rich man to enter into the Kingdom of God," he expressed the central doctrine of the Christian Revolution. It was the first time since the days of the old Hebrew prophets that a religious or government leader expressed the concept of [the] equalitarian status of the ancient lowly or the common laborers, the camel drivers, the publicans and sinners with the high priests of the scribes and Pharisees, Sadducees, the conquering warriors, philosophers and kings.

Even the great Athenian philosophers, Socrates, Plato and Aristotle, voiced no concern about the cruel oppression of the poor. Verily, the democracy of Athens and the Golden Age of Pericles, with its superlative excellence in art, literature, science and philosophy, were based upon human slavery. But Jesus made it unmistakably clear where he stood with respect to the house of "haves" and the house of "have nots" when he cried out: "Woe unto you Scribes and Pharisees, hypocrites, for you devour widows' houses and for a pretense make long prayer; therefore you shall receive the greater damnation." And when Jesus came to Nazareth where he had been brought up, as his custom was, he went into the synagogue on the Sabbath day and stood up for to read. And there was delivered unto him the book of the prophet Esaias. And when he had opened the book, he found the pages where it was written: "The spirit of the Lord is upon me because he hath anointed me to preach the gospel to the poor; he hath sent me to heal the brokenhearted, to preach deliverance to the captives, and recovering the sight to the blind, to set at liberty them that are bruised."

Such was the mission of the Christian Revolution well-nigh two thousand years ago. This is the mission of the Civil Rights Revolution today. Not only is the Civil Rights Revolution, through sit-ins, wade-ins, lie-ins and lie-downs, marches, boycotts and picket lines, shaking America, if not the world, into consciousness of the black Americans' will to win freedom, racial and social justice and human dignity, but it is awakening and arousing the white workers, white liberals, leaders of the church of the Protestant, Catholic and Jewish faiths, and the white poor, to the magnitude and importance of the problem of poverty to Negroes and white Americans alike.

Yes, in this age of revolutions, this time of trouble, in this era of restless man, Asian and African revolutions of rising expectations against colonialism and imperialism have shaken and continue to shake the world. Out of these upheavals have emerged independent, sovereign Afro-Asian nation-states, and now, as nonaligned political international forces, are playing a significant role in the United Nations. But the rising winds of change have not only swept across the ancient world of color, the winds of change have swirled through the Americas, fanning the fires of revolution for civil rights and civil liberties.

Practically contemporaneously the revolution of science, technology and industrialism is transforming the world and creating new crucial crises of change, including nuclear war weaponry and the revelation of the possibilities of the discovery of new worlds of the universe. This revolution of technology, variously known as automation or cybernation, is creating the foundation of a social revolution, the fundamental mission of which is the achievement of a more equitable distribution of the wealth of our affluent society, which constitutes problems which the Civil Rights Revolution cannot reach. Although the Civil Rights Revolution has the limitations of a bourgeois revolution that provides primarily the attributes of first-class citizenship, it has brought about a revival of the fires of a fighting faith in freedom in America for all men. It has stressed the truism that freedom is not free; it must be fought for. It has a price; namely, struggle, sacrifice and suffering. . . .

[The] continuing growth of the Negro population, resulting in overcrowded housing, *de facto* segregation in the schools, police brutality, unemployment and teenage dropouts, tends to make for social unrest eventuating in frustration, violence, resentment, outbreaks of gathering crowds on street corners upon the least provocation, [and] culminating in the throwing of bricks, bottles, Molotov cocktails at citizens, white and black, [and] windows of stores, [the] overturning of garbage cans and [the] looting of stores. But long hot summers of lawlessness, looting riots, vandalism, with attacks upon person and property, for any reason or cause, cannot and should not be condoned, excused or tolerated, for freedom and civil rights are impossible of realization without law and order, and law and order is impossible of realization without freedom and civil rights.

Of course, because of the complexity and variability of the nature of social phenomena, whether the coming summer will be long or hot, and in which areas the so-called long hot summer will occur, is highly unpredictable. However, unless some meaningful action is taken to provide some jobs and hope for an increasing population of unemployed teenagers and adults, the probability is that there may be intermittent riotous, racial eruptions of lawlessness and ugly scenes of violence which could get out of hand.

Both the Negro community and the law enforcement agencies of the big cities should cooperate to prevent these manifestations of socio-racial sickness from afflicting the communities. Some teenagers and adults who participate in these riots are well meaning but misguided. Others are drug addicts and hoodlums who take advantage of these racial upheavals to pillage and loot stores, have no interest whatever in the freedom movement and neither care [n]or know anything about the Negros' struggle for civil rights.

Unfortunately, because of the long reputation of the police for brutality [enacted] upon the poor, especially the black poor, the great mass of Negroes in the ghettoes look upon the police as their enemy and, therefore, the police encounter suspicion and distrust and sometimes opposition when they attempt to enforce the law. In fact, the history of the police has been to protect property, not human rights. They brutalize white and black workers on the picket line during strikes for the benefit of employers. They evict tenants at the behest of the landlords. In the South, following the Civil War, the job of the police was to oppress, suppress, intimidate, harass, beat up, shoot and jail the black freedmen in order to break their spirit and reduce them to the status of segregated serfs, sharecroppers and peons.

Thus, police review boards that are established agencies of the city government to which a citizen—Negro, Puerto Rican or white—may present a complaint about police brutality, which will fairly and impartially analyze and weigh the evidence with a view to giving both the complaining citizen and the accused policeman in question a fair and impartial hearing and assess a just discipline or acquittal, should be set up. Such a board will tend to eliminate police brutality on the one hand and mob brutality against the police on the other. It will enable the minorities' communities and the police to cooperate on a basis of mutual interest for the maintenance and protection of civil rights and civil liberties of citizens, regardless of color or status, and maintain law and order. . . .

These periodic summer riots must not be identified with civil rights demonstrations. Civil rights demonstrations constitute a major tactic of the Civil Rights Revolution. They are the most effective social instrumentality for awakening and arousing the public conscience to express its commitment against race bias. Of course, this is not to suggest that all demonstrations advance the cause of the black freedom movement. Some demonstrations do and some don't, because they reflect emotionalism and irrationality—or [are] mere gimmicks. But as a rule, tactical maneuvers that smack of the ridiculous meet with public scorn and rejection, as they, of course, deserve. We cannot afford to demean the dignity, nobility and high moral promise of the Civil Rights Revolution by short-cut, ill-advised improvisation of action of extremist orientation.

Demonstrations are all the more a basic force of the Civil Rights Revolution because it is only through marches in the streets that the so-called lower-lower stratum of the race, the unskilled and illiterate, unemployed and unemployable black workers, can play an effective role in the fight for their own liberation. The so-called talented black tenth don't represent large numbers [which are] necessary to change and shape the course of American social-racial history.

Verily, the talented black tenth need the non-talented nine-tenths, and the nine-talented black nine-tenths need the talented tenth of the black bourgeoisie. Unfortunately, the black untalented nine-tenths have not had much faith in the black talented tenth, not without some good, varied and various reasons, and the black talented tenth have tended to discount the non-talented black nine-tenths because of their lower level of literacy. But, the Civil Rights Revolution is beginning to change the fallacious and regrettable status-oriented interracial outlook at the problem. In very truth, there is no hope for the Civil Rights Revolution without a working and effective unity between these two basic forces. One indispensable factor of a creative unity is that the talented tenth tell the untalented nine-tenths the truth about the promises and limitations of the Civil Rights Revolution, even when it is unpopular. They must not be lulled into a false sense of security by glowing, glittering generalities about racial progress that cannot eventuate into reality, nor be thrown into the desperate darkness of despair by descriptions of inevitable racial hopelessness.

Negroes must be made to understand that there is no one panacea for the solution of the race or American problem. It is not the ballot, or education, or jobs, or freedom to enjoy public accommodations, or school integration, or business development, but all of these factors are necessary for a solution of the problem. They must be informed of the fact that the lot of the civil rights movement is tied up with the lot of [the] labor's rights movement because neither labor [n]or the Negro is fully free and both have a stake in the maintenance and strengthening of our political, democratic system, within the framework of which alone can civil rights and labor's rights be realized. Thus, they must be alerted to the folly, fallacy, futility and danger of black racism as well as white racism, and of the menace of Communism, either of the Peking or Moscow vintage. . . .

It will be obvious to him who runs and reads the signs of the times that in this world where machines displace men and have shown capabilities for decision making, no one group struggling for a place in the sun of opportunity, freedom and achievement can win its goals alone. Thus, just as the civil rights movement needs the power of organized labor, so organized labor needs the power of the Negro civil rights movement. Hence, an alliance between these two forces is natural.

Be it said to the great credit of the American Federation of Labor and Congress of Industrial Organizations, it has put, under the leadership of George Meany, its full weight back of the Civil Rights Act of 1964 and the Voting Rights Act of 1965. By the same token, the civil rights movement must place its full weight back of labor's fight to repeal Section 14(b) of the Taft-Hartley Act, which is the basis of the deceptive and sinister anti-labor and anti-civil rights "right-to-work" laws that are on the statute books of 19 states. The "right-to-work" laws are backed by the Ku Klux Klan, the White Citizens Councils and the John Birch Society—the known enemies of civil rights and labor's rights. Practically all of the southern states have "right-to-work" laws as well as Jim Crow laws, and also the highest poverty level and lowest literacy rate.

And now, let me hail and salute our great President of the United States, Lyndon B. Johnson, upon the fact that he has demonstrated a high order of statesmanship in placing the full power of the federal government, and his own brilliant genius in the art and science of government, back of the struggle for civil rights by the Negro Americans and their white allies of labor and the Church, Jewish, Catholic and Protestant, and the liberal intellectual community. In the President's recent speeches before both Houses of the Congress and at Howard University, he gave a new momentum to, and fired the faith of, the most humble men of color in the Civil Rights Revolution of rising expectations.

Be it said to the great honor of the President that in these times of trouble, trial and tension, he has maintained an uncompromising position of support for full, first-class citizenship for black Americans, and wisely proposed a White House Conference on Civil Rights in September 1965 to draft a program of action to give reality to the promise of civil rights legislation. This is a tribute to his greatness as an American and World Statesman. It is his finest hour. He has also courageously placed the bill for the repeal of Section 14(b) of the Taft-Hartley Act before the Congress, a major goal of labor. May God give him the faith, courage and strength to bear the cross history has placed upon his shoulders.

Let me also hail and salute our great Vice-President Hubert H. Humphrey, an honored son of the Twin Cities. He led the fight in the Congress for the Civil Rights Act of 1964, and has brilliantly over the years served as one of the champions of liberalism in America.

In honor of the great heroic struggle of the Civil Rights Revolution, I salute those young, brave, dedicated, fallen warriors in the memorable cause of civil rights, liberty, and the indestructibility of the human spirit: Andy Goodman, James Reeb, Viola Luizzo, Medgar Evers, and a gallant host of unknown soldiers who gave their all for human dignity, regardless of race, color, religion or national origin.

Although the North cannot be said to be thoroughly anti-segregationist, the great March on Washington and the Selma-Montgomery crusade showed that there is a minority of whites in the North who view racial segregation and discrimination with perfect hatred and who publicly bear witness of commitment to human dignity.

It is these white leaders and ordinary men of labor, religion, business, government and education who constitute the marching millions throughout the nation and who, with their black brothers and sisters, sing the stirring lines "We Shall Overcome" and the noblest war song of the ages to the tune of "John Brown's Body":

> *Mine eyes have seen the glory of the coming of the Lord,*
> *He is trampling out the vintage where the grapes of*
> *wrath are stored,*
> *He hath loosed the fateful lightening of his terrible*
> *swift sword,*
> *His truth is marching on!*

SOURCE: Box 36, folder: Speeches, January 30, 1965–September 17, 1965, A. Philip Randolph Papers, Library of Congress.

Black Power—A Promise or a Menace (1966)

Stokely Carmichael's popularization of the phrase "Black Power" struck like a thunderclap and gave voice to previously unarticulated nationalist impulses among many in the civil rights movement. This article, one of the longest Randolph wrote for *The Black Worker* in the 1960s, analyzes the movement's new direction and offers a stolid counterpoint that coalition politics are the most promising vehicle for changing America's still problematic racial order. Like many commentators, Randolph criticized "Black Power" as being an empty slogan devoid of constructive plans—something Carmichael addressed at length in a book he coauthored with Charles Hamilton later in 1967.

"Black power" is an unhappy combination of words. It has overtones of black racism just as "white supremacy" has overtones of white racism. The behavior patterns of black racism are similar to the behavior patterns of white racism. Both black racism and white racism are indefensible and dangerous to social peace and progress. Moreover, the cry of black racism is only an emotional slogan. It has no programmatic plan to successfully grapple with the basic problems of unemployment, segregated housing and schools. It reflects the concepts of Negro salvation through racial isolation, a condition which is both impractical and impossible in the operation of the process of the market economy at the point of production and distribution in this age of advancing democracy.

The revolution of science and industrialism has given birth to the city and urbanization, with a population explosion which has rendered rural life with its great spaces between dwellers no longer feasible or possible. Racial segregation, a social weapon of oppression and subjugation of the Negro by the southern plantation slave economy, is unnatural and had to be bolstered up by the anthropological myth of hereditary racial inferiority of persons of color. Hence, the cry of "black power" has not only broken with the Civil Rights Revolution, the basic objective of which is to complete the incompleted Civil War Revolution, but rejects its unfulfilled mission, which is the transition of the Negro from the status of second-class citizenship to first-class citizenship.

Thus, "black power" is bent upon turning back the clock of the Civil Rights Revolution and embarking upon a course of voluntary segregation upon the unsound assumption that the road to "black power" is a black political party, black labor unions, black schools with black teachers, black businesses and a black community, if not a black state. Such is a course of action which amounts to an exercise in frustration, fantasy, if not futility. But this is not to say that the idea of the Negro developing power in politics, labor unions and businesses is unimportant or unnecessary; it is important, necessary and desirable. But the question is how is it to be done. The employment of the method of racial segregation and isolation to achieve "black power" is not only unsound but anachronistic. It has no rational relation to existing social and racial realities.

Verily, power is not something anyone can seize with a slogan, however dramatic. Power must be built. It results from organizing people or material things with respect to certain relationships and purposes, such as labor unions, businesses and political action. For instance, the various parts of an automobile lying around on the ground, together with gasoline, cannot function as an automobile. But if you assemble the parts into a certain pattern of relationship, with the application of gasoline, the parts and gasoline become a functioning automobile; they will develop the power to run. Disassemble or separate the parts of the automobile from the gasoline and the power will vanish.

This illustration applies also to the Negro and the workers, neither one of which is fully free. Both Negroes and workers, having large numbers, have potential power, just as the unassembled parts and gasoline of an automobile have the potential power to run. Hence, the cry, "we want black power," has little meaning. Negroes already have kinetic power. They have greater potential power by virtue of their unorganized numbers. The basic and urgent problem of the Negro is the wise use of power for his advancement. The workers have developed power with the formation of trade unions and the utilization of the principle of collective bargaining, the strike, picket line, consumer boycotts and the ballot.

Now, inevitably, the cry of "black power" will provoke the countercry of "white power." This has already occurred in the march led by Dr. Martin Luther King for open occupancy in housing in Chicago, and by the Congress of Racial Equality in Cicero, Illinois. The danger lies in the possibility of the propaganda of "black power" and "white power" degenerating into black terror in confrontation with white terror. This kind of irrational black and white racism runs the dangerous risk of overheating the black ghettos and the white poor and can eventuate and escalate into a race war, which would be catastrophic to the Negroes and devastating to the country.

Unfortunately, tensions, uncertainties, division on strategy and tactics and even conflicts on goals, plague the Civil Rights Movement. There needs to be a moratorium on inflammatory racist propaganda against white people merely because they are white.

Efficiency is known to be impaired in people who are mentally sick, and people are mentally sick who are afflicted by the social disease of human hate and prejudice because of race, color, religion or national origin. Whites and Negroes who are in the pathological group of Negrophobia, anti-Semitism or anti-whiteism are prevented by their consuming obsession from seeking rational and permanent solutions to their social, economic and political problems.

A crucial crisis of disastrous proportions is the developing, deepening hatred and bitterness between the black and white poor. Not only will racial warfare between the black working poor and white working poor create a black and white backlash which can stop the Civil Rights Revolution dead in its tracks, but it can also halt the progress of political and economic liberalism in the Congress, state and city governments of the nation.

One of the most disquieting, disturbing, distressing and saddening spectacles I have ever witnessed was [that of] the faces, ugly with hate, of white spectators watching and shouting curses and threats at the Negroes in Chicago who were merely exercising their constitutional right of protest against racial discrimination in housing by marching in the streets. It is a chilling and frightening feeling to read the graphic comments of Rabbi Robert J. Marx about his experience in his participation in the march in Chicago under the leadership of Dr. King. Said he: "What I saw in Gage Park seared my soul in a way that my participation in no other civil rights event has done. I was afraid and I am afraid now. I saw how the concentration camp could have occurred and how man's hatred can lead him to kill. I saw Catholic priests reviled and nuns spat upon. I found myself—a rabbi—standing guard like a policeman over a pile of rocks, for fear that grown men, and mothers dragging little children around with them, would seize those rocks and throw them at demonstrators." Such is the fearful and terrifying state of mind and spirit of grown-up white men and women in America today concerning the Civil Rights Revolution, one of the greatest human events of social change involving freedom, racial and social justice of the twentieth century.

Obviously, these average white Americans are obsessed and inflamed with the myth that the presence of a Negro family in a white community will cause a decline in the value of a property. While this is not true, they believe it is true, and the beliefs of people are what counts. They determine human action. Thus, the Civil Rights Movement, the church, organized labor, government at all levels, the intellectual and liberal movement, face a monumental and grave challenge of immediate urgency.

Instead of joining the cry of "black power" by well-meaning, dedicated but misguided young Negro militants following the illusion of racial separatism, the civil rights leaders must rebuild the national coalition of conscience which was back of the Montgomery Bus Boycott of Dr. King in 1955, the brilliant Birmingham battle against racial segregation in 1963 and the tremendous civil rights challenge by the Selma-Montgomery March of 1965, together with the great Job-Freedom March on Washington, August 1963. This civil rights, labor, church and student coalition won the Civil Rights Act of 1964 and the Civil Rights Act of 1965. But now the coalition has collapsed. Some liberal, church, labor and student groups have either turned against the civil rights cause or have lost interest in the struggle.

Obviously, the announced rejection of white liberals in particular, and white civil rights activists in general, as participants in the Negro freedom movement by the Student Nonviolent Coordinating Committee, riots in the streets and the sensational cry of "we want black power" have had no little effect in driving out white friends from the civil rights struggle. Needless to say this was a grave mistake in strategy, tactic and policy, especially in the light of the great sacrifice young adult and white civil rights activists have made with their lives and freedom in Alabama, Mississippi and other areas of the South. I have only to mention the names of young Andy Goodman and Michael Schwerner.

Naturally, I deplore riots and disorders in the streets. The throwing of bricks, bottles of Molotov cocktails into store windows, setting buildings afire, turning over automobiles, looting stores, vandalism and lawlessness are no answer to the problem of racial oppression. Riots cannot win civil rights but they can lose them. They have already caused the Civil Rights Movement to lose support of the national public consensus. They result in the destruction of the Negroes' own communities, loss of jobs and loss of lives, for they are chiefly the sole casualties of racial violence. The tragic convulsions in Watts, Chicago, San Francisco and other areas leave only bitter ashes of disillusionment, wounded hearts, hopelessness and despair. The brash statement "burn, baby, burn" is more witless than wise. It may make the fickle laugh but it can only cause the judicious to grieve. The paraphrase of Whitney Young, Jr., national director of the Urban League, "learn, baby, learn," is more apt and timely. . . .

When it is understood that Negroes are the only people in this country who have been held, owned and sold as slaves, not for a day but for a quarter of a thousand years, one can understand how they may come to point of the strain of their patience and submissiveness. When it is known that after slavery was abolished in 1865, Negroes have existed only as second-class citizens for a hundred years without the right to vote, without the right to work at decent jobs, without the right to quality education, without the right to rent or buy houses of their choice even if they possessed the money, without the right to public accommodations, it ought not be difficult for white America to realize that the time would come when Negroes would stand up on their feet and fight back for their rights. When white American citizens possess this information, they will understand why Negroes are marching in Alabama, Mississippi, Washington, Chicago and San Francisco. They will begin to be aware of the reason why Negroes are in motion and why there are riots and disorders in the streets.

It is a matter of common knowledge that the rate of unemployment of white workers and white teenagers is now going down while the rate of unemployment for Negro workers and Negro teenagers is now going up. This information will show white America why Negroes do such incredibly senseless things as tearing up and burning down their own community, and why they fight the police and militia even at the sacrifice of their own lives. When it is understood that Negroes were subjected to the oppression and persecution and brutalization and humiliation of a system of slavery maintained under law and order, driven from the ballot box by the Ku Klux Klan under law and order, mobbed and lynched under law and order, it will not be difficult to comprehend why Negroes are not impressed by sermons on law and order. Verily, riots in the streets, however unwise, proceed from racial and social injustices. Remove the causes of the riots and they will vanish.

I make these judgments by way of explanation, not justification. Just as water in a kettle on a hot stove will begin to boil at a certain time if it remains there long enough and the fire is kept burning, and unless the lid of the kettle is removed, the expansion of the steam in the kettle will either blow the lid off or burst the kettle; so long as harsh oppression of a people continue, regardless of race, religion, national origin or class, they will eventually and inevitably resist, resent and reject the said oppression in the form of uprisings and rebellions.

One has only to look at the history of the British oppression of the American colonies, through taxation without representation, to know only the awakened and aroused oppressed can and will disturb their oppressors and drive them to abolish oppression. The Founding Fathers created riots and disorders in the streets of Boston. They resorted to civil disobedience by seizing the tea of British merchants and throwing it into Boston Harbor. They staged a massacre on Boston Commons and launched a full-scale war against King George III. Look at the history of our country. American patriots waged a Civil War for four years, with Americans murdering Americans, to abolish slavery in order to save the Union. Irish patriots staged an Easter rebellion against the oppression of British landlords in 1916, and manifested signs of violence against Queen Elizabeth of Great Britain on her recent visit to Ireland. . . .

White America must realize that the Negroes' battle for equality, freedom and human dignity is in the great tradition of American history, and that they should be supported and not condemned and attacked, for they are as American as any white American and have paid the price with their blood and tears and lives in every war, from the Revolutionary War of 1776 to Vietnam, to make this country free, strong and great. When the Polish, Italian, Irish, Hungarian,

British, French, and German-Americans realize that the Civil Rights Revolution for first-class citizenship for Negroes will never end until they are fully free and equal, they will recognize the futility of attacking Negro marches for open occupancy in housing with bottles, bricks, curses, hate and scorn.

Verily, the moral basis of the Civil Rights Revolution is the source of its power, hope and promise. It is the expression and philosophy of the universal moral imperative that all men, Negro and white, Jew and Gentile, Catholic and Protestant, African and Asian, are members of one common human family of which God is the Father and Creator. It follows that if all men are members of one common family, then all men are brothers; if all men are equal, all men are entitled to equal treatment; if all men are entitled to equal treatment, then discrimination and segregation based on race or color, religion or national origin are morally wrong; if discrimination and segregation of any human being are morally wrong, then they should be abolished.

The fact that the Negro's right—like the rights of white, brown and yellow races—to life, liberty and the pursuit of happiness is God-given and not man-made. No law, constitution, or state can give any human being this right; it is a natural right, and Negroes, like other human beings, possess this right as a result of their being human. They were born with it, and the role of government is to protect Negroes and all other human beings in the exercise and enjoyment of this right. This is why the Civil Rights Revolution demanded and secured the Civil Rights Act of 1964, Civil Rights Act of 1965, and also fought for the Civil Rights Act of 1966 (which was filibustered to death). The basic evidence of the recognition of one's status of manhood, whether Negro or white, is that he receive respect for the dignity and infinite worth of his personality as a human being. . . .

As a matter of fact, the use of the instrument of demonstrations in the streets in any form should be determined in response to the existing social and racial realities in any particular place or at any particular time. It is obvious that it is time to suspend demonstrations in the streets, for they are provoking counterdemonstrations from white spectators and deepening currents of racial hate. The basic strategy at this stage of the Revolution is to rebuild the coalition with its three faiths, Jewish, Catholic and Protestant, students, liberals, intellectuals and sympathetic business forces. This is necessary since the coalition has collapsed as a result of the division within the ranks of the freedom movement and growing overtones of black racism against white people merely because they are white. This is an unfortunate development which has practically emasculated the strength and force of the Civil Rights Revolution. Moreover, it has resulted in reversing the direction of the Revolution, not on a big scale, but by a small group of militant civil rights activists who have elected to set forth the hysterically, emotionally-packed slogan, "black power."

But this is not to suggest that differences in tactics, strategy and achievements with respect to even the direction of the Revolution should be suppressed. Great mass movements reach a stage of proliferation which gives birth to pragmatic expressions and groups. Ideas that are regarded as sound must be subjected to competition in the arena of public discussion in order to establish their strength and force. No movement which is based on a monolithic foundation can liberate the disadvantaged and semi-free people, because it smacks of totalitarian structure and function in the struggle. This is the way of life of the totalitarian social order, Fascist, Nazi and Communist. The Civil Rights Revolution is essentially a product of the struggle within a free democratic society and cannot exist under a totalitarian system, just as the labor movement cannot exist under such a system. This is the reason why civil rights leaders who have expressed opposition to the slogan "black power" consider that the direction of the slogan is unsound.

SOURCE: *The Black Worker* 38 (December 1966), 4–7.

Freedom Budget (1966)

Randolph unveiled the Freedom Budget for All Americans during this October 26, 1966, press conference at Salem Methodist Church in New York City. Although this massive poverty eradication program was never implemented, it was just as radical as the call for Black Power articulated by Stokely Carmichael in the same year. With "freedom" attained through the 1964 Civil Rights Act and the 1965 Voting Rights Act, Randolph wanted to fulfill the agenda announced by the 1963 March on Washington for Jobs and Freedom.

Brothers and Sisters:

Let me express my deep appreciation to you for joining me today in the launching of "The Freedom Budget for All Americans." Many of you have come a long distance to be here—and not for the first time. For I see in this audience the faces of many men and women, black and white, who came together three years ago to realize another great dream—the 1963 March on Washington for Jobs and Freedom.

In a very real sense we have gathered today to undertake the redemption and the completion of the goals set forth on that historic day in August of 1963. Since that day much has changed. There are signs of a new resistance to our struggle. We face more complex and difficult problems. A weary, but no less cruel, indifference has settled upon elements in the Congress. And, within our own ranks, confusion and division have been exploited by our enemies.

But I believe, and profoundly hope, that from this day forth the opponents of social progress can take comfort no longer, for I am proud to announce to you, brothers and sisters, and to the members of the press, that not since the March on Washington has there been such broad sponsorship and enthusiastic support for any undertaking as has been mobilized on behalf of "The Freedom Budget for All Americans."

We have the support of every national civil rights organization, of the united labor movement, of the major Protestant, Catholic and Jewish Institutions, of forward-looking business leaders, of the most prominent economists and academicians, of students and intellectuals. These forces have not come together to demand help for the Negro. Rather, we meet on a common ground of determination that in this, the richest and most productive society ever known to man, the scourge of poverty can and must be abolished—not in some distant future, not in this generation, but within the next ten years!

Negroes, of course, are no strangers to poverty. Two-thirds of our families have an annual income of $4,000 or less. This at a time when the latest studies show that an urban family of four requires $6,800 a year for a "modest but adequate" standard of living. But while most Negroes live in poverty and deprivation, it is not true that most of the poor and deprived are Negroes. We must not forget that 75 percent of the poor are white. No less than Negroes are they denied adequate income, decent housing, quality education, sufficient health care and security.

The tragedy is that the workings of our economy so often pit the white poor and the black poor against each other at the bottom of society. The tragedy is that groups only one generation removed from poverty themselves, haunted by the memory of scarcity and fearful of slipping back, step on the fingers of those struggling up the ladder. And the tragedy is that not only the poor, the nearly poor, and the once poor, but all Americans, are the victims of our failure as a nation to distribute democratically the fruits of our abundance. For, directly or indirectly, not one of us is untouched by the steady spread of slums, the decay of our cities, the segregation and overcrowding of our public schools, the shocking deterioration of our hospitals, the violence and chaos in our streets, the idleness of able-bodied men deprived of work, and the anguished demoralization of our youth. No more than the Western migrants of generations ago can today's affluent migrants to the suburbs build a privileged utopia apart from the cities darkened by blight. For better or worse, we are one nation and one people. We shall solve our problems together or together we shall enter a new era of social disorder and disintegration.

The "Freedom Budget" demonstrates that the abolition of poverty—its causes and symptoms—is not only morally right but economically imperative. It demonstrates that we can achieve full employment and full production if we will meet our unmet social needs, if we will clear the slums and rebuild our cities, if we will provide the schools and hospitals we need, if we will purify our air and water, if we will bring our transportation systems and natural resources development into line with our needs. We cannot achieve these goals through haphazard, piecemeal efforts. We cannot solve the problems of the schools while leaving the slums intact. We cannot train people for jobs when there are no jobs. And so, brothers and sisters, what we need is an overall plan of attack, a coordinated mobilization of our natural resources. We need, in short, not a skirmish, not a battle—but a real *war* on poverty. This is what the "Freedom Budget" is. It is not visionary or utopian. It is feasible. It is concrete. It is specific. It is quantitative. It talks dollars and cents. It sets goals and priorities. It tells how these can be achieved. And it places the responsibility for leadership with the federal government, which alone has the resources equal to the task.

The question is not whether we have the means. Before 1975 we will have a one trillion dollar economy. The question is whether we have the will. Ten years from now, will two-fifths of our nation still live in poverty and deprivation? This is, above all, a moral question. And upon the answer hangs not only the fate of the Negro—weighted down by centuries of exploitation, degradation and malice—but the fate of the nation. The "Freedom Budget" is not a call for a handout. It is a challenge to the best traditions and possibilities of America. It is a call to those who have grown weary of slogans and gestures to rededicate themselves to the cause of social reconstruction. It is a plea to men of good will to give tangible substance to long-proclaimed ideals. The "Freedom Budget" does not ask for the moon, but only for justice here on earth, in a land so well able to afford it.

SOURCE: Box 37, folder: Speeches, 1966, A. Philip Randolph Papers, Library of Congress.

Speech at White House, "To Fulfill These Rights" (1966)

As honorary chairman of the conference, Randolph joined Thurgood Marshall and Roy Wilkins on the list of major African American leaders who gave addresses at this benchmark event on June 1, 1966. Coming on the heels of the Civil Rights Act and Voting Rights Act, "To Fulfill These Rights" sought to implement a broad plan for racial equality that included educational opportunities, investments in economic development, improvements in public housing and municipal services, and enforcement of recently passed progressive legislation. Whereas "To Secure These Rights" was a veritable blueprint for the civil rights movement and cemented President Harry Truman's reputation as a statesman committed to desegregation, "To Fulfill These Rights" solidified President Lyndon Johnson's place in history as a leader whose idealistic Great Society was undermined by a stubborn insistence on maintaining a costly war in Vietnam.

Of particular importance in Randolph's remarks here is the theme of African American exceptionalism, wherein he postulates that, because of race, the black experience in the United States is fundamentally different from that of the various European ethnic groups that comprise the nation's cultural fabric. As he often did, Randolph draws upon historical knowledge to buttress his arguments. In this case, he cites the collapse of Reconstruction and betrayal of freedmen and -women, the hardening of the color line and creation of racial ghettos, and the persistence of discrimination as examples of injustices that only applied to African Americans.

In the spirit of the conference "To Fulfill These Rights" I welcome you. I welcome you to share in the enriching fellowship of the great and rewarding and creating experience, and the marvelous, wondrous, moral adventure, in a social enterprise to mark and achieve a new era of acceptance of the principle of the unity of the human family, and the dignity of the human personality—irrespective of race or color, religion or national origin or ancestry.

Let me hail and salute the President of the United States, whose vision and wisdom expressed in that historic speech at Howard University, June 1964, provided the inspiration and foundation for this conference when the President stated in that speech, with boldness and humility, "But freedom is not enough. You do not wipe away the scars of centuries by saying 'Now, you are free to go where you want, do as you desire, and choose the leaders you please.' You do not take a person who for years has been hobbled with chains and liberate him, bring him up to the starting line of a race, and then say, 'You are free to compete with all others,' and still justly believe that you have been completely fair. Thus it is not enough just to open the gates of opportunity. Your citizens must have the ability to walk through those gates."

These declarations express a profound moral commitment to the highest ideals of the brotherhood of man. And here we are, men and women of the church, labor, business, and government, assembled in a great conference, to become more deeply involved in what we more and more recognize to be the most tremendous social challenge of conflict and change in our country today—the Civil Rights Revolution. It is our fervent plea for strong voices to be raised from all areas of our society, out of varying traditions and interests, to arouse the conscience of our land, in order to achieve in fact that which has already been won in law, and what always has been in the hearts of good men—equality, justice, freedom, and human dignity for all men regardless of color or country.

To millions of people of the Old World, America represented a land of promise, a land where people were free, a land where the individual could move about and up in his opportunities, his job, his income, and his social status. America was hope, it was promises. This meant horizontal and vertical mobility. Where a man could better himself, the level he could find was largely up to him. It was this vision of a land of promise that drew men and women from the Old World. True, practically all these people lived in ghettos. Some of them may still persist. But for most of them the nationality ghettos were only way stations, thresholds inviting the newcomer to make his adjustment and then move out into membership in the larger American community.

But the problem of the Negro is different. The ghettos we are concerned about are neither voluntary nor temporary. They are, for the most part, compulsory and permanent. Precisely because the Negro is a substantial part of the total population, and because it presents the critical problem and extreme challenge to American democracy, this conference, "To Fulfill These Rights" seeks to awaken and cause all Americans to make a serious effort to understand and face up to their moral responsibilities.

Of all the groups who have settled in the United States and have become a part of this nation, Negroes are one people who were brought here originally against their will. They were brought here in chains. The slave trade was a profitable business. Much of the culture of New England, and the life of Southern aristocracy were based on it. No other people were in slavery and exploited so mercilessly, even by the founding fathers of the nation. Although slavery had existed in the ancient world and down through the centuries in many parts of the world, the American institution of slavery was the worst. Slaves had no rights in American laws, moral codes or customs. Husbands and wives became separated, and children could be taken from their parents. They were denied education and any hope of a better life.

The people had a Civil War fought over their condition, a war which divided the nation with a bloody and bitter conflict, kept the slaves landless, moneyless, friendless, voteless, and hopeless. To their deprivation was added the loss of the Reconstruction Revolution by the rise of the Confederate counter-revolution, which virtually nullified the Thirteenth Amendment of 1865, the Fourteenth Amendment of 1868, the Fifteenth Amendment of 1870, and the Civil Rights Act of 1875 by a United States Supreme Court decision of 1883, and the decision of *Plessy vs. Ferguson* in 1896, which handed down the doctrine of "separate but equal," which provided the foundation of racial segregation and discrimination in this country. Thus, after over three hundred years of slavery, the mass of Negro people were the victims of segregation and inequality for another hundred years.

And to these human agonies of physical brutalization and mental humiliation which were suffered by no other group in the population, I must add the mark of color. Other groups had moved out of the ghettos—the Irish, the Germans, the Jews, the Polish, the Italians. They had moved ahead in education and employment. They enjoyed exposure to the stimuli of America's material and spiritual development. They could better themselves and become part of the mainstream of American civilization. If they suffered from the prejudices of their neighbors, they still had a fighting chance of changing, of overcoming the barriers of discrimination. But for the Negro, discrimination and segregation and organized persecution and intimidation were a part of a conscious and determined plan to hold the Negro down.

During the First World War, masses of Negroes fled from the Southern plantations and rural and urban areas to seek jobs and a new life in the North. They were forced to settle in restricted areas in the great cities of the North. Here again they ran into the same patterns of Jim Crow—these patterns of housing and employment, deprivation and rejection were not written in laws. But prejudice, custom, practice, made for the same thing. Indeed, many will testify that the Negro ghettos in the cities are firetraps; mice, rats and vermin multiply due to lack of adequate sanitation. The increase of the Negro population through migration from the South and the increased birth rate result in extreme density of population and overcrowding. People are hemmed in, unable to move out or escape the slums even if they have the money to move. The rents they pay are higher than those paid by their white neighbors. They get less of housing for the dollars they pay for rent. Instead of paying a fourth of their income for rent, they often have to pay as much as a third, leaving them with less money out of low wages for food, clothing, medicines, education, and recreation.

Racial ghettos suffer a double evil. They suffer from racial segregation, and also from poverty. The people have no margin of security. There are no shelves with extra food for the next meal or the next day. There are no bank savings or insurance policies, for the starvation wages require a weekly supplement of welfare. There is nothing the people can show as security for loans in times of unemployment, family sickness, accidents, or other misfortunes. There is no wonder that life expectancy is shorter than that in a white community. The incidence of disease and death due to tuberculosis and cancer is many times that of the white community. Child death in the first days of life, in the first months of life, and year of life is over twice that for other parts of the city.

To the physical illnesses we have to note the ill effects of family life. The man of the family is supposed to be the protector and support of the family. But if he is denied education and employment, if he cannot play his role as a husband or a father, the family breaks down. Thus, men plagued with forced idleness, women have to carry the burden of providing the income, and at the same time caring for their children. Is it any wonder that alcohol and narcotics and gambling and various forms of antisocial action are found in the black ghettos? And is it any wonder that children and youth are damaged emotionally and mentally? The destructive and devastating impact of the ghetto too is frightfully continuous and total. There are families that have been on welfare rolls for two, three, four generations. The result is a sense of hopelessness and helplessness and powerlessness.

But despite the seemingly insurmountable obstacles, most of the men and women of the black ghettos struggle to find work and maintain family life. And despite adverse conditions, most youth remain in school and strive to better their condition. They try to believe in the American promise, and they try to obey the law and look forward to participation in the political, economic and cultural life of the nation. But the youth that are damaged are incalculable.

First are those who lose faith in their families, in themselves, and in the larger community. They reject themselves and develop a sense of self-hate and despair. They accept any evaluation of themselves. Those who suffer from self-rejection tend to withdraw from the community. They undergo an inner death. They lose an appetite for learning. Some end with mental illness, and seek escape in suicide.

Second are those who react with bitterness and rage. They are ready to strike against others. Their respect for life and law is destroyed. They fill the jails and houses of detention and the prisons. Their hatred is against authority, and especially the police, who they consider their enemy and oppressor. They hurt not only the white population, but also they strike against the life and property within the ghetto.

Third are those whose anger becomes a social force of mass proportions. This is the volcanic force which builds its explosive power to such a pitch that it breaks out into race riots, and in violence, such as is symbolized by events in the summer of 1965 in Watts, a ghetto in the city of Los Angeles. It took only a trivial incident involving police ineptness to light the flames of racial violence.

Those who participated in the riot were chiefly youth. They set fire to 600 buildings, destroyed 200 completely. They broke store windows and looted the shops. Thirty-six persons were killed. A thousand were injured. Four thousand were arrested. Over 150 million dollars' worth of property was destroyed or damaged. It took the National Guard to restore order. Let me warn this conference that the Negro ghettos in every city throughout the nation are areas of tension and socio-racial dynamite, near the brink of similar racial explosions of violence.

What can be done to right the wrongs of the Negro people of this country? What can be done to bring about social and racial justice and fulfill the promises of American life for all our people, both the black working poor and the white working poor? Is there any hope we can solve a deep-rooted and complex problem which affects the life of every American and threatens the survival of this nation? How can we abolish the racial ghettos?

Let us realize that children learn their prejudices. They are not born with them. They learn the ways of racial inequalities from their parents, from their attitudes and words and behavior patterns. And they learn from the experience of racial inequality, from the television, radio, press, church, school, playgrounds, employment, and government. Can we re-educate our children? Can we re-educate ourselves? Americans tend to believe in education as the cure-all for all ills. We must realize that the relations of the races and the roots of racism in the American culture are deep. . . .

Thus the purpose of this conference is to involve all Americans in the great social enterprise of [demonstrating] respect for the sacredness of the dignity of the personality of every human being, which is reflected in recognizing the rights of every person to life, liberty, and the pursuit of happiness. Every day's delay in breaking down the barriers of segregation in housing, schools and discrimination in jobs means irreparable damage to hundreds of thousands of human beings. The damage is not merely to the Negro; it is a liability to white people as well. For we live in a world whose population is 80 percent colored. It is no rational kindness to permit a white child to grow up in a home which is segregated, or in a school which is segregated, and in a white community which is an isolated sector in the total world community.

In the large cities where white people, white families, have moved to the suburbs, the white child has been brought up without knowledge or understanding of his colored neighbor. A white youth rarely if ever meets or communicates with a Negro youth, though both are fellow citizens of this nation and fellow human beings. How can persons or property be secure in a community where invisible racial walls keep children and youth and adults apart? Tension, fear and hate are likely to plague personal lives in communities for generations unless we equalize conditions and plan for the transformation of urban life so that the great metropolitan complexes are more truly democratic places of human habitation.

Finally, this is a difficult age, made so by the revolution of science, technology, and industrialism, and the revolution of the colored world for freedom and status, peace and plenty. Insecurity and conflict throughout the world have made it an age of anxieties. Yet for each of us there are compensations. This is an exciting time, a time of changes and new possibilities. If there is insecurity, anxiety, and fear, there is also a tremendous sense of possibilities beyond what men dared to hope for in the past.

This conference to "Fulfill These Rights" will broaden the horizon for the Negro and white American, and the entire world of color now in the revolutionary flames of discontent. All honor to the President for his imagination and sense of innovation which made this conference possible. He will be remembered in history as the President of Human Rights, Education, and Anti-Poverty. And the civil rights revolution gave him inspiration and motivation. The implementation of the Report of the Conference "To Fulfill These Rights" will constitute a major and powerful thrust giving Negroes the ability to walk through the gate of opportunity and achieve first class citizenship in America. To the men and women, black and white, Catholic, Jew and Protestant, participating in this Conference: "Quit ye like men! Be strong! We shall overcome!"

SOURCE: *Major Addresses at the White House Conference, "To Fulfill These Rights," June 1–2, 1966* (Washington, D.C.: GPO, 1966).

Letter to Layle Lane on the Ocean Hill–Brownsville Crisis (1968)

In this correspondence between two long-term veterans of the black freedom struggle and the labor movement, Randolph minces no words in describing his position: "Black Powerites" are in a battle that, even if they win, will be to their detriment. Never a fan of provincialism, and distrustful of local communities' ability to act in any ways other than fundamentally insular and xenophobic ones, Randolph derides the push for local control of schools as being as "irrelevant . . . as Zoroastrianism is to the Space Age." The letter was sent to Lane's eastern Pennsylvania home in Doylestown, a city that has honored her legacy as a civil rights activist and union organizer by naming a street in her honor: "Layle Lane."

May 22, 1968

Miss Layle Lane
R.D. #1, Ferry Road
Doylestown, Pennsylvania 18901

Dear Layle:

I was glad to get your letter of May 15, with your comments on the school situation and your suggestion that the A. Philip Randolph Institute hold a conference on the matter to develop discussion and dialogue.

I think something will have to be done, otherwise there will be utter chaos and anarchy in the Negro community as the result of the efforts of the Black Powerites to take over the schools in the ghettos on the grounds that white teachers don't give Negro youth proper education and inspiration. Of course I think this position is entirely ridiculous because if it is proper and sound to exclude whites from the Negro communities (people who have passed examinations and are hired to positions in the schools) what are Negroes, who get ninety percent of their income from jobs that are not in the Negro communities, going to do?

Moreover, the whole idea of contending that power can be created by people in one area, on a basis of racial organization, is as irrelevant to economic and social justice as Zoroastrianism is to the Space Age.

Anyone who will take the time to read any treaties on economics will find that power springs from the ownership of property, and the organization of labor, business, consumers, and tenants into movements to fight for their interests. Business people will naturally fight for profits; labor for wages; tenants for lower rents; and consumers for lower prices.

Then, there is the need for community organization to improve the conditions in the community, including schools, not for any particular group but for the children of anybody who lives in the community.

Well, Layle, it has been a long time since I have heard from you and I hope you are well and enjoying life. Some time when you are in New York I hope you will come to visit me as you used to do.

Sincerely yours,
A. Philip Randolph

SOURCE: Box 3, folder: General Correspondence, 1957–1968, C-W, A. Philip Randolph Papers, Library of Congress.

7

Randolph, War, and the Fight to Desegregate the United States Military

A. Philip Randolph had mixed ideas about the U.S. military and the extent to which African Americans should support various wars. He was chiefly interested not in *who* was being fought against but *what* was being fought for. Randolph firmly believed in democracy, and he saw little hope for racial or ethnic minorities under any variant of dictatorial or totalitarian rule. As a keen observer of international affairs, he resented the platitudes that saber-rattling warmongers used to justify their actions overseas. He was convinced that freedom was worth fighting for, but he knew hypocrisy when he saw it. Why should African Americans take up arms to ensure the rights of Europeans, Randolph reasoned, when racial conditions in the United States so clearly undermined the very principles that his country professed to be fighting for?

Randolph was troubled by the question of whether or not to support a specific war, but he was especially interested in the status of African Americans in the armed forces. The military's long-standing pattern of racial segregation represented the nationalization of ostensibly local and regional racial patterns. By enforcing the color line in the military, he argued, the federal government was giving greater credibility to segregation and nationalizing a "Southern" pattern. Integrating the military was an unfulfilled goal of the March on Washington Movement and just about every other African American organization during the 1940s. Like Sisyphus, Randolph tirelessly and fruitlessly worked on advancing this cause for most of that decade. He eventually succeeded when President Truman signed Executive Order 9981. By the end of the Korean War, America's next major conflict, the armed forces were almost completely desegregated.

The primary sources featured in this chapter are a combination of ruminations on the expediency of particular wars and a statement of the resentment that African Americans felt about serving their country as second-class citizens. This ambivalence is manifest in the chapter's first document. "The Negro and the War" typifies Randolph's speeches and writings about the Second World War, a conflict to which he said the African American "must give freely and fully his blood, toil, tears and treasure to the cause of victory for the United States over Japan, Nazi Germany, and world Fascism." Disillusioned with the absence of progress despite the noteworthy achievements of African Americans in that war, Randolph escalated his position and defiantly went in front of Congress with his plans to actively organize against conscription if the military persisted in its segregationist policies. He was fully aware that organizing takes more than words, and the correspondence that is included in this chapter provides us with an inside glimpse of the various networks he tapped to advance this cause.

Randolph said comparatively little about the Vietnam War, but the final document in this chapter illustrates where his primary concern lay. As Randolph saw it, the peace movement was diverting attention from the "Civil Rights Revolution" and the costly war was channeling resources away from the Great Society.

FOR FURTHER READING

Astor, Gerald. *The Right to Fight: A History of African Americans in the Military.* Novato, Calif.: Presido, 1998.

Dalfiume, Richard. *Desegregation of the U.S. Armed Forces: Fighting on Two Fronts, 1939–1953.* Columbia: University of Missouri Press, 1969.

Gardner, Michael R. *Harry Truman and Civil Rights: Moral Courage and Political Risks.* Carbondale: Southern Illinois University Press, 2002.

James, Jennifer C. *A Freedom Bought with Blood: African American War Literature from the Civil War to World War II.* Chapel Hill: University of North Carolina Press, 2007.

Mershon, Sherie, and Steven L. Schlossman. *Foxholes and Color Lines: Desegregating the U.S. Armed Forces.* Baltimore: Johns Hopkins University Press, 1998.

Nalty, Bernard C. *Strength for the Fight: A History of Black Americans in the Military.* New York: Free Press, 1989.

Phillips, Kimberley L. *War! What Is It Good For? Black Freedom Struggles and the U.S. Military from World War II to Iraq.* Chapel Hill: University of North Carolina Press, 2012.

Westheider, James E. *The African American Experience in Vietnam: Brothers in Arms.* Lanham, Md.: Rowman and Littlefield, 2008.

The Negro and the War (1941)

Race relations were far from ideal in North America, but in this document Randolph makes the case that black people were better off in a severely flawed United States than under rule of Communist Russia, totalitarian Italy, or fascist Germany. Democratic ideals, Randolph argues, at least gesture toward the concept of equal rights—and that is essential for any minority group's security.

Japan has fired upon the United States, our country. We, all of us, black and white, Jew and Gentile, Protestant and Catholic, are at war, not only with Japan but also with Hitler and the Axis powers. What shall the Negro do? There is only one answer. He must fight. He must give freely and fully his blood, toil, tears and treasure to the cause of victory for the United States over Japan, Nazi Germany, and world Fascism. There is no alternative to this decision. There should be no alternative to this decision. We are citizens of the United States and we must proudly and bravely assume the obligations, responsibilities, and duties of American citizenship. We cannot escape this fact. We ought not to want to escape it. Happily, the Negro has never sought to escape it in the wars and crises of the past of our country.

Moreover, the Negro has a good stake in this war. It is the stake of democracy—at home and abroad. Without democracy in America, limited though it be, the Negro would not have even the right to fight for his rights. Under the rule of Japan, Nazi Germany, or Fascist Italy minority groups like the Negro and organized labor are not only without rights, such as freedom of speech, the press, assembly, petition, trial by jury and habeas corpus and so forth, they don't have the right to exist. They are liquidated or put into concentration camps for non-conformity to the pattern of totalitarian regimentation.

If the democratic nations are swept under the sword and fire of Hitler and Japan, our America is not secure; and if the United States goes down, the Negro is through in the western world. But the fight to stop and destroy totalitarian Japan, Nazi Germany, and Fascist Italy and their Axis partners also involves the obligation, responsibility and task for the Negro people to fight with all their might for their constitutional democratic rights and freedoms here in America—including equality of opportunity to work in all categories of skills upon a basis of ability and merit in the defense and non-defense industries; to full and equal integration and participation in the army, navy, air corps, and marines; in short, the rights to the full statute of constitutional citizenship, free from discrimination, segregations, and Jim-Crowisms of any kind and all kinds.

Negroes cannot ask for anything more, nor can they accept anything less. Yes, Negroes must fight. We might answer the call for national unity. We must see to it that the United States wins this war and wins the peace. For the interests, future and destiny of the Negro are fundamentally tied up with the interests, future and destiny of our country; and the interests, future and destiny of the United States are tied up with the interests, future and destiny of Great Britain and her allies.

We must fight to preserve democracy and liberty such as we now have in the world so that we may make it sounder and better. And Negroes must demand the right to fight and work alongside their fellow white Americans as full and equal citizens, workers and soldiers, sailors, air, and marine men. If we fail to fight to make the democratic process work in America while we fight to beat down Japan and Hitler, we will be traitors to democracy and liberty and the liberation of the Negro people.

SOURCE: *The Black Worker* 13 (November 1941): 4.

The Negroes Fight for Democracy Now! (1942)

Randolph staunchly advocated the desegregation of America's armed forces, and his interest in this cause heightened at the onset of World War II. In this September 11, 1942, speech at the Golden Gate Auditorium sponsored by the March on Washington Movement, Randolph argued that the war's magnitude necessitated the full utilization of African American soldiers and posited that the conflict's ideological underpinnings demanded that the military abandon its color line. This issue was one of Randolph's initial demands when the original threat to march was made in 1941, but it was not addressed by Executive Order 8802.

Mr. Chairman, Fellow Marchers, Comrades, Workers and Citizens:

We have come together at an hour when the skies are darkened with the horrors and tragedies of war. The outcome of this war may mean a new order of enlightened democracy and civilization, or it may mean the advent of another Dark Ages. If the United Nations win, there is the hope and the possibility, but not the certainty, of a new order of democracy and humanitarian enlightenment; if the Axis forces triumph, our prospect is totalitarian reaction and tyranny. We are therefore, as a minority group in America and as one of the great sections of the dark races of the world, and also as a group the large majority of whom are workers, our interest lies on the side of the United Nations. We want to see the victory of the arms of America, Great Britain, Russia, China and their allies.

But we know that a military victory is not enough, for the object of the United Nations must not merely be the victory of the United Nations, but the victory of the democratic forces. Be assured that it is possible for the United Nations to win and the cause of democracy to lose. "How can this be?" the question is asked. The answer is pure and simple. If the United Nations win and the old imperialisms continue, the cause of democracy will not have been served. The history of the old imperialisms represents some of the most unhappy chapters of the human race. Under it, 1,700,000,000 people of color have been sentenced to walk in darkness at noonday. Their countries have been scenes of the world's worst crimes against humanity committed in the name of Christianity, civilization and democracy. Hundreds of millions of human beings have been murdered and mutilated in India, China and Africa to satisfy the power-hungry nations of monopoly capitalism and the vile philosophy of racism. And these power-hungry nations are now dominant forces of the United States.

It is possible that the victory of the United Nations may perpetuate the Anglo-American empire systems and set up a world state whose purpose will be to serve as an agency for the maintenance and perpetuation of a world hegemony of the same old doctrines of white supremacy, and the continued subjugation, exploitation and oppression of the darker races. If this happens, this Second World War will not be the last World War, but it will simply serve as a basis for a Third World War of increasing severity, cruelty and destruction. Not only will the victory of the United Nations fail to consolidate the forces of democracy if the old Anglo-Saxon imperialisms are not destroyed, but the units of the Anglo-American imperial order—Great Britain, America, Canada, Australia, New Zealand and their allies—will become centers of a devastating and ferocious fascist militarism and administration by men on horseback whose Machiavellian doctrines will be the absolute emasculation of all democratic ideals, institutions, heritages, and faiths that have inspired the hearts of men for 150 years.

Thus the central question with the liberal and democratic forces, minority groups and darker races of our contemporary is twofold: one, the victory of the United Nations over Hitler's Nazism, Mussolini's Fascism, and Hirohito's Militarism, but a victory without the Anglo-Saxon imperialism and the recognition and acceptance of the principles of the equality of races, nations and people. Two, the maintenance of the democratic spirit, that the United Nations may be spiritually and morally qualified and worthy of the trusteeship of the jewel of democracy when victory comes.

Unless the Anglo-American empire systems are ready to accept the peoples of color in the struggle for democracy as equals now, the Atlantic Charter and the declarations about the Four Freedoms and that this war is a people's war is but as sounding brass and tinkling cymbal, and are preachments that the people of color neither believe [n]or respect, for they are the veriest hypocrisies, just words without meaning to the disinherited millions of the darker races of the world. It is because the faith in American democracy by the Negro people is strained to the breaking point, if, indeed it is not already broken, that they are calling upon the President and the congress for democracy now. . . .

But Negroes also realize that their fight for freedom here in America is tied up with the fight of the Indian people for freedom. As long as one section of the darker races, or any people regardless of color, is in bondage, the freedom of the Negro is not secure. Freedom, democracy and peace are indivisible. The March on Washington Movement demands independence for India and the release of their nationalist leaders, Gandhi and Nehru, and the abandonment of the wanton murder of Indian people by British soldiers. We call upon President Roosevelt to call upon Prime Minister Churchill to let the Indian people go. Let them be free. We call upon President Roosevelt to call upon Prime Minister Churchill to grant the Negro people in the West Indies wide suffrage and Dominion status. Release our brave and militant fighter for Negro rights, W. A. Domingo, now languishing in a concentration camp in Jamaica for no other crime than that he seeks more freedom for the West Indies.

Thus, fellow marchers, let us build our great movement to secure the adoption of our eight point program [see chapter 5] by our government, to fight to protect our interest in a post-war world and win racial, economic, political and social equality, and abolish exploitation of man by man. For this job let us dedicate our hearts to the spirit reflected in this poem of that militant singer of Negro people, Claude McKay:

If We Must Die

If we must die
Let it not be like hogs
Hunted and penned
In an inglorious spot
While round us
Bark the mad and hungry dogs
Making their mock
At our accursed lot.

If we must die—
Oh, let us nobly die,
So that our precious
Blood may not be shed
In vain, then even
The monsters defy
Shall be constrained
To honor us though dead!

Oh, kinsmen! We must meet the common foe;
Though far outnumbered
Let us show us brave.
And for their thousand blows
Deal one death blow!
What though before us lies the open grave?
Like men we'll face the murderous,
Cowardly pack
Pressed to the wall, dying, but fighting back!

SOURCE: Box 34, folder: Speeches, September 11, 1942–November 1, 1942, A. Philip Randolph Papers, Library of Congress.

Our Battle on the Home Front (1942)

Randolph cheers heroic fighters in allied forces, whether they are from Russia or Great Britain, and pledges that African Americans in the United States are doing their part to spread liberal democratic values. In this short editorial, Randolph draws upon Claude McKay's classic poem "If We Must Die" (see previous document) and argues that African Americans must sacrifice to prove their worth as citizens.

Now, to set at rest rumors that I have some hidden ambition for political place and preferment, let me assure you that I don't want anything the President has to give. I don't want to be in the Cabinet. I don't want to be ambassador to any nation. I don't want to go to Congress. I only want one thing and that is: I want to dedicate my life to the task of helping stop these white people from pushing colored people around.

The Communists of all shades and wings who have sought to sabotage this meeting say the time and money and effort put into this meeting should be put into helping to win the war. We reject this advice. Our reply is that not only are we staging this meeting, but one in Chicago and Washington, the District of Columbia and all government departments and the armed forces. Colored people are going to MARCH and we don't give a damn what happens.

While we want to see Russia defeat Hitler, we are not going to let the Communists of Russia or the Communists of America who take orders from Russia, or Fascists or Nazis tell them what to do about their problems in America. We are determined that this war shall not end and our boys now going to Burma and Australia to give their lives for democracy return and not find democracy at home. It is our responsibility to them that they shall not have fought in vain for a democracy which they cannot enjoy in their own country.

We don't propose to permit this war to end and find colored people in the same fix they were in when it began. We are not going to fight for democracy and then live under mob rule, lynching, the poll tax, white primaries and jim crow. We are not going to continue to tolerate the injustices meted out to Odell Waller and the Scottsboro boys.

Yes, we know that to break down jim crow and bury it in the same grave with Hitler's Nazism, Mussolini's Fascism and Hirohito's Militarism means struggle and trouble. But what difference does it make? We are having trouble anyway. Better that we face extermination than a life of segregation with its degradation and bitter humiliation. Rather that we die standing upon our feet fighting for our rights than to exist upon our knees begging for life. Only brave men can build a new world. If colored people are not willing to fight, suffer, sacrifice, and if need be, go to jail and even die for a place of equality in this new world, we are not worthy of it. Believing in the will to struggle and die for democracy, liberty and peace, the March on Washington Movement, militant, dauntless and honest, hails and salutes the colored masses of America, the West Indies and Africa and bids them forward!

We hail the fearless stand of the people of India against British imperialism. We hail the courageous legions of China and bid them to fight on against the sinister imperialism of Japan! We hail the intrepid workers of England whose spirits rose above the tragedy of Dunkirk! We hail the heroic people of Russia standing firm in defense of their land! We hail the embattled warriors of Ethiopia and the Philippines in this crucial hour to put down totalitarian tyranny.

We send greetings to our black and white boys in the camps and on foreign battle fronts! We shall not fail you. We are buying government war bonds to send you guns and food and we propose to break our bonds of bondage here so you will return to a land that is truly brave and free to all men, regardless of color.

SOURCE: *Baltimore Afro-American*, August 8, 1942.

The Negro in War and Peace: No More Important Question Confronts the World Today than the Adjustment of Racial Relations (ca. 1940s)

In this short speech, Randolph makes clear his understanding of how large-scale war disrupts the racial status quo and provides an opportunity to fight more effectively for freedom.

From casual survey of conditions throughout the countries of the world, racial and color tensions are on the increase. The riots in Detroit, Beaumont, Texas, Mobile, and New York, together with the outbreaks of violence against Jews in New York and Boston, attest to this distressing fact. Unless out of this war comes along a durable and just peace and the extension of democracy and freedom for the common man and smaller nationalities, ethnic democracy or the recognition of the equality of the races and peoples, which can only come as the result of the change in policy of the existing empire systems, a racial and color war may follow this one and sweep the world back to the midnight of barbarism.

The remedy for racial, color, nationality and religious hatreds is not tolerance alone but cooperation based upon the Christian Hebraic doctrine of the organic unity of mankind. Today democracy in the world is threatened by the aggressive menace of Christian Fronters, Ku Kluxers, Fascists and Labor Baiters. To meet this problem, the country must devise a Fair Racial Practices Act that will give life and force and reality to our Bill of Rights and the Thirteenth, Fourteenth, and Fifteenth Amendments to the Constitution and the principles of the Declaration of Independence and the Four Freedoms of the President. Every group—racial, religious, labor, business and etcetera faces the moral obligation, in the interest not only of themselves but the survival of American democracy, to join hands in sweeping anti-Semitism, anti-Negroism, anti-unionism, anti-Catholicism and anti-foreignerism.

SOURCE: Box 38, folder: Speeches, Undated, A. Philip Randolph Papers, Library of Congress.

The Negro, the War, and the Future of Democracy (ca. 1940s)

Unlike his attitude toward the First World War, a pronounced patriotism marked Randolph's reaction to World War II. A quote from this speech, "If America goes down, the Negro goes down," exemplifies his view about the pessimistic prospects minorities would have under any political system other than democracy.

During this World War in which two powerful forces are in conflict; namely democracy and totalitarianism, the Negro—[an] oppressed and exploited minority—has no other choice save to throw his lot in with the democratic powers and join in an all-out struggle to save the democratic system, however it may be. The Negroes' hope, future and destiny are tied up with the hope, future and destiny of American democracy; and the hope, future and destiny of American democracy are tied up with the hope, future and destiny of the democratic powers of the world.

If America goes down, the Negro goes down. If it stands, his right to fight for his rights continues. What is true with respect to the Negro is [also] true with respect to organized labor. Under the totalitarian system, minority groups and labor have no rights for freedom such as assembly and the press, trial by jury, right of petition and freedom of worship.

And it is a matter of common knowledge that the salvation of an oppressed minority lies in its opportunity to present its cause to the world. This can only be done within the framework of a democratic state.

SOURCE: Box 38, folder: Speeches, Undated, A. Philip Randolph Papers, Library of Congress.

Socialism for Peace and Plenty (ca. 1940s)

Impressed by the efficiency of the partnership between the federal government and private industry during the World War II defense production, Randolph saw the possibility that greater centralization of a highly planned economy could yield full employment. This, he hoped, would be the key ingredient of shared prosperity that he saw as the foundation of a lasting peace.

This is an hour of a world-war-peace crisis. The conflict on the Western Front is about over, and it may not be long before the guns will be quiet in the Southwest Pacific, but the war systems that bred wars still remain. While the plans for a world security council, started at Dumbarton Oaks and further developed at San Francisco, are a necessary, important and a valuable contribution to the peace, the causes and cure of our war-peace crisis go deeper than any form of international machinery for peace, however perfect in workmanship it may be. The problem of our war-peace crisis is the problem of the dominant world economy. This is the economy of the profit system and the struggle for wealth and power. Hitler, Mussolini and Hirohito may go, but there will be no peace so long as the driving motivation of the great power nations is the quest for new world dominion.

The fight for wealth and power by the modern state and empire systems requires that they employ war as an instrument of national policy, foreign and domestic. Foreign adventures unify a people behind their war-lords under the smoke-screen of national defense, manifest destiny, freedom, master-race doctrine, democracy, victory, glory, empire and world domination. Thus, while peace will come, it will neither be just [n]or durable, because it will rest upon the might of the three great powers, the United States, Great Britain and Russia, and not upon freedom and justice for all the peoples of the world. The peace, say the great power nations, is a problem of governments. Thus, the cause of the teeming millions of darker peoples, oppressed and disinherited, will have no voice in the making of the peace.

Can the Anglo-American-Russian empire systems achieve a just and durable peace? Not so long as they hold any people in subjection against their will. Let Gandhi and Nehru speak. Listen to the story of the dominated blacks of South Africa. Our own Puerto Rico is ill at ease. The challenge of Poland to the ethics of the peace, like Banquo's ghost, will not down. But, the nature of an empire is to oppress as it is the nature of a snake to bite. An empire, whether British, Japanese, American or Bolshevik Russian, can no more build a just peace than a sewing machine can grind corn. This has been so for more than four thousand years of historical man. The empires of Egypt, Babylonia, Persia, Aegea, Rome, Spain, France, Britain and the United States were built by armed force. The empires of superior arms grabbed the territory, colonies, concessions, dictated the lines of frontiers, seized the mineral deposits, coaling stations, landing fields, trade routes and investment markets.

But, the verdict of history is clear. You cannot build human brotherhood upon monopoly, exploitation, race discrimination, oppression, coercion, murder, rapine, fear, hate, blood-feuds and vengeance. However, after [Edward] Stettinius of America, [Anthony] Eden of Great Britain and [Vyacheslav] Molotov of the Soviet Union shall have built their world security council, these countries will face the problems of economic security and freedom for their own workers.

In government and labor circles, discussion waxes hot and heavy around the controversial question of full employment, or the creation of 60,000,000 jobs. It is therefore pertinent to ask the question, can there be full employment in the United States of America? The answer is yes. The war has shown that the United States of America has sufficient farms, experienced farmers, factory technicians, mechanics, and natural resources, such as coal, iron, oil, lumber, textiles and so forth. In spite of having 11,500,000 men and women in our armed forces, our production is such as to enable the majority of our people to enjoy the highest standard of living in the world, and still send food to our allies, at a time when we are producing enormous quantities of guns, ships, airplanes and munitions. But, here is the rub. This miracle of production for war was not the handiwork of private enterprise for profit solely. No, not at all. It is a matter of common knowledge that many of our manufacturing capitalists wouldn't convert from peace production to war production until the government guaranteed them prices to cover all costs, costing the taxpayers billions of dollars.

It is important to emphasize that the government planned and directed war production. And the planning of war production is more difficult than planning peace production, because of the shifts in war strategy and fighting, unpredictable destruction of goods, casualties and great distances that upset calculations. The government has taken and is taking all of the risks in the war. The government has planned and directed distribution of both war and civilian goods and services. Now, just as we have become the arsenal of democracy in war, we can become the storehouse of democracy in peace, which would provide full production, full employment and adequate consumption. . . .

SOURCE: Box 38, folder: Speeches, Undated, A. Philip Randolph Papers, Library of Congress.

Testimony before the Senate Armed Services Committee (1948)

MOWM's campaign against military segregation during World War II stalled, but the issue remained important to Randolph because it represented a "federally enforced pattern of segregation." This 1948 statement before the Senate Armed Services Committee is Randolph at his most bold. Knowing that he could be charged with treason, Randolph nonetheless told the committee, "Negroes are in no mood to shoulder a gun for democracy abroad so long as they are denied democracy here at home," and he went on record affirming plans to urge African American draft resistance through civil disobedience. There were many reasons behind President Truman's decision later that year to issue Executive Order 9981, which called for desegregation of the armed forces, but the threat of black militance articulated by Randolph was surely a factor.

Mr. Chairman:

Mr. Grant Reynolds, national chairman of the Committee against Jim Crow in Military Service and Training, has prepared for you in his testimony today a summary of wartime injustices to Negro soldiers—injustices by the military authorities and injustices by bigoted segments of the police and civilian population. The fund of material on this issue is endless, and yet, three years after the end of the war, as another crisis approaches, large numbers of white Americans are blissfully unaware of the extent of physical and psychological aggression against, and oppression of, the Negro soldier.

Without taking time for a thorough probe into these relevant data—a probe which could enlighten the nation—Congress may now heed Mr. Truman's call for Universal Military Training and Selective Service, and in the weeks ahead enact a Jim Crow conscription law and appropriate billions for the greatest segregation system of all time. In a campaign year, when both major parties are playing cynical politics with the issue of civil rights, Negroes are about to lose the fight against Jim Crowism on a national level. Our hard-won local gains in education, fair employment, hospitalization, [and] housing are in danger of being nullified—being swept aside, Mr. Chairman, after decades of work—by a federally enforced pattern of segregation. I am not beguiled by the Army's use of the word "temporary." Whatever may pass in the way of conscription legislation will become permanent, since the world trend is toward militarism. The Army knows this well. In such an eventuality, how could any permanent Fair Employment Practices Commission dare to criticize job discrimination in private industry if the federal government itself were simultaneously discriminating against Negro youth in military installations all over the world?

. . . I reported last week to President Truman that Negroes are in no mood to shoulder a gun for democracy abroad so long as they are denied democracy here at home. In particular, they resent the idea of fighting or being drafted into another Jim Crow Army. I passed this information on to Mr. Truman not as threat, but rather as a frank, factual survey of Negro opinion. Today I should like to make clear to the Senate Armed Services Committee and, through you, to Congress and the American people, that passage now of a Jim Crow draft may only result in a mass civil disobedience movement along the lines of the magnificent struggles of the people of India against British imperialism. I must emphasize that the current agitation for civil rights is no longer a mere expression of hope on the part of Negroes. On the one hand, it is a positive, resolute outreaching for full manhood. On the other hand, it is an equally determined will to stop acquiescing in anything less. Negroes demand full, unqualified first-class citizenship.

In resorting to the principles of [the] direct-action techniques of Gandhi, whose death was publicly mourned by many members of Congress and President Truman, Negroes will be serving a higher law than any passed by a national legislature in an era when racism spells our doom. They will be serving a law higher than any decree of the Supreme Court, which in the famous Winfred Lynn case evaded ruling on the flagrantly illegal segregation practiced under the wartime Selective Service Act. In refusing to accept compulsory military segregation, Negro youth will be serving their fellow men throughout the world.

I feel qualified to make this claim because of a recent survey of American psychologists, sociologists and anthropologists. The survey revealed an overwhelming belief among these experts that enforced segregation on racial or religious lines has serious and detrimental psychological effects both on the segregated groups and on those enforcing segregation. Experts from the South, I should like to point out, gentlemen, were as positive as those from other sections of the country as to the harmful effects of segregation. The views of these social scientists were based on scientific research and on their own professional experience.

So long as the Armed Services propose to enforce such universally harmful segregation not only here at home but also overseas, Negro youth have a moral obligation not to lend themselves as world-wide carriers of an evil and hellish doctrine. Secretary of the Army Kenneth C. Royall clearly indicated in the New Jersey National Guard situation that the Armed Services do have every intention of prolonging their anthropologically hoary and untenable policies. For twenty-five years now the myth has been carefully cultivated that Soviet Russia has ended all discrimination and intolerance, while here at home the American Communists have skillfully posed as champions of minority groups. To the rank-and-file Negro in World War II, Hitler's racism posed a sufficient threat for him to submit to the Jim Crow Army abuses. But this factor of minority group prosecution in Russia is not present, as a popular issue, in the power struggle between Stalin and the United States. I can only repeat that this time Negroes will not take a Jim Crow draft lying down. The conscience of the world will be shaken as by nothing else when thousands and thousands of us second-class Americans choose imprisonment in preference to permanent military slavery.

While I cannot with absolute certainty claim results at this hour, I personally will advise Negroes to refuse to fight as slaves for a democracy they cannot possess and cannot enjoy. Let me add that I am speaking only for myself, not even for the Committee against Jim Crow in Military Service and Training, since I am not sure that all its members would follow my position. But Negro leaders in close touch with GI grievances would feel derelict in their duty if they did not support such a justified civil disobedience movement—especially those of us whose age would protect us from being drafted. Any other course would be a betrayal of those who place their trust in us. I personally pledge myself to openly counsel, aid and abet youth, both white and Negro, to quarantine any Jim Crow conscription system, whether it bear the label of UMT or Selective Service.

I shall tell youth of all races not to be tricked by any euphonious election-year registration for a draft. This evasion, which the newspapers increasingly discuss as a convenient way out for Congress, would merely presage a synthetic "crisis" immediately after November 2nd, when all talk of equality and civil rights would be branded unpatriotic while the induction machinery would move into high gear. On previous occasions I have seen the "national emergency" psychology mow down legitimate Negro demands.

From coast to coast in my travels I shall call upon all Negro veterans to join this civil disobedience movement and to recruit their younger brothers in an organized refusal to register and be drafted. Many veterans, bitter over Army Jim Crow, have indicated that they will act spontaneously in this fashion, regardless of any organized movement. "Never again," they say with finality.

I shall appeal to the thousands of white youth in schools and colleges who are today vigorously shedding the prejudices of their parents and professors. I shall urge them to demonstrate their solidarity with Negro youth by ignoring the entire registration and induction machinery. And finally I shall appeal to Negro parents to lend their moral support to their sons—to stand behind them as they march with heads high to federal prisons as a telling demonstration to the world that Negroes have reached the limit of human endurance— that is, in the words of the spiritual, we'll be buried in our graves before we will be slaves.

May I, in conclusion, Mr. Chairman, point out that political maneuvers have made this drastic program our last resort. Your party, the party of Lincoln, solemnly pledged in its 1944 platform a full-fledged Congressional investigation of injustices to Negro soldiers. Instead of that long overdue probe, the Senate Armed Services Committee on this very day is finally hearing testimony from two or three Negro veterans for a period of twenty minutes each. The House Armed Services Committee and Chairman [Walter G.] Andrews went one step further and arrogantly refused to hear any at all! Since we cannot obtain an adequate Congressional forum for our grievances, we have no other recourse but to tell our story to the peoples of the world by organized direct action. I don't believe that even a wartime censorship wall could be high enough to conceal news of a civil disobedience program. If we cannot win your support for your own Party commitments, if we cannot ring a bell in you by appealing to human decency, we shall command your respect and the respect of the world by our united refusal to cooperate with tyrannical injustice.

Since the military, with their Southern biases, intend to take over America and institute total encampment of the populace along Jim Crow lines, Negroes will resist with the power of non-violence, with the weapons of moral principles, with the good-will weapons of the spirit, yes, with the weapons that brought freedom to India. I feel morally obligated to disturb and keep disturbed the conscience of Jim Crow America. In resisting the insult of jim crowism to the soul of black America, we are helping to save the soul of America. And let me add that I am opposed to Russian totalitarian communism and all its works. I consider it a menace to freedom. I stand by democracy as expressing the Judean-Christian ethic. But democracy and Christianity must be boldly and courageously applied for all men regardless of race, color, creed or country.

We shall wage a relentless warfare against Jim Crow without hate or revenge for the moral and spiritual progress and safety of our country, world peace and freedom.

Finally, let me say that Negroes are just sick and tired of being pushed around and we just don't propose to take it, and we do not care what happens.

SOURCE: Senate Committee on Armed Services, *Hearings on Universal Military Training*, 80th Cong., 2nd sess. (Washington, D.C.: GPO, 1948), 685–94.

Letters to President Harry S. Truman on behalf of Committee against Jim Crow in Military Service and Training (1947–1948)

The following letters sent to President Truman preceded the signing of Executive Order 9981 on July 26, 1948. In a memo attached to this correspondence is a January 20, 1948, note written by White House aide David Niles that reads: "Phil Randolph, the signer of this letter, is an important Negro. He is the head of the Negro Pullman Porters Union, and is not a left-winger." Randolph's careful positioning of himself as a protest leader whose ideology was essentially democratic and whose campaigns were generally reformist was why he had access to power. Understood properly, Randolph's threat that "Negro youth will have no alternative but to resist" compulsory Selective Service if they were drafted into a segregated military was only in opposition to federally sanctioned segregation, and was not against universal military service.

December 28, 1947

Dear Mr. President:

On December 10, Grant Reynolds and I wrote you requesting an appointment.

On December 17, we received a reply from Mr. David K. Niles, one of your administrative assistants, indicating that he would "be glad to talk to a delegation at any time that is mutually convenient."

There may be several matters which we would be happy to talk over with Mr. Niles. However, the two hundred Negro leaders who comprise our Committee feel that the matter of discrimination and segregation in the Armed Forces and in particular in prospective UMT legislation is a grave threat to Negro youth and to the internal stability of our nation. Segregation becomes all the more important at a time when the United States should be assuming moral leadership in the world.

We consider the matter serious and urgent as to require a personal conference with the President.

Representative Negro leaders have indicated that they stand ready to come to Washington at any time. I trust that you will find time to see us at your earliest convenience.

Cordially,
A. Philip Randolph
National Treasurer

January 12, 1948

Dear Mr. President:

On December 10, 1947, Mr. Grant Reynolds and I wrote you requesting that you receive representative Negro leaders to discuss your proposed UMT bill, which if adopted as drawn would subject American youth, Negro and white, to compulsory jimcrow. Mr. David K. Niles replied on December 17, 1947, that he stood ready to receive a delegation.

On December 28, 1947, I wrote you again pointing out that our emergency committee of 225 Negro leaders feels that the matter is of such extreme concern as to require an interview with the President himself.

On January 7, 1948, your secretary, Mr. Matthew J. Connelly, wrote that an interview with you is not "possible to arrange in the near future." It is difficult to believe that there can be matters before you at this time which in urgency exceed the just concern and long-accumulated grievances of one-tenth of our population.

One might reason that consideration of the European Recovery Program and other matters require such time as to make a meeting of Negro leaders impossible. Might I remind you, on the other hand, that the success of many internal and foreign programs finally depends on a healthy state of the body politic. Such a state requires the elimination of, rather than the extension of, segregation and discrimination in military training and the armed forces.

May I ask when it will be possible for you to receive us?

Sincerely yours,
A. Philip Randolph
National Treasurer

June 29, 1948

Dear Mr. President:

Because Congress enacted, and you have now signed, a Selective Service bill devoid of any safeguards for Negro youth, we should like to request, at your very earliest convenience, a conference with you to discuss the issuance of an executive order abolishing all *segregation* and discrimination from the armed forces.

In the light of past official civil rights pronouncements, it is our belief that the President, as Commander-in-Chief, is morally obligated to issue such an order now. Unless this is done, Negro youth will have no alternative but to resist a law, the inevitable consequence of which would be to expose them to the un-American brutality so familiar during the last war.

America must not subject one-tenth of its population to such treatment again. Knowing that you have it in your power to prevent this, we are seeking an opportunity to confer with you on implementing this essential part of your civil rights program.

Sincerely yours,
Grant Reynolds, National Chairman
A. Philip Randolph, National Treasurer

July 15, 1948

Dear Mr. President:

We were indeed happy that you decided to call Congress back into special session in order to act on civil rights legislation, among other matters. We trust that in your message to Congress on July 26 you will specifically ask for legislative approval of anti-lynching and other safeguards for Negro draftees. You are undoubtedly aware of the intense bitterness on the part of Negro citizens because of the bi-partisan "gentlemen's agreement" to scuttle the Langer amendments to the draft bill early in June.

The action most necessary today to strengthen the fabric of democracy is of the type that would enhance the dignity of second-class citizens. Because the 1948 Republican platform expressed its disapproval of army segregation and because the recently adopted platform of your own party in essence called for the abolition of racial distinctions within the military establishment, we feel that you now have a bi-partisan mandate to end military segregation forthwith by the issuance of an Executive Order.

May we take this opportunity to renew our request for a conference with you in the immediate future to discuss such an Executive Order. The date for registration under the draft is only a month away and it is the hope of all Negro youth that there will be an alternative beyond submission to a discriminatory law and imprisonment for following the dictates of self-respect.

Sincerely,
Grant Reynolds, National Chairman
A. Philip Randolph, National Treasurer

SOURCE: Official File #93-B, Harry S. Truman Library.

Letter to George Houser (1949)

This letter to George Houser, an esteemed pacifist and head of the Fellowship of Reconciliation, offers an insider's view of tactical fissures in the network of activists working for the cause of military desegregation. As he did in response to the aborted 1941 march on Washington, Bayard Rustin criticized Randolph for calling off a national campaign and thus squandering an opportunity to build a larger movement.

Randolph writes of having "high hopes" that nonviolent direct action could "abolish jim crow." Of course, in less than a decade Randolph and Rustin would collaborate in support of numerous civil rights causes—and with a great deal of success.

April 26, 1949

Mr. George Houser
The Fellowship of Reconciliation
2929 Broadway
New York, New York

Dear George,

Thanks a lot for your letter of March 30th presenting your attitude with respect to certain aspects of the civil disobedience campaign which was conducted by the League for Non-Violent Civil Disobedience Against Military Segregation.

I keenly regret that conflicts arose within the small group which was charged with the responsibility of waging a civil disobedience campaign against military segregation. It is true, as you suggest, that if it is not possible for persons committed to the principle of civil disobedience against military segregation to work in faithful cooperation, it will certainly be difficult to enlist persons unfamiliar with the non-violent good-will movement to work together in the spirit of brotherhood.

I think the basic cause of the trouble was the apparent position of Brothers Muste and Rustin who did not want to call off the civil disobedience campaign after the President issued an Executive Order banning discrimination and segregation. It seems to me that an important and valuable moral victory was forsaken by way of building the basis for an effective civil disobedience non-violent good-will movement in America against discrimination and segregation for a temporary and transitory advantage. No doubt, the disposition to construe success in the civil disobedience campaign as being tied up only with the continuance of the campaign[,] despite the issuance of the Executive Order by President Truman, was responsible for the trouble.

I consider the essence of the Gandhian civil disobedience movement is faithful adherence to truth, and to moral commitments, even though the full and complete objective of the campaign be not realized. It is this position, which I think gives moral strength to a movement.

Because of the obviously reckless manner in which the principle of non-violent civil disobedience was handled, taking the form of a rumpus movement, although no civil disobedience campaign had been officially called off by its leaders, it is certain to set back the cause of civil disobedience and non-violent good-will direct action among minorities in the United States, for some time. I keenly regret this, because I have high hopes for the application of the philosophy of civil disobedience and non-violent good-will direct action as a way of abolishing Jim Crow in the United States. Of course, I have absolutely nothing against any of the Brothers who are opposed to my philosophy in this matter.

It is my hope that the civil disobedience method may be employed in various areas of America against Jim Crow, by groups such as the Fellowship of Reconciliation, the March on Washington Movement, and others. But, whatever steps are taken in the future to develop civil disobedience against jim crow in the United States, there must be unequivocal agreement that under no condition will our moral commitment be denied or abandoned even though total victory may not be achieved. This is the only approach to this method of fighting injustice to minorities through civil disobedience which will develop moral strength.

Sometime in the future when it is convenient, I hope to have a chat with you.

Sincerely Yours,
A. Philip Randolph
International President

SOURCE: Box 17, folder: Committee to End Jim Crow in the Armed Services, Correspondence, 1949, A. Philip Randolph Papers, Library of Congress.

Letter to Jackie Robinson (1949)

Randolph's ongoing push for military desegregation inevitably brought him into contact with Jackie Robinson, a World War II veteran and icon of integration. As the first African American player in the modern era of Major League Baseball and a star for the Brooklyn Dodgers, Robinson symbolized the untapped potential of talented African Americans whose abilities were overlooked because of the color line. As a veteran who had served in a segregated army, Robinson was in a position to speak against the military's racial policies without being attacked as unpatriotic. In the letter below, Randolph courts Robinson to help advance the cause of the Committee against Jim Crow in Military Service and Training.

February 3, 1949

Mr. Jackie Robinson
Station WMOA
1697 Broadway
New York 19, New York

Dear Mr. Robinson:

You probably recall that you told our executive secretary, Mr. Worthy, over the telephone that you would be willing to make a wire recording of Jim Crow highlights in your Army experience, inasmuch as you were unable to testify in our Washington, D.C., public hearing on January 8.

We have spoken to Mr. Arthur Garfield Hays and Mr. John Finerty of the American Civil Liberties Union, and both of them would be delighted to arrange with you a mutually convenient time for such wire recording at WMOA. Mr. Hays, as the enclosed article from the *New York Post* indicates, cross-examined the witnesses at the Washington hearing, and he and Mr. Finerty would use the same technique if that would be agreeable to you.

We should like to make your testimony part of the record and also use it for publicity and educational purposes in various cities throughout the country. I am asking Mr. Worthy to give you a ring in a few days to ascertain a convenient time. We appreciate your interest in this matter.

Cordially,
A. Philip Randolph

SOURCE: Box 17, folder: Committee to End Jim Crow in Armed Services, Correspondence, 1949, A. Philip Randolph Papers, Library of Congress.

Should Negroes Help the U.S.A. Win the Cold War against the U.S.S.R.? (n.d.)

Randolph viewed the cold war in much the same way as he saw World War II: African Americans should support the United States because it represented their best hope for advancement, but they should never cease their demand for the ending of racial segregation and discrimination. In juxtaposing the American tradition of putting the individual before the state with the Communist tradition of putting the state's interest ahead of that of the individual, Randolph looks toward the lessons of history. Slavery was a terrible blight on the nation, he reasons, but at least America's commitment to freedom of speech gave the abolitionist movement room to blossom. As vehement as Randolph's anticommunism often was, he remained wedded to preserving the liberty of individuals, and he was never on the side of McCarthyism. As he pragmatically put it, "attempts to eliminate Communists by law will only drive them underground and deprive the country of the effective weapon of public identification."

The question here stated grows out of a mortal and crucial conflict between the U.S.A. and the U.S.S.R. as a result of a struggle for world power by these two great nations and a consequent bid for the minds and allegiance of Negroes by Communism and Democracy.

This conflict shapes up as follows:

Russia employs satellite strategy to expand her political influences and power by the conquest of smaller and weaker peoples whom the Soviet Union sets up as puppet states, such as Bulgaria, Romania, Hungary and Czechoslovakia and China. These states are bound by the Stalinist Line, deviation being rewarded with the Tito treatment. . . . No one can deny the existence of grave grievances of Negroes in our country. No one can deny that the United States has been distressingly recreant to its duty and moral responsibility in meeting the Negro problem with a view to affecting the situation. No one can deny that the United States, in view of its record with its own citizens of color, does not come into the world court with clean hands when she presumes to teach the people of Europe and Asia lessons of democracy. The most ardent American patriot must admit the shortcomings, limitations, inconsistencies, contradictions and failures in the great American enterprise of democracy. However, it must also be conceded that in the United States, Negroes, Jews, Catholics, foreigners and labor, by virtue of the Bill of Rights and our traditions of a free way of life, *possess the right to fight for their rights.* This is priceless, for the only way to get rights and hold them is to fight for them. Rights, freedom and justice are never given. They are won.

Even if Russia had the power to give Negroes their rights in the United States, a fantastic notion, Negroes, not having developed strength by fighting for them, could not hope to keep them. *But, nowhere in the totalitarian Communist world do minorities or labor possess the right to fight for their rights.*

They take that which is given by the dictator and keep what is permitted. Within the framework of the American democratic system, Negroes have made significant progress in industry, business, labor, education, government, science, art, the professions, religion and philosophy.

But to hold their gains and win others, Negroes who have, despite discrimination, made basic progress under democracy are compelled by enlightened self-interest to help the United States win the cold war, and a hot one if it should come against Soviet Russia, which is the only way to keep the jewel of democracy in the firmament of government. . . .

Since in order to win this cold war, the heads and hearts of the people of color, who constitute two-thirds of the population of the world, must be won, the most powerful moral and spiritual force the United States has today is the active, dynamic support and cooperation of black America. It is quite doubtful that the United States can win the cold war, which is a conflict of ideas and the things of the spirit, without the Negro, the measure and test of the American ideal and faith.

Only the Negroes who have known and know their times of trouble, and who are the only people in the Western world that, in the crisis of a Civil War to achieve "their freedom," refused to hate their enemy, the slave masters, can give America the preparation for the spiritual and moral leadership of the democratic forces of the world in a crusade against the Russian Communist religion, a preparation which can only result from a relentless and uncompromising fight for civil rights, the most effective propaganda weapon the United States has in its arsenal of ideas.

Thus, it is the moral responsibility of the Negro to give reality, strength and integrity to American democracy, which will enable her to win the ideological war for world democracy, humanity and the good life. Negroes can only carry successfully through this role and challenge if they remain true to the faith of democracy and a free society and shun the false gods of Russian Communist totalitarianism with its gospel of hate and blood and sword in recognition of the truth that the salvation of a people must come from within, with the resources of love and fellowship and good-will. Negroes who are without great material power, or the record and guilt of discrimination against or exploitation of any people at any time, and who are the most lowly and oppressed of all workers in the Western world, have been selected by history to teach white America in particular and the world in general the lessons of democracy and Christian brotherhood. Black slaves, with their blood and faith, had to be called in by Abraham Lincoln to save a tottering union, abolish bitter slavery and establish democracy and give moral idealism and strength to the United States. . . .

SOURCE: Box 38, folder: Speeches, Undated, A. Philip Randolph Papers, Library of Congress.

Vietnam and Freedom Movement at Crossroads (1966)

In this 1966 speech before the Negro American Labor Council, Randolph appraises the roots of the "Civil Rights Revolution" and presents a program for the next steps of the movement. He takes the position that the "freedom movement" was being drained of zeal by the shifting of political passions to the peace movement. For further analysis by Randolph of the Vietnam War, see "Lincoln University Commencement Address" (chapter 3).

Now, the freedom movement at the crossroads is faced with the possibility of the Civil Rights Revolution failing to fulfill its mission because of a failure to employ sound, pragmatic judgment. It is for this reason that I warn the Civil Rights Movement against becoming involved in the Vietnam Peace Movement, either against or for the war in Vietnam. Let me make it clear that I certainly don't advocate that Negroes refuse to answer the call of their country to fight in the war in Vietnam along with other Americans. This is their responsibility and obligation. But, since Negroes are the only second-class Americans in the country, denied equality of opportunity for jobs, integrated quality education and integrated decent housing, they have a right to safeguard and protect the Civil Rights Revolution.

Now, with the black revolt steadily moving toward a state of increasing relaxation, a natural result of any social movement which has reached a high level of tension, emotionalism and disillusionment and also because of a widespread belief among black and white Americans that on account of the enactment of Civil Rights legislation by the Congress, the Revolution is over, care should be taken to avoid any strategy and tactics that may tend to split and weaken the national consensus for civil rights and the Civil Rights Movement itself. This is certain too if the Civil Rights Movement undertakes to fight on two fronts, for or against the Vietnam War and the race war in Alabama and Mississippi, at the same time. In the nature of things, major emphasis will be placed on one at the sacrifice of the other.

When Dick Parrish, Treasurer of the Negro American Labor Council, and myself visited Jackson and Meridian, Mississippi in 1964, a period when the flames of the fires of the Civil Rights Revolution were mounting high, hundreds of young, white, dedicated students, together with hundreds of liberal white teachers, lawyers, even some doctors and many ministers of churches, were down there doing everything they could to advance the cause of the Civil Rights Revolution. Go down there now. They are not to be found. Where are they? They are marching in the streets against the war in Vietnam. Even the liberal-radical Negroes are not down there in the numbers they represented when the black revolt was blazing in Alabama and Mississippi. But the racial war is still going on there. The enemy is still there. The Alabama-Mississippi front is exposed.

Now, I don't deplore or condemn this. White liberals and Negroes have a moral right and are justified in participating in the Peace Movement, especially in this age of nuclear weaponry, if they desire to do so. But I cite these facts to demonstrate that the Civil Rights Movement is not strong enough to fight on the Vietnam and Alabama-Mississippi fronts and do justice to the cause of the Civil Rights Revolution—which is the Negroes' primary concern and urgency. Already the Civil Rights Revolution has frightfully fallen far too low on the scale of the national priorities. Verily, just as the black freedmen were pushed from the center of the stage of American history by the Confederate Counter-Revolution following the Civil War, the revolt of the workers and farmers through national strikes, and the Populists and Granger propaganda for Greenbackism for cheap money, so today the War in Vietnam, the revolution of science, technology and special exploration are taking the center of the stage of American history from the Civil Rights Revolution. This development could result in the catastrophic failure of the Civil Rights Revolution to fulfill its mission. This would constitute a mortal blow to the Black Americans' fight for freedom and first-class citizenship, halt the march forward to economic and social justice of the black and white working poor, and hurt the image of America as the leader of the free world.

SOURCE: Box 37, folder: Speeches, 1966, A. Philip Randolph Papers, Library of Congress.

8

A. Philip Randolph on International Affairs

Like many African Americans, A. Philip Randolph closely followed international affairs because he believed that global events impacted race relations in the United States. This interest peaked in the 1950s and 1960s, when African nations were gaining independence and the cold war created a political climate that put a spotlight on civil rights in America. Advancing free and independent trade unions in the developing world was Randolph's chief interest, and this position coincided with his sometimes dogmatic anticommunist position. Only through progressive and effective trade unions, he argued, could prosperous economies be developed and the spread of communism be thwarted.

The documents in this chapter begin in the 1920s, at the height of the "Garvey Must Go" campaign, which arose in backlash to questionable decisions made by Marcus Garvey and the outlandish dreams of the Universal Negro Improvement Association. This early piece from *The Messenger* shows Randolph at his most histrionic and reveals how bombastic one needed to be in order to command attention in the crowded field of Harlem Renaissance commentators.

Speeches Randolph made during the years that paralleled the civil rights movement in America are the core of this chapter. Equal parts political commentary and observations on international developments, threads of anticolonialism and anticommunism are woven into Randolph's democratic socialist ideology. He believed strongly in African independence and sovereignty, but he was just as stridently opposed to emerging nations aligning themselves with the Soviet Union. He called for an outpouring of international aid to support nation building in Africa, Asia, and Latin America. If the Marshall Plan could rebuild a war-ravished Europe and create prosperity for all of its partners, Randolph reasoned, why not do the same for the nations whose predominantly black and brown citizens inherited the legacy of colonial exploitation?

Other documents in this chapter attest to Randolph's travels overseas. His witnessing of Kwame Nkrumah's inauguration alongside Martin Luther King Jr. is a historical highlight of these selections, but Randolph's participation in, and observations of, international labor organizing as an ambassador of the AFL-CIO are also significant. Randolph traversed countless miles in North America through his work with the BSCP, but these unique travelogues document his impressions of the wide world beyond the United States.

FOR FURTHER READING

Anderson, Carol. *Eyes off the Prize: The United Nations and the African American Struggle for Human Rights, 1944–1955.* Cambridge: Cambridge University Press, 2003.

Arnesen, Eric. "Civil Rights and the Cold War at Home: Postwar Activism, Anticommunism, and the Decline of the Left." *American Communist History* 11, no. 1 (April 2012): 5–44.

Borstelmann, Thomas. *The Cold War and the Color Line: American Race Relations in the Global Arena.* Cambridge, Mass.: Harvard University Press, 2001.

Bush, Rod. *The End of White World Supremacy: Black Internationalism and the Problem of the Color Line.* Philadelphia: Temple University Press, 2009.

Dudziak, Mary L. *Cold War Civil Rights: Race and the Image of American Democracy.* Princeton, N.J.: Princeton University Press, 2000.

Prashad, Vijay. *The Darker Nations: A People's History of the Third World.* New York: The New Press, 2008.

Singh, Nikhil Pal. *Black Is a Country: Race and the Unfinished Struggle for Democracy.* Cambridge, Mass.: Harvard University Press, 2005.

Skrentny, John. *The Minority Rights Revolution.* Cambridge, Mass.: Harvard University Press, 2002.

Von Eschen, Penny M. *Race against Empire: Black Americans and Anticolonialism, 1937–1957.* Ithaca, N.Y.: Cornell University Press, 1997.

The Only Way to Redeem Africa (1922–1923)

The rivalry between Randolph and Garvey is renowned for its name-calling, but real ideological and practical differences lay behind the vitriol. In this article, Randolph surveys recent developments in Africa and concludes that Garvey's "Africa for Africans" nationalist program is pragmatically untenable. Evolving beyond capitalism is one solution, Randolph argues, but he makes a case that real improvements in Africa can better be made by abolishing all forms of unfree labor, respecting tribal sovereignty and land rights, and making strides toward fostering a genuine cross-cultural understanding based on mutual respect.

The proposition of Africa for the Africans is not new. Even before the Civil War, groups of whites, both friend and foe, favored schemes for the colonization of American Negroes in Africa. The establishment of the Republic of Liberia grew out of the idea that Africa was the best place for the Negro. Plans for carrying all of the Negroes back to Africa were freely discussed with President Lincoln, but were shown to be impracticable. Only recently, an idiot known by the name of Chief Sam promulgated schemes not much more feasible than Garvey's for shipping all Negroes to Africa.

Fundamentally, the idea of Africa for the Africans is accepted, endorsed and advocated by all Negroes as well as by the liberals, radicals and labor sections of the whites. Of course there are various and varying interpretations of the phrase. A word, then, about its meaning. To Mr. Garvey the phrase means Africa for the Negroes, as shown by his perfervid reference to 400,000,000 Negroes establishing an empire there. Of course, brother Bark-Much Garvey is something over 100,000,000 off in his figures. But he should worry! What's a hundred million to this imperial Don Quixote? Even if we allow 200 million to Africa, which is 50 million too many; 15 million to the United States; 3 million to the West Indies; and 30 millions to South and Central America whose actual populations are much less, His Majesty's Highness would have just 102 millions of Negroes more in the world than actually exist. But, you know, that is jolly darn good propaganda to make claims to that which no other sane and honest person will make claims to. It attracts attention, and the ignorant will believe it; verily, they will not only believe it, but they will come across with their cold cash for this sort of sensational stuff. But it will be seen later on that to view the idea of Africa for the Africans to mean Africa for Negroes only is the essence of error and folly.

To Mr. Marcus also the phrase Africa for the Africans carries with it the hope of isolation from the white world. His anti–white man's doctrine indicates as much. He is ignorant of the fact that such cannot be done in this period of modern industrial inventions that facilitate transportation and communication. The steamship, airship, and railways, together with the cables and wireless means of communication make the most distant peoples neighbors.

But even were it possible to separate the Negro peoples from the white world such would not be desirable or beneficial. The isolation of any people from the society of other races and nations would result in an inevitable racial and national decay, the arrest of their economic, political and social progress. Witness China for centuries. Also note the difficulties of Russia as a result of a world-wide blockade, preventing her from establishing complete trade relations with the great world powers. And it is a matter of common knowledge that the German debacle grows out of her inability to set up commercial and political contact with whomsoever she chooses. Japan only rose to national greatness upon her recognition that isolation was suicidal, studied the methods and ways and entered the councils of the white nations, even though she didn't love them. I think it's logical to ask that if isolation is against the interests of China, Japan, Germany and Russia, wherein and why will it benefit Africa? If the yellow, brown and white peoples of the world have fought against segregation, why should the black peoples invite it? To separate the Negro peoples from modern, scientific Western Civilization and culture would wreak irreparable injury upon their progress, in fact, they would relapse into barbarism and savagery. It is to the interest of the weaker peoples always to maintain contact with the peoples of power. To disjoin them is like segregating intelligence from ignorance, light from darkness, undeveloped children from educated grown-ups. Nor is it sufficient to justify segregation upon the plea that the strong will exploit the weak, the intelligent, the ignorant. Though this be generally true, it is only out of the exploitation of the weak by the strong, a sort of struggle between the classes, that the weak will even prepare itself for achieving its own emancipation. Such has been the inexorable law of social progress. It is not a question of right or wrong. It is purely a brutal question of advantage. Progress is only possible through intelligence, and intelligence is only possible through contact between those who have and those who haven't information, [and that is] power. Thus, from the point of view of isolation, Mr. Garvey's interpretation of Africa for Africans is un-sound and inimical to the interests of Africans in general and Negroes in particular.

The only rational interpretation of the phrase "Africa for Africans" is from the point of view of ultimate-ness. It is a condition "devoutly to be wished." But the fact that we desire "Africa for the Africans" does not imply that we recognize the ability of the Africans to assume the responsibilities and duties of a sovereign nation, at the present. To illustrate: we may desire a boy someday to become a man, to assume the responsibilities and duties of manhood, still we realize that he is not yet a man. To make it known that he is not a man is no reflection upon the boy, nor does it indicate that he will not become a man or that he does not possess the qualities and capacity for the ultimate assumption of the duties and responsibilities of a man. Again, [this] writer cannot speak the Chinese language. But that does not prove that I cannot learn to speak it. Nor is it any reflection upon my intelligence to admit that I cannot speak Chinese. But for me to pretend that I can when I can't tends only to mislead and to confuse; and, perhaps to shut me off from the agencies from which such knowledge may be secured. Moreover, a belief that I know when I don't know a given subject tends to disincline me to seek to learn that subject. Such is the situation with Africa. In terms of wisdom, skill and power, Africa is a child continent. This does not indicate, however, that she will always be so, that she is incapable of the highest lights of modern civilization. Numberless causes are responsible for the backwardness and unprogressiveness of Africa, a discussion of which is beyond the purview of this article.

While we all recognize and advocate Africa's right to self-determination, it ought to be clear even to a child's mind that the recognition and advocacy of "Africa for the Africans" is not tantamount to the achievement of "Africa for the Africans." The recognition and advocacy of the thing and the achievement of that thing are two different propositions. For instance, we all desire always to be in perfect health, but the how we are to effect it is another issue. Again, we all would like to become millionaires, but the becoming millionaires is a different song. Thus the method, the how, by which we are going to redeem Africa is the chief question. . . .

Besides, sincerity of intent is not sufficient. Garveyites cannot meet the issue merely by claiming that His Excellency is sincere, that he has good intentions. While I deny that he is sincere about his cry of "Back to Africa," even if he were sincere it would not change the prospects in the least. He never expects to land there himself, or to get any of his followers there for that matter. He is simply exploiting it as a grand slogan with which to fire the imagination of the unthinking to lure them to pour their sweat and blood dollars into the Black Star Line "Sea."

But even granting that his intent were good, what about the result? Though intent be good, intent will not redeem Africa. It is no substitute for knowledge, for correct forms of action. Mere intent to go somewhere or do something, however sincere, is not sufficient to take you there or to have that something done. Thus the followers of Garvey are in for a rude awakening if they think that Brother Garvey's alleged good intentions will conquer Africa. What do the British and the French care about his good intentions? The more sincere he is in his desire to conquer Africa, the harder they will fight him. It is a well-recognized fact that good intent won't cure Influenza. Ignorance of the science of medicine may lead one, with perfectly good intentions, to take the [im]proper medicine, to take bi-chloride of mercury, a poison which results in his death. His desire to get well was good, but his knowledge of medicine was faulty, and hence he was the victim of his own honest ignorance. From the foregoing it is obvious that the entire problem of achieving "Africa for the Africans" hinges upon the question of method, method with respect to the construction of the phrase "Africa for the Africans," and method with respect to the execution of every phase of the program of the UNIA or of any other movement.

But before entering upon a searching examination of the Garvey program, let us consider briefly what the true meaning of the phrase Africa for the Africans is.

First, Africa is a continent, not a nation. It comprises many nations and races. Its area is 11,500,000 square miles. It is a continent like Europe, Asia, America, South and North, and a continent is a vast area of land in which numberless nations and empires, races and religions may exist. History records no case where a continent has been conquered and made into an empire. Even the Holy Roman Empire under Charlemagne failed to achieve this mighty end. A nation may exist in a continent, but not a continent in a nation. A continent is a natural product of nature; a nation is an artificial product of man. Not a cubic foot can be added to a continent by the ingenuity of man, but the area of a nation may be increased, almost at will. Nations rise and fall; not continents. Yet, the conquering of a continent for the erection of an empire is the fantastic project of Garvey. From his ignorant sputterings one would think that the terms nation and continent may be used interchangeably. While it may be possible for a continent to be controlled by one great empire, it is not probable. In fact, we have grounds a plenty for maintaining that this crowd of Garvey maniacs who can't operate three rickety old ships will never establish any such empire when it is remembered that the 11,500,00 square miles of Africa is controlled, every inch of it, by the following powers:

Nation	Area	Population
France	4,200,000	25,000,000
Great Britain	3,300,000	35,000,000
Germany*	1,100,000	12,000,000
Belgium	900,000	7,700,000
Portugal	800,000	8,800,000
Spain	750,000	200,000

* Now [ca. 1927] in the hands of Great Britain, France, and Belgium.

These figures represent every inch of land in Africa. Even the mythical Provisional-President of Africa can't create another inch of territory. And, besides, this land is no more available than land in Wall Street, New York City.

It is guarded by six powerful navies and armies, one of which would be sufficient to protect it from invasion by the formidable Garvey Black Star Line and Black African Legion. In very truth, one good-size airplane could prevent the Garvey hot-air-brigade from landing. . . .

A word now about the term Africans. The word African, like European, Asiatic, or American, has general, composite connotation. When we say that we stand for Africa for the Africans we mean black, yellow, brown, white Africans. Negroids, Mongoloids, Mediterraneans, Alpines, Nordics, Mohammedans, Christians, Buddhists, etcetera. We recognize that in Africa today there are several nations that are distinct, separate and different in customs, traditions, manners, culture, language, race and religion, as are the nations of Europe. For example, Liberia is as different from Abyssinia in history, policy, language, customs, etcetera, as Germany is from Italy. Egypt is as different from the Republic of South Africa as Great Britain is from France. And a native of Abyssinia is just as much a foreigner in Liberia as a Russian is a foreigner in Spain or an American is a foreigner in Mexico. But this bit of ethnography and lines of nationality demarcation mean absolutely nothing in the Black Infernal Buzzard's young life. To him, every African is a Negro and every Negro is black. To him there is a racial and nationality homogeneity in Africa; all tribes possessing one mind, awaiting the time when, according to the Garveyites, Brother Marcus will pull the Houdini stunt and touch a cable button from his imperial dais in "Slavery Hole" (misnamed "Liberty Hall") on 138th Street, New York City, and instantaneously, through his magic power, millions of African Legionaries will spring forth out of the region of nothingness and pass thousands of miles through thin air, land upon Africa and, presto! All of the armed forces of Great Britain, France, Portugal, and Spain will get scared and skiddo. Don't laugh! Honest Enjun, it's no stage stuff! Garvey is a live one whom some "Nutiacs" follow. Comedy, did you say? Of course it is; but it is tragedy, too, when one considers the economic disasters and moral demoralization that he is bringing upon the Negroes, to say nothing of the joke which he is making of them.

II

Of course, there is nothing more normal and logical than that the idea of building up a Negro empire that should flow from the "Back to Africa" movement. A word about the difficulties to be overcome. First, with the opposition of the white powers, it would not be possible for the Garvey crowd to even land in Africa. Second, granting that they were allowed to land, they would have nothing to conquer Africa with, for it is not conceivable that Great Britain, France, Italy or America would supply their foe with the means for overthrowing their own dominion anywhere; and there is no spot in Africa where a landing can be effected which is not controlled by a great white power. In Africa, three obstacles would have to be overcome by the Garvey group, namely, the great white powers, the natives who are opposed to alien rule, and nature in Africa, such as the intensely hot tropical climate, the uncultivated soil, the wild beasts and deadly reptiles, together with a forbidding forest. Neither one of these three obstacles could a group of uneducated, unarmed and unorganized Negroes—such as the Garvey crew—overcome.

In view of the foregoing difficulties, it ought to be clear to the most Africoid-Negro Garveyite that it would require unlimited technical, scientific skill and knowledge, together with billions of dollars of capital to subdue, harness up and develop the nature aspect of Africa alone, to say nothing of driving out the entrenched white powers and subjecting the intractable natives. Conquering Africa is not any less difficult than conquering Europe.

Thus, I think that we are justified in asking the question, that if Mr. Garvey is seriously interested in establishing a Negro nation why doesn't he begin with Jamaica, West Indies (not Jamaica, Long Island). Jamaica is but a small island with a population of 850,000—the white population consisting of less than 20,000. Obviously, on a small island where the ratio of black and white inhabitants is 42 to 1, the Negroes ought to be able to overcome the whites and establish control. Then, too, Jamaica is Mr. Garvey's home. He ought to know the geography of the island, the language and customs of the people. In other words, he is far better qualified to establish a Negro nation in Jamaica than he is in Africa—a land which he has never visited, the customs and language of whose inhabitants he is entirely ignorant. Besides, I submit that it is much easier to overthrow one white power such as controls Jamaica, than it is to overthrow six white powers equipped with the greatest armies and navies the world has ever known, such as to control Africa. And, too, it requires much less capital, less brains, less power. . . .

There is also Liberia, who tried to sell her independence to the investment bankers of America for a loan of $5,000,000. If Mr. Garvey is so interested in a Negro nation, why didn't he come to the rescue of Liberia by raising five millions to save her from being gobbled up by the American Imperialist Eagle? No, he didn't do that, but responsible persons say that he raised money presumably as a loan for a redemption fund for Liberia and that only an insignificant part of it was ever used in the interest of Liberia. As an evidence of the thought which Liberia gave the Garvey movement, when President King of Liberia was in the United States seeking a loan of five million dollars, he never had the slightest association in any way with the Garvey outfit. Besides, Haiti is a struggling black nation which needs help. Why doesn't Mr. Garvey expel the United States from Haiti? Here is a black people who won their liberty over a hundred years ago. Now they are under the imperial heel of the United States. Why doesn't Brother Marcus help keep a Negro nation independent instead of trying to build up a new one? For if a Negro nation is all he wants, then he has two: Liberia and Haiti.

But granting that it were possible to establish a black empire in Africa, would it be desirable. *Black despotism is as objectionable as white despotism.* A black landlord is no more sympathetic with black tenants than white landlords are. A Negro is no more interested in having his pocketbook stolen by a black thief than he is in having it stolen by a white thief. Death is no sweeter at the hands of a black murderer than it is at the hands of a white murderer.

Again, empires are passing. Witness Russia, Germany and Austria-Hungary. Garvey has begun empire building too late. Even Germany started in the empire business too late. She wanted to build a "mittel europa" from Berlin to Bagdad, but she was thwarted. Great Britain, France, Italy, and Russia of the Czar were not interested in having any more competitors in the empire business. Hence they crushed her. Such would be the fate of an African empire, granting that one could be established. It is also of special moment to note that no people love empires save the ruling class who live by the exploitation of the subject or working class. Such was the reason for the revolt of the Russian people against the Russian empire. The ruling and subject classes were both white, but that fact did not keep back the revolution. Note also the revolutions in Germany and Austria-Hungary, and the revolts in Ireland, India and Korea against empire-rule. Then there is Mexico under [Porfirio] Diaz. Oppression produces revolutions whether in white or black empires. Thus, an African empire would last no longer than [until] the African workers became conscious of oppression and their power to remove it, and then, they would overthrow and decapitate a black king as quickly as they would overthrow and decapitate a white king. . . .

It would appear, then, that Mr. Garvey is not so much concerned about the soundness, feasibility or value of a project as he is about getting together something that will duplicate the efforts and works of the whites. As fortune or misfortune would have it, he always selects the most impossible things among the whites to imitate. His policy is to run the entire gamut of slavish imitation from empire building, ship lines, a Black House in Washington, D.C., a Black Cross Nurse, a Provisional President with Royal Court. . . . The Garveyites are so strong on imitation that they attempt to justify the Black Star Line disgrace by pointing to the millions of dollars that the United States Shipping Board lost. In other words, if a white man takes arsenic, a Negro ought to take it too. A sort of getting even policy, with the Negroes always the victim. Think of Negroes competing in losing money with the United States Government, which has the power to tax both white and black to raise revenue.

III

(This final installment speaks for itself. If there are any sinners in the congregation, will they kindly stand up? . . . There seem to be none.)

It would certainly be unnecessary for Brother Marcus to end his weekly front page braying with constant begging for the wherewithal with which to run the convention, the hundred and one different slippery jokers, and incidentally himself. Thus, the only logical conclusion is that the dear Brother is either a consummate liar or a notorious crook. If he were getting $21,600,000 a year from 4,500,000 members, certainly he would not be constantly pressed into the courts by enraged creditors; if he is not getting it, he is lying about the membership of the UNIA, the only motive I can assign for which is that he has a mania for wanting to appear as a great man—a man who could organize 4,500,000 Negroes. But this membership is about as real as the number of delegates who attended his convention. He advertised that 150,000 delegates would be at the convention. Responsible delegates at the convention state that there were not more than 300. According to this mountebank, 15,000 Negro preachers alone would attend. A canvass of the delegates disclosed that not a single responsible, respectable, intelligent Negro preacher in America was at the convention. Hence, a sound policy for one to adopt is to accept with a grain of salt everything that emanates from that "Temple of Ananias" on 138th Street, New York. It is just that irresponsible method of misrepresentation and exaggeration of Mr. Garvey's that is expressing itself in a vicious policy which introduces dissension and suspicion as between blacks and mulattoes. Still, this is in harmony with this "Back to Africa" idea out of which the "anti–white man's" doctrine grows; for if it be a sound policy to oppose all white men, then it follows, as night the day, that it is also a sound policy to oppose everything which possesses any of the so-called white man's blood. Consequently, Garveyites denounce all non-blacks. How foolish, how vicious! If such inanity gained much headway in America, it would well-nigh wreck every Negro home, setting brother against sister and husband against wife.

Yet even the dividing of the Negro into shades of color does not complete the vicious circle of Garveyism. Perhaps the "most unkindest cut of all" is the fostering of intra-racial prejudices such as color and nationality. Still, it is not unnatural that nationality prejudice should spring from the "Back to Africa" bogey. Why? If Negroes are bent upon going back to Africa, they will not prepare to remain in America; and, if they don't plan to remain here, they will not strive to acquire rights and privileges, economic, social or political; they will not fight groups or forces that would seek to deny them such rights. In fact, they will combine with agencies that desire to get rid of the Negro. Such is the logical "Back to Africa" reason for Garvey's alliance with the Ku Klux Klan. Of course, there may have been other reasons, and doubtless there were.

Now, it is a matter of common knowledge that the Ku Klux Klan is the historic enemy of the American Negro. It was organized to destroy Negro suffrage, to re-enslave him. It has murdered, burned up and lynched thousands of innocent, defenseless Negroes. Southern Negroes, with a spark of manhood in them, would suffer their tongues to be torn from their mouths before they would dare to give any color of support to this bank of criminal, cut-throat bandits. Yet, Mr. Garvey found it necessary to hold a secret interview with the King Kleagle [Edward Young] Clarke (an interview, by the way, which he promised to publish, but which has not yet seen the light of publicity) after which he had the unmitigated effrontery to come before the American Negroes and advise them not to fight the Klan. He says it is not an alliance. But note this illustration: During the war if anyone in America had advised anyone else not to fight Germany, what would he have been considered as? Obviously, a spy—an ally of Germany. Certainly he would have been recognized as the enemy of America. So it is with Mr. Garvey. He has joined the enemy of the American Negro, and, consequently, can only be considered as the enemy of the American Negro. But you ask what relation has this to prejudice between the American and West Indian Negro? This: Mr. Garvey is a West Indian. As the leader of the Universal Negro Improvement Association, it is assumed that the followers endorse his policies. It is also assumed by American Negroes, wrongly, of course, that all West Indians are followers of Garvey. Thus, the deduction of the American Negro is that all West Indians, like Garvey, are their enemy. While this is not true, it is believed to be true; and people act more strongly upon belief than they do upon fact and truth. The most prominent, intelligent West Indians are opposing Garvey. Garvey does not represent all West Indians any more than did Booker T. Washington represent all American Negroes. . . .

Now, it is recognized that political power makes legislation, and that legislation can modify the social and economic life of groups for good or ill. It is also a matter of general understanding that political power can only be acquired by meeting the conditions of citizenship. It is also elementary that whether one be a citizen or not, he is affected by the legislation of the country where he happens to be residing. Thus, upon the basis of enlightened self interest, the West Indian Negro should meet the conditions of citizenship in order that he may acquire political power with which to protect and advance his own economic and social life, and also to increase the political power of the Negro group in the United States of America, which would go farther toward improving the condition of the Negro in Africa, Haiti and the West Indies, than a thousand UNIAs. Thus Garvey's blustering talk about citizenship in Africa at the sacrifice of citizenship in America is a decidedly pernicious example.

Witness the attitude of the Jews. They know an advantage when they see one. They immediately become citizens and employ their political power to assist their plan to build up a Jewish home in Palestine. But of course, no Jewish leader advocates any "back to Palestine" slogan. Nor do they build any Jewish steamship lines, or Jewish House in Washington, D.C. Still, the Jews have their problems here and elsewhere. No Jew would drop so low as to join the Klan, and especially, no leader. What is true of the Jews is also true of the Irish. They never fail to exercise their political power, which means they never fail to become naturalized. Nor do the Irish propagate any "back to Ireland" doctrines. They build no Irish ship-lines and establish no "Irish Houses" in the capitals of various nations. . . .

Now, as to the remedy for the redemption of Africa.

First, the cause of the African question is "world imperialism." Africa is exploited just as China, the Philippines, Haiti, Cuba, Korea, Ireland, India are exploited. The issue is not race, color or nationality, but economics. Africa is held in subjection because it is the home of rubber, gold, diamonds, cocoa, kernels, iron, coal, etcetera. These raw materials are necessary to the western capitalist European and American powers. The investment bankers send millions of dollars into these undeveloped countries, and in order to protect the said investments, huge navies and armies are built up and maintained. Militarism, the handmaiden of financial imperialism, is developed to insure the safety of the Western European and American powers' economic spheres of influence, where labor is cheap, raw materials plentiful, and, consequently, the return on capital high.

The method of imperialism consists in making loans to certain tribal chieftains, heads of weak governments, such as Morocco, Egypt, Haiti, Santo Domingo, Liberia, China, India, etcetera. When default in payments is made, the great power steps in and establishes control. Africa then will never be free so long as financial imperialism holds sway in society, and financial imperialism will hold dominion just so long as the resources and means of wealth, production and exchange are privately owned. As long as surplus wealth is created in the capitalist countries of the world, that wealth will be invested in countries where the profits are high, and one of those countries happens to be Africa [*sic*]. So long as investments are made in Africa or China, neither Africa nor China can be free, because whoever controls the economic power will control the social and political power. *Thus the problem consists in overthrowing capitalism.* Of course, this is an ultimate matter. For the present, only reforms can be adopted which may improve the status of the Africans. For instance, the abolition of "forced labor," the retention of fertile land for the African for his own cultivation, the recognition of tribal polity, the establishment of an International Commission composed of African, American, West Indian, South and Central American Negroes, together with certain experts, white or black, to study African life, language, customs, culture, traditions, history, etcetera in order that it may make reports, upon which constructive social, economic and political policies of reform may be based. Such is the only way to redeem Africa, Mr. Marcus Garvey to the contrary notwithstanding.

SOURCE: *The Messenger 6* (November 1922): 540–42; 7 (January 1923): 568–70; 7 (March 1923): 612–14.

March on Washington Leader Sees Danger of Race Losing the Peace (1942)

Randolph was fundamentally concerned with dismantling racial discrimination in the United States, but, as this *Chicago Defender* editorial indicates, he understood the global context of any contest against the color line. To Randolph, fighting racism in America was analogous to fighting colonialism in India—both were campaigns against entrenched inequality and institutionalized white supremacy.

Negroes are fighting on two fronts. This is as it should be. They are fighting for democracy in Europe. They are fighting for democracy in America. They are trying to stop Hitler over there, and they are determined to stop Hitlerism over here. These are the horns of the dilemma. There is no alternative. Were Negroes not to fight for democracy on the world front, in Europe and Asia, their fight for democracy on the home front would be in vain. Conversely, were they not to fight for democracy on the home front, their fight on the foreign front would be a farce and a mockery, without point or meaning. That this is so is a blessing to the Negro and the world today. While the old medieval doctrine of salvation through suffering and sacrifice may have only relative validity, it is, perchance, written in the stars that the "peoples who walk in darkness at noonday," must point and lead the world to democracy and freedom, justice and decency, peace and love, today. This is the high task and mission of a humble but not docile, serving but not servile, democratic but not demagogic, plain but not pliant, compassionate but not compromising, people. Such are the people of India, Africa, China and the Negro people of America.

Those proud, pretentious and powerful leaders of the empire systems, resting upon the slavery, squalor and suffering of the colonial masses of Africa, India and China, who are guilty of bringing the world to the brink of destruction, are hardly fit to lead it to freedom, peace and plenty. Winston Churchill still resents the just claims of Gandhi and Nehru for the independence of India. Even Sir Stafford Cripps seeks to smear the sainted leader Gandhi of the Indian people before the bar of world opinion, by charging him with unloosing a violent revolt against the fight of the United Nations for Victory over Axis powers. Nor has one word been heard from the British Trade Union Congress condemning the wanton murder of the Indian people and the imprisonment of the Nationalist leaders for their projection and execution of the movement of civil disobedience against the continued tyranny of the British Empire. Callous, indifferent, and apathetic to the cries of the people of India for freedom, and although aware of the strategic importance of the geographical position of India to the victory of the arms of the United Nations, British political leaders still cling with a death-like grasp to the old mores . . . and carry on the imperialistic culture responses.

Verily, intolerance of the struggles of India for independence has become so dominant in the British imperial mind that there is what the psychiatrist calls a paranoid coloring in all of the thinking and pronouncements on India which take the form of a pathological distortion, magnification and misrepresentation of every legitimate and normal effort of the Indian leaders to secure a fair world audience on their case. So completely delusional has the mentality of the British government become on India and her colonial possessions, and obsessed with the mythical postulates of a superiority racial complex, that the United Nations may lose the war because of their dangerous culture and mindset against [the] equality, freedom, and independence of the darker races.

Apparently, wholly incapable of learning their lesson from the tragedy of Singapore, Malaya and Burma, English war-leaders go on repeating over and over again the same mistakes and blunders by disregarding the significance of 1,700,000,000 of people of color in the world, and sabotaging the moral and spiritual front, the real foundation of a nation's power for survival and progress.

Withal, the patterns of oppression and exploitation are brutally similar throughout the world. This is doubtless due to the fact that the distinctive areas of oppression stem from a world-wide monopoly capitalist economy. The forms of oppression may be more subtle in one country than another or in different sections of the same country, but in the main, the oppression of a people or a class does not materially differ either in kind or degree. Look at America, our own country; witness the problem of the Negro. What basic difference is there between the problems of the Indian people under British rule and the Negro people under American rule? The answer is, "none." Both countries are greatly influenced by the doctrines of racism. Both countries have highly developed forms of monopoly capitalism, with Great Britain's highly decadent, and America's still in the last phases of progressive monopoly capitalism but swiftly moving toward a period of decadence. Both the Indian people and the Negro people are subject peoples, lacking the constitutional civil and political rights of free people. The Indian and Negro people insist upon their right to fight for democracy in the true spirit of democracy, namely, as a free people. Neither Britain nor America is willing voluntarily to concede this right. To secure it, the Indian people have been forced to declare and conduct a social, political and economic program of civil disobedience. And in America, to secure their rights as American citizens, the Negro people have been compelled to threaten to march on Washington. Both of these challenges won some concessions from Britain and America. In India, the movement of civil disobedience hurried Sir Stafford Cripps from England with a belated proposal for dominion status. It was rejected. . . .

This raises the question: What are the United Nations fighting for? What kind of victory and peace should the people fight for? Obviously, the freedom-loving people of the United Nations do not want to bleed and die for a victory and peace which only serves to entrench the old imperialism of the United Nations or the Axis powers. All imperialisms are oppressive and exploitive and do not only serve to rob the darker races of their land and labor, but by the arrogance and smirking manner and satirical insolence of the imperial agents of the colonial apparatus, humiliate and insult the very souls of the natives.

Another type of victory and peace which is possible is one which destroys all imperialisms and accepts, recognizes and adopts the principle of the equality of all races, peoples and nations. If the Axis powers should win, the principle of racial equality will not get a hearing at the peace table. If the United Nations win, the principle of racial equality will only get a hearing if and when the oppressed peoples of color in India, Africa, the West Indies and the Negro people in the United States fight for equality now.

It is quite possible that the Anglo-American-Austrian-Canadian-Alliance or Anglo-Saxon systems may win the war and the darker races lose the peace. If the darker races are to accept the Atlantic Charter as a symbol of the Anglo-American philosophy of victory and peace, it is apparent that no democratic, free world awaits the people of color. For the Atlantic Charter expressly states its concern only about the fate of the European peoples that are now subjugated by the Nazis. No thought is given to the hundreds of millions of brown, yellow, and black peoples who are under the yoke of despotism of the United Nations. Thus, India and the Negro people of the America call for freedom now. And the Negro and Indian people are not fighting for freedom now for themselves alone, but for the moral and spiritual salvation of America and England, if not western civilization.

SOURCE: *Chicago Defender*, September 26, 1942.

My Trip Abroad (1951)

Randolph's duties with the BSCP took him all around the United States and Canada, but he had never gone overseas until he traveled to France as a delegate for the AFL's 1951 Congress of the International Confederation of Free Trade Unions. Randolph kept a log of his activities and his impressions of the journey, and he published it as a series for *The Black Worker.* Comments on the grandeur of ocean travel and comparisons of various dishes to his wife's cooking reveal sides of Randolph's personality rarely seen elsewhere. The same can be said of the underlying distaste that colors his observations on the behavior of American travelers that he observed while abroad.

I.

Bon voyage! Bon voyage! Bon voyage! These greetings and salutations represented the climate of goodwill, interest and affection which prevailed at the "going away" party Brotherhood officials and members arranged for me the day before sailing to Europe on the S.S. Queen Elizabeth. Though I had no happy thrills about the trip to Europe, when I was aboard the ship, there was a sort of zest that no doubt comes to one when about to launch upon some adventure. There was an interest, a profound interest, in going places I had never known or seen.

Going away to Europe was an event to me and our Brotherhood people. At the pier where the big ship, like a mighty sea beast, stood waiting for the signal to put out to sea, people, our Brotherhood people and friends, stood waving farewell. [Milton Webster] Webb had come from Chicago and Bennie [Smith] from Detroit to bid me their best. Vernelle Turner, one of Washington's outstanding and charming teachers, and a friend of the family and the Brotherhood, had driven up from Washington to join the bon voyage party. For the Brotherhood, it was a party, and the office girls made the most of it.

Not long after the huge pile of steel began ploughing her path to the sea, I began exploring the various areas of the ship. The Cunard's S.S. Queen Elizabeth is a veritable city afloat with a maximum of everything to provide comfort, convenience, safety and relaxation. The crew from top to bottom was friendly, courteous and accommodating. No signs of discrimination anywhere, and of course, I was naturally looking for old man James H. Crow. The food was good and plentiful. Of course, it was not so tasty as that which Buddy, my wife, fixes for me at home. Traveling first class, one is told and urged to ask for anything you wish to eat though it may not appear on the menu. Speaking of first class passage, it may not be amiss to add that too much ado is made over first class passengers. Even the Captain, in addressing the passengers in the safety drill, went to great pains to tell the tourist and second class passengers to stay in their places and not to go, as he put it, rolling all over the ship, which appeared to me both unnecessary and a bit snobbish. It didn't take me long then, from a casual glimpse of the so-called first class breed, to discover that they were stuffed shirts with pockets full of dollars, journeying to Europe to suck up culture through the doubtful process of osmosis, and to appear important; but of course primarily, to play with the bankrupt European smart set and titled gentry. . . .

After the first night, dinners became a social event, with women in their evening fineries and men in "tucks." A cameraman scampered up and down the spacious and decorative dining hall shooting the pictures of vain women and vainer men. The following morning large groups of both sexes could be seen excitedly examining the pictures on a long table to find out if their mugs were in evidence, so they could take the number of the photographer and hustle off to buy it at any price. One need not observe that the ship's photographer did not hesitate to exploit this human weakness of egocentrism. Since photographers cannot provide a face for people that they don't have, many a person, with a sprightly, eager quest for his picture became quite forlorn upon finding it. While, probably, no human being is without some measure of social-me-tooism, I never spent any time searching for my photo. . . .

Although from early childhood I had a sort of fear fixation of bodies of water, especially large ones, nightly I gazed out upon the roaring seas under the starless skies with a certain enchantment and assurance with the definiteness of eternity and the certainty of uncertainty. I thought of the awkward fact that, unlike [conveyances that] travel by land, the great leviathans of ocean transportation never stop moving toward their port of landing for repairs or for any cause except disaster upon the medium—the water—through which they sail. Traveling by sea gives one time, much time, for thinking and contemplation.

II.

From Cherbourg, I took the boat train to Paris, a trip of some four hours, more or less. The Cherbourg railway terminal station, well set-up and quite large, was under repair because of damage inflicted by Herr Hitler's Luftwaffe during the war. I approached the platform to board the train, whose engines and cars are a bit smaller than the engines and cars in the United States, though the cars' "first class" are not bad, and the speed of the train is comparable to our best, and as a rule leave and arrive on scheduled time. I found my luggage, consisting of three bags in order and placed before the car, indicated by my ticket and trip card. The Red Cap, who usually hands passengers' baggage to them through the windows of the cars, carried my bags to my compartment, for which I gave him a tip of 400 francs. On the basis of exchange there, an American dollar was worth 350 francs.

Being curious about the workers and make-up of the train, I leisurely strolled through its thirteen or fourteen cars and found them crowded to capacity first and second class. Soon after the Customs Officers had inspected your passport, something a person while traveling in Europe must keep ever close to him, a waiter from the dining car inquired if you wished to be among the first to dine. If so, he gave you a little coupon marked "First," whereupon, you were expected to go to the diner immediately for dinner, or whichever meal was being announced. While not too hungry, I went to the diner at first call. Every seat was taken. Bottles of wine were on the table, two hard rolls of bread wrapped in paper napkins were placed by each set-up, there being four at each table. Promptly, the waiters began serving the meal, beginning with soup which was quite tasty, followed by a large plate of a bread-like affair, or a sort of boiled dough, seasoned with cheese. While I, a little suspicious in a strange land, ate sparingly of it, other passengers especially of the native tongue, licked it up voraciously. The next course was a good dish of veal with gravy, potatoes and peas, coffee, tea or beer, the last of which one could buy. One of the choice courses is composed of cheeses of various kinds and is served as a desert topped off with fruit. Water was never served except upon request. Everybody, that is, the French people, drinks wine. I was told by the seasoned travelers not to drink the regular water but to purchase mineral waters to avoid dysentery. But I got it just the same. When I finished my meal, which is served at an unusually rapid pace, I requested the check, which was more than eleven hundred francs, or a price little less than three dollars in American money. This is a reflection of just one aspect of the high cost of living in France. This bill also contained a fifteen percent service charge. But the waiters, who were friendly and accommodating, still expect a tip. I gave a tip of a hundred francs.

When I had finished my meal, which was quite nice, I returned to my compartment to observe the countryside. To my surprise the country appeared to be rich and well cultivated with good looking cattle. I saw no great farms such as one finds in the United States and Canada. They appeared to be largely family farms which were not worked with any large amount of hired labor. On the whole, the countryside looked very much like Connecticut, Pennsylvania or New York.

No one can arrive in Paris without knowing it, for there is endless din, hustle and bustle, the congestion of taxis and chatter of people, not much different from terminal stations in New York, Chicago and Montreal. . . . The Crillon Hotel, one of the oldest, about a hundred years or more and one of the first class, is located on a sort of circle, the Place de la Concorde, from which may be seen the Arc de Triomphe which leads on to the Champs-Élysées, one of the great highways of personality of times ancient, medieval and modern, and down which Hitler's legions marched upon Paris. Glancing to the left from the Crillon may be seen the Tuileries, Garden of the Kings; straight-away, the building of the National Assembly; and, to the right, the American Embassy. Around this circle are huge statues, symbols of the glory that was France. It is said that the bloody Guillotine upon which King Louis XVI lost his head stood nearby this circle, and the famous revolutionist Robespierre lived behind this hotel.

After dinner, Bill and I did a bit of Paris, that is, in harmony with social fashion, drank beer at one of the side-walk cafes in the well-known Saint-Germaine-des-Prés, where artists and poets, indigent but proud, offer their wares for a few francs. This is one of the spots where the true flavor of France may be scented. Americans, easily identified by a sort of reckless, confident, cultural air of amateur-ness, were rolling all over the place, as ever anon, a shiny Cadillac, filled with rotund, well-fed citizens from the States, aped by. Bill and I spent a pleasant evening discussing the problems of the International Confederation of Free Trade Unions and the workers of France. . . .

III.

Because of my long Socialist activities and interest in the United States, I was given a warm and delightful welcome at a luncheon in one of the first class restaurants by some of the leaders of the Socialist Party, perhaps, the third political party in France in numbers and influence, the De Gaullists' rally of the French people and the Communist parties running neck and neck for first place. Here I heard the soundest and most brilliant analysis of the problems of France and Europe I had heard given with expansiveness, charm and logic, if not optimism, and esprit de corps. At the luncheon was Jean Louguet, Jr., son of the grandson of Karl Marx, a genial and loveable personality with whom I talked at length. While here was a group of European Socialists in the midst of a national and world crisis, you heard none of the resonant clichés of orthodox Marxism. Although France is under the deepening shadows of a red Russian blitz, no one gave expression to war scares. While there appeared to be a logical commitment to preparedness for war, one was sharply impressed with the feeling there was greater concern about making peace than making war, halting a declining standard of living, which has not, according to labor and Socialist leaders, been greatly helped by the Marshall Plan. . . .

SOURCE: *The Black Worker* 23 (August 1951): 6; (November 1951): 6; (December 1951): 6.

The World Challenge of Ghana (1957)

Accompanied by Martin Luther King Jr., Randolph was present at the festivities surrounding Ghana's independence from British rule. Impressed by the mood of the masses, or, as he called it, "the fires of nationalism," he predicted that Ghana would lead the way toward self-rule for emerging nation-states throughout Africa.

I saw the birth of Ghana, a new African nation, 12:01, March 6, 1957. It was this hour when the ceremonial lowering of the Union Jack and the red, green and gold flag of Ghana was raised. Like the roaring and rushing waters of a mighty river over a dam, the beginning of the hauling down of the British flag touched off a thunderous and resounding burst of pent-up, pressure-packed emotions of independence and freedom of thousands of jubilant, but earnest and determined, black men, women and children who thronged the Polo Grounds and streets of Ghana. The people shouted, sang, danced and wept for freedom and independence. Long chains of men and women were seen marching and chanting, "freedom—freedom—freedom!" Verily, mine eyes had never before beheld such a spectacle.

No one could witness this vast mass of humanity of recent colonial bondage stirred, aroused and moved by the fires of nationalism and a brave new vision of hope and freedom and progress, without being profoundly shaken by the powerful impact of the burning and universal passion of man for self-rule. This is a proud day for Ghana with its background of a thousand years of ancient glory. It was its finest hour, not only for Ghana, but all Africa. It was a symbol of hope. It was an unmistakable expression of the aspirations of all Africa, eighty percent of whose land and ninety percent of [whose] people are still under colonial rule.

While the ceremony of installing Ghana into the honorable estate of membership and brotherhood of the free, independent, and sovereign nations of the world was one of grandeur, majesty and pomp, the driving motivation of this moving human drama was reflected in the eloquent and masterly policy speech of the Prime Minister, Kwame Nkrumah, the man of the hour, when he exclaimed to the rapturous cheers of the great concourse of people: "Ghana is from today and forever free!" With a deep sense of prophecy, he pointed out that: "Ghana may serve as a center to which all the people of Africa may come and where all the cultures of Africa may meet . . . it will show them that there is a peaceful road to independence and that brains, not bombs, win freedom. . . ."

Well might it be said that Nkrumah is a sort of combination of George Washington and Abraham Lincoln to his country. One senses in the climate of the population that he is revered by his people with as much authentic respect and devotion as was Lincoln or Washington in the United States. In fact, the jailing of Nkrumah, because of his aggressive leadership of the Gold Coast revolution for the transition of power from the colonial order to the African people, is, perhaps, the outstanding romantic event in Gold Coast history. It conveys to the Ghanians what Paul Revere's Ride, Custer's Last Stand, Valley Forge and the Alamo mean to Americans. The most casual contact with the Prime Minister impresses one with the fact that, in addition to his great dedication to the liberation of his people, he is a man of homely virtues, massive integrity, and granite-like resolution to stand steadfast in the challenging enterprise of building a free nation. He also possesses warmth of heart and spirit, essential qualities for the equipment of any man to lead and win the veneration and affection of a people.

Like a political magnet, the celebration for independence attracted delegates from fifty-eight countries. And they did not come merely to witness the colorful pageantry of the new order of freedom displacing the old order of colonialism when the Union Jack fluttered from the forts that were once slave depots. No, not at all. These delegates had come not only to offer the greetings and goodwill of their respective nations, but not the least of their interests was to seek a friendly gesture of association from this new nation.

While, unfortunately, President Eisenhower has mistakenly failed to speak out against southern race terror and hate, he has shown great wisdom and foresight, as well as full appreciation of the magnitude and far-reaching significance of the celebration of the independence of Ghana by dispatching Vice President Nixon, second in command of the United States, to carry the blessings and respect of this great republic to the leaders and peoples of Ghana. And, although there were some complaints by some Americans that Vice President Nixon was being a bit bypassed and not given the focus of attention commensurate with his high government station, it is a matter of common and general agreement, regardless of political overtones, that in his genial, friendly, and approachable manner, he has made an effective ambassador of goodwill for the United States. Naturally, Soviet Russia, with an eye to winning this new country to the orbit of the Kremlin, was represented by a delegation which remained behind after most of the other delegations had departed and offered an invitation to the leaders of Ghana to send a delegation to Moscow. Well might the free world keep its eyes upon the machinations of the Soviet Union on the continent of Africa. While Ghana is small and new, it may be that the change in the balance of power between the USSR, Communist China, and the Russian satellites and the USA and her western allies will be effected by a small power which has access to the world forum, the United Nations.

Now, the major lessons this historic event will teach the world is: (1) that all

Africans are now in the mood and intend to make a bid for a place in the sun of independence and freedom, (2) the capacity of African people for self-rule, (3) the possession of the genius to achieve freedom and independence without recourse to violence and bloodshed, and (4) the disposition to pay the price of suffering and sacrifice for equality and freedom. As I sat in contemplation of this nationalist revolution and miracle in statecraft, my mind went back to the Pan-African Conference called by Dr. W. E. B. Du Bois, great scholar and prophet of the new Africa. I also, in retrospect, reconstructed the massive demonstrations for the cause of Africa for the Africans, by the incomparable crusader and organizer, Marcus Garvey.

My trip to Ghana was a revealing and delightful experience. Viewing the city from our airship presented a spectacle of dazzle and glitter, order and charm, and moving among the people and surveying various phases of the community, one was struck by the coexistence of manifestations of tribal traditionalism and industrial and political modernism. I was veritably bewildered in finding Accra a real city; a city which is tough, confident, energetic and dynamic, and in the momentous occasion of the hour of transition from the old order to the new, it stood out as a beautiful queen with radiance, grace and dignity. Now that a free and independent Ghana is a reality, Nigeria, Kenya, Uganda, the Rhodesias, Nyasaland, Tanganyika, Gambia, South Africa, Somalia, the Portuguese colonies of Mozambique and Angola, and the Spanish colonies will not be far behind.

SOURCE: Box 38, folder: Speeches, Undated, A. Philip Randolph Papers, Library of Congress.

Statement at Histadrut Humanitarian Award Dinner (1964)

As a trade unionist and believer in independence for the colonial world, Randolph looked to Israel as an example in nation building. Predictably, he praises the Histadrut, an Israeli labor union whose name translates as "General Federation of Laborers of the Land of Israel." Randolph saw great value in Israeli collective farming practices and the potential of consumer co-ops to empower the working class.

It is with deep humility and gratitude that I accept this award from Histadrut, the authentic voice of the workers of Israel. I do so in the name, not of or for myself alone, but of and for the members of the organizations I have the honor to be associated with—the Brotherhood of Sleeping Car Porters, the Negro American Labor Council, the American Federation of Labor and Congress of Industrial Organizations, and the two hundred fifty thousand black and white

Americans who marched on Washington, August 28, 1963, to bear witness to their commitment to the God-given right of every human being, regardless of race, color, religion, national origin or ancestry, to life, liberty and the pursuit of happiness. . . .

Both the Negroes and the Jews are fighting for freedom. It was Rabbi Judah L. Magnes, first president of the Hebrew University of Jerusalem, who declared: "The destiny of Israel, more than any other people, depends on the establishment of universal freedom." To this end, the Histadrut, the Israeli Labor Federation organized in 1920, and one of the great social forces of these times, built a great welfare republic in Israel, sometimes referred to as an act of faith. In confrontation with a hostile environment and, no doubt, considerable natural skepticism among some of the followers, limitless initiative, invincible courage, and an everlasting faith were required of the pioneers of the Histadrut when they put their hands and hearts to the monumental task of building a new self-governing state in Palestine. . . .

Accordingly and properly, the American Trade Union Council for Histadrut has called upon the American government "to guarantee the territorial integrity and independence of Israel and all other countries of the Middle East and to use its good offices to reduce tensions in that area by withholding economic aid from any nation which continues to violate the spirit of peaceful coexistence in the Middle East."

The AFL-CIO Executive Council, in its May 1962 session at St. Louis, issued a statement urging the United States government to discontinue all aid to any country in the Middle East which refuses to pledge complete compliance with the United Nations Charter and its provisions for maintenance of peace. The Executive Council declared it was deeply disturbed by the ambitious nuclear armament program of Egypt's President Nasser and equally dismayed by the United Arab Republic's constitutional provision stating the avowed purpose of destroying another member state of the United Nations—the Republic of Israel. . . .

Now, I hail and salute Kibbutzim, an outstanding landmark of social invention for the advancement of community development and economic security. It is a monumental tribute to the creative capacity of the Israeli society. And let me applaud our trade union brothers and sisters of Histadrut upon the conception and building of the Afro-Asian Institute, which is appropriately described by Henry C. Fleisher as "alma mater" for hundreds of students from Africa and Asia, and a point of interest for labor and government officials throughout the entire free world. While financial aid is needed by the emerging new nations of Africa, nothing can serve the young men and women of Africa and Asia and the coming leaders more than to be exposed to and learn how modern Israel has tackled the problem of building up from scratch.

For the Afro-Asian students to watch the operation of the cooperative farms or consumer co-ops, or trade unions at work in factories and shops, to look at the projects for irrigation and the experiments in scientific agriculture, and to discuss how the same techniques may be used back home in Nigeria or Kenya or Ceylon, in fact, in practically all of the Afro-Asian countries where freedom is new and fragile and the problems are big, is a valuable lesson in self-help. Association by African and Asian leaders with the purpose and spirit, as well as the pragmatic life of Histadrut, is a basic lesson in creative experience. The heart of the lesson is the wisdom of one's "letting his bucket down where he is."

While the new Afro-Asian states may not posses the technology and capital to build a steel mill today, all of them can build producers' and consumers' cooperatives and credit unions, schools and health centers, so as to vigorously and successfully tackle poverty, illiteracy and disease. An evidence of the practical, sound value of the Institute is the fact that the alumni have become advocates of the principle that trade unionism is indispensable to the formation of a democratic society and should cooperate with but not be the instrument of government; that the small farmer and Labor should work jointly towards common goals, and that cooperatives offer the best means for efficient farming in underdeveloped territories.

Ladies and gentlemen, I propose a toast: to the independence, stability and progress, freedom, peace and plenty for the State of Israel, one of the pillars of the free world.

SOURCE: Box 36, folder: Speeches, May 29, 1964–November 28, 1964, A. Philip Randolph Papers, Library of Congress.

Africa: Challenge and Crisis (1967)

In his 1967 speech at the American Negro Leadership Conference on Africa, Randolph calls for economic divestment in Rhodesia and South Africa, where white minorities dominated the government and instituted apartheid regimes. Seeing the persistence of white supremacy in what remained of colonial orders, he reminds his listeners that "the defeat of Nazism is not the final chapter of the struggle against tyranny." To preserve a global peace, he appeals to the United Nations for a "Marshall Plan" that would help African nations rebuild from the ashes of colonialism, and he urges African Americans to "lead the way." In his concluding remarks, Randolph calls on black scholars to carry on W. E. B. Du Bois's "Encyclopedia Africana," an uncompleted scholarly venture cataloging all things African that the "great scholar of sorrow and light" was working on at the time of his death in 1963.

Africa is a vast human volcano seething with unrest which threatens eruption at any time into a massive, violent, catastrophic race war between black and white Africans. An irrepressible bloody conflict looms upon the horizon of Southern Rhodesia and South Africa. South of the Zambezi River, which divides Zambia from Rhodesia, is a hotel which overlooks the vast expanse of Kariba Lake. At the entrance to the hotel is a sign which reads: "This hotel is not multiracial." This is a warning of "ne plus ultra," or no further beyond, to the traveler who may entertain beliefs in the idea of the brotherhood of man, for he is crossing the divide of Africa into two completely different worlds. To the north as far as the Sahara Desert virtually all of the continent, as a result of the sweep of the fires of nationalist revolutions of rising expectations, is ruled by Black Africans. To the south lies the white man's Africa. Four million whites of Rhodesia, South Africa, Angola and Mozambique live among and dominate, exploit and oppress 30 million Black Africans.

The impending hostile racial confrontation stems from two dynamic forces:

One, the determination of Black Africans to rule all Africa south of the Sahara Desert.

Two, the equal determination of White Africans to maintain their control of southern Africa at any cost. The danger of armed conflict between Black and White Africa escalated and became more acute when the Rhodesian Government, representing 220,000 whites, on December 5, rejected British terms for ending a year old dispute over Rhodesia's unilateral declaration of independence without regard to the wishes and interests of 4 million Black Africans.

President Johnson is to be commended upon his constructive, wise and timely act of statesmanship in supporting the highly sensitive policy of mandatory sanctions against the rebel regime of Rhodesia voted by the United Nations. It is not surprising that the John Birch Society–Barry Goldwater reactionary wing in the Senate should intemperately denounce President Johnson's order invoking sanctions against Rhodesia as "dictatorial, deceitful and dangerous." These anti-Black African critics and partisans of the white African school of thought contend that the Ian Smith white government of Rhodesia has only exercised the right of self-determination and that does not constitute a threat to the peace. While Ambassador Arthur Goldberg has brilliantly answered the opponents of President Johnson's Administration's position on Rhodesia, support is needed and required, especially from the Black American community as a catalyst for mobilizing public opinion in support of the cause of Black Southern Rhodesia in particular, and Black Africa in general. Well does the *New York Times* editorially observe in a recent issue: "And anyone who argues that this illegal act aimed at perpetuating the rule of the 6 percent white minority over the 94 percent African majority is not a long-run threat to peace simply ignores the realities in Southeast Africa."

Moreover, in view of the growing mood of anger of Black Africans and the widening credibility gap between Black and White Africa, as well as between Black Africa and Western Man, it is a serious question as to whether the sanctions will be vigorously enforced and, if adequately enforced, whether they can bring down the rebel Smith regime of Rhodesia.

Certainly there is little faith among Black Africans in sanctions alone as an effective weapon to topple White Rhodesia. Black Africans take the position that the only answer to white Rhodesia's refusal to agree to Britain's demands for guarantees of majority rule for the country's four million blacks is the use of military force by Great Britain of the military peace-keeping forces of the United Nations. Verily, there is considerable justification for the skepticism of Black Africans in the capability of sanctions alone to overthrow Rhodesia. Black Africans understand that white governments in southern Africa are realizing that survival is only possible, at least for some time to come, if they unite into a white bastion, for a defeat for one is a defeat for all. Thus, until sanctions are extended to South Africa, a great industrial power and the heart of the alliance of southern White African governments, Rhodesia is not likely to fall under the pressure of UN sanctions. There is, of course, another weapon in the arsenal of the UN, namely, international military force. But unless much greater pressure of world opinion is mobilized to defeat the white rebellion in Rhodesia, its implementation is quite unlikely. If the UN venture against Rhodesia should succeed, it will have established its importance as an instrument for the peaceful settlement of one of the last stubborn problems of world decolonization. If it should fail, it will have reduced the UN to a sounding board for world problems and an agency for occasional voluntary peace missions.

Because of long historical and political domination and economic exploitation of Black Africans in southern Africa by Great Britain, it is the responsibility of Britain to employ her military power to strike down the Rhodesian government. But Britain evinces a lack of will to send expeditionary forces to Rhodesia to bring down the white Rhodesia government in the interest of the Black Africa majority. Britain just cannot stomach white British soldiers shooting their white kith and kin in Rhodesia for Black African majority rule. But, at the turn of the century, British troops went to South Africa and fought for three years against the Boers before achieving a doubtful victory. The Boers used guerilla war tactics and, although the British were much stronger, the war dragged on. Thousands lost their lives. There is no reason to assume that it would be different today. While Britain stressed its appalling financial plight as a reason for not embarking upon military action against the rebel Ian Smith regime, one might inquire where Britain found the money to support the Malaysian operation, and to send troops to Aden, and to pay for the support of the puppet states in the Persian Gulf.

Obviously, because of South Africa's strong army, viable economy and prosperous export and import trade with Great Britain, the United States, West Germany and Japan, Black Africa cannot win the fight against the evil racialism of apartheid of South Africa and Rhodesia alone. Britain has 3.5 billion dollars worth of investments, and the United States 700 million, in South Africa. More than 200 U.S. companies are doing business with South Africa. A revolving credit of 40 million dollars has been extended to South Africa by ten great American banks, including Chase Manhattan, First National City, Chemical, Bankers Trust, Morgan Guaranty, Manufacturers Hanover Trust, Irving Trust in New York, Continental of Illinois, National Trust and Savings, and First National in Chicago. This economic blood of the banks of the United States helps to give [to] and maintain the life of apartheid. Despite the utter horror of the Sharpeville Massacre of 1960 and the unspeakable degradation of the racial separatism of the system of Bantustans, it will take nothing less than a major revolution to break the grip of South Africa on the financial lifeline of American business. Of course it can be done if the American churches, unions, educational and fraternal institutions could be aroused to withdraw large amounts of their accounts in these giant banks because of their support of apartheid. There is no nerve so sensitive as the nerve of the pocketbook.

The fight against apartheid has been waged not only inside South Africa but in almost every part of the world, be it said to the great credit and racial pride of Black Africans. A veritable deluge of information and propaganda has been disseminated pointing out the evils and inhumanities of apartheid. This has resulted in an unparalleled growth of repugnance to apartheid and total commitment by its victims to fight for its eradication.

The South African government has now taken steps to counter this rising tide of propaganda against apartheid. Her information services are expending millions of pounds on counterpropaganda. Semi-government bodies are hard at work trying to sell apartheid to the world. This is proof of the value of, and need of, Negroes of the United States and the West Indies joining hands with our Black African brothers in warning the world of the grave dangers of apartheid to the peace of the world.

The life of a non-European under apartheid is very cheap in South Africa, as cheap as the life of a Jew in Nazi Germany. But if the Buchenwald in South Africa, the sadistic fury with which the Herrenvolk policemen belabor the Black African—guilty or not guilty—is comparable only to the brutality of the S.S. Guards, and if we accept the premise—as I hope the nations of the world do—that peace is indivisible; if we accept the moral concept that there should be no peace as long as the scourge of Nazism exists in any corner of the globe, then it follows that the defeat of Nazism is not the final chapter of the struggle against tyranny.

To the Black Africans, and to us of African descent, there can be no peace in the world as long as the tyranny of apartheid remains. One of the grossest insults, not only to the millions of Black Africans and non-Europeans of South Africa but to all those who are honestly striving to shape the world upon new foundations of freedom, equality, and racial and social justice, occurred when, in 1945, Jan Smuts, Prime Minister of South Africa, who had once declared that "every white man in South Africa, believes in the suppression of the Negro, except those who are mad, quite mad," stood before the assembled peoples of the world and pleaded for an article on human rights in the United Nations charter.

Nothing so vividly illustrates the twisted contradiction of thought in the minds of white Western man. What brought it about? What caused the paradox? I believe it was the slave trade commerce in human beings between Africa and America, which flourished between the Renaissance and the American Civil War, which is the prime and effective cause of the contradictions in European and American civilization and the illogic in modern thought and the collapse of human culture. Nor are Nazi Germany and South Africa alone guilty of this grave moral contradiction. How can we account for the Founding Fathers of the United States writing the Declaration of Independence, in which they asserted, "We hold these truths to be self-evident, that all men are created equal, that they are endowed by their Creator with certain unalienable Rights, that among these are Life, Liberty and the pursuit of Happiness," while they owned slaves.

While the freedom fighters of Black Africa, the West Indies and the United States must not cease in their crusade against apartheid in white South Africa, it must not be forgotten that Black Africa, Asia and the Caribbean countries are in the category of "have-nots." They are developing countries yet seeking

A. Philip Randolph at his 80th birthday celebration, shaking hands with Coretta Scott King and standing with Bayard Rustin, George Meany, and Nelson Rockefeller. (Library of Congress, Prints & Photographs Division, A. Philip Randolph Papers, LC-USZ62-125025)

to enter the twentieth century while many of them, in many respects, have not yet reached the nineteenth. Many still need to achieve the precondition of industrialization, including stable government and the capacity of advancing technology. It, too, is important to recognize that the price of admission to the industrial society is much higher today than it was a century ago. Technology is costlier, capital requirements are greater, established producers are harder to overtake in world commercial competition. The fact is, the poor nations are getting poorer while the rich nations are getting richer. Of the 80 or more developing countries of the world, 30 or so depend for more than half their foreign exchange earnings on exports of a single crop or commodity such as cocoa or sugar.

Just as a Marshall Plan was necessary to help rebuild Europe out of its ashes of economic exhaustion and despair, it is obvious that Africa, Asia and the Caribbean areas of the world, whose people have been exploited and oppressed for centuries by imperialistic colonialism, must be lifted up by another world Marshall Plan, under the aegis of the United Nations, or the world may set afire with a conflict of catastrophic dimensions between the "have" and "have-not" countries. The United States, the richest and most powerful nation in the world, should lead the way. It is the responsibility of Negro Americans to point the way.

I therefore want to commend the Negro leaders who have seen the wisdom of forming and developing this movement to awaken, inform and arouse the mind and conscience of black and white America to the menace of apartheid. A strong, aggressive and dedicated Negro movement committed to the abolition of apartheid in Africa can exercise effective and meaningful influence on the foreign policy of the United States in behalf of Black Africa. Such a movement can give help and hope to the brave and dedicated black African freedom fighters in the resistance movement against apartheid in South Africa and Angola, Rhodesia and Mozambique.

Negroes in the United States and West Indies have exhibited pride in the great aboriginal cultural endowment and heritage of Africa, which well might be the original home of homo sapiens. Dr. W. E. B. Du Bois' imperishable work for the recognition of the monumental contribution of ancient and medieval Africa to civilization must ever live in the book and memory of all black men. He held five Pan-African conferences during his lifetime for the memorialization of the priceless treasures of art, science and philosophy of our African forebears. His last creative effort was the conception and building of the *Encyclopedia Africana* in Ghana. Let us hope that African, American and West Indian Negro scholars will not permit this great work to die. It will be of incomparable value, not only to all Africa and the black men and women and youth of America and the West Indies, but to modern man. . . .

SOURCE: Box 37, folder: Speeches, 1967, A. Philip Randolph Papers, Library of Congress.

Index

ANDREW E. KERSTEN is dean of the College of Letters, Arts & Social Sciences at the University of Idaho. As an undergraduate he attended the University of Wisconsin–Madison and earned his MA and PhD from the University of Cincinnati. Among his books are *A. Philip Randolph: A Life in the Vanguard*, *Clarence Darrow: American Iconoclast*, and *Reframing Randolph: Labor, Black Freedom, and the Legacies of A. Philip Randolph* (with Clarence Lang).

DAVID LUCANDER is assistant professor of Pluralism and Diversity at SUNY Rockland Community College. He majored in history at Westfield State University and earned a PhD in Afro-American studies at University of Massachusetts Amherst. Lucander is author of *Winning the War for Democracy: The March on Washington Movement, 1941–1946*.